Evidence-Based CBT S

BPS Textbooks in Psychology

BPS Wiley presents a comprehensive and authoritative series covering everything a student needs in order to complete an undergraduate degree in psychology. Refreshingly written to consider more than North American research, this series is the first to give a truly international perspective. Written by the very best names in the field, the series offers an extensive range of titles from introductory level through to final year optional modules, and every text fully complies with the BPS syllabus in the topic. No other series bears the BPS seal of approval!

Many of the books are supported by a companion website, featuring additional resource materials for both instructors and students, designed to encourage critical thinking, and providing for all your course lecturing and testing needs.

For other titles in this series, please go to **http://psychsource.bps.org.uk**.

Evidence-Based CBT Supervision

Principles and Practice

Second Edition

Derek L. Milne

The British Psychological Society

WILEY

This edition first published 2018 by the British Psychological Society and John Wiley & Sons Ltd
© 2018 John Wiley & Sons Ltd

Edition History
British Psychological Society and Blackwell Publishing Ltd (1e, 2009)

Registered Offices
John Wiley & Sons, Inc., 111 River Street, Hoboken, NJ 07030, USA

John Wiley & Sons Ltd, The Atrium, Southern Gate, Chichester, West Sussex, PO19 8SQ, UK

Editorial Office
The Atrium, Southern Gate, Chichester, West Sussex, PO19 8SQ, UK

For details of our global editorial offices, customer services, and more information about Wiley products visit us at www.wiley.com.

Wiley also publishes its books in a variety of electronic formats and by print-on-demand. Some content that appears in standard print versions of this book may not be available in other formats.

Library of Congress Cataloging-in-Publication Data

Names: Milne, Derek, 1949- author.
Title: Evidence-based CBT supervision : principles and practice / Derek L. Milne.
Description: Second edition. | Hoboken, NJ : Wiley, 2018. | Series: BPS
    textbooks in psychology ; 2380 | Includes bibliographical references and
    index. | Description based on print version record and CIP data provided
    by publisher; resource not viewed.
Identifiers: LCCN 2017013978 (print) | LCCN 2017029758 (ebook) | ISBN
    9781119107637 (pdf) | ISBN 9781119107606 (epub) | ISBN 9781119107521 (pbk.)
Subjects: LCSH: Mental health personnel–Supervision of.
Classification: LCC RC440.8 (ebook) | LCC RC440.8 .M55 2018 (print) | DDC
    616.890092–dc23
LC record available at https://lccn.loc.gov/2017013978

ISBN 9781119107521

Cover images: (Watercolour spot) © itskatjas/Gettyimages; (Galaxy) © Attila445/Gettyimages
Cover design by Wiley

Set in 10.5/13 pt MinionPro-Regular by Thomson Digital, Noida, India
Printed in Singapore by C.O.S. Printers Pte Ltd

1 2018

The British Psychological Society's free Research Digest email service rounds up the latest research and relates it to your syllabus in a user-friendly way. To subscribe go to http://www.researchdigest.org.uk or send a blank e-mail to subscribe-rd@lists.bps.org.uk.

*This book is dedicated to my father, Alec Milne.
Like a good supervisor, he taught me to value
both evidence and experience.*

Contents

About the Author

Dr Derek L. Milne (BSc, MSc, DipClinPsych, PhD, C Psychol, FBPS) was a Consultant Clinical Psychologist with Northumberland, Tyne & Wear NHS Trust, and Director of the Doctorate in Clinical Psychology at Newcastle University in England, until his retirement in 2011. His previous experience included 12 years as a Clinical Tutor (Newcastle and Leeds Universities). Prior to this he also gained valuable experience in the roles of clinical supervisor, teacher, tennis coach, sport psychologist, mentor and as an action researcher (on staff development generally, but focusing on clinical supervision latterly). Since 1979 he has published 10 books and over 200 scientific and professional papers, many on staff development and supervision.

Preface

Preface to the First Edition

One of the fascinating aspects of writing this book on evidence-based clinical supervision (EBCS) has been to experience the interplay between theory and practice in clinical supervision at a personal level, as if writing this book was one great big learning exercise. This came about because I adopted the evidence-based practice framework, a broad approach to problem-solving which required me to repeatedly adopt alternating and rather different ways of understanding supervision. As a result, I spent a year revolving around an extensive experiential learning cycle, during the time that was devoted to preparing this book. Much of this period was occupied with discussions with experts in clinical supervision, in order to develop guidelines and to continue my own research programme. But there was also the protracted process of studying relevant theories and research findings in a particularly systematic way, whilst preparing and submitting some of the articles that are embedded within this book for peer review, in relation to publishing in scientific journals. This personal journey of discovery can be seen explicitly in some passages of the book (e.g. in Chapters 3 and 9), where my grasp of similar approaches, such as cognitive-behaviour therapy (CBT) supervision, challenged my assumption that EBCS was a distinct approach. Ultimately, I reasoned that EBCS was sufficiently distinctive to merit its own brand name. For example, by comparison with CBT supervision, EBCS has a wider range of theoretical roots, entails working explicitly with the supervisee's emotional material, draws systematic analogies with related literatures (especially staff development and therapy process–outcome research), and has broader objectives than CBT (e.g. educational goals, especially the development of 'capability').

I appreciated that these apparent distinctions may simply be differences of emphasis, as there would appear to be nothing in EBCS that is fundamentally contrary to CBT supervision. But careful scrutiny of the evidence from observations of CBT supervision and surveys of CBT supervisors indicated that EBCS really was different (Milne, 2008a). By the end of my year's adventure, I came to view EBCS as subsuming CBT supervision, as well as a range of related supervision models. This is largely due to its integrative, 'bigger picture' approach (i.e. seeking out the core psychological and social factors within supervision, based on a fairly general search). Indeed, the original title for this book was *The Psychology of Supervision*. Thus, I believe that EBCS is unique, but affords a suitable way of revitalizing CBT and related approaches to clinical supervision (i.e. modern professional practice; applied science).

The book aims to provide clinical supervisors, and those who support them, with the best-available evidence to guide their work (which is assumed to be primarily CBT in Britain), as practised within the mental health field. This includes empirical knowledge derived from the latest research, and guidance from expert consensus. Such material addresses the 'restorative' and 'normative' functions of supervision, but priority is given to the supervisor's 'formative' or educative role. The resultant material was also sifted and sorted by drawing on my 25 years of relevant experience, moderated by regular interaction with colleagues with a similar investment in developing supervision (at conferences, workshops, etc.). This includes the detailed feedback I received from the referees and editors of scientific and professional journals, as a result of submitting much of the original material in this book as research papers for peer review. Taken together, these aims and methods are intended to address a paradox in the supervision field. This is that, despite its manifest importance, supervision is a sorely neglected topic. As Watkins (1997) has put it, 'something does not compute' (p.604). This paradox has been a spur to my work, as reported in this book.

Based on this evidence-based process of attempting to make things compute, Chapter 1 reviews how supervision has been defined to date, offering a more rigorous definition, derived from a systematic review of 24 recent studies of effective clinical supervision. I describe this particular review approach, the best-evidence synthesis (and continue to draw on it in subsequent chapters). I also question the conventional historical account, which identifies Freud as the first to explicitly utilize and report clinical supervision. Rather, applying the definition of supervision precisely and delving into pre-Freudian history, it seems to me that the Ancient Greeks got there first (again!). Chapter 2 summarizes the main types of models (conceptual frameworks) that are intended to help us understand supervision. They are mainly ones that are either based explicitly on therapies (where CBT is a strong example), or on developmental models, or are supervision-specific ones. In Chapter 3, I draw on these models to propose my own EBCS approach, which (following a critical review) then colours the remainder of the book. The important role of the learning alliance in supervision is recognized in Chapter 4, alongside some challenges to its creation and maintenance (i.e. the 'rupture and repair' cycle; power dynamics). The first of my four EBCS guidelines is introduced here. These guidelines were designed following the National Institute for Health and Care Excellence (NICE) methodology, but revised as necessary to make the approach as relevant as possible to supervision (what we termed the NICE(R) guideline development procedure). Over a hundred clinical supervisors and tutors helped to refine these guidelines. Chapter 5 sets out the supervision cycle, namely: conducting a learning needs assessment; negotiating the objectives (learning contract); utilizing different methods of supervision; and evaluating progress. Three EBCS guidelines are introduced in this chapter, as it is the heart of routine supervision. All four guidelines are part of the EBCS training manual, which is accessible from www.wiley.com/go/milne2e. The EBCS model has been represented physically as a tandem, according to which reasoning the front wheel of the bike is controlled by the supervisor. This then casts the rear wheel (and the back seat) as the supervisee's province, set out as the Kolb (1984) experiential learning cycle. Chapter 6 details this cyclical process, furnishing supportive evidence and illustrating how supervisees are essential collaborators in the business of supervision. But this tandem duo are insufficient to develop and maintain effective supervision within complex workplace systems, so Chapter 7 reviews the ways in which supervision can be supported, especially through the dominant intervention of supervisor training. Chapter 8 returns to the task of evaluation, offering the 'fidelity framework' as a coherent, step-wise way to view and practise the evaluation of supervision. Implementation issues are also addressed, in order to increase the likelihood that evaluation serves a useful purpose. In the ninth and concluding chapter I tease out the main principles of EBCS, adding reflective commentaries where there is unfinished business, such as the overlap between EBCS and CBT supervision, and I offer a specification for career-long supervision.

The method I've used to tackle these chapters has also been CBT compatible, as in adopting the evidence-based practice model (Roth & Fonagy, 1996), then using it as a framework to guide a process of scholarly review, featuring:

- critically analysing and constructively re-synthesizing the research literature;
- integrating research findings with knowledge from textbooks and from formal consensus statements by experts;
- relating this knowledge-base to the contexts in which supervision occurs (e.g. organizational and professional influences on supervision);
- reviewing the nature and effectiveness of supervisor training and support arrangements;
- comparing closely related approaches to supervision; and
- auditing the fidelity of supervision, and evaluating its results.

This method enabled me to draw out numerous practical implications, and to summarize a comprehensive approach to supervision as an applied psychological science. As a result, I believe that this book is original yet accessible, detailed yet coherent, critical yet constructive. It offers a rounded rationale and a systematic guide for evidence-based supervision, and, more generally, it offers a way of making the vital business of supervision 'compute' (Watkins, 1997). I hope that you will also enjoy the experience of discovery, as you read the book.

Preface to the Second Edition

It gives me great pleasure to present this new edition, which includes a substantial body of additional research findings that have been published since the 2009 edition. This literature has greatly strengthened and enriched the contents of this second edition (e.g. regarding measurement tools), broadening the content to reflect the growing field of clinical supervision. It is stronger because the research literature has continued to grow, sometimes buttressed by expert consensus (e.g. competence-based supervision; evidence-based training; outcome monitoring procedures). It is broader by incorporating far more on the restorative function of supervision (i.e. supporting supervisors emotionally), and by drawing on the expertise literature (including fresh theories of experiential learning).

Also, the passage of time, and not least my continued involvement in supervision since 2009, have also enabled me to review critically the material within the first edition. Like the first edition, this new volume also benefited from my engagement in extensive experiential learning. For the two years leading up to this new edition I was co-authoring (with Robert Reiser) a manual for evidence-based CBT supervision, complete with guidelines, video demonstrations and an extensive review of the best-available evidence (Milne & Reiser, 2017). This work included linked workshops with supervisors throughout the UK, including the guideline development work. The collaborative effort involved working with the British Association for Behavioural and Cognitive Psychotherapies (BABCP) on the design and broad strategy behind the manual. In effect, the two-year stint was like an action-research project, though with the greatest emphasis on reviewing the supervision literature. Some examples of this manual are included here, and this new edition has benefited greatly from that two-year effort. Specifically, that experience further developed and refined my understanding of the status and nature of evidence-based clinical supervision. As a result, this second edition adopts a cognitive-behavioural therapy (CBT) orientation to supervision, while still exemplifying the evidence-based clinical supervision approach. It is because of this more specific focus that the title of this second edition has become *Evidence-Based CBT Supervision*, as well as to try to signal the strong link to the above manual. In effect, this book provides a theoretical companion to the manual, offering a much broader review of the supervision literature. However, it retains the practical emphasis of the first edition, both in its tone and through again linking to supervisor training guidelines and other resources for developing and supporting supervisors.

The net result is a much improved statement of evidence-based clinical supervision, a distinctive and much-needed perspective required to guide the essential business of supervision within modern mental health services. All-in-all, this second edition represents a much more rounded account, portraying supervision as a mature and internationally recognized specialization within professional practice (Watkins & Milne, 2014).

Acknowledgements

As already touched on, the parallel between the experience of writing this book and the experience of supervision appears strong to me: I have grappled with some suitably challenging and perplexing material, learning much along the way, and have been supported and guided by those who have written about supervision (in texts, journal papers and consensus statements). I have also had the benefit of receiving encouragement and feedback from numerous colleagues, locally and nationally. I am grateful to the main local allies for their interest (Peter Armstrong, Helen Aylott, Nasim Choudhri, Tonia Culloty, Chris Dunkerley, Mark Freeston, Ian A. James, Dominique Keegan, Caroline Leck, Chiara Lombardo, John Ormrod, Roger Paxton, Alia Sheikh and Colin Westerman). Nationally, I have felt aided and influenced by Dave Green's DROSS group (i.e. the Development and Recognition of Supervisory Skills initiative, based in northern England, latterly rechristened STAR), by those colleagues who write about supervision (e.g. Joyce Scaife and Graham Sloan), and by my Clinical Tutor colleagues within the Group of Trainers in Clinical Psychology (GTiCP). I am grateful to them all for their collaboration, and for their encouragement to reflect on supervision as a serious academic topic. I am especially grateful to them for their help in developing the guidelines on EBCS (and please note that many additional individuals have had their input acknowledged within the original EBCS training manual, available from www.wiley.com/go/milne).

But the greatest regular impetus I should acknowledge was the stimulating interaction that arose through the EBCS consultancy that I provided to Californian Robert Reiser, during the year when I was writing the first edition of this book. This fortnightly engagement in listening to and discussing tapes of his ongoing supervision provided a vital practical dimension to the book, enlivening the theoretical information that I was trying to process. As a consequence of this quasi-supervisory experience, I felt energized and supported, and learnt much about this young but essential field of professional practice. Since 2009 I have continued to collaborate with Robert Reiser over EBCS, and would like to thank him for his continued stimulation, general enthusiasm, and for specific help in commenting on revisions to some of the chapters in this second edition. Our intensive collaboration over the co-writing of the manual for evidence-based CBT supervision (Milne & Reiser, 2017) was another major inspiration for this second edition. Helpful comments and material towards this new edition were also received from Craig Gonsalvez, Russell Hawkins, Kieran O'Donoghue, Priya Martin, and Ed Watkins.

Learning is one thing, producing the goods is quite another, and so in relation to the first edition I must also acknowledge the massive assistance received from the secretarial staff at the Newcastle Doctorate in Clinical Psychology programme (Lynne Armstrong, Karen Clark, Kathryn Mark and Barbara Mellors); I am also grateful to Amy Lievesley, for acting as my 'production assistant' (i.e. obtaining articles and checking the manuscript) and Judy Preece (graphic artist, Newcastle University) for drawing many of the figures in the book. Assistance also took the form of grants from the Higher Education Academy (Psychology Network) and the British Psychological Society (Division of Clinical Psychology).

Finally, I must say a heartfelt thanks to my partner Jan Little for her steadfast and warm support, and to my daughter Kirsty for her unstinting encouragement and unfaltering belief. I hope that all these wonderful people will see in this book some worthwhile return for their much-valued help.

Derek L. Milne
Morpeth
Northumberland
31 December 2016

1

Recognizing Supervision

Introduction

Sitting squarely at the crossroads between professional development and professional practice, clinical supervision continues to cry out for study and enhancement. Clinical supervision is defined as the formal provision, by approved supervisors, of a relationship-based education and training that is work-focused and which manages, supports, develops and evaluates the work of colleague/s (Milne, 2007b). This definition is described later in this chapter.

Supervision merits scholarly attention because it helps to ensure safe and effective practice (Falender & Shafranske, 2004), partly by fostering treatment fidelity (Inman *et al.*, 2014), which in turn helps to maximize the outcomes for clients (Callahan *et al.*, 2009). It also offers support to supervisees (Knudsen *et al.*, 2008) and represents the foremost 'signature' method and most critical part (Watkins & Milne, 2014) of teaching clinical skills to mental health practitioners. Duly perceived as the main influence on clinical practice amongst qualified staff and their trainees (Lucock *et al.*, 2006), it also helps to address the growing emphasis on clinical accountability (Wampold & Holloway, 1997), is required for the accreditation of initial professional training (e.g. British Psychological Society: BPS, 2002), is necessary for continuing professional development and regulation (e.g. British Association for Behavioural and Cognitive Psychotherapies: BABCP, see Latham, 2006) and is an accepted defence against litigation (Knapp & VandeCreek, 1997). Not surprising, then, that Britain's Department of Health (1998) should regard effective staff training that subsumes

Evidence-Based CBT Supervision: Principles and Practice, Second Edition. Derek L. Milne.
© 2018 John Wiley & Sons Ltd. Published in 2018 by the British Psychological Society and John Wiley & Sons Ltd.

supervision as one of the 'ten essential shared capabilities' of mental health practitioners (Department of Health, 2004a). For such reasons, supervision has now achieved international recognition as a distinctive and essential professional role (Watkins & Milne, 2014).

Yet, in spite of its critical and valued role, the development of supervisors has long been a neglected research area, one that has 'generated only a modicum of research' (Holloway & Poulin, 1995, p.245), research that has been judged inadequate scientifically (Ellis *et al.*, 1996; Ellis & Ladany, 1997) and narrow in focus (Milne & Reiser, 2016a). Russell and Petrie (1994, p.27) found this neglect 'alarming', and Watkins (1997) noted how this neglect simply 'does not compute' (p.604) with the important role supervision has in professional life. Since 1997 the number of papers on supervision has increased dramatically, but unfortunately the methodological weaknesses remain marked (Inman *et al.*, 2014). For example, there appear to have been five studies of supervision within the otherwise impressive Improving Access to Psychological Therapies (IAPT) programme: McFadyen *et al.* (2011); Newman-Taylor *et al.* (2013); Richards *et al.* (2013); Green *et al.* (2014); and Waller *et al.* (2015). This is disappointing, given that the cognitive-behaviour therapy (CBT) model that underpins IAPT is devoted to an empirical approach. But more worrying is the unsystematic nature of this research. Table 1.1 provides an illustration of the omissions within this small literature. By applying some important questions about these five studies (from the fidelity framework: see Chapter 8), and doing so leniently (see key to Table 1.1), it appears that none of these studies has conducted a thorough evaluation of supervision. In two cases there was reason to believe that supervision had even been implemented in a faulty manner. For example, in the McFadyen *et al.* (2011) study supervision only seemed to include one feature of IAPT supervision (agenda-setting); in the Waller *et al.* (2015) study there was poor attendance at group supervision. Furthermore, only one of these studies utilized a controlled research design (Richards *et al.*, 2013), and none of these studies manipulated supervision or employed direct observation. Indeed, the controlled study (Richards *et al.*, 2013) was focused on patients' clinical outcomes, with only passing mention of supervision (clarification that IAPT style supervision was included was only obtained by personal correspondence between the author and Professor Richards on 16 April 2015).

In relation to Table 1.1, it should be acknowledged that these studies had other important foci, and made an impressively rigorous job of analysing

Table 1.1 An illustration of the methodological weaknesses of supervision research.

Study	Right thing?	Right thing done?	Done right?	Right receipt?	Right outcome?
Green *et al.* (2014)	?	?	?	✓	✓
McFadyen *et al.* (2011)	×	?	✓	✓	?
Newman-Taylor *et al.* (2013)	✓	✓	✓	?	?
Richards *et al.* (2013)	✓	?	?	?	✓
Waller *et al.* (2015)	?	×	?	✓	✓

Key: ✓, clear claim or demonstration (any measure *or* qualitative data); ×, not right (some evidence of low fidelity); ?, not known: no data.

one or more of the fidelity criteria. For example, Richards *et al.* (2013) provided very rare and interesting information on the economics of therapy, including estimating the cost of supervision (£40.50 per patient). However, the overall conclusion I draw is that we still do not know if IAPT supervision works. Whilst there are rigorous clinical outcome evaluations that indicate that IAPT is an effective approach (e.g. Clark *et al.*, 2009; Richards & Suckling, 2013), as far as I know it has not been shown that IAPT supervision contributes to these outcomes. In short, the 'modicum of research' decried by Holloway and Poulin (1995) appears to still hold true more than 20 years later, even for a 'flagship' development like the IAPT programme.

It should not be surprising, then, to learn that supervision models do not correspond to the complexities of professional practice (Cleary & Freeman, 2006), and that the adequacy of supervision has been rated as 'very poor' in 20–30 per cent of cases, according to a national inquiry concerning junior doctors in the UK (see Olsen & Neale, 2005). In the presence of such damning views, and in the absence of a well-developed toolkit of psychometrically sound instruments, long-standing concerns that the practice of clinical supervision may generally be poor are difficult to dispel (Worthington, 1987; Binder, 1993). To illustrate the validity of such concerns from my own experience, $N = 1$ observational analyses of experienced CBT supervisors have always indicated surprisingly low levels of competence at baseline assessments.

An Evidence-Based Framework for CBT Supervision

In order to address some of these concerns and to introduce a systematic approach, the present book adopts the evidence-based practice (EBP) approach and applies it to supervision, using an evidence-based clinical supervision (EBCS) framework to guide the development of CBT supervision (i.e. the best-available research, expert consensus and theory). In this sense, EBCS is a research and development rationale or practice development philosophy, similar to 'Best Evidence Medical Education' (Harden *et al.*, 1999), in that both treat professional development in a systematic way, based on the highest quality and most relevant research. It differs most markedly from intensively personal (humanistic) approaches to the development of supervision, which assert, for instance, that 'good supervision, like love . . . cannot be taught' (Hawkins & Shohet, 2000, p.195). As described in the next chapter, the EBCS framework is based on the use of a range of research activities, expert consensus and relevant psychological theories which address the development of 'good supervision' through the applied science of training.

The EBCS framework is therefore a specialized example of EBP (see Parry *et al.*, 1996), a prominent objective in health services, and part of an international effort to ensure that patients have access to the best-available care. For example, in the USA, the American Psychological Association (APA) has developed a policy for EBP (APA, 2006), and international scientific journals published in the USA have carried special issues to foster understanding and to promote EBP (e.g. see Thorn, 2007). Internationally, definitions differ minimally, as in the APA (2006) definition of EBP emphasizing individual and situational differences: 'Evidence-based practice is the integration of the best-available research with clinical expertise, in the context of patient characteristics, culture, and preferences' (p.273). The result of applying the EBCS framework leads to a firm theoretical basis in the form of a supervision model, a conceptualization called the tandem model. This model helps researchers to study supervision, and guides CBT supervisors in their practice, as described in the remainder of this book.

In practice, supervisors draw on the tandem model in making considered decisions in relation to supervisory events (e.g. how best to help the supervisee to formulate a client's presentation). Therefore, through the convenient and accessible tandem model, these decisions draw on a range of evidence, especially the best-available research evidence. This definition is explained and elaborated in Chapter 3. For example, Figure 3.4 indicates how research is supplemented by relevant theory and by expert consensus statements, and so on. The EBCS framework is integrative in nature, so the evidence-base is not restricted to material from CBT supervision, and not even to material within clinical supervision, drawing judiciously on evidence from neighbouring literatures (e.g. research findings on feedback from the educational literature). The EBCS framework also integrates practice-based evidence (PBE) alongside EBP (Barkham *et al.*, 2010). Figure 3.4 sets out the EBP framework of Parry *et al.* (1996), adapted only slightly by replacing 'therapy' with 'supervision'. This EBCS framework helps to clarify the different factors that we should consider in relation to supervision, together with the way that they should relate to one another, so as to develop supervision (e.g. the relationship between research findings and professional consensus on what represents best practice). As the guiding rationale, the EBCS framework underpins this book, as summarized shortly under the 'Aims' section, and as detailed in Chapter 3.

On this definition, EBCS could take a number of forms, provided that there was an evidence-base. In this book I adopt a CBT orientation, so I selectively attend to the research and other evidence of most relevance to that approach, and I emphasize how a CBT supervisor might best practise CBT supervision. This is why the book is called 'evidence-based CBT supervision'. Perhaps one day someone will write a book called 'evidence-based systemic supervision', drawing on the evidence that is appropriate for that theoretical orientation. Thus, whereas the first edition of this book avoided adopting a theoretical orientation, this second edition adopts a CBT model, but other models could in principle be developed in this way. The resulting nature of evidence-based CBT supervision is described more fully in Chapter 3.

The extent to which CBT supervision can properly be described as 'evidence-based', given the much-lamented state of the research literature, is discussed in the final chapter. For now let me say simply that my EBCS strategy is to highlight seams of better quality supervision research using the 'best-evidence synthesis' approach to the systematic review, as illustrated below in relation to defining supervision (Milne, 2007b). As already noted, this selective approach is combined with extensive reference to several neighbouring research literatures, for relevant theories (e.g. leadership), and for evidence-based methods or specific technical details (e.g. how exactly to provide feedback). These findings are interpreted in the light of professional and expert consensus statements, and by means of relevant theory (e.g. lifespan development: see Chapter 3 for a full rationale). My belief is that this can provide a satisfactory evidence-base for the current implementation of policy directives, moving CBT supervision into the era of evidence-based practice.

A result of this EBCS development process has been the clarification of a model of supervision, the 'tandem' model (Milne & James, 2005), also described in Chapter 3. The theoretical foundation is 'experiential learning', broadly as summarized by Kolb many years ago (1984), but still endorsed within the mental health professions (e.g. the BABCP, see BPS, 2003; Lewis, 2005). As detailed in Chapter 3, and in keeping with the evidence-based approach, the emphasis on Kolb (1984; 2014) has been reduced in this second edition, replaced by reference to recent empirical accounts of experiential learning. This is appropriate, as clinical supervision is primarily a form of experiential learning (Carroll, 2007). However, I still draw on Kolb's (1984; 2014) experiential learning model, because it offers some helpful details that can be missing from recent research. In particular, I have retained the fundamental idea that supervisees acquire competence by learning from practical experience, and that this learning results from the necessary combination of five learning modes: reflection; conceptualization (thinking); planning; experimenting; and experiencing (feeling and doing). According to this view, professional competence is achieved most efficiently when the supervisee is given regular opportunities to use all five modes in a balanced or integrated way. Drawing on this theory and on the most recent research literature, it appears that the supervisor needs to use a range of methods to succeed in enabling the learner to utilize these different modes of experiential learning (Milne & Reiser, 2014). To restate this in traditional behavioural terms, supervisors are initially judged competent and effective when their supervision draws on such methods, and when this successively serves the function of facilitating this kind of experiential learning in their supervisees (i.e. a functional definition of competence). Additionally, supervision should also be judged in terms of its influence on the work of the supervisees, characteristically the development of their therapy skills and its clinical effectiveness. Chapter 8 elaborates this argument, in discussing the evaluation of supervision. Several studies that I conducted with collaborators have indicated the value of this model for the development of supervision, and they are described later in this book (especially in Chapter 6), together with related research, theory and expert consensus. In summary, according to the tandem model, effective and competent supervision will be characterized by the use of a range of supervision methods (e.g. collaborative goal-setting), ones selected by the supervisor in order to increase the supervisees' use of these five learning modes (i.e. a structural and a functional definition of effective supervision, respectively), and consequently their capacity to work competently, safely and effectively.

Chapter 3 also contains a discussion of what makes the tandem a distinctive CBT supervision model, deriving as it does from a systematic, EBCS framework (as opposed to the therapy-based approach in CBT supervision; Milne, 2008b). The supervision methods should be selected intelligently, partly in a responsive way to best meet the supervisees' learning needs as they unfold (e.g. to address a weak grasp of a relevant therapy technique); and partly to blend these methods to obtain the best results (e.g. following the explanation of a technique with a demonstration). The success of such responsivity and blended training should then be judged by the supervisees' use of the learning modes, which in turn should result in learning episodes and the improvement in the targeted competencies.

The Significance of Supervision

The regular media attention to examples of professional misconduct provides a powerful reminder of the importance of supervision within EBP. The 'Bristol case' is an illustration, a case in which unusually high death rates amongst infants following two types of heart surgery led to doctors being struck off the medical register. The inquiry dramatically highlighted how the traditional trust placed in doctors needed to be replaced by systems for monitoring competence and for providing relevant training, amongst other things (such as effective quality-control procedures within professionals' organizations; Smith, 1998). Supervision would logically form a central part of that training, and should draw on any monitoring data. There is reason to fear that some supervisors also practice in harmful ways. In a survey of 363 multidisciplinary supervisees in the

USA, Ellis *et al.* (2014) reported that 35% of these supervisees reported currently receiving harmful supervision, such as emotional or physical harm, for instance through negligence or by violating professional standards.

It is unfortunate that supervision is a neglected research topic, despite considerable investment in staff development. In the UK alone, the Department of Health spends about £2 billion per year on the training of clinical staff (Department of Health, 2000). In 2007, this investment was described as 'huge' (Department of Health, 2007, p.3). Although only a small part of this is likely to relate to the training of supervisors, supervision is surely the major form of continuing professional development (CPD) for clinical staff and therefore the greatest practical investment that healthcare providers like the National Health Service (NHS) make in staff support and development. This investment was justified within a modernization agenda in which the development of the workforce was emphasized (e.g. see *A First Class Service*, Department of Health, 1998). Over time, the UK government's interest in CPD has become increasingly specific, detailing its nature, content and process (for a thorough review of these policy refinements see Gray, 2006). A case in point is supervision, which needs to be regular and to be available to all staff as it can 'ensure a high quality of practice' and 'will encourage reflective practice', at least in relation to the psychological therapies (Department of Health, 2004a, p.35). More generally, 'recognizing the importance of supervision and reflective practice' (p.18) became one of 'the ten essential capabilities' (Department of Health, 2004b), and a core national standard was that 'clinical care and treatment are carried out under supervision' (Department of Health, 2004c, p.29). Latterly, the contract specification for training clinical psychologists in the UK (which presumably applies equally to all staff groups) added that this should be 'effective' supervision, developed through CPD (BPS, 2007). This is consistent with recent policy guidance on initial training and CPD, which indicates a major shift in contracting and monitoring by stressing, for instance, the need for all training to be 'of high quality', within a system that raises the importance of training to be 'core business' (Department of Health, 2007, pp.26–27). As a result of investing heavily, the NHS expects staff to be motivated, confident and skilled, so that they can provide appropriate care, treatment and support to patients throughout their careers (Department of Health, 2007).

Apart from the explicit functions it serves, such as ensuring safe and effective clinical practice (see the next chapter for a full breakdown of these functions), supervision is also significant in terms of attracting new recruits (Lavender & Thompson, 2000), affording job satisfaction (Milne, 1991), providing status and enhanced pay, helping therapists in managing their caseloads, and as part of the natural career development of professionals. According to the Care Quality Commission (2013, p.6):

> Clinical supervision has been associated with higher levels of job satisfaction, improved retention, reduced turnover and staff effectiveness. Effective clinical supervision may increase employees' perceptions of organizational support and improve their commitment to an organization's vision and goals. It is one way for a provider to fulfil their duty of care to staff. Importantly, clinical supervision has been linked to good clinical governance, by helping to support quality improvement, managing risks, and by increasing accountability.

Because of such considerations, the Care Quality Commission (2013, p.6) added that 'Clinical supervision is considered to be an essential part of good professional practice by a range of different professional bodies.'

Therefore, although there are concerns about the generally poor quality of research on supervision, there is a markedly greater emphasis on the professional importance of supervision, both in developing initial competence (so that trainees become qualified as independent practitioners), and as a major way to ensure CPD. But next I want to try to understand how we arrived at the present situation: how did supervision become so valued, despite being so poorly understood? How can we make sense of the present significance of supervision, in terms of the past? The next section takes a brief look at the early forms of supervision, based on some literature relating to the mental health field.

The History of Supervision

Given the widespread use of the apprenticeship approach in society, exemplified by the learning of a trade or profession from a more skilled practitioner or employer, it seems likely that supervision has been practised since ancient times. How else would those with the necessary skills and the responsibility for providing specialist services ensure that they had a skilled workforce, one that was working to the required standard? It appears that the first faint examples of clinical supervision date from the eighteenth century, when charity workers and philanthropists within European charity organizations provided moral treatments to the poor and sought to ease their poverty (Harkness & Poertner, 1989). Over time, the training of staff and 'friendly workers' (volunteers) in such organizations became increasingly formal, including more systematic approaches to education and supervision ('overseers'), and with it the emergence of the profession of Social Work (White & Winstanley, 2014). Perhaps for this reason, Social Work has remained one of the most impressive disciplines in fostering the practice of supervision, as indicated by Kadushin's (1976) noble efforts to professionalize supervision.

The next development appears to have been the training clinics in psychology, dating back at least to the late nineteenth century, when Witmer (1907) utilized case-based instruction. Shakow (2007) dates the emergence of proper psychological clinics from Witmer's time, noting that 'with respect to training, there was a consistent recognition of the importance of providing systematic education in applied psychology and supplying facilities to psychologists, educators, and other students for study in the practical setting. Courses, demonstrations, and practicum facilities in the clinical field for the study of exceptional children were a regular part of the programme' (p.2). Shakow (2007) believed that Witmer's early emphasis on training led universities to establish clinics and formal training courses. He noted that, by the time of a survey reported in 1914 (but referring to practices some time prior), there were 26 university clinics, and many related courses in the USA. However, according to Shakow (2007), training remained generally unsystematic, relying on individual trainees to organize their own programme of professional development. In the USA, it was not until 1945 that training in clinical psychology was formalized into university-based, four-year PhD programmes. Seemingly for the first time, clinical supervision was a clearly specified requirement within this training programme: students were first to receive teaching, then were supposed to acquire clinical skills in diagnosis and therapy under 'close individual supervision' (Shakow, 2007, p.7).

It appears that the first clear-cut example of clinical supervision for mental health problems arose in Freud's Zurich clinic in 1902, when a group of physicians studied analysis with him at regular meetings (Kovacs, 1936). Indeed, it appears that the need for a personal analysis of the therapist began to appear within these study circles. According to Kovacs (1936), Freud 'noted certain disturbing factors, which proved a great hindrance to harmonious co-operation, and he began to surmise that this disharmony was mainly due to the unresolved psychic conflicts of his fellow workers' (p.347). The first international conference took place in 1908, including a report on this Zurich clinic. This had been founded by Bleuler, and was the first place where psychoanalysis was officially taught and practised (Kovacs, 1936). The main methods of supervision at the time were guided reading of the current psychoanalytical literature, plus word association tests, designed to give the trainee analyst a first-hand experience of the workings of the unconscious mind. It soon became established that, for psychoanalysis to be successful, the therapist first needed to undergo psychoanalysis. By 1922, it was further established that 'only those persons should be authorized to practice psychoanalysis who, as well as taking a theoretical course of training, had submitted to a training analysis conducted by an analyst approved by the Society at the time. A training committee was set up within each Society for the purpose of organizing a system of training' (Kovacs, 1936, p.25). The training analysis was based on the supervisee analysing one or two patients, under the supervision of an experienced colleague. This was believed to develop the 'right attitude' towards patients, and to help in the acquisition of techniques.

In summary, 'almost from the beginning of organized teaching, supervision has been accorded an important place in the training programme' (DeBell, 1963, p.546). According to DeBell, the essential method of apprenticeship amongst healthcare professionals was to use case material to draw out relationships between theoretical concepts and the specific practicalities of a clinical case. Supervisors reportedly used the methods of feedback, self-disclosure, didactic teaching, encouragement, reflection on material and the translation of the case into relevant theory. Other methods included confrontation and clarification, in order to formulate the case from the supervisee's written notes of therapy (process notes), and work on the supervisee's account of therapy within the subsequent supervisory hour (especially the use of interpretations; Bibring, 1937). At that time, a total of 150 hours was regarded as the minimum for effective supervision. The goal was to enable a less experienced therapist to become effective in the task of benefiting patients (DeBell, 1963).

While research on therapy dates from the 1940s, research on supervision first appeared in the 1950s (Bernard & Goodyear, 2014). I next bring this review up to date, drawing carefully on the research available at the start of the twenty-first century to address another important building block for supervision, its proper definition.

The Definition of Clinical Supervision

It is evident even from these historical accounts that supervision was a complex intervention, defined and practised in a wide variety of ways. To this day there remain significant differences in what is meant by the term 'supervision', resulting in a surprisingly diverse range of practices. For instance, in the UK it has been defined within the NHS as: 'A formal process of professional support and learning which enables practitioners to develop knowledge and competence, assume responsibility for their own practice, and enhance consumer protection and safety of care in complex situations' (Department of Health, 1993, p.1). The most widely cited definition of clinical supervision, popular in the USA, is the one provided by Bernard and Goodyear (2014). According to them, supervision is:

> an intervention provided by a more senior member of a profession to a more junior colleague or colleagues who typically (but not always) are members of that same profession. This relationship is evaluative and hierarchical, extends over time, and has the simultaneous purposes of enhancing the professional functioning of the more junior person(s); monitoring the quality of professional services offered to the clients, she, he, or they see; and serving as a gatekeeper for the particular profession the supervisee seeks to enter (p.9).

The evidence that this definition is widely embraced in the USA is indicated by its acceptance within a consensus statement (Falender *et al.*, 2004) and in the *Handbook of Psychotherapy Supervision* (Watkins, 1997).

However, numerous prior reviews have noted that such definitions of supervision are problematic (e.g. Lyth, 2000; Hansebo & Kihlgren, 2004; Milne, 2007b). Additionally, surveys of practitioners indicate that they are unclear over the nature and purposes of supervision (e.g. Lister & Crisp, 2005). There are related challenges for researchers. To illustrate, Ellis *et al.* (1996) conducted a systematic review of 144 empirical studies of clinical supervision, concluding that hypothesis validity was not properly specified within this body of literature. They also noted that this poor precision and vague or absent specification meant that supervision cannot readily be manualized or replicated. In turn, this hampers the interpretation of results from research, and the clarification of practice implications.

For these kinds of reasons, I conducted a systematic review in order to develop an empirical definition of clinical supervision, building on the above definitions in an integrative, constructive fashion (Milne, 2007b). In the first part of that review I examined the logical requirements of a sound definition, then looked hard at a carefully selected sample of successful supervision studies. These steps are now summarized.

Logical basis for a definition

According to philosophy and general scientific convention, a definition needs to state the precise, essential meaning for a word or a concept in a way that makes it distinct (*Concise Oxford English Dictionary*, 2004). I refer to this as the 'precision' criterion. Precision can be enhanced by drawing out comparisons and citing examples, in order to distinguish one concept from another. A clear instance in the case of supervision is attempting to draw out meaningful boundaries between supervision and closely related concepts, such as 'therapy', 'coaching' or 'mentoring'. To illustrate, coaching has been defined as the provision of technical assistance, in order to model, simulate and practise, with corrective feedback, so as to improve the transfer of learning to the workplace (Joyce & Showers, 2002). These features are part of supervision too, so the distinction would appear to be that supervision subsumes coaching, as supervision has additional features and functions. Similarly, there are aspects of therapy and mentoring in supervision, such as the emphasis on the relationship and on reflection, respectively. However, there are important distinctions between these concepts and supervision, in terms of such aspects as the formal authority required to supervise, and the formal evaluative ('summative') function of supervision.

This discussion indicates that we also need 'specification', namely a detailed description of the elements that make up the concept of supervision (*Concise Oxford English Dictionary*, 2004). Within research, the term 'hypothesis validity' defines the extent to which a study accurately relates different concepts to the development of hypotheses, and to the way that these are tested and the results interpreted (Wampold *et al.*, 1990). That is, according to theory-driven research, the sequence is first to adopt a theoretical model of a concept like supervision, then to specify which panels (also known as boxes or variables) within the model are the subject of a particular investigation, and what relationships are predicted between these panels. The next task within an empirical, science-informed approach is to suitably operationalize the key relationships in the model, so that appropriate forms of measurement are planned.

To emphasize this point, consider the summary provided in Table 1.2. This sets out supervision following the specification provided within four illustrative texts. It can be seen that none of these textbooks actually identified the same variables when they came to specify the supervision intervention. That is, although there was precision (different concepts or elements of supervision were noted, such as the basis of supervision being the working alliance or relationship), there was a lack of consistent specification of such elements of supervision. Such a fundamental lack of consensus makes the whole foundation on which research and practice might be based insecure and indefinite: Just what is 'clinical supervision'? In addition, Table 1.2 presents a disappointing picture in relation to whether the variables that each of these four books specified within their definition of supervision were actually capable of being measured, or indeed were actually measured. This brings me to my third logical requirement of a sound definition: 'operationalization'. For instance, none of these authors noted an instrument that might measure their definition of supervision. This is unfortunate, as an instrument will tend to delimit a concept to some critical parameters, enabling supervisors to see more clearly what is meant when an author uses the term 'supervision'. Also, vague definitions do not enable researchers to manipulate or measure a loosely bounded, murky concept. What is needed is a statement of supervision in a form that enables sensitive measurement to occur. Additionally, an operational definition enables one to state valid hypotheses, and it guides us in manipulating the independent variable (supervision) with fidelity. Reliable manipulation of supervision is then possible, a key element in enabling the intervention to be specified in a manual and administered in a consistent, replicable way (Barker *et al.*, 2002). In turn, such careful operationalization allows us to determine whether supervision is indeed being delivered as it is specified in a manual (termed variously an adherence, audit or fidelity check). It also allows the subsequent outcomes to be attributed in a precise way to that intervention, assuming a suitable research design. The concept of intervention fidelity is helpful at this point, as it distinguishes usefully between five aspects of a properly specified intervention (Borelli *et al.*, 2005). This concept is discussed and illustrated with supervision research in Chapter 8.

The fourth and last of the necessary conditions for an empirical definition of supervision is that it has received clear support from empirical research: that there exists some persuasive information that helps to justify a given definition. Unfortunately, none of the texts in Table 1.2 satisfied any of the three evidential criteria. For example, no mention is given to supportive

Table 1.2 Testing some textbook definitions of 'clinical supervision'.

Criteria for an empirical definition of 'supervision'	Textbooks			
	1 Bernard and Goodyear (2014)	*2 Fall and Sutton (2004)*	*3 Falender and Shafranske (2004)*	*4 Hawkins and Shohet (2000)*
A Operationalized?				
1. Senior person	✓	✓	×	×
2. Relationship prioritized	×	×	✓	✓
3. Educational	✓	✓	✓	✓
4. Longitudinal	✓	×	×	×
5. Evaluative	✓	✓	✓	×
6. Quality control (protects clients, et al.)	✓	✓	✓	✓
7. Gate-keeping role	✓	✓	×	×
8. Objectivity of role	×	✓	×	×
9. Supportive	×	×	✓	✓
10. Experienced person	×	✓	✓	×
11. Develops competence	✓	✓	✓	×
12. Science-informed	×	×	✓	×
13. Develops confidence	×	×	✓	×
B Measured?				
14. Defined in observable terms	×	×	×	×
15. Instrument/s specified/exist	×	×	×	×
16. Conducted assessment	×	×	×	×

Table 1.2 (*Continued*)

	Textbooks			
Criteria for an empirical definition of 'supervision	*1 Bernard and Goodyear (2014)*	*2 Fall and Sutton (2004)*	*3 Falender and Shafranske (2004)*	*4 Hawkins and Shohet (2000)*
C Supported (by evidence)?				
17. Consensus claimed (e.g. 'widely accepted')	×	×	×	×
18. Cites corroborating literature (e.g. a text or review paper)	×	×	×	×
19. Notes at least one empirical study as supporting definition	×	×	×	×

NB: This assessment is based on the part of the text that explicitly presents the authors' definition of clinical supervision. It is acknowledged that some or all of these criteria may be met elsewhere in the text. Also, criteria judged to be subsumed by the above categories have not been elaborated. For example, in Falender and Shafranske (2004) various ways of 'educating' and 'developing confidence' are noted (e.g. instruction and modelling), which are subsumed under these broad categories.

Source: Milne, D.L. (2009). Reproduced with permission of Derek Milne.

studies. I refer to this as the 'corroboration' criterion: something that confirms or gives support to a concept (*Concise Oxford English Dictionary,* 2004). Logically, a definition could in principle meet the earlier three criteria (i.e. be precise, specified and operationalized), yet lack an evidence-base. Systematic reviews like the one by Ellis *et al.* (1996) address this criterion directly. Indeed, this is surely the most firmly established of the four criteria for an operational definition, as it is customary for textbooks and review papers to give systematic attention to the available evidence-base.

In summary, if we apply these four tests to the above definitions, it can be seen that they are incomplete, leading to major practical and scientific difficulties. It is surely time to tackle this impediment to good supervisory research and practice by developing an integrative and suitably empirical definition.

An improved definition of clinical supervision

Thankfully, the texts noted in Table 1.2, together with definitions provided by professional bodies and by the NHS, do give us a full range of concepts with which to develop an improved definition of supervision. This builds on the NHS (Department of Health, 1993) and the Bernard and Goodyear (2014) definitions. On this basis, the following appears to be an improved definition (the tests of a definition are noted in bold):

> The formal provision, by approved supervisors, of a relationship-based education and training that is work-focused and which manages, supports, develops and evaluates the work of colleague/s (**precision**). It therefore differs from related activities, such as mentoring and therapy, by incorporating an evaluative component (**precision by differentiation**) and by being obligatory. The main methods that supervisors use are corrective feedback on the supervisees' performance, teaching, and collaborative goal-setting (**specification**). The objectives of supervision are 'normative' (e.g. case management and quality control issues), 'restorative' (e.g. encouraging emotional experiencing and processing) and 'formative' (e.g. maintaining and facilitating the supervisees' competence, capability and general effectiveness) (**specification by identifying the functions served**). These objectives could be measured by current instruments (e.g. 'SAGE: Milne & Reiser, 2014; **operationalization**).

This definition is supported by recent reviews of the empirical literature (e.g. Watkins, 1997; Falender & Shafranske, 2004; Watkins & Milne, 2014), and by a consensus statement (Falender *et al.*, 2004; **corroboration**). This empirical definition not only integrates the main current options (i.e. Proctor, 1992; Department of Health, 1993; Watkins, 1997; Bernard & Goodyear, 2014), but also embraces various supervision formats, professions, therapeutic orientations and stages of provision (pre-qualification and CPD). It excludes staff training, consultancy, performance management, mentoring, coaching and other variations on the supervision theme that do not satisfy the above definition. The most recent definition affecting England's NHS was provided by the Care Quality Commission (2013), the independent regulator of health and social care in England. The definition was based on the lessons learned from the Winterbourne inquiry into criminal abuse by staff of patients at Winterbourne View, a private hospital for patients with a learning disability situated near Bristol. The Care Quality Commission (2013) definition also strongly corroborates the improved, empirical definition immediately above, including an emphasis on the normative ('managerial supervision'), restorative ('clinical supervision') and formative functions of supervision ('clinical or professional supervision').

Testing this definition: a systematic review

The above is an improved definition in logical and scientific terms, but does it withstand empirical scrutiny? In order to test the definition a systematic review was conducted, using the 'best evidence synthesis' approach (Petticrew & Roberts, 2006) to examine a representative sample of the clinical supervision literature. This approach stands in stark contrast to reviews that attempt to scrutinize all studies within an area, regardless of considerations like their rigour or effectiveness (e.g. Ellis & Ladany, 1997). In the example that follows, the aim was to test whether this working definition was sufficiently precise to capture the definitions that were used explicitly or implicitly in the selected sample of empirical studies, and was specified and operationalized in ways that also corresponded with these studies (i.e. a carefully selected group of 24 research papers in which clinical supervision was studied within interpretable designs, and where it had proved successful; for details see Milne, 2007b). Lastly, I wanted to see whether the findings from these 24 studies corroborated the working definition. It should be borne in mind that one of the criteria used to select these 24 studies was that the supervision had proved successful (as defined by the authors and supported by the findings: outcomes included the learning of the supervisee, the transfer of that learning to therapy, or other aspects of the supervisee's work). This therefore provided a very practical test of the working definition.

I found that explicit definitions were largely absent within these 24 studies: only six papers specified what they meant by clinical supervision (25 per cent of the sample). Five of these papers specified at least two methods and one function of the supervision as manipulated in their studies, but none of the authors differentiated this definition from closely related educational activities (like mentoring). I therefore concluded that this literature corroborated the working definition as far as it went, but was basically inadequate to provide a proper test. The next test was to examine how this body of scientific literature specified its supervision intervention. It was found that 23 of the 24 studies specified some of the variables making up their supervision manipulation, and these agreed with those in the working definition. The exception was the lack of emphasis on the normative or restorative functions of supervision. However, these are retained in the working definition on the basis of expert consensus (e.g. Care Quality Commission, 2013). Sixteen of the 24 studies (67 per cent) measured all or most of the variables specified within their application of supervision. The measures used were consistent with the outline in the working definition. For example, Fleming *et al.* (1996) measured the competence of the four supervisors in their study using a nine-item observational checklist (e.g. assessing 'participative goal-setting' and 'provides feedback'). Lastly, in order to assess corroboration for the working definition, a simple, seven-point summary rating was made across all 24 studies, in order to gain a general sense of their effectiveness. A value of 2.4 for supervisees (i.e. the amount of learning for the therapist) and 2.3 for patients (clinical outcomes) indicated that these studies were generally very successful, equivalent to an 80 per cent and 77 per cent effectiveness of supervision score, respectively. Overall, these systematic review data indicate that supervision, as per the working definition, is associated with positive outcomes, giving it empirical support. In conclusion, having passed these various tests, the working definition will be accepted as the definition of clinical supervision to be used within this book.

Aims of This Book

In order to build on this empirical definition and to redress the imbalance between research and policy that was noted earlier, this book will collate the best available evidence on clinical supervision (usually referred to simply as 'supervision' from now on) in order to aid our understanding of what it is and how it works, so that research and practice can benefit, and so that policy can be translated into practical interventions. Therefore, the main purpose of this book is to enhance the practice and study of supervision, especially CBT supervision. In effect, this book represents the theoretical companion to the CBT supervision manual (Milne & Reiser, 2017). A supporting aim is to describe fully the way that the EBCS framework has been applied, over many years, within my highly collaborative and pro-grammatic research activity. Another aim is to describe the tandem model that resulted from this application of the evidence-based practice approach, together with the materials that support and guide it (e.g. supervision guidelines). As part of my aim to enhance supervision, I will outline and make accessible the most relevant original material (e.g. instruments for measuring key aspects of supervision, and a manual for training supervi-sors). To contribute to the study of supervision, I will also provide a critical, scholarly and evidence-based review of this vital activity as it stands at the start of the twenty-first century.

In particular, I draw extensively on my own work on supervision, both the sustained and concerted research and development programme described in this book, and also my professional experience as a clinical psychologist. I have been fortunate to have occupied the role of clinical tutor for over a decade (effectively a consultant to supervisors), and to have spent 33 years working within Britain's NHS, including periods in higher education, contributing to the training of mental health professionals. As a result, the basic psychological principles and practices will be clarified in a searching yet constructive way, so that we can understand and apply supervision more effectively. Although the focus is on one-to-one supervi-sion, other formats will be discussed, such as group and peer-consultation arrangements. Also, the prime emphasis is on the supervision of the clinician's caseload for normative (management) and formative (develop-ment) reasons, although I also attend to the traditional concern with the clinician's well-being (restorative supervision). This foundation for improved supervision practice is fostered by presenting and elaborating some supervision guidelines, part of the linked manual for training new supervisors (Milne, 2007a). That manual is supplemented and updated in Milne and Reiser (2017). Another neglected aspect of the training of supervisors, and of routine supervision, is the emotional dimension. There is a 'tyranny of niceness' (Fleming *et al.*, 2007) that can stifle supervision, dampening down in particular the exploration and effective use of emotional experiences within supervision. Therefore, another aim is to give due weight to developing supervision, by attending to the relevant thoughts, feelings and behaviours.

Although you may already sense a definite psychological emphasis, this book is written for all those involved in supervision, not just psychologists, and not just supervisees or those who train supervisors. The emphasis is on isolating the basic, essential ingredients of effective supervision, drawing primarily from the relevant multidisciplinary research literatures, so as to provide an enhanced, evidence-based and novel account of supervision. This information should therefore be relevant to everyone involved in supervision (and not just to supervisors in the mental health field, though that is the assumption). As a result, there are also implications for supervisees, researchers, commissioners, programme reviewers, patients and others with an interest in supervision. This, then, is psychologically informed supervision for the evidence-based practitioner or scientist-practitioner, particularly suitable for the modern healthcare organization. Supervision will be regarded as a complex intervention within health systems and treated with the aim of applying some long-overdue scientific rigour, as a core part of the business of delivering high-quality, evidence-based health services.

In summary, in this book I aim to provide the reader with an experienced guide's approach to supervision as an applied science, in a way that is intended to show how CBT supervisors in particular can better integrate theory and practice in this vital professional activity, consistent with the era of evidence-based practice.

Plan for the Book

The remaining eight chapters are suitably businesslike, stressing informed action within a coherently structured, logical approach. To summarize, Chapter 2 outlines a basic, evidence-based model of the factors that govern supervision, and Chapter 3 goes on to reconstruct an experiential 'tandem' model. Recognizing the importance of the relationship between the supervisor and the supervisee (typically, a therapist) is far from novel, but it merits serious attention. Therefore, I review recent work on this interpersonal professional 'alliance' in Chapter 4, where I introduce the first of four guidelines. These early chapters prepare us to address the technical tasks faced by supervisors, and Chapter 5 sets these out as the 'supervision cycle'. Drawing on the staff training literature, supervision is regarded as a closely related series of activities: assessment of the supervisee's learning needs; collaborative goal-setting; applying methods to facilitate learning; and evaluation. Further guidelines on these topics are introduced. Chapter 6 then mirrors this emphasis on the supervisor by giving attention to the part played by the supervisee, a strangely neglected player in most published accounts of supervision. I detail how supervisees can be understood to learn from their experience through supervision, affording a psychological map of the unfolding journey of professional development. Related to this understanding, some instruments with which to capture this process are noted (to be discussed in Chapter 8, alongside a wider summary of the available tools and associated issues). Chapter 7 notes the need to ensure that professionals are properly supported in their emotionally demanding work. This aspect of supervision has been called the 'restorative' or 'supportive' function, complementing the 'formative' focus of Chapters 5 and 6. In Chapter 7 I deal with the various practical arrangements that need to be addressed by those who appoint, support and guide supervisors, such as regular peer support groups and training workshops. Chapter 9 draws together the essential principles and implied practices covered within the book.

Summary

Supervision is deemed essential by all professional groups and by health service organizations such as Britain's NHS. It is internationally recognized as having a pivotal role in professional development, and in the maintenance of competent, ethical practice (Watkins & Milne, 2014). But there is a surprising gulf between these endorsements and the available research and practical resources to develop and deliver supervision. To bridge this gulf, this book draws on the evidence-based practice framework to set out a systematic approach called evidence-based CBT supervision. Using techniques such as the 'best evidence synthesis' to review the core literature, by drawing on professional consensus statements, and by conducting programmatic research and development activity (using the EBCS framework) has resulted in a supervision-specific approach to CBT supervision: the tandem model. This model provides a feasible way to bridge the theory–practice gulf, is evidence-based and represents the most contemporary approach to competent CBT supervision. This book is written in a scholarly, scientist-practitioner style, as illustrated above when defining supervision empirically. This specifies what supervision entails, how it can be measured and what it is known to achieve. I next consider the various popular models of supervision, before describing in detail the tandem model.

2

Understanding Supervision

Introduction

In order to make sense of the complex intervention known as clinical supervision, authors have produced a wide range of descriptions, formulations and theoretical models. These models set out the different factors or variables that are thought by the authors to explain their preferred understanding of supervision. In addition, models suggest how these variables relate to one another. Models are tentative theories, requiring corroboration from a compelling body of research before they can achieve the status of a theory. Typically, a general, established theory may be drawn on (i.e. treated as an analogy) to provide a coherent framework for the specifics of a supervision model. For example, the most popular type of supervision model is the developmental model, which is based on lifespan development theory (Baltes *et al.*, 1998). It draws on our general understanding of how humans grow and mature, so that the developmental model of supervision can then introduce key concepts from the general theory. For example, developmental theory suggests that, in addressing life's tasks successfully, we stimulate progression from one phase of growth to another (see, for example, Kaufman & Schwartz, 2003). When applied to supervision, this general theory encourages us to assume some lawful pattern in how supervisees become competent professionals, and to attend to stages, phases and tasks in their continuing development.

Alternatives to the developmental model of supervision include those that simply extend the concepts and practices of therapy to the business of

Evidence-Based CBT Supervision: Principles and Practice, Second Edition. Derek L. Milne.
© 2018 John Wiley & Sons Ltd. Published in 2018 by the British Psychological Society and John Wiley & Sons Ltd.

supervision. In practice, this reflexivity is thought to be one of the main guides that professionals use in their supervision. A strong example is the cognitive-behaviour therapy (CBT) model, which explicitly extends key concepts used in therapy to propose how supervision should be conducted (e.g. utilizing processes such as collaboration and guided discovery: Padesky, 1996; Liese & Beck, 1997; Reiser, 2014). I will refer to these as therapy models.

Thirdly, there are models that propose altogether different constructions of supervision, going beyond developmental prototypes and therapy extensions to introduce unique or integrative accounts: the supervision-specific models.

Fourthly, it should be acknowledged that there are approaches to supervision that dispense with the need for theoretical models altogether, adopting a pragmatic approach instead. For instance, it appears that the most popular model of all is simply drawing on how one was supervised during one's own training (Falender & Shafranske, 2004). Another pragmatic example is outcome-oriented supervision (Worthen & Lambert, 2007), which advocates tracking clinical outcomes as the way to understand and practise supervision. On this logic, good supervision is supervision that produces the desired results. Such data serve as systematic feedback to therapists, to let them know how they are succeeding, together with suggestions about possible interventions (especially for patients who are failing to benefit from therapy).

Finally, we should acknowledge that some eclectic mixture of these models is a further option, one that after all appears popular in conducting therapy, as in bolting one or more of these pragmatic options together, or blending this with an explicit theoretical model, to augment it in a congruent, personally meaningful way. For example, CBT supervision is developed naturally by incorporating an outcome emphasis, combined with its other guiding principles. However, this chapter focuses on the most popular and professionally appropriate options. In the next chapter I will propose an integrative tandem model, which combines what appear to me to be the essential elements of the reviewed models, adding helpful ideas from parallel literatures (e.g. expertise).

Chapter Plan and Objectives

In order to develop a better understanding of clinical supervision, this chapter first goes back a step, to clarify what is generally meant by a psychological model. This will draw on basic reasoning and philosophical premises (as per Chapter 1), in order to define the criteria by which the above models can be best grasped and assessed.

Having clarified the nature and parameters of a model, I will next summarize the developmental, therapy and specific models. Part of this synthesis will entail mapping the models against a basic training model, so as to clarify where they place their emphasis and what they omit or minimize. In this way I will be trying to establish a basic model of supervision, one that clarifies the essential factors and processes. Given that one of the criteria for a model is the degree to which evidence is available to support or refute it, this essential model will also be evidence-based. The choice of the term 'essential' is deliberately chosen to draw out the idea of a distillation of the best ingredients from these models (the essence), to recognize the growing pressure to be able to justify one's methods in relation to the evidence (having a rationale or justification), and to convey the idea that having such a model to guide one's practice is vital ('nothing as practical as a good theory'). Having constructed an essential model (for more background see Milne *et al.*, 2008a), this will then be critiqued against some of these criteria for a good model. It will be suggested that, although there is a wide and helpful range of concepts and relationships within the existing models of clinical supervision, some significant deficiencies remain (e.g. the lack of a sufficiently detailed account of how development occurs within supervision; the limited research support). This critical review therefore collates what is known and suggests some explicit requirements for further model-building, which are then addressed in the next chapter (at which stage the criteria for a good model will be applied more carefully). This chapter closes with a discussion of some emergent issues.

Theoretical Models

We draw on theoretical models throughout our clinical and professional practice, because models are helpful devices for gaining an improved understanding of phenomena. Amongst other things, models help by allowing us to represent things that we struggle to understand and hence a model can help us to develop a coherent, cumulative knowledge-base, particularly in terms of guiding our causal thinking. In this sense, models help to make information meaningful (e.g. identify non-random patterns), highlighting what is important and identifying what is irrelevant (random) to supervision. The parallel with a cognitive schema is strong (e.g. as 'lenses' through which we perceive the world, seeing connections between events and identifying causes), but models differ in being in the public domain and also because they should be meticulously specified. Models also aid decision-making, action-planning (e.g. by highlighting mechanisms of change), monitoring of success (by pinpointing likely effects, or guiding judgements) and shaping research, training and other related activities (Bennardo, 2014). In short, they exemplify the saying that 'there is nothing as practical as a good theory'. For example, research on supervision draws on models to generate hypotheses, define suitable interventions, select instruments and interpret results. Without an explicit model, research is hard to design or conduct intelligently. Unfortunately, models are absent or poorly explicated in the majority of supervision studies (Ellis & Ladany, 1997), leading to problems with these vital benefits of a model. In Chapter 8 I use the fidelity framework to consider the implications of this sorry state of affairs.

Models can be mechanical or concrete, like the DNA double helix, mathematical (like some representations of memory functioning), or conceptual, where variables and their relationship are depicted in words and diagrams (Warr, 1980). In the next chapter I detail the tandem model, which is an example of a mechanical model of clinical supervision. By contrast, CBT has traditionally adopted the conceptual approach, epitomized by the diagrammatic formulation of the basic cognitive therapy model (see, for example, Liese & Beck, 1997, p.116). A model therefore provides us with the basic elements (variables) that we require to make sense of something, like the schemas, triggers and automatic thoughts in the CBT model. These are then arranged into some kind of order, so that the way that they interact is clear; for example, by the sequencing of these variables within the diagram, and the use of directional arrows in CBT. Some of these variables and processes (represented by the arrows) may be common to several models. In the case of supervision, it appears that all models include variables like a relationship variable (often specified as a learning or supervision alliance), some techniques to promote reflection and development in the supervisee and some evaluative work to clarify whether supervision is progressing as it should. However, to complicate matters, the different models will naturally select different terms, to reflect different concepts. For example, a supervision model based firmly on a particular therapy, like CBT, should have an appropriately distinctive (and internally consistent) idea of the nature of variables like the supervision alliance, as in stressing the importance of guided discovery in defining the shared goals of supervision. In a good model, such specifications will distinguish approaches like CBT from the way that the psychodynamic model (for instance) treats the alliance. As we saw in Chapter 1, the recent history of supervision has been dominated by the psychodynamic model. This approach requires the supervisee to undertake a personal analysis, as the individual's personality might otherwise influence the alliance adversely, without the supervisee's conscious awareness. By contrast, the CBT model generally discounts the presence of unconscious influences in the alliance, viewing the relationship in terms of such observable factors as warmth, empathy, trust and rapport (Padesky, 1996). This illustrates how the same broad concept needs to be framed within a given theory. In addition to these theoretically shaped core concepts, the different models of supervision introduce additional variables, in an effort to provide a satisfactory explanation of the operation of supervision. These will be detailed shortly.

Therefore, a model of supervision needs to satisfy a number of criteria, and to pass some long-established tests before it can be granted the status of a model (by comparison, drawing on a framework, or some hunches that derive from clinical experience, is preliminary to a model). The criteria for a model are that it offers a theoretically grounded (i.e. logically plausible) analysis of the elements required to explain how supervision should be practised, how such practices come to operate (i.e. mechanisms or processes of change) and the kinds of outcomes that are prioritized. In addition, a sound model of supervision is a tentative theory, an internally consistent proposition regarding the explicit relationships between variables (i.e. precise assertions, with proper elaboration), one that is expressed in a way that is amenable to scientific analysis (i.e. falsifiable, for example through suggesting new hypotheses, and through being quantifiable). This implies the need for elegance or parsimony in the expression of the essential ingredients. Additional criteria are that models should have a focus (a delimited, bounded area of application); be justified by supportive evidence; aid understanding (e.g. by indicating how change occurs); and have action implications (Popper, 1972; Warr, 1980). Such criteria allow different models to be contrasted and evaluated on logical, scientific and practical grounds, so that we can decide objectively whether some models are 'better' than others (because they satisfy more of these criteria, or 'correspond better to the facts'; Popper, 1972, p.232; and thereby enable practitioners to improve their understanding and practice).

These criteria will next be used in relation to the three broad types of model that are popular in supervision. This critical review process will enable us to judge the strengths and weaknesses of the respective models, leading to the view that none are wholly satisfactory. This provides the rationale for a fresh synthesis and extension of these models, the subject of the next chapter.

The Developmental Model of Clinical Supervision

According to this model, supervision is an example of lifespan development, namely 'the description, explanation and optimization of . . . individual change . . . from birth to death' (Sugarman, 1986, p.2). The assumptions that underpin this optimization process are that the potential for develop-ment extends throughout the lifespan; that there is no specific route that development must or should take; that development occurs on a number of different fronts; and that the individual and the environment influence each other – there is a reciprocal relationship between a changing being and a changing context. Sugarman's (1986) account remains contemporary, as these assumptions are reflected in more recent summaries of the develop-mental perspective. Although using different terms for the same concepts (i.e. plasticity, diversity, relationism and temporality, respectively), Lerner (1998) has underscored Sugarman's (1986) assumptions. According to these assumptions, the essential message for supervisors is to adopt a stance in which the potential for change always exists, recognizing that it will occur at multiple levels, within a complex system (relationism). The system will have change as an inevitable and necessary feature, promoting development (temporality or 'historical embeddedness'). As a result of individual differences in the supervisor and the supervisee, a dynamic interaction arises that drives development (Lerner, 1998).

In terms of the moment-to-moment process that enables development to occur, the model takes the view that, fundamentally, development hinges on selective adaptation. This involves three essential activities: the selection of courses of action, based on option-appraisal relative to one's goals; the active use of coping strategies; and the selection of optimal environments, so as to optimize the attainment of these goals and what is referred to as 'compensation', namely responding to the unfolding situation so as to adjust coping and effort in a way that minimizes losses and maximizes success (Baltes *et al.*, 1998).

Let us now apply these assumptions from the general developmental theory to supervision. A classic example in supervision is the work of Heppner and Roehlke (1984) on the stages of supervisee development. They studied counsellor supervisees over a two-year period, in order to analyse the change process, focusing on how supervisees judged effective supervision over time. Beginners valued support and simple concrete skills-enhancement work, but later in their development they appreciated more attention to understanding the basis for their actions (e.g. conceptualization skills, such as the formulation of cases). Only after two to three years of training were the supervisees interested in personal issues, developing their individual approaches and other 'meta' issues. As a result of this kind of analysis, the different stages can be defined according to the developmental model (the following breakdown is from Hess, 1987):

Stage 1 (inception): This features insecurity and considerable dependency on the supervisor, with an onus on defining the role and building relationships, so that competence is demonstrated to an adequate level.
Stage 2 (skill development): At this point there is a shift to an apprenticeship model, and a greater involvement of the supervisee in identifying goals and selecting strategies.
Stage 3 (consolidation): Now supervisees are developing what is termed a 'therapeutic personality' – they are beginning to specialize, and to show some confidence in their practice.
Stage 4 (mutuality): The supervisee can next begin to demonstrate some creativity, working with increasing independence and relating to the supervisor in terms of a 'mutual consultation among equals'. Collegiality succeeds the apprentice status.

Heppner and Roehlke's (1984) analysis was based on the self-reported frequency of developmentally critical instances over training for beginning ($N = 15$), advanced ($N = 14$) and Doctoral intern trainees ($N = 12$), and illustrated these stages. For example, whereas no personal issues were noted by beginners, the Doctoral interns reported these to be frequent. Conversely, competence issues decreased over time, ceasing to be a significant incident for the Doctoral interns.

Perhaps the best-known contemporary developmental model within clinical supervision is the integrated developmental model (IDM; Stoltenberg & Delworth, 1987; Stoltenberg *et al.*, 2014). Characteristically for this model, different levels of development are delineated, in which 'level 1' (unfortunately, no descriptive label is offered for these levels) involves supervisees having a primary focus on themselves, particularly their need to develop skills whilst managing their performance anxiety and evaluation apprehension. By 'level 2', skills are developing and anxiety and apprehension are decreasing. As a result, awareness of the other (the client, primarily) can emerge, allowing empathy and understanding to blossom. But some destabilization (i.e. temporary loss of confidence and competence) is a feature of level 2, as motivation is more variable and some confusion and ambivalence predominate. Equally, there is variability in the supervisees' need for autonomy, including swings from inappropriate independence to excessive dependence. 'Level 3' represents the successful resolution of the issues of level 2 and, by this stage (benchmarked against the third year of initial professional training), motivation stabilizes and the supervisee develops appropriately autonomous and individualized role performance with an acceptable degree of insight.

In order to depict these levels with what they regard to be the necessary complexity, their account covers assessment, intervention, ethical practice and other dimensions of professional activity for each of the above three levels of development. This is because there needs to be a degree of specificity to enable an adequate assessment of the supervisee's developmental level. Thus, for example, a level 1 supervisee will tend to try to apply diagnostic categories and assess clients strictly 'by the book', looking for a fit between general theory and practice. By level 2 the focus will shift towards a more personal account of the client, although there may be a lack of understanding of how diagnostic labels affect the client and others with whom the supervisee needs to communicate. By level 3 the supervisee is thought to develop a much better-grounded grasp of the options for assessment, and to use things like diagnostic categories more flexibly, depending on factors such as the setting and the client. Other qualities emerge, such as greater self-awareness and reflective practice (Stoltenberg *et al.*, 2014).

This model is evaluated later, after the other two popular models have been described.

Therapy-Based Models of Clinical Supervision

Accounts of supervision that are based on therapy draw an explicit analogy between the critical assumptions and practices within therapy with those of supervision. Probably the dominant example of this analogy is the importance accorded to the therapeutic or 'working' relationship. The following are considered to be 'demonstrably effective' relationship variables in therapy by the American Psychological Association Task Force (APA; Norcross, 2001):

- Therapeutic alliance;
- Cohesion (in group therapy);
- Empathy;
- Goal consensus and collaboration;
- Dealing with resistance; and
- Addressing functional impairments.

In addition to these demonstrably effective relationship variables, the APA Task Force listed a further seven variables that were promising and 'probably effective' relationship variables:

- Positive regard;
- Congruence/genuineness;
- Feedback;
- Repair of alliance ruptures;
- Self-disclosure;
- Management of counter-transference; and
- Quality of relational interpretations.

By contrast, it was thought that there was insufficient research to judge whether customizing therapy for the following characteristics of the patient would improve outcome: attachment style; gender; ethnicity; religion and spirituality; preferences; and personality disorders.

Linking several of these variables together within an explanatory, evidence-based model, Norcross (2002) defined the therapeutic relationship in terms of 'the feelings and attitudes that therapists and clients have toward one another, and the manner in which these are expressed' (p.7). He proposed that the relationship was 'like a diamond, composed of multiple, interconnected facets' (p.8).

Some therapy-based models of clinical supervision apply such thinking and research directly, as in CBT supervision. For example, Liese and Beck (1997) note that the 'therapeutic relationship is *highly* important in cognitive therapy' (p.119, italics in original), featuring a collaborative stance. According to them, the relationship can become a central focus in therapy if necessary, and therapists will naturally pay attention to the interpersonal processes that occur (even including transference and counter-transference; Safran & Segal, 1990). This kind of link between the therapy and its supervision is made strongly by Padesky (1996), who stated that 'cognitive therapy supervision parallels the therapy itself' (p.281), and that 'the same processes and methods that characterize the therapy can be used to teach and supervise therapists' (p.289). As noted by Padesky (1996), Beck's initial manual for CBT (Beck *et al.*, 1979) had a chapter on the necessity of a positive therapeutic relationship, founded on warmth, empathy and genuineness. There was also an acknowledgement of difficulties in the relationship, and a discussion of transference and counter-transference issues. Therefore, according to Padesky (1996), competent cognitive therapists were always expected to be able to develop and sustain effective therapeutic relationships.

The working relationship (usually referred to as the 'learning alliance' in supervision) is only one example of a direct parallel being made between therapy and supervision. Perhaps the clearest and most thorough explication of the link between CBT and its supervision is a table provided by Liese and Beck (1997) in the *Handbook of Psychotherapy Supervision* (Watkins, 1997). This table (8.1 on p.121) helpfully provides a direct comparison of nine steps that characterize CBT, showing the equivalent step within supervision. To illustrate, the first step in CBT is agenda-setting, followed by a mood check and bridging with previous therapy sessions. The parallel steps in supervision are check-in, agenda-setting and bridge from previous supervision session. Equally strong parallel steps continue through to the final one which is, in both instances, eliciting feedback (throughout the session, and at the end). Interest in the supervisory relationship has continued within the CBT tradition (e.g. the rupture and repair cycle; Safran & Muran, 2000), but close inspection of the available CBT literature up until 2016 suggested that the CBT supervision alliance should have a narrower scope than in the original (and dominant) psychodynamic definition (e.g. less emphasis on the 'emotional bond', and more on the 'task alliance'; Milne & Reiser, 2017).

Other therapies also stress the importance of the relationship or alliance in supervision. This is most pronounced within the psychoanalytic tradition, where the supervisor is first trained as a psychoanalyst, based on the completion of a didactic programme, the analysis of several patients under the supervision of a senior analyst, and then through the candidate's personal therapy (Dewald, 1997). These traditional three elements in the development of a psychoanalytic supervisor are expected to be synthesized and applied within therapy. But, by contrast with CBT, it would appear that there are fewer parallels between therapy and supervision, as Dewald (1997) notes that 'most psychoanalytic supervisors consider supervision to be a process in some ways similar and in other ways quite different from therapeutic psychoanalysis' (p.33). Similarities include the need for an alliance and a place of comfort and safety, to promote open and honest interaction. Also, the needs of the patient/supervisee are important and take priority within the alliance. Other analogies within psychoanalysis include the recognition of the need for empathic recognition and acceptance (of some of the issues and conflicts experienced by the supervisee/patient) and transference/counter-transference phenomena (these may be drawn to the attention of a supervisee, though these would conventionally be addressed within the private analysis). In short, such is the overlap between therapy and supervision that it has traditionally been assumed that 'if one were a skilled analyst one would be able to do skilled supervision' (p.41). However, it is now being recognized that, whilst some analysts may be effective, others will have difficulty communicating concepts in an effective way as a teacher, necessitating some training.

Therefore, both CBT-based and psychoanalysis-based supervision treat the relationship as necessary for effective supervision, and both import concepts and practices directly from therapy for use in supervision. But, reflecting the need for internal consistency, in psychoanalysis the relation-ship that develops is a relatively intense, long-term and more significant component than in CBT supervision (Eagle & Long, 2014; Milne & Reiser, 2017).

Another major therapy model is based on systems reasoning. Within the systemic model there is also a close correspondence between the therapy and supervision, referred to as an 'isomorphic translation' (Rigazio-DiGilio *et al.*, 1997, p.224). Supervisees are seen as developing a complex, recursive pattern which requires a highly personalized approach. Within this developmental path, supervision is seen as a 'co-constructive process', meaning that a dialectic relationship between the supervisor and supervisee needs to emerge. In Holloway's (1997) systems approach the relationship 'is the container of dynamic process in which the supervisor and the supervisee negotiate a personal way of utilizing the structure of power and involvement that accommodates the trainee's progression of learning. This structure becomes the basis for the process by which the trainee will acquire knowledge and skills – the empowerment of the trainee' (p.251).

Although there is a difference of emphasis amongst these rather different therapies, the integrative model of supervision (which appears at the end of this section of the *Handbook of Psychotherapy Supervision*; Watkins, 1997) regards nurturing the supervisory relationship as one of the 'cardinal principles' of integrative supervision (Norcross & Halgin, 1997, p.208). They note that the therapeutic relationship has long been regarded as a primary curative factor in therapy, so conclude that 'it does not involve a great leap of understanding to perceive the supervisory relationship as being comparably important in fostering growth in clinical trainees' (p.212). Not surprisingly, this integrative model also draws parallels between therapy and supervision. Like good therapists, 'good supervisors are those who use appropriate teaching, goal-setting and feedback; they tend to be seen as supportive, non-critical individuals who respect their supervisees' (p.212). According to the integrative model, some of the same methods that are used to promote the therapeutic relationship are appropriate in supervision, with caveats. In this sense, the supervisor should aim to be supportive and use interpersonal techniques, so that the supervisee feels supported, understood and well educated. The aim is ultimately to reduce the inherent power imbalance, working towards an empathic and collaborative relationship in which insecurities, disagreements and alternatives can be discussed. A guideline on the alliance within CBT supervision can be found in Milne and Reiser (2017).

Other Commonalities Between Therapies and Supervision

Whilst the relationship or alliance features prominently in all accounts of supervision, we have already seen that there can be a considerable extension of the other therapeutic methods to supervision. Indeed, an interesting corollary becomes the question of the appropriate boundaries between therapy and supervision. In order to capture both the commonalities and these limits, Table 2.1 summarizes how the main therapeutic orientations explicitly transfer methods to supervision, but also where they place the limits, or make modifications to these extensions.

As Table 2.1 indicates, whilst both supervision and therapy would emphasize agenda-setting in the case of CBT (patient and the supervisee are active collaborators, contributing agenda items), this would be limited to what the therapist/supervisor deemed to be an appropriate focus. In this

Table 2.1 Examples of the overlaps and distinctions between therapy and supervision.

Therapy (source reference)	Identical (therapy and supervision are isomorphic/ indistinguishable)	Modified for supervision (exclusions/extensions)
CBT (Liese & Beck, 1997)	• Agenda-setting (patient and supervisee contribute items) • Feedback (elicited throughout and at end)	• Focus (on patient, i.e. excluding the supervisee as the 'patient' as an agenda item) • Includes formal (standard documentation) and summative evaluation (pass/fail judgement)
Psychoanalysis (Dewald, 1997)	• Goal of accessing internal experiences and functioning (e.g. counter-transference) • Building a working alliance (to provide comfort and safety, so promoting open and honest interaction)	• Boundary – but only access experiences specific to impaired learning in supervision. Personal issues of supervisee to be addressed within the separate personal analysis
Systemic (Rigazio-DiGilio et al., 1997)	• Assumed that change/ development is an individual but co-constructed journey, complex, holistic and recursive in nature	• This assumption is a topic for explicit, educational discussion in supervision (e.g. impact of culture and ability on use of model)
Integrative/ Eclectic (Norcross & Halgin, 1997)	• An eclectic blend of methods should be used pragmatically (i.e. in response to the patient's/ supervisee's needs at the time) • Evaluation of outcomes	• Methods like 'case discussion conferences' are presumably excluded from therapy; as are the roles of 'lecturer, teacher and collegial peer'. Also, the adequacy of supervision is 'typically assumed, rather than verified' (p.214)

Source: Milne, D.L. (2009). Reproduced with permission of Derek Milne.

sense, the supervisee would not normally be permitted to include their personal functioning or personal growth as an agenda topic. Similarly, whilst feedback is integral to both, only the supervisee would expect to have their performance recorded on standard documentation forms provided by a local training programme, and to have that performance judged in terms of whether or not it was up to a required standard. Other examples include the goals and the importance of the alliance. All of these examples are taken for convenience and ready comparability from the *Handbook of Psychotherapy Supervision* (Watkins, 1997). However, a defining characteristic of the supervision models summarized in Table 2.1 (and of others that draw on therapy for their inspiration) is that these methods transfer to supervision, and to a large extent. That is, far more unites the two areas of practice than divides them, and locating examples bounding or limiting the extension of therapeutic methods to supervision is relatively difficult. Personally, I agree with this explicit use of reasoning by analogy, because it is a useful skill when addressing new problems (itself a common topic in supervision), and it is also a highly professional way to think about how activities that may seem distinct are actually better understood as different points on related continua (for a detailed justification for utilizing analogies see Milne, 2007c; Milne & Reiser, 2017).

Supervision-Specific Models

Social role models

A social role model specifies the roles that a supervisor performs, together with the associated functions (Beinart, 2004). They are basically pragmatic, placing little explicit emphasis on a governing theory. For example, according to a popular model, the supervisor partly plays the manager role, serving a 'normative' set of functions (e.g. ensuring that paperwork is completed and that the organization's policies and procedures are followed). This is complemented by the therapist role, in which the supervisor performs a 'restorative' function (providing support and care to the therapist), and the teacher role (carrying out the 'formative' function, in which the supervisee is educated and trained; Kadushin, 1976; Proctor, 1988). A fourth role that has been defined is that of consultant, someone who allows supervisees to share responsibility for their development, to become a resource, whilst encouraging supervisees to take responsibility and to trust their own ability to resolve work issues (Bernard, 1997). In playing the consultant role, the supervisor will encourage discussion of different options (e.g. different therapeutic possibilities) and encourage reflection on the pros and cons. Another consultant activity would be to encourage the conceptualization of work problems, and to consider the emotional aspects of such work.

Another major role that has been delineated is that of evaluator or monitor (Bernard & Goodyear, 2014). Holloway (1997) also emphasizes the task of working on the professional role, including emotional awareness and self-evaluation. As do several authors, she generates a matrix to show how these different tasks relate to roles, trainee factors, client factors and organizational or contextual factors. Holloway (1997) refers to her model as a dynamic one, in which her Systems Approach to Supervision (SAS) provides a frame of reference that allows supervisors to perform their roles systematically. The model is also meant to be pan-theoretical and practical, highlighting the work that needs to be done, pivoting around the quality of the supervisory relationship, with the familiar objective of enabling the supervisee to become competent. These broad roles can be subdivided and expressed in terms of the behaviours that make up the larger roles. For example, the teacher role can be based on instruction, advice, modelling and so forth (for an explication and update see Holloway, 2014).

Whilst the dominant role categorization of teacher, therapist and manager appears to survive empirical scrutiny, for example withstanding factor analytic testing (Winstanley, 2000), the role of consultant and these other subsidiary roles (consultant, evaluator, monitor) do not appear to be as well defined (for a critical review see Bernard & Goodyear, 2014).

Supervision task models

The social roles (and the different styles or orientations that supervisors use to perform them) necessarily link to the related tasks of supervision. This is because one's orientation dictates that certain activities have priority, as in a CBT supervisor adopting the formative role and a task-orientated style in order to develop an agenda collaboratively. Because of these important links to a different theoretical framework, these supervision-specific models are not subsumed under the developmental model, although the notion of 'tasks' is also commonly used within that approach.

Examples of these task-orientated models include Bernard's (1997) discrimination model, in which the three topics of 'interventions, conceptualization and personalization' are emphasized. The focus of intervention concerns discussion of all aspects of therapy, such as attempts to greet, empathize, confront or interpret within therapy. Conceptualization refers to the efforts that the supervisee makes in therapy (or their other work) to make theoretical sense of phenomena and to generate predictions or hypotheses. In supervision this becomes a joint activity and is referred to as the conceptualization task. Finally, the supervisee's functioning as an individual makes up the personalization focus (including their personality, culture and other individual differences). This latter category would also subsume professional behaviour or personal professional development, namely aspects of ethical functioning and the interface between the individual and their professional persona (Gillmer & Marckus, 2003).

For Hawkins and Shohet (2000) there are seven distinguishable topics or 'modes' within supervision: the content of therapy; the strategies and interventions used within therapy; the therapeutic relationship; the therapist's process (i.e. phenomena such as counter-transference and parallel processes); the supervisor's own processes (including reactions to the supervisee); the supervisor–client relationship (e.g. attending to fantasies the supervisor and client may have about one another); and the wider context (i.e. attention to the professional community and other aspects of the environment that relate to the supervisee, like the service organization in which they both operate). This longer list of tasks can be seen to overlap closely with, and essentially extend, those within Bernard's (1997) discrimination model, subdividing some activities like therapy, and providing a much clearer account of the context within which this would be addressed. According to Hawkins and Shohet (2000), good supervision involves the use of all seven modes over time (i.e. not necessarily occurring in every single supervision session). They suggest that the use of the different modes should be related to considerations such as the developmental stage or readiness of the supervisee for the different modes. But, as a general rule, they suggest starting with mode 1 (focusing on therapy with the client and the details of each session's work). With growing sophistication in the supervisee, they believe that the other modes become more prevalent and appropriate (echoing the developmental model material presented earlier). Other considerations are the nature of the work being undertaken, the quality of the alliance between supervisor and supervisee (especially openness and trust) and the respective styles of the parties (e.g. learning style and cultural background). Although they do not furnish any empirical data, they are strongly of the view that all seven modes are necessary for successful supervision: 'we have become increasingly convinced that to carry out effective supervision . . . it is necessary for the supervisor to be able to use all seven modes of supervision' (Hawkins & Shohet, 2000, p.87).

These task models can, in turn, merge with process and functional models. For example, consider the work of Shanfield *et al.* (1989). They trained raters to use the Psychotherapy Supervision Inventory to reliably distinguish the different styles of 34 supervisors who worked with supervisees whose style was held constant. Supervisors judged to be excellent used a lot of empathy to enable supervisees to detail their therapy work, attended to the emotional accompaniments that the supervisees experienced and focused their remarks on the clinical material that was provided, in order to help the supervisee to understand the patient (Shanfield *et al.*, 1993).

Functional models

One way of clarifying these diverse models and their numerous dimensions is to distil them down to their core functions. Clarity about one's functions as a supervisor can greatly enable decisions about the most appropriate topics, styles, and so on (a truth from biology: 'form follows function'). As touched on a moment ago, Holloway's (2014) SAS model identifies five supervisory functions: those of monitoring/evaluating, advising/instructing, modelling, consulting, and supporting/sharing. She offers a wheel diagram to show how these functions would be related to different tasks and the other dimensions of her model. For example, the supervisee's experience and the client's problems combine in a dynamic process, in which the seven different dimensions of her SAS model mutually influence one another. The SAS delineation incorporates the traditional Kadushin (1976) breakdown, in terms of the normative, formative and restorative functions, adding detail on how development can be supported (i.e. the modelling and consulting functions). Combined with the above tasks, a supervisor's efforts to fulfil these five primary functions represent supervision 'process' to Holloway (2014).

Despite the multitude of tasks, roles and functions, they can be brought into a relatively clear focus by working back from the primary purposes of supervision, including the provision of safe and ethical therapy, and the development of competence and capability in the supervisee. Other functions, labelled 'outcomes' and 'tasks' in Figure 2.1, are set out to illustrate how the different levels of supervisory function can be thought to contribute to these primary purposes. This analysis of the functions of supervision is based on collating illustrative material in the supervision literature (Binder & Strupp, 1997; Holloway, 1997; Lambert & Ogles, 1997; Falender & Shafranske, 2004; Ladany *et al.*, 2005; Bernard & Goodyear, 2014). This wealth of material was then organized around the four kinds of broad

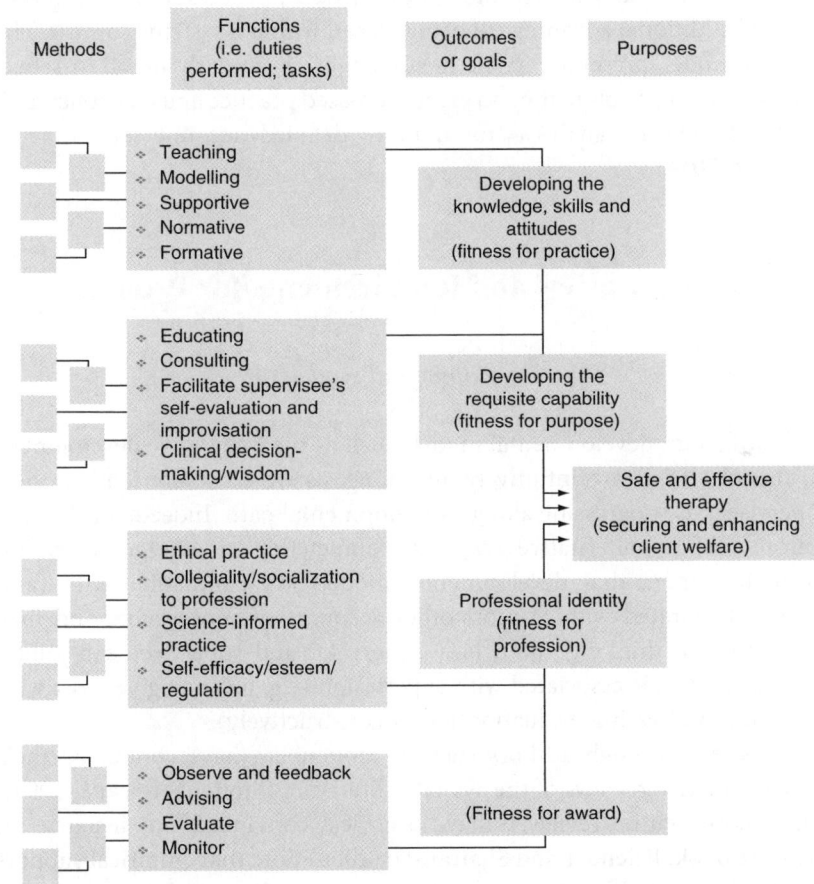

Figure 2.1 A thematic summary of the related functions of supervision.
Source: Milne, D.L. (2009). Reproduced with permission of Derek Milne.

educational outcomes (i.e. the second-order themes) that are identified by the Quality Assurance Agency (QAA, 2005). This has everyday parallels in how individual and collective behaviour is organized as a hierarchy. For example, a university has the purpose of generating knowledge that is relevant to society, which is pursued primarily through the functions of teaching and research, with specific outcomes (such as training health practitioners to be fit for practice). A popular analogy can be made with the *Canterbury Tales*, in which Chaucer's characters can be thought of as quite distinctive, yet to share a common destination.

Holloway's (2014) systems approach to supervision (SAS model) is a particularly well-articulated integration of tasks, processes and functions, with the additional advantage of being placed within a systems context. The tandem model, presented in the next chapter, is similarly broad in scope, but has a stronger foundation in evidence-based practice and an explicit link to this functional analysis (for a more detailed account see Milne & Watkins, 2014).

Critical Review and Requirements for Progress

Developmental models

In their favour, developmental models such as the integrative developmental model (IDM) are intuitively appealing, as we naturally tend to view supervisees as progressing along a developmental path. Indeed, it is hard to conceive of an alternative way for competence to emerge. It is not surprising, then, that developmental models are compatible with (and even incorporated within) most other accounts of supervision, and they are helpful in thinking about how supervisor and supervisee can jointly address the issues associated with supervision (e.g. balancing support with challenge; addressing evaluation issues constructively).

However, although authors such as Stoltenberg have conducted their own affirmative reviews of the available literature (Stoltenberg *et al.*, 1994), other more neutral reviewers have been less convinced. For instance, in their textbook, Falender and Shafranske (2004) note that empirical support for developmental models has not been obtained, as the literature is a 'methodological morass' (p.15). The exhaustive and meticulous systematic review by Ellis and Ladany (1997) similarly concluded that the rigour of the relevant research was 'sub-standard' (p.493). They concluded that the central premises of the developmental model remained untested. A later review by Ellis and colleagues (Inman *et al.*, 2014) reiterated these concerns. These impartial reviews question the empirical support for the developmental model. Furthermore, there are theoretical concerns that the model is fundamentally simplistic and vague (Russell *et al.*, 1984). In model criteria terms, there is a lack of 'elaboration'. Another long-standing criticism, dating from Worthington's (1987) early review of 16 developmental models, is that little explication is offered as to how transitions are made between the different stages of development (i.e. weak 'causal precision'). Other weaknesses of this approach include the reliance on self-report and experience (time served) as the way in which development is operationalized (Bernard & Goodyear, 2014: i.e. poor 'assumptions').

These concerns make one question the strong conclusion from the Stoltenberg *et al.* (1994) review, namely that 'evidence appears solid for developmental changes across training levels' (p.419). In summary, whilst the developmental model makes intuitive sense and provides a useful basis for organizing supervision (i.e. good 'heuristic value'), even advocates of the developmental approach conclude that a more precise theory is required if we are to clarify how specific thoughts, feelings and behaviours, occurring at the different developmental stages, predict patterns of development (Watkins, 1997). It is Watkins' view that, to realize the promise of developmental models, we require a much clearer focus on the actual behaviours of both supervisors and supervisees, over specified developmental passages and incorporating superior methodologies.

Therapy models

Turning to the therapy-based models, it is evident that much overlap can be defined between a therapy and its supervision. This is indicated by Table 2.1, and by the emphatic quotes cited above (from the proponents of particular therapies). Adopting one's preferred therapy model as one's model of clinical supervision has considerable advantages. These include automatically importing a coherent, acceptable and well-understood model to the complex business of supervision (as shown earlier by the explicit 'compatibility' of the CBT models of therapy and supervision). Also, one similarly imports well-honed skills, in relation to the different methods that are shared by supervision and the specific therapy (i.e. the 'action implications'). However, a challenge for every therapy-based model is to be clear about the boundaries of this extension to supervision (i.e. 'focus' issues). This is touched on in Table 2.1, and indicates the nature of the challenge, but in routine supervisory practice such grey areas will at times become a vexatious issue, meriting greater clarification of boundaries.

We can illustrate some of these difficulties if we adopt the traditional distinction between the normative, formative and restorative functions of supervision (Kadushin, 1976; Proctor, 1988). In normative terms we should acknowledge that there are important power differences between therapy and supervision: whilst the client can opt out of therapy, the supervisee is normally obliged to remain in supervision (Newman, 1998; Bernard & Goodyear, 2014). This involuntary or mandatory aspect is typically most evident in pre-qualification supervision, and although more experienced practitioners may exercise more choice over their supervisor and the content and methods of supervision, the different professional bodies and the supervisee's employers tend to require career-long supervision (at least in the UK). This power difference can have a significant differential impact within supervision, negating therapy-based approaches. For example, there are no precedents in therapy for the situation where a supervisor might insist that a supervisee discontinues something that is judged to be inappropriate, or for the possible sequel, a disciplinary or course continuation (progress) episode. It follows that within this rather differently charged environment there arise various thoughts, feelings and behaviours that would be unusual in therapy. This includes negative aspects, like professional rivalry and deception ('faking good' in relation to evaluation), and positive ones like informal collegiality (which tends to characterize established supervisory relationships, but which would be inappropriate in therapy).

In terms of the formative function of supervision, these examples touch on the important distinction around the presence of evaluation: whilst both supervisors and therapists are supposed to evaluate their work routinely, in the case of supervision the instruments and procedural details (e.g. the frequency of assessments, and who is privy to the information) are dictated by the local training programme (pre-qualification), or by the profession (post-qualification: continuing professional development, CPD), and to an extent that usually exceeds national (e.g. managed care) or employer requirements. Also, in supervision the competence of the professional providing the service is an explicit focus, which in therapy is rarely a criterion (outside of some research trials). Given the summative function of evaluation, this can lead to supervisors being 'blacklisted' by training programmes to an extent that seems far more common than their being 'struck off' for incompetence by their profession or 'fired' by their employer.

Finally, from the restorative perspective, therapy techniques are inappropriate in supervision when they represent treatment for the supervisee's personal functioning or growth, because these should not be part of the contract between supervisor and supervisee, nor are they part of the expectations that authorizing organizations have of supervision. Rather, supervision is primarily an educational enterprise, focusing on the therapy that is provided, rather than the therapist who provides it. This is not to say that there are not therapeutic elements and features within appropriately focused supervision (e.g. the non-specific factors, such as warmth and concreteness), but rather that the boundaries between these activities need to be monitored and maintained. To quote Watkins (1997), 'supervision may have its therapeutic elements, but it is primarily education' (p.606). This is a boundary that is also acknowledged within the psychodynamic tradition, through its use of a separate arrangement for personal issues (i.e. the training analysis), and through the clarification of the goals of supervision: 'the typical supervisor applies psychodynamic clinical theories and methods usually associated with therapy to achieve the educational goals of supervision' (Binder & Strupp, 1997, p.45).

Overall, however, there is much to commend the reasoned, cautious transfer of therapy to supervision, and it is perhaps because of the extensive and highly plausible parallels between the two professional activities that using therapeutic thinking is one of the most popular models of supervision (competing with that of supervising as one was supervised).

Supervision-specific models

Task models have been criticized on the grounds that they omit key activities. For example, in her review of the different models, Beinart (2004) points out that the discrimination model (Bernard & Goodyear, 2014) fails to take account of evaluation as part of the supervisor's role, and also gives little attention to relationship qualities.

In general terms, these models are probably better described as frameworks or practical schemes for organizing supervision. This is because they tend to lack any theoretical basis, deriving instead from experience and expert consensus on what is important (e.g. topics for the agenda; awareness of roles, contexts and systems). Whilst this will make them serviceable (i.e. high on the 'action implications' criterion), and perhaps particularly appealing to the novice supervisor (given their concreteness, and their 'compatibility' with their existing understanding), there appear to be no carefully developed guidelines or manuals that set out such things as how supervisors should behave, or how they should be trained (Milne, 2016). This omission (poor intervention 'elaboration') is tackled in Chapter 5 (supervision methods), but at least there has been progress with CBT supervision latterly (Sudak *et al.*, 2016; Milne & Reiser, 2017). I describe these manuals in Chapter 5. Without a clear, written statement about what a model is meant to include, research on its effectiveness is severely hampered. For example, there is the real risk that outcome evaluations are fatally flawed by the lack of specificity as to what the particular 'supervision' process should look like (i.e. weak intervention 'fidelity'; Borelli *et al.*, 2005). This may seem obvious, but it is surprising how few outcome evaluations even describe their intervention in outline terms, far less provide data on what actually happened within the study (i.e. 'quantification' is absent). Such process-outcome evaluations are necessary if a specific model is to move forward. Chapter 8 picks up this issue, describing ways to pursue these and related types of evaluation.

Another kind of problem with specific models is that the absence of a guiding theory makes such pragmatic approaches of limited value (e.g. in not having some core principles or understanding that can be deployed in complex, novel or difficult situations). By contrast, a supervisor who is working from a therapy model will have the option of considering an issue from that guiding theory. For example, CBT suggests how one might address difficulties in forming and maintaining an effective working alliance, because this is also a common issue in therapy (for details see Chapter 4).

The limited, rather concrete level of generality of specific models is a further concern, as it fails to suggest exactly how the functions of supervision are achieved (i.e. low 'causal explanation'), the ways in which they might be researched are unclear (i.e. 'assumptions' about the most appropriate research methods do not follow from the framework), and, in particular, it is not obvious which predictions follow (i.e. they have limited 'potential').

I want to close this critical review by mapping these three broad types of supervision model onto one that is derived from the neighbouring staff development literature. This represents a critical evaluation and integration of all three types of supervision models. If they are sound, they should surely address the majority of themes within the comparatively well-developed field of staff training.

An Essential, Staff Development Model of Supervision

A helpful framework against which to map the three types of supervisory models is the model of staff training and development (e.g. Colquitt *et al.*, 2000; Goldstein & Ford, 2002). This allows us to draw on a highly relevant neighbouring literature in order to specify the essential variables that logically should be in a general supervision model, at least as far as the formative/educational function of supervision is concerned. Figure 2.2 depicts this model, showing a classic conceptual model made up of boxes or panels (i.e. the variables) and arrows linking these variables (i.e. the

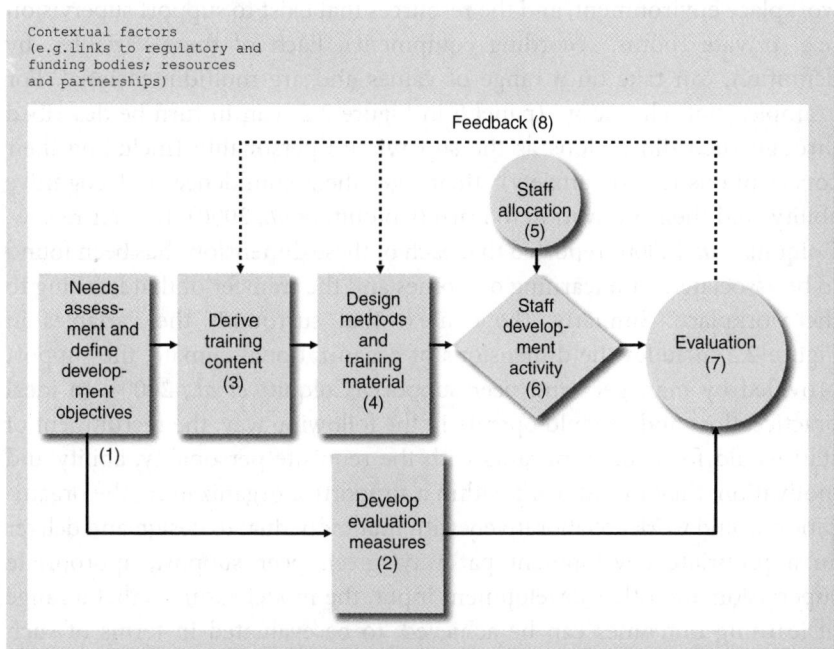

Figure 2.2 The essential model of staff development.
Source: Milne, D.L. (2007). Reproduced with permission of Taylor and Francis.

causal mechanisms or generative processes by which the variables influence each other, to promote development).

According to this general model (Milne, 2007b), supervision can be understood as requiring: a process of needs assessment, so that learning objectives can be specified (panel 1 in Figure 2.2); the development of instruments to measure and evaluate the extent to which these objectives have been achieved; the designing of a syllabus or programme of activity, and a related design effort to specify the supervisory methods and supporting materials that are indicated. Once this work has been done, the supervisory activity can commence with suitably allocated supervisees (panels 6 and 5 in Figure 2.2, respectively). As indicated in a partial way within Figure 2.2, each of these panels or variables should be linked to one another by feedback loops. This provides the essential means by which the supervision system can adapt to its changing context, and monitor the supervisee's development. Lastly, as indicated by the heading 'contextual factors', the eight defined elements that make up this general supervision model need to be considered within such contextual considerations as the workplace environment, and the resources that exist to support supervision (e.g. private rooms, recording equipment). Each of these variables, by definition, can take on a range of values and are multidimensional. For example, 'staff allocation' (panel 5 in Figure 2.2) can in turn be described through such dimensions as the supervisee's personality (including their conscientiousness or anxiety), their age, their confidence and cognitive ability, and their motivation to learn (Colquitt *et al.*, 2000). In their review, Colquitt *et al.* (2000) reported that each of these dimensions has been found to be associated with learning outcomes and the transfer of that learning to the workplace. Similarly, the context that surrounds the variables in Figure 2.2 includes the dimensions of organizational climate, the support provided by managers and peer support (Colquitt *et al.*, 2000). In ideal practice, this model would operate in the following way: the recruitment of staff would focus on applicants with the requisite personality, ability and motivation; they would work within a supportive organization; the organization would work collaboratively with that individual to design and deliver an appropriate development pathway; given peer support, appropriate supervision and other development input, the model assumes that a range of learning outcomes can be achieved, to be evaluated in terms of such dimensions as the supervisee's reactions to supervision and their acquisition of relevant skills. The extent to which these become part of that individual's job performance represents the degree to which supervision has resulted in successful transfer to the workplace (technically referred to as generalization, across time and settings).

How do the three broad types of models we have just considered map onto this essential one? In general terms, pretty much everything that is specified within the essential model is present to some extent within the three models discussed earlier. However, the degree to which the nine different variables are emphasized (treating 'context' as the ninth factor) understandably varies. For instance, the systemic approach (as per the SAS model) gives most emphasis to this supervision context, whereas the developmental model would lay greater stress on the individual characteristics of the supervisee. Therefore, in a general sense, it seems that these three models duly reflect the staff development one (which, it is only fair to note, is itself open to the criticism that it places relatively little emphasis on the restorative or normative functions of supervision).

In summary, I believe that the essential model of supervision set out in Figure 2.2 can be thought of as compatible with the three broad types of supervision models that we have considered, capturing at least the core variables and processes that are necessary to understand supervision. However, more elaborate models are needed, such as the one developed by Colquitt *et al.* (2000), to account better for staff development. In this sense, I will treat the essential model as the basis for reformulating supervision, the task of the next chapter.

Discussion

It has been said that supervision 'can be as complex and challenging as . . . therapy itself' (Liese & Beck, 1997, p.114) and this brief overview of the different models within clinical supervision surely underlines that view. Indeed, logically one might suggest that it is even more complex than therapy itself, because supervision subsumes therapy (i.e. in terms of 'treating' the therapy, necessarily overlaying therapists' issues, such as parallel processes or personal professional development). One could reasonably argue that, amongst the challenges faced by mental health professionals, supervision is second only to organizational change in complexity.

I have tried to ensure that this complexity has been duly reflected in this chapter, as even my brief analysis of the different supervision models indicates the wide variety of theories and concepts that drive equally diverse notions of the roles, tasks and methods of supervision. If one simply thinks about the therapy-based supervision models then there are surely dozens of variations on the supervision theme, given that there are so many different therapies. Add to this the differences, theoretical orientations, preferences and styles that individual supervisors have, and then multiply that by the emphasis within different training programmes, and one can begin to envisage the complexity of the supervision business.

But perhaps this complexity (which violates some of the criteria for a good model, such as parsimony and falsifiability) can be whittled down to a more concise, elegant model of supervision? After all, the history of science is replete with instances where hugely complex phenomena are ultimately reduced to their essence through research (e.g. the incredible diversity of planet Earth's organisms ultimately being comprehensible by reference to natural selection). The essential model is an example of how this might eventually be achieved in relation to supervision, although of course we have a long way to go yet, awaiting much better research.

In addition to recognizing the daunting complexity of supervision, there are other reasons to feel uncomfortable about the current status of supervision. For instance, applying the criterion of empirical support, these popular models do not appear particularly promising. For instance, Ellis and Ladany's (1997) systematic review found that one of the most widely cited approaches, the IDM (Stoltenberg & Delworth, 1987), 'has not been adequately tested and no tentative inferences seem justifiable given the poor rigour of the two studies' (p.480). Ellis and Ladany (1997) opined that their review of the developmental model led to 'disheartening' (p.482) conclusions (e.g. because significant difficulties had not been resolved in relation to hypothesis validity, and there has been a heavy reliance on cross-sectional research to test the longitudinal inferences that are integral to a developmental model). A second issue that they raised, and which applies to all three types of models, is that of fidelity; it is rare for researchers to demonstrate objectively that supervisors are adhering to the given model, as opposed to studies that provide outcome data purportedly showing that their model was successful. A number of studies of the fidelity of therapists and supervisors bear out this caution, and I have certainly found this to be an issue in my own collaborative research (e.g. Milne & James, 2002). Such over-simplification is unlikely to give supervision the complex modelling needed for its full comprehension or successful implementation. What we require are carefully specified models of the kind that allow measurement of precisely how different supervisory activities or relationship qualities relate to specific changes in the supervisee (Gonsalvez *et al.*, 2002). There is a need to focus on the actual behaviours of supervisors and supervisees, in their context (Watkins, 1997). Unfortunately, supervision research has itself continued to neglect models (Barker & Hunsley, 2013), further compounding the problem.

These and other criticisms lead us smoothly into the next chapter, which puts forward a partial solution to several of these issues. In order to provide a general working model and a fresh point of reference, I will again draw on the staff training literature for more building-blocks, developing the essential model of supervision that was set out above. This tactic (another example of reasoning by analogy) is used explicitly because it allows us to draw on a closely related but surprisingly distinct literature. In particular, I will try to show how this essential model can be developed by drawing on the best of the above supervision models, becoming an integrative and (through further careful scrutiny of the research literature) evidence-based approach to CBT supervision, the tandem model. I believe that this is the kind of model that is required to take supervision further down its own developmental path.

3

Reframing Supervision

The various models of clinical supervision noted in the previous chapter afford many ways of thinking about how supervision works, but there is a general lack of conceptual rigour to these models. Although there is a strong tendency to judge research and theory on the basis of the outcomes (e.g. statistically significant findings that support a theory), research needs to start with careful reasoning, as in utilizing clear concepts, acknowledged assumptions, and proper arguments (Machado & Silva, 2007). In general, the models that were summarized in Chapter 2 do not withstand such basic logical tests. For instance, there is a lack of internal consistency and insufficient elaboration to make many of the models useful and testable (Warr, 1980). As a result, the models lack the degree of precision needed for supervisors to know what to do in specific situations, and it also means that research work is hampered. Specifically, this imprecision compromises the hypothesis validity of research (Wampold & Holloway, 1997), in the sense of making it difficult to set out hypotheses that are based on the model and which are appropriately explicit and relevant. According to a review of 144 studies of clinical supervision conducted up to 1993, it was judged that at least 80 per cent of these studies had poor conceptualization (i.e. inconsequential or ambiguous hypotheses; Ellis *et al.*, 1996). To overcome these difficulties, Ellis *et al.* (1996) suggested that future research would be better served by an explicit model that defines the constructs that are involved, so that appropriately clear hypotheses can be explicated and tested. Although the number of supervision research studies has multiplied

Evidence-Based CBT Supervision: Principles and Practice, Second Edition. Derek L. Milne.
© 2018 John Wiley & Sons Ltd. Published in 2018 by the British Psychological Society and John Wiley & Sons Ltd.

since 1996, in general there has been little progress in incorporating explicit models (Watkins & Milne, 2014). This chapter addresses that neglect by considering in detail successive versions of the cognitive-behaviour therapy (CBT) supervision model.

Of course, this kind of conceptual detail is also a great help to those who practise supervision, as it specifies exactly which variables are thought to be important and how they are understood to interact. This relates to another criticism of current models, namely that they are not sufficiently complex to reflect the realities that envelop supervision in typical mental health service settings. Because models are typically set out in rather general terms, for example with only a few interacting variables, those with an awareness of the business of delivering supervision in the 'real world' believe that these models fail to recognize its inherent complexity (Worthington, 1987; Watkins, 1995). In addition to recognizing the complex work environments in which supervisors operate, there is also a need for models to clarify the way that moment-to-moment supervisory interactions are supposed to unfold. Models need to specify what it is that supervisors are supposed to be doing within a supervision session, and the anticipated effects that this will have on the supervisee, during and after the session.

Given these concerns about current models, one option is to abandon them in favour of a more pragmatic approach, one that simply builds on experience and consensus to test a simplified framework, with only a limited number of concepts. An example is the outcome-orientated approach, in which the focus is on guiding therapy through corrective feedback, based on the therapists' clinical effectiveness (Harmon *et al.*, 2007). But this sort of theory-free approach seems fraught with difficulty. For one thing, it is inconceivable that supervisors could somehow empty their minds of theory whilst engaged in their professional duties. But even if that were possible, reliance on simple technologies like feedback would fail to furnish supervisors with the information needed to solve new problems in the present. Also, the history of science indicates that conceptual analysis is required to develop and test knowledge, as in knowing how to interpret information and feedback (Machado & Silva, 2007). In this sense, abandoning models appears problematic, making the issue one of trying harder to establish which concepts and factors are critical to supervision in its complex context (e.g. in relation to the generalization of supervision to routine work, especially therapy).

Therefore, the assumption made in this book is that an appropriately detailed model is the proper basis for taking forward both research and practice in supervision. But this needs to be evaluated rigorously, within complex settings (i.e. naturalistically), if it is to develop the requisite specificity and relevance to practice. An approach called theory-based evaluation (Chen, 1990) can provide the necessary balance. As Falender and Shafranske (2004, p.232) put it: 'An empirical, evidence-based, theoretical foundation is required.' Having a sound theory is, of course, something that many educationalists have advocated for many a long year. In his classic book, *Experience and Education*, Dewey (1938) described the need for a model in these terms (I have substituted the term supervision for education):

> The issue is not one model or another, but what is worthy of the name supervision. The basic question concerns the nature of supervision, pure and simple. We shall make surer and faster progress when we devote ourselves to finding out just what supervision is – and what conditions have to be satisfied in order that supervision may be a reality, and not a name or a slogan. We need a sound philosophy.
>
> *(Dewey, 1938, pp.90–91)*

This, then, is the goal of this chapter: what is a sound philosophy, one that overcomes these difficulties with current models?

In order to address this challenging question, the remainder of this chapter recounts my collaborative work on the evidence-based approach to developing clinical supervision. As I illustrate, this includes drawing very carefully on the existing evidence in order to set out the important variables, trying to indicate how they interact. As a result, an integrative, evidence-based, tandem model of supervision will be articulated, with experiential learning at its heart. In order to address the traditional problems over imprecision, this model will be presented in a variety of ways (i.e. graphically, mechanically and metaphorically), and contrasted with the CBT supervision model, to maximize its comprehension and precise application (to research or practice). This tandem model builds on the general definition of clinical supervision (Milne, 2007b), adding the empirical (applied science) perspective on supervision, as set out in Chapter 1.

This conceptualization work is just the beginning of the scientific journey, and will lead into the manualization of the approach ('implementation'). This is another important step, one that allows practitioners and researchers to see exactly how the model might be applied. But before the intervention we need to have 'operationalization', namely a stage in which we specify how the model can be measured. In order to address this additional scientific requirement, a number of processes and outcomes will be specified from the tandem model, and an instrument described for the measurement task. In the final phase of this research agenda, evidence bearing on the 'evaluation' of this model in routine practice will be presented. Based on this analysis, the final part of this chapter will be a critical review of this tandem model.

Conceptualizing Supervision

A basic model of supervision

I have already described the 'best evidence synthesis' approach to the literature review in Chapter 1, in working up an empirical definition of clinical supervision. It will be recalled that this approach focuses on a carefully selected sample of key papers (i.e. research that is highly relevant to the question at hand). These selected papers are then scrutinized thoroughly, in a consistent way, in order to help us clarify what is known (and remains to be found out) about the topic at hand. This is the basic systematic review method (Petticrew & Roberts, 2006), a cornerstone of evidence-based clinical supervision (EBCS). This best-evidence synthesis approach was therefore repeated so that an evidence-based model of supervision could be clarified (for more detail see Milne *et al.*, 2008a). That is, we restricted our analysis to studies of supervision that had occurred in naturalistic work settings and which had demonstrated effectiveness in terms of their intended educational or clinical outcomes. In this way, we aimed to pinpoint a crystallization of the variables and interactions that had proved effective, integrating the inductively to indicate how supervision could be understood.

We found 24 such evaluations of supervision, most of them coming from the learning disability field, but involving a range of professional groups. These studies had used a wide range of instruments to assess the effectiveness of supervision, including supervisees' reactions, measures of the supervisees' learning, and the transfer of such learning to therapy. Most of these studies were drawn from residential settings, and the key variables manipulated through supervision were feedback, support and instruction. We used a coding manual to review the 24 papers, looking for three fundamental kinds of information. In order to address the need for a more complex model of supervision, we summarized the 'moderator' variables noted in the 24 studies. A moderator is a background factor that effects the direction and/or strength of the relationship between an independent and a dependent variable (Barron & Kenny, 1986; Kraemer *et al.*, 2002). Thus, the way that feedback or instruction is used might be moderated in one study by local history, by the personalities of these involved or by the physical environment in which supervision takes place. Such factors are usually subsumed under the term 'context', meaning that there is assumed to be an influential system within which supervision occurs. Indeed, several nested layers of systems are assumed, including primarily the social and physical ones, and these are thought to be evolving and influencing one another over time (Reis *et al.*, 2000). These authors quote Capra (1996) as observing that: 'Throughout the living world we find living systems nesting within other living systems' (p.28). A familiar example of this kind of nesting is the relationship between the 'common factors' of therapy, such as the alliance, which is understood to operate independently of the specific, technical aspects of a therapy (e.g. 'guided discovery' in CBT; see Nathan *et al.*, 2000). Another term for this nesting relationship is that of 'coupling' – the idea that all variables are continually linked and mutually interactive (Thelen & Smith, 1998). In supervision, a major example concerns the format that is utilized, such as the traditional one-to-one and group arrangements. Milne and Oliver (2000) enumerated seven such formats, surveying 24 supervisees, supervisors and their managers in order to get a sense of their popularity. They reported that the one-to-one approach was endorsed by everyone they asked, followed by the use of individual supervision in a group (e.g. 30 minutes per supervisee per week, on a rotational basis, within a 90-minute group) and co-therapy. These formats can be regarded as the inner 'nest' or micro-context for supervision, moderating it in significant ways. Because of its popularity, plus the present book's emphasis on clarifying the essential elements of EBCS, the one-to-one format will be given greatest emphasis. However, this is not intended to diminish the status of other formats and group-based formats in particular, which are clearly an important option, as well as being popular amongst supervisees, complementary to individual supervision, and a seemingly effective format (Liness *et al.*, 2016).

A second and highly topical moderating influence on supervision concerns its goals. In the UK, the government's Improving Access to Psychological Therapies (IAPT) initiative has shifted attention from the supervisor to the patient. Termed 'clinical case supervision' (Richards, 2008), this minimizes the traditional emphasis on caring, supportive interactions (intended to recognize and reduce therapists' burnout, through emotional support and strengthening their personal coping strategies) in order to re-prioritize problem-solving work addressing the challenges associated with the therapist's caseload management and clinical effectiveness. Therefore, the goals of clinical case supervision are to try to ensure treatment fidelity, in order to maximize the welfare and safety of all clients. In this context, the convention of supervisee-led case discussion is succeeded by supervisor/ service-led review of the supervisee's entire caseload. Case-based (or 'case-management') supervision is therefore 'high volume' and outcome-linked, representing a key part of the 'collaborative care' approach (an enhanced, multi-professional service system, featuring primary care-based help from mental health specialists operating through a case-manager arrangement; Katon *et al.*, 2001). This is discussed in greater depth later, for example in relation to the outcome-monitoring aspect (see Chapter 8). In summary, it is not difficult to imagine how innovations like case-based supervision, applied within flexible formats, could have a major moderating impact on both supervision and therapy.

The 'mediators' were the second type of variable that we sought to isolate in our review of the basic model of supervision. A mediator is an event occurring during supervision (the intervention, technique or independent variable), such as Socratic questioning or the use of an instructional method. By definition, mediators link cause (i.e. supervision) to effect (e.g. learning outcomes); these are therefore the methods that are used in supervision.

In turn, these methods, operating under the effect of moderator variables, achieve their effect through what are called 'mechanisms' – the generative explanation for a change process, such as learning as a result of Socratic questioning. A famous example in biology was Mendel's discovery of genes, which are the mechanism of heredity (for a gripping account see Bryson, 2004). Classic examples of mechanisms of change in therapy are exposure, developing a fresh understanding and re-experiencing something. Therefore, a mechanism is the means through which a mediator has its effect on outcomes, typically a learning process in the case of supervision.

Moderating factors

Having established that we could code these papers in a reliable way, following a coding manual, we were able to clarify the moderators, mediators and mechanisms within these 24 carefully selected studies. As far as moderators were concerned, some 35 different moderating variables were noted by the authors of these studies. These included general organizational factors, like staff turnover and administrative support. We also found reference to aspects of the intervention itself that were thought to be influential, such as the complexity of the task and the researcher's ability to persist with it. There were also research factors and learning factors (e.g. how reactive participants were to observation; the presence of game-playing and collusion). Depending on how the authors described these moderating factors, they were given a simple grading as facilitating (a positive '+' symbol) or impeding the supervision intervention (symbolized by a negative '−' symbol). As set out in Figure 3.1, it can be seen that the different moderating variables described within our sample of 24 studies were largely facilitating. For example, administrative support was reported in 5 of these 24 papers (each positive or negative symbol within the figure represents a study).

These many and various moderating variables can be thought of as providing the kind of complex modelling of supervision that reviewers have been requesting (Worthington, 1987; Watkins, 1997). Although the causal influence of these moderators on the supervision that was studied was not manipulated (or related to an explicit effect) in these 24 studies, Figure 3.1 does at least provide a contextual map for the kinds of factors that these researchers thought were important. The implication for practitioners is to try to ensure that as many as possible of the positive variables are present in their efforts to make a success of supervision. For researchers, the implication is to look more closely at how these factors actually operate on supervision. Although by definition rather general and difficult to manipulate, these moderators do appear to be significant: a mean of 2.1 moderators were identified per study, and only 2 of the 24 studies failed to identify a moderator. Consistent with the fact that these studies were educationally and/or clinically effective, 68 per cent of these identified moderators were judged as being facilitative.

To bring these data to life, consider one of these 24 studies. Hundert and Hopkins (1992) noted how the nature of administrative support, and indeed the process by which it was provided, may have affected their supervision intervention. This can be negative in its influence, as illustrated by the Demchak and Browder (1990) study, where it was noted that 'staff turnover influenced this study' (p.161).

Ordered Themes

First	Second	Third	Fourth

1 Staff turnover –
2 Scheduling problems –
3 Admin support +++++
4 Progressive organizational culture +
5 Orientation of school +
6 Diametrically opposed model –
7 Competing contingencies –
8 Insufficient organizational support –
9 Settings favourable (e.g. 'inclusive living') +
10 Support from visitors +
11 Problems in homes –

A
General (naturalistic) context.

General organizational context [A + E]

12 Complexity of task –
13 Persistence/negative attitudes – –
14 Generalization to other staff +
15 'Proctoring' effect ++
16 Incentives (£/manual free) +
17 Acceptable approach +
18 Brevity –

B
Intervention factors

'Intervention' factors [H + B]

19 Burden of study –
20 Reactivity to observation + & –; +; ++
21 Unreliable observation tool –

C
Research factors

Research influences

22 Game playing and collusion –
23 Training needed +
24 Needs led ++
25 Socialization to model necessary –

D
Learning factors

Learning

26 Changing ward organization +
27 Team approach +
28 Systems approach +; +; +; +

E
General (manipulated) support II

General organizational context [A + E]

29 Experience +
30 Ability and psychological mindedness +
31 Motivated ++

F
Supervisee factors

Participants [F + G + I]

32 Client outcomes ++
33 Patient reactions +

G
Patient factors

34 Consultant's facilitation +
35 Skills and experience +

H
Consultant factors

'Intervention' factors [H + B]

36 Anxiety (threat of new method) –

I
Supervisor factors

Participants [F + G + I]

MODERATED THE EFFECTS OF SUPERVISION

[+ or – influences; each symbol = freq. mentions]

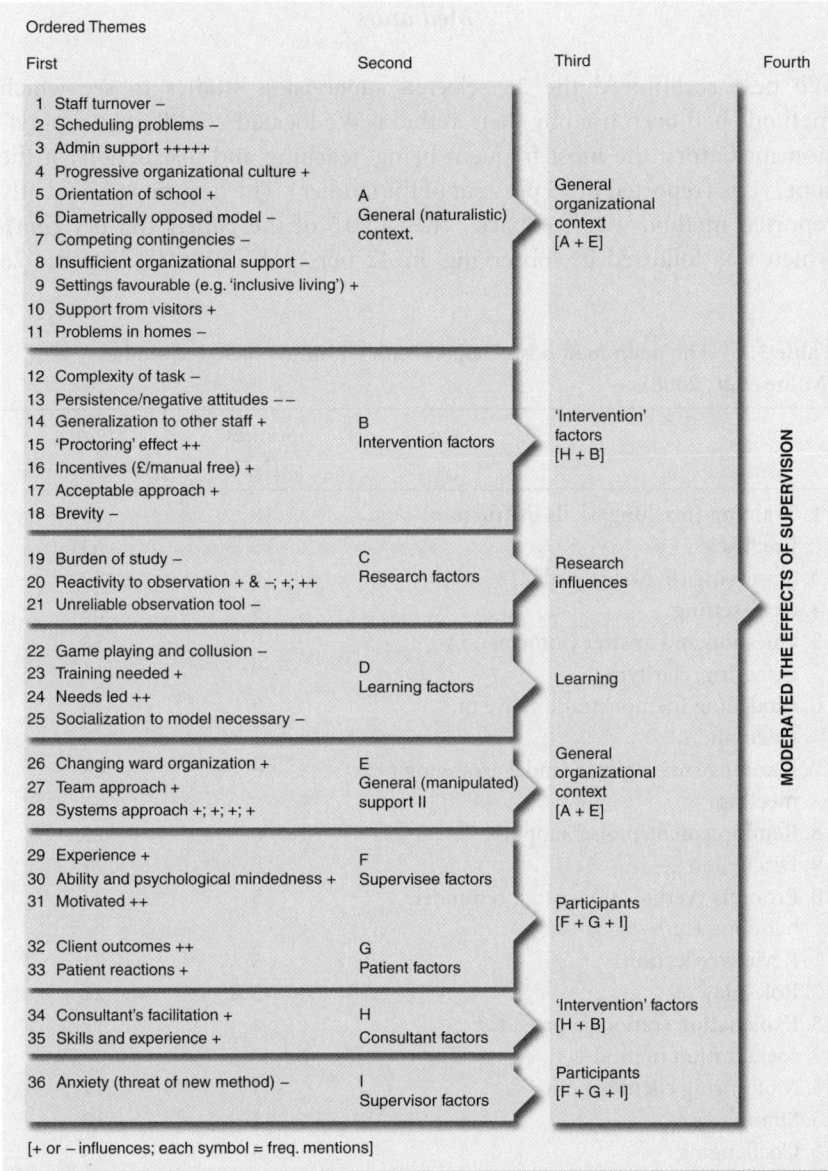

Figure 3.1 A dendrogram, depicting the 36 moderating factors identified in 24 reviewed studies.

Source: Milne *et al.* (2008a). Reproduced with permission of Taylor and Francis.

Mediators

We next scrutinized the 24 selected supervision studies to see which methods had been used by their authors. We located 26 different supervision mediators, the most frequent being 'teaching and instruction' of the supervisee (reported in 75 per cent of the studies). The next most frequently reported method was 'feedback', cited in 15 of the papers (63 per cent), which was followed by 'observing' in 42 per cent. Table 3.1 lists the 26

Table 3.1 The main methods of supervision within 24 reviewed studies (Milne *et al.*, 2008).

	Studies (N)	Studies (prevalence; %)
1. Training (teaching; skills instruction)	18	75
2. Feedback	15	63
3. Observing (live or recorded)	10	42
4. Goal-setting	9	38
5. Question and answer (information-gathering; clarifying)	9	38
6. Modelling (demonstration, live or video/audio)	7	29
7. Planning (managing agenda; arranging next meeting)	6	25
8. Reinforcement/praise/support	6	25
9. Discussion	5	21
10. Prompts (verbal and written reminders, handout, etc.)	5	21
11. Review/reflection	5	21
12. Role-play	5	21
13. Explanation (rationale provided; socialization to model)	4	17
14. Monitoring client benefit	4	17
15. Summarizing	4	17
16. Challenging	3	13
17. Self-disclosure	3	13
18. Listening	2	8
19. Problem-solving	2	8
20. Rehearsal of skills	2	8

Source: Milne, D.L. (2009). Reproduced with permission of Derek Milne.

different methods that were cited. In total, 130 methods were used within the 24 studies, an average of 5.4 supervision methods per study. This means that different supervision methods were combined in order to achieve the successful outcomes. For example, Miller *et al.* (2004) used 'instruction' to get supervisees up to a standard level of understanding over a two-day period, then engaged in 'collaborative problem-solving', the use of educational 'role play rehearsal and modelling', supplemented by 'feedback' (in the form of favourable comments when the supervisees made approximations to competent practice).

The list of supervision methods in Table 3.1 is consistent with current thinking on good practice in supervision, both in terms of the types of methods that were used and in relation to being combined together to form educational packages (Bransford *et al.*, 2000; Kaslow *et al.*, 2004; Watkins & Milne, 2014). It is also worth noting that in using such packages (i.e. multiple methods of supervision), these studies are manipulating a range of ways in which the supervisee can learn from the experience (i.e. through words, actions and feelings). This reflects conventional wisdom (Bruner, 1966), as combined within the 'structured learning format' (Bouchard *et al.*, 1980). Not listed in Table 3.1 are a number of methods that were only used in one of the 24 studies: challenging (inviting supervisee to rethink something); collaborating (joint-working); confidence-building (self-efficacy); disagreeing; formulating; self-monitoring; and checking understanding.

Mechanisms

Finally, we found that the studies we analysed defined 28 different mechanisms of change in order to explain how the different methods of supervision (as listed in Table 3.1) could enable supervisees to develop competence, and apply it in their workplace. These included changes in supervisees' emotional self-awareness, their motivation and their skills. Although a daunting number of mechanisms were noted and a diverse terminology used, we were able to accommodate 23 of these 28 mechanisms to the experiential learning model (Kolb, 1984). Table 3.2 summarizes these data, which indicate that the most widely used mechanism was 'experiencing' (i.e. working on the attitudes, affective awareness and motivational dimensions within the supervisee). This emphasis on experiencing was present in half of the studies, whereas 'planning' and 'reflection' were explicit in only a

Table 3.2 Mechanisms of change reported in the 24 reviewed studies (Milne *et al.*, 2008).

	Studies specifying (N)	Studies (%)
Experiencing (attitude change; affective awareness; motivation/reinforcement)	12	50
Planning (increased attention to goals/focusing)	4	16
Reflecting	3	12
Conceptualizing	2	8
Experimenting	2	8
Other (general 'learning'; self-monitoring)	5	20

Source: Milne, D.L. (2009). Reproduced with permission of Derek Milne.

minority of studies. However, this crystallization by means of the experiential learning model is encouraging, as it provides a clear account of how supervision appears to work, one that is precise enough to enable research hypotheses to be generated and clear enough to be practical within the moment-to-moment process of supervision practice (see Chapters 7 and 8 for illustrations).

Based on the information gleaned from this systematic review, a basic model of supervision can be sketched out (basic in the sense that it draws on the variables that are common to the reviewed studies). This is set out in Figure 3.2, which notes the different numbers of people involved at each stage, and the frequency with which different methods were employed. The figure indicates how the moderators bear down upon the mediators and mechanisms, indicating the general influence that they might have on the speed or direction of supervision. Supervisors use a wide range of popular methods, and these, according to this model, have their intended effect through the process of experiential learning (for additional details see Milne *et al.*, 2008a; Table 3.2 is a summary of this 2008 review paper).

Although the basic model does have some advantages over those discussed in Chapter 2 (e.g. supported by some empirical evidence), it is still rather general (i.e. the parsimony is poor) and it lacks the kind of elaboration needed to set out explicit predictions. There is also an absence of implied research methods and types of evidence (i.e. its assumptions are weak). On the other hand, it is compatible with many of the models summarized in Chapter 2 and it does provide an explanation as to how causal processes occur (i.e. mainly through experiential learning). Also,

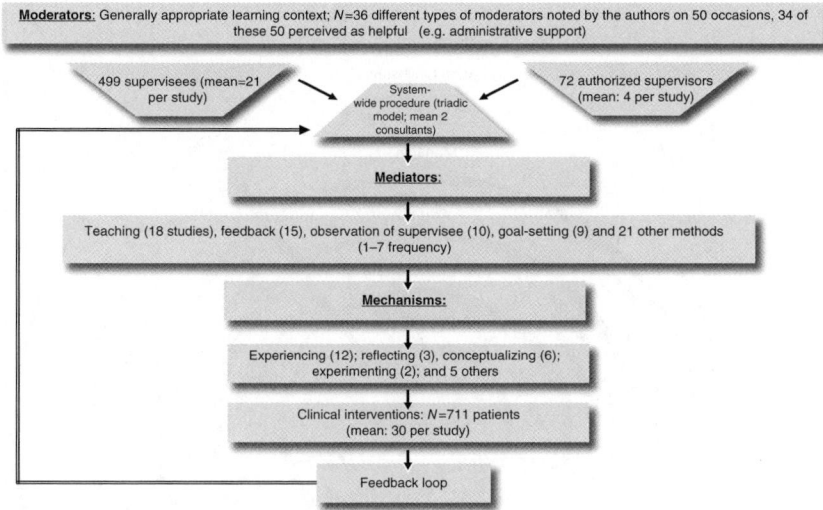

Figure 3.2 The basic model of clinical supervision.
Source: Milne *et al.* (2008a). Reproduced with permission of Taylor and Francis.

clear action implications are included (e.g. try to ensure that favourable moderators are present, utilize a range of supervision methods and facilitate experiential learning).

A Circumplex Model of Supervision

In order to bring greater precision and parsimony to the basic model above, a traditional model-building method known as the 'circumplex' was next utilized to develop an evidence-based approach (Kiesler, 1983; for a more recent application see Faith & Thayer, 2001). A circumplex model depicts the relationship between key variables in terms of successive, nested layers of interaction. For instance, in one of the earliest applications, a circumplex model was used to try to capture the spectrum of interpersonal behaviour (Leary, 1957). Cross-cutting axes were used to divide a circle into the main variables/dimensions (e.g. concerning the degree to which a person exerts or cedes control; is warm or cold) and their resultant segments (e.g. supervisors who are directive but nurturant, involved and accepting, could be characterized interpersonally as akin to 'guides'). More importantly, as

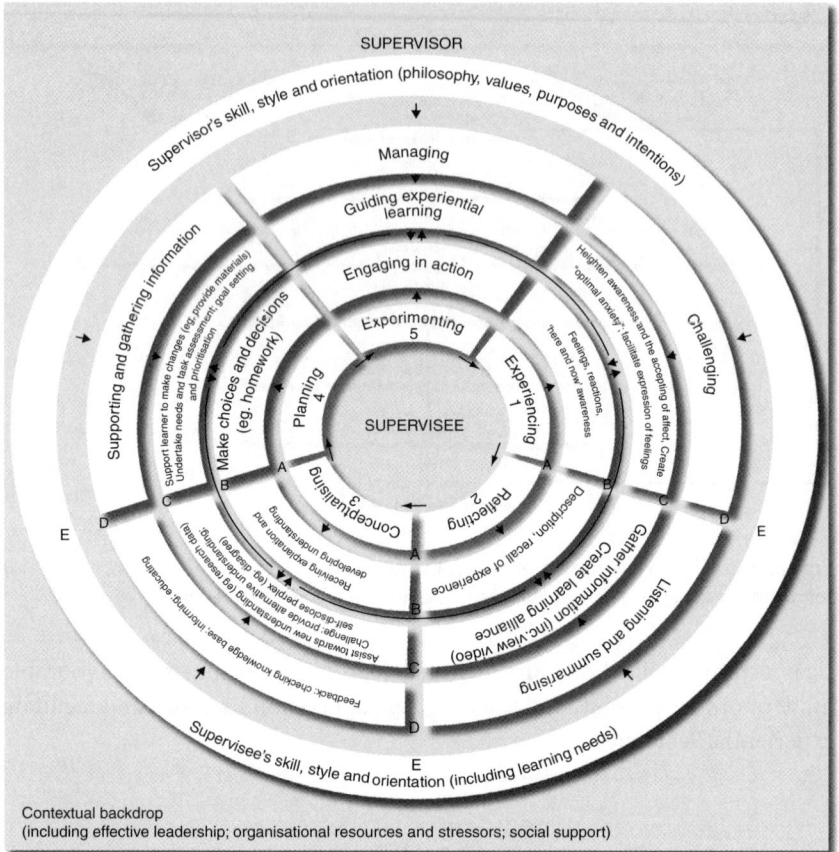

Figure 3.3 The circumplex model of evidence-based clinical supervision.
Source: Milne and Westerman (2001). Reproduced with permission of John Wiley & Sons Ltd.

illustrated in Figure 3.3, each of the variables (represented by boxes in this figure) within the circumplex should be thought of as capable of operating independently in relation to every other panel. This approach recognizes the dynamism and inherent complexity within the basic model, but adds a greater degree of specificity by indicating how the numerous moderators, mediators and mechanisms might interact. The moderating variables noted in Figure 3.1 are thought to concern the contextual background to supervision, such as staff turnover and administrative support. This context influences how the supervisor exercises his or her skills (the outer ring of the circumplex), as in a service environment that requires the adoption of case-based supervision within group formats, a context that necessarily shapes the selection and use of the different supervision methods (such as ensuring that outcome data are included in the review of all a supervisee's cases). In turn, this engages the supervisee in a particular trajectory of experiential learning (the inner circle of Figure 3.3). Unlike the basic model, this circumplex model gives equal weight to the supervisee and the supervisor as contributors to the necessary experiential learning interactions, in the context of their workplace. Not depicted here, but logically nested within the centre of the diagram, would be the subsequent interactions between the supervisees (i.e. therapists) and their clients. Similar interactions would be expected to occur at that level (e.g. there would be a moderating influence present, because of the client's characteristics, history, etc.).

The more precise, subtle and complex modelling of supervision that is shown in Figure 3.3 provides supervisors with much greater clarity than is available from the basic model (see Figure 3.2) and from the essential model described within Chapter 2. For researchers, the circumplex model suggests what might be important to study, allowing consequential hypotheses to be constructed. For instance, the circumplex model indicates that the relationship between 'challenging' and 'experiencing' is mediated by specific kinds of questioning, and that the mechanism for this process is heightened awareness (creating optimal anxiety and a 'here and now' engagement in supervision.) This circumplex model of EBCS was first published by Milne and Westerman (2001), when it was also given an initial and positive $N = 1$ evaluation. This will be discussed shortly, but for further detail on the model, the interested reader is again referred to this original paper.

A Tandem Model of Evidence-Based Clinical Supervision

Subsequently, a more explicitly dynamic account of supervision, still based on the circumplex model, was developed with my colleague Ian James (Milne & James, 2005). This tandem version of supervision is an elaborated analogy (an example of a mechanical model) which enhances the thinking in the circumplex model, and which provides a more accessible, dynamic representation of the model than in Figure 3.3. There are numerous important assumptions within the tandem model. As the tandem model is integrative, these assumptions can be contrasted readily with the types of supervision models described in Chapter 2.

Therapy model

The assumption in the tandem model is that the supervisor, as the leader, occupies the front seat of the tandem. This is the seat that allows the vehicle to be steered and the controls to be used appropriately (e.g. brakes and gears). This reflects the assumption that the supervisor is a guide, ultimately responsible for the direction and pace entailed in supervision (as per the therapist in CBT). Like effective therapists, supervisors must occupy this position with due authority, and must have the power to discharge their responsibilities. Of course, as the supervisee develops, it is only natural that they should be given more autonomy and even episodes of leadership. The model allows for this, in that literally a tandem can be cycled solo, or the roles reversed (e.g. for the purposes of a specific learning assignment). A second fundamental analogy is that through this highly interactive process the supervisor and supervisee have the capacity to shape one another's learning and development, a transactional process. This idea is drawn from the transactional stress model, which underlies most approaches to therapy (Lazarus & Folkman, 1984). The tandem model assumes that successful supervision shares this dynamic, organic quality, operating as an open system that fosters development (i.e. 'reciprocal' and 'circular' causality).

Developmental model

Another useful analogy that comes from the tandem metaphor is that the supervisor and supervisee are both on a journey of learning and development: there will be tasks and challenges to master. However, it is assumed that supervisors either know the path moderately well, or are experts in finding their way. The metaphor of travelling seems to be highly appropriate, drawing as it does on such notions as coming across unfamiliar issues and having to work jointly to optimize the available resources and solutions. The process is also recognized as progressing through phases, as in the developmental stages, and is unending, leading to progressively greater skill. Another implication of the travelling idea is that the amount of effort made by the two parties will significantly influence how much travelling occurs.

Supervision-specific model

Just as social role models emphasize leadership relationships, in the tandem model both supervisor and supervisee need to be active contributors to supervision for it to be effective. A collaborative alliance is essential, and the role relationships are fundamentally those of teacher–pupil (in relation to the formative supervision function); manager–staff member (the normative function); and therapist–client (the restorative function). Task models are represented within the tandem in such terms as 'scaffolding' supervision (learning requires a clear structure, proper resources and personalized learning opportunities; Vygotsky, 1978) and through addressing contextual challenges, such as inadequate learning resources (likened to dealing with bad weather on the tandem).

Functional model

The tandem model explicitly sets out two complementary wheels of activity, linked to the functions of supervision. The front wheel of the tandem, being under the immediate control of the supervisor (as leader), is taken to represent the wheel of supervision. This then is the business of establishing learning needs, negotiating supervision objectives, and utilizing different methods of supervision to facilitate progress down the developmental path, all guided by regular evaluation and feedback. This wheel is a direct use of the staff development model (Goldstein & Ford, 2002), and is elaborated in Chapter 5. The back wheel, being closest to the supervisee's seat on the tandem, is taken to represent the experiential learning cycle (Kolb, 1984). It is understood also that the back wheel provides the drive that propels the tandem, so that it can progress down the developmental path. This reflects Kolb's emphasis on a spiral curriculum, in which different levels of engagement with reflection, conceptualization (and the other modes of experiential learning) will ultimately determine the supervisee's development.

Definition of Evidence-Based Clinical Supervision

The basic, circumplex and tandem models were successive ways of conceptualizing clinical supervision, increasingly based on the evidence-based

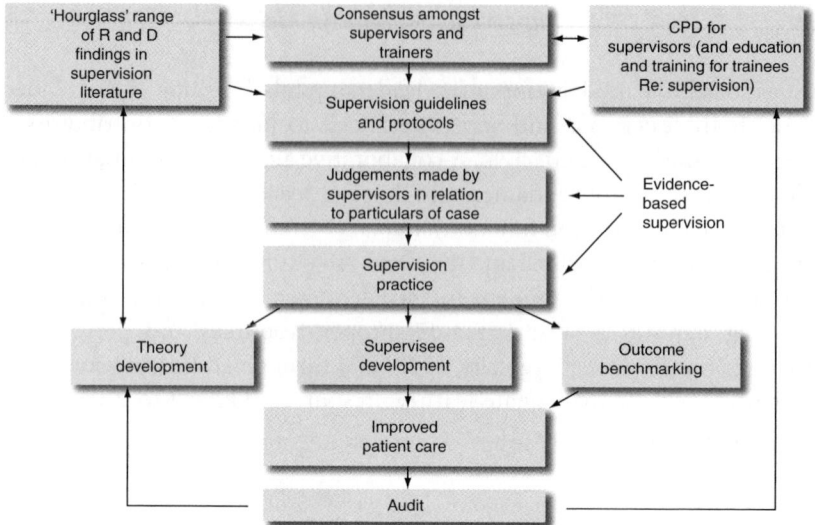

Figure 3.4 The EBCS framework, the guiding evidence-based practice rationale behind the development of the tandem model of CBT supervision.
Source: Parry *et al.*, (1996). Reproduced with permission of Guilford Press.

practice (EBP) framework (Parry *et al.*, 1996). These successive models were driven by the ongoing EBCS research and development activity, following the EBCS framework. As set out in Figure 3.4, this EBP framework simply replaces the term therapy with that of supervision, otherwise being exactly as per the original version. In this sense the tandem model is the best-developed model of EBCS, because it builds on these earlier models. Each successive EBCS model resulted from following the steps in the EBP framework, as set out in Figure 3.4. The clearest examples of these developmental cycles were the five successive $N = 1$ studies, starting with Milne and Westerman (2001), and continuing until Milne *et al.* (2013). An important point about this tandem model development process is that the $N = 1$ studies were based on naturalistic CBT supervision (supervision provided by multidisciplinary colleagues who were providing CBT supervision of supervisees' CBT: Stan Graham, Ian James, Robert Reiser, Brian Rowley and Colin Westerman). At the time of this $N = 1$ research, all of these supervisors were working within the UK's NHS, except for Robert Reiser, who worked in a community clinic in the USA. Related iterations took place in relation to the seven systematic literature reviews published to date, starting with Milne and James (2000), up to Reiser and Milne (2014). This development process is reflected in the definition of EBCS provided in Chapter 1 and explained now. According to this procedure, EBCS is defined as the judgements that are made by supervisors in relation to each particular supervisory event (e.g. how best to help the supervisee to formulate a client's presentation), judgements that draw on a range of evidence, especially the best-available research evidence. Therefore the tandem model offers the evidence-based supervisor a quick reference guide to the best available and most essential evidence, a rationale for making such moment-by-moment judgements (e.g. deciding that the supervisee needs to stop conceptualizing and start experimenting). At other times, the tandem model is a guide to research and the other parts of the EBCS framework.

Figure 3.4 indicates that research is supplemented by relevant theory and by expert consensus statements. EBCS is integrative in nature, so the evidence-base is not restricted to material from within clinical supervision or to cognitive theory, but draws on evidence and theories from neighbouring literatures (e.g. research findings on feedback from the educational literature). This emphasis on using neighbouring literatures recurs within this book, and is especially explicit in the evidence-based CBT supervision manual (Milne & Reiser, 2017). EBCS also integrates practice-based evidence alongside EBP. Practice-based evidence (PBE; Barkham *et al.*, 2010) is regarded as an integral element within the 'hourglass' spectrum of research with which mental health practitioners should be engaged (Salkovskis, 1995), as indicated in the top left panel in Figure 3.4, and also by the panels below the panel 'supervision practice'. In this sense, PBE explicitly and necessarily complements EBP by recognizing the value of clinicians gathering relevant data on their effectiveness from their own routine practice, especially when it comes to addressing the pragmatic challenges of implementing the findings from randomized controlled trials, or translating for their purposes other aspects of the more academic and efficacy-focused explanatory research that typically characterize EBP (Sackett *et al.*, 2000). Therefore, in terms of the individual supervisor working within a healthcare context, this combination of EBP and PBE equates to the scientist-practitioner approach to advancing one's practice (Barlow *et al.*, 1984). This integrative EBP rationale has shaped the tandem model (Figure 3.5), making it a distinctive example of a supervision-specific model. Whether the tandem model is distinct from modern versions of CBT supervision will be discussed shortly. Therefore, this tandem model provides supervisors with the essential information needed to engage in EBCS.

Clinical supervision

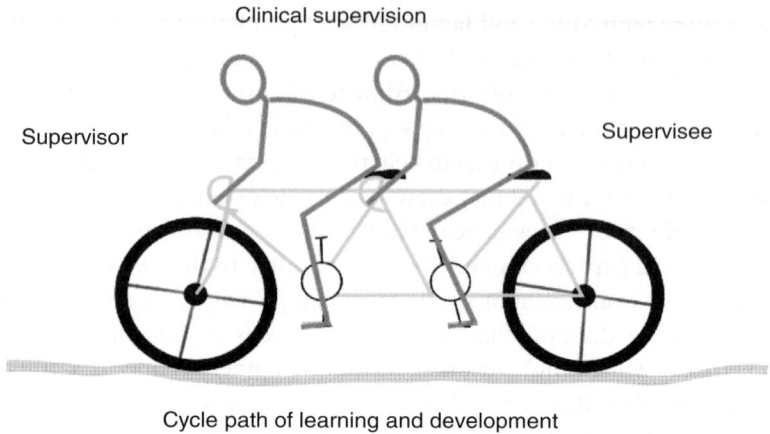

Supervisor

Supervisee

Cycle path of learning and development

Figure 3.5 The tandem model that guides evidence-based clinical supervision (EBCS).
Source: Milne & Reiser (2017). Reproduced with permission of John Wiley & Sons Ltd.

The tandem model is explained and described more fully in the rest of this book.

These three fundamental forms of evidence (research, theory and expert consensus) underpin a range of materials and activities that offer practical support for supervisors' judgements, including supervision guidelines and supervisors' workshops, the continuing professional development aspect of the EBCS framework (the EBCS manual linked to the 2009 edition of this book is effectively replaced by Milne and Reiser, 2017). Following on from supervisors' considered decisions and judgements, Figure 3.4 indicates that supervisors next engage in relevant supervisory practices, in order to foster the development of their supervisees' competence. This typically takes the form of applying supervision methods, such as goal-setting and feedback (Table 3.1), to facilitate the supervisees' experiential learning (Table 3.2). Subsequently, Figure 3.4 suggests that a complementary range of outcome evaluation methods conclude the steps within the EBCS framework (i.e. outcome monitoring, audit and improved patient care).

Note that each such sequence of steps represents a problem-solving cycle, which should contribute to developments in all aspects of this system, including enhanced supervision. In this sense, the EBCS framework encompasses three successive problem-solving cycles. At the outer layer are the evidence-bases and support activities, being a series of public organizational systems (research, continuing professional development, etc.). The intermediate layer is the heart of EBCS, namely how supervisors form judgements, decide what to do next, apply suitable methods with their supervisees and monitor the outcomes. Nested within this supervision cycle is the supervisee's cycle, mirroring the supervisor's tasks and activities, primarily at the level of the more private, personal system that is an individual's experiential learning and developmental experience. This reasoning is detailed more fully in Milne and Reiser (2016b).

All of these steps within the EBCS framework will be addressed more fully later in this book. For instance, considerable work has gone into developing guidelines on best practice in supervision, based on a consensus amongst multidisciplinary colleagues in the UK (i.e. the top of Figure 3.4), and these will feature in the next three chapters. The theory-development aspect of EBCS has come from systematically reviewing the best available literature with colleagues in the UK and the USA, as already illustrated at the start of this chapter and in Chapter 1 (the definitional work). Of course, many relevant reviews have been conducted by other researchers, and these will also be drawn on, as will the intensive ($N = 1$) case studies and our larger scale, pragmatic surveys and evaluations. Figure 3.4 specifies this EBCS framework, indicating where these various activities fit into the development of the tandem model.

In summary, this tandem model (Figure 3.5) is my preferred current conceptualization of how the EBCS framework links to supervision. Note that, like the EBCS framework, the tandem model is not necessarily aligned with any one theoretical orientation. Indeed, in its development it was tested against CBT supervision as a distinct model (e.g. Milne *et al.*, 2013). I now take the view, explained below, that the tandem is an enhanced version of CBT supervision, a fourth wave in the same way that new forms of CBT are referred to as fourth wave. The tandem improves on previous models in a number of critical areas, including having greater internal consistency, better precision and by specifying how the moment-to-moment supervisor–supervisee interactions can result in experiential learning, all within an open, complex system. However, there are some other key challenges that need to be addressed if the tandem model is to be considered a genuine competitor, in relation to the better established models. Paramount amongst these challenges are the conventional scientific tasks of manualization, operationalization and evaluation. I will now detail how the EBCS framework addresses these challenges, leading to a critique of the current model.

Manualization of evidence-based clinical supervision

As we have seen, several of the criteria by which any model should be judged relate to setting out a model explicitly in the first instance (i.e. having an appropriate focus; being duly elaborated; specifying the action implications: Warr, 1980). Manualization is the second major challenge we face in applied science, which is the detailing of an intervention in a form that allows it to be replicated. So, having constructed a working conceptualization (the tandem model), we now need to show how that model can be delivered faithfully. Within the mental health/social science field, the convention is to draft a document such as a manual, guide or protocol. As per Figure 3.5, the convention in evidence-based practice is to refer to this documentation as 'guidelines'. According to the National Institute for Health and Care Excellence (NICE, 2007), guidelines are systematically developed recommendations that are based on the best-available research evidence, moderated by expert consensus, containing a list of suggested actions intended to improve interventions and their associated outcomes. By reviewing and interpreting the extant literature, guidelines are intended to be a service to clinicians, 'capturing optimal performance expectations', whilst acknowledging the importance of clinical judgement (in order to factor in client characteristics, the context of application, etc; APA, 2015, p.33). For example, the second APA (2015) guideline on supervision states that 'Supervisors seek to attain and maintain competence in the practice of supervision through formal education and training' (p.36). Subsequent guidelines spell out how competence in supervision can be demonstrated (e.g. by clarifying goals and establishing a collaborative relationship).

I reviewed these and other guidelines on clinical supervision recently, alongside the available supervisor training manuals (Milne, 2016), concluding that they only succeeded in improving supervision when they were part of a broader innovation effort. Although not popular (Lucock *et al.*, 2006), and often misunderstood and misused (Parry, 2000), guidelines represent an integral part of modern healthcare. They offer the individual practitioner a summary of otherwise overwhelming amounts of knowledge, and they can also help to ensure that some evidence-based practices exist within clinical services. But it seems clear that the 'top-down' dissemination of guidelines and manuals, while necessary components, is insufficient to improve supervision. It appears that we also require complementary and systemic 'bottom-up' interventions, such as action research and supervisor training, followed by ongoing support in the workplace (Milne & Reiser, 2016b).

In keeping with this reasoning, and consistent with the approach used by NICE, four guidelines on clinical supervision were prepared for the first edition of this book, followed by six guidelines for the manual prepared by Milne and Reiser (2017). These guidelines are noted in the relevant sections of this book. These first four guidelines are included in the EBCS manual, which has been drafted to detail how novice supervisors can be trained in the EBCS approach (Milne, 2007a). Supplementing the guidelines are PowerPoint slideshows to introduce the six parts of the linked three-day workshop. These presentations lead into demonstrations of the methods, through naturalistic video recordings of the key aspects of supervision (e.g. goal-setting). Next are some suggestions for how workshop leaders can engage the participants in experiential learning about the material. Sessions end with a summary and the opportunity for some discussion. This manual can be found on the Wiley website (www.wiley.com/go/milne). The guidelines within the manual (which cover the supervisory relationship; establishing the learning contract; facilitating learning; and evaluation) were developed with the help of over 100 multidisciplinary colleagues, and included careful evaluation and redrafting.

The manual, which was prepared with a grant from the Higher Education Academy (Psychology network), underwent piloting with 10 Doctorate in Clinical Psychology courses within the UK (Milne, 2010). The results of this pilot evaluation indicated that others could follow the manual successfully, and provided feedback so that the manual could be improved (the audit part of EBCS; Figure 3.5). From a practical point of view, the manual makes explicit what is meant by EBCS. From a research standpoint, the manual enables the approach to be implemented with fidelity, and hence evaluated properly. Of course, none of this work assumes that the tandem is superior to competing models, but rather it represents a starting point from which we can begin to examine their relative effectiveness. This is a necessary step in our efforts to improve the quality of supervision.

As already noted, a significantly updated manual (Milne & Reiser, 2017) has recently been developed, with guidelines intended to specify and enhance CBT supervision in particular. It incorporates a review of the recent work on supervision competencies (Roth & Pilling, 2008; APA, 2015), an expanded set of six guidelines and includes 18 new video demonstrations. This more recent manual (Milne & Reiser, 2017) is entitled 'evidence-based CBT supervision', because we utilized the EBCS framework to develop it (e.g. literature reviews and expert consensus, as per the original tandem model). Specifically, we again engaged in extensive consultation, involving over 100 supervisors and supervisees, asking them as workshop participants to evaluate the guidelines and to suggest refinements. Therefore, I recommend that readers who wish to implement the tandem model of CBT supervision use the training manual developed by Milne & Reiser (2017).

Operationalization of EBCS

A clear model of supervision (the conceptualization phase) and an explicit method with which to implement it (the manualization phase) leads to the next task in applied science, clarifying how the model should be measured. Which kind of measurement approach is appropriate? The first instrument that was developed to measure the tandem model was 'Teachers' PETS' (Process Evaluation of Training and Supervision; Milne *et al.*, 2002). This was an observational tool which required recorded samples of supervision, so that we could code the techniques used by the supervisor, together with the reactions of the supervisee (i.e. a process–outcome evaluation). The instrument was first reported by Milne *et al.* (2002), and the present summary draws directly from that paper. The main purpose here is to show how the tandem model is capable of being measured through Teachers' PETS. The tandem-style logic applied, in that the front wheel (representing the training cycle) was set out in terms of 13 common methods that are used by supervisors (defined through a literature review). These methods are very similar to those appearing in Table 3.1, and also correspond to accounts of CBT supervision (e.g. Rakovshik *et al.*, 2016), including 'feedback' and 'guiding experiential learning' (i.e. the use of simulations, modelling, educational role-plays, behavioural rehearsal and similar learning tasks). Related to this list of supervisor activities is the experiential learning cycle (by analogy, the back wheel of the tandem). In order to better observe this learning phase, we elaborated Kolb's (1984) four modes to become five modes, by distinguishing between 'experiencing' (the emotional accompaniments to action) and 'experimenting' (the behavioural aspect, such as watching a video or engaging in a role-play). The other modes from Kolb (1984) were retained: 'reflecting', 'conceptualizing' and 'planning'. This five-mode breakdown of experiential learning is represented in the innermost circle in Figure 3.3. In keeping with the convention in using the direct observation measurement approach, we added the category 'other' (an item included also for the supervisors, to allow the observer to record other kinds of activities, such as social chat).

Drawing on these two complementary lists, the observer (following a manual) alternately records what the supervisor is doing (the supervision process) and then, a few seconds later, the mini impact that this appears to have on the supervisee (the outcome). This allows a profile of supervision to be constructed, and so in the Milne and James (2002) evaluation of EBCS we were able to present baseline data on supervision to illustrate how often the supervisor (Ian James) used different methods over the period of the study. This showed that his most frequent behaviour was that of 'listening' (coded on 142 of the 358 occasions observed; 40 per cent). By comparison, he used 'informing/educating' on 14 per cent of occasions, 'supporting' 12 per cent of the time, followed by several lower frequency behaviours (such as 'observing a video', 'gathering information' and 'checking theoretical knowledge': all around about 6 per cent of observed occasions). Because Teachers' PETS also codes the supervisees' behaviour, we could also provide a contingency table, to express the relationship between these activities and the sought-after instances of experiential learning by the supervisee (the mini-outcomes). During the same baseline period, by far the most common impact was on the supervisees' reflection (302 instances were observed, 84 per cent of all mini-outcomes). Very few incidents of the supervisees' 'experimenting', 'conceptualizing', 'experiencing' or 'planning' were observed (there were three supervisees in this intensive case-study design, all qualified mental health practitioners undertaking a Diploma course in CBT). As the Milne and James (2002) study illustrated, the variables within the tandem model could be set out and observed with Teachers' PETS. Furthermore, this could be done with satisfactory inter-rater reliability, a further criterion in applied science (for further details see Milne & Westerman, 2001; Milne & James, 2002; Milne *et al.*, 2002).

However, PETS is a labour-intensive instrument to apply, and it also requires extensive training, making it best-suited to a research context. Another weakness is that PETS does not use the kind of competence-based approach now popular within the supervision field (Milne & Watkins, 2014; APA, 2015). For these reasons we revamped PETS and created a new measurement instrument (SAGE), as described below.

Implementation and evaluation of EBCS

With a clear concept of what is to be done, some clear guidance in the form of a manual on how to do it and a suitable measurement tool to detect the intended effects, the next stage is to evaluate the tandem in action. Various versions of EBCS have been applied, in keeping with the basic, circumplex and tandem models described earlier. The first published implementation and evaluation was by Milne and Westerman (2001). In that study (also an intensive, case-study $N = 1$ design), a supervisor, Colin Westerman, was studied in relation to his three supervisees, all qualified mental health nurses. An earlier, more rudimentary version of the EBCS manual was used to guide this work, and consultancy was provided by the present author to ensure that the method was applied faithfully. Teachers' PETS was used to detect whether the intervention had any effect. This provided data that described the supervisor's profile, and the relationship this had with the supervisees' learning, for each of the three phases of the experiment (a nine-session baseline period, then nine sessions of EBCS and then a 12-session maintenance phase). To quote that report: 'The main findings from this study were that clinical supervision could be measured systematically, could be enhanced to a small extent and in a predicted direction through consultancy, and could result in slightly improved learning for the supervisees. Supervisee satisfaction was also very high throughout the year long study' (Milne & Westerman, 2001, pp.453–454).

Learning lessons from that initial evaluation, Milne and James (2002) conducted a similar analysis, again using Teachers' PETS as the main measure, plus a supervisee satisfaction instrument. In this instance the supervisor (Ian James) had six supervisees (supervised in three pairs). To quote again from the paper itself: 'supervision improved during the experimental phase, but most markedly during the maintenance phase. The results appear to reflect a lag effect for the intervention, which can be most readily explained in terms of a socialization period during which both supervisor and supervisees adapted their styles of interaction' (p.55). The interventions referred to were 'general consultancy' and 'consultancy plus feedback' (feedback came from the results from Teachers' PETS, plus a summary of the supervisees' satisfaction, session upon session).

To be more explicit about the findings, during the baseline period we found that the supervisor's profile was weak in relation to the tandem model, featuring only a limited use of the vital experiential learning methods (referred to as 'guiding experiential learning' within Teachers' PETS). By contrast, considerable use was made at this stage of the less potent verbal methods (e.g. teaching, informing, advising). As predicted by the tandem model, this had the effect that most of the supervisees' time was spent in 'reflection' (84 per cent of observed occasions), whilst engaging in the essential 'experiencing' and 'experimenting' modes was only observed on 4 per cent of occasions. With consultancy and feedback during the intervention phases these figures improved, and with them the impact on the supervisees' learning became more balanced (i.e. featured all five learning modes). Thus, whilst 'reflection' decreased over time, 'experiencing' and 'experimenting' increased (from mean values of 1.8 and 0.8 during the baseline period, to 7.5 and 1.3 during the consultancy phase). These figures improved slightly more during the subsequent consultancy plus feedback and maintenance phases (e.g. 'experimenting' rose to a mean of 17.2, whilst 'experiencing' remained stable). By this stage 'reflection' had reduced from a mean of 50.3 to 35.2. Supervisee satisfaction remained stable and high throughout, indicating that these changes were acceptable.

Subsequent to the first edition of this book, we conducted a literature review to assess the need for a new measurement tool (Milne & Reiser, 2011). Although PETS fared fairly well in comparison with the other available observational tools, we decided to revamp PETS by incorporating items that mapped closely on to the Pilling and Roth (2014) competence framework for supervision (for sight of this map, see the appendix to Milne & Reiser, 2017). Also, we incorporated the most popular competence rating scale (Dreyfus & Dreyfus, 1986). The new instrument was Supervision: Adherence and Guidance Evaluation (SAGE). I describe SAGE in Chapter 8 (further details can be found in Milne *et al.*, 2011b, and Milne & Reiser, 2014). SAGE is especially suitable for measuring the tandem model (see the $N = 1$ study by Milne *et al.*, 2013), but can also capture aspects of systemic and psychodynamic supervision (Cliffe & Milne, 2012).

Critical Review

Testing the tandem

Whilst the tandem model is promising, it is appropriate to engage in some critical reflection. It is also appropriate to apply the same criteria to the tandem model as were applied previously to the other models (see Chapter 2). In terms of the tandem model, 10 such tests were tackled fairly well by the model, when applied in a fairly unsystematic and no doubt biased way (i.e. it was undertaken by the model's proponents; Milne & James, 2005). Therefore, there is a need to strengthen the model to withstand these tests, as well as a need to develop the model in other respects, encouraging independent review. This includes attending to the logical weaknesses, such as the imprecise meaning of some of the concepts (e.g. 'experiencing') and the unacknowledged assumptions (Machado & Silva, 2007). This kind of rigorous conceptual analysis should accompany the familiar emphasis on experimentation.

More research

On the subject of data collection, the EBCS model needs further support, as there are only five $N=1$ analyses to date. However, these were rigorous evaluations of the EBCS model (i.e. high internal validity) and they all yielded similar findings (i.e. Milne & Westerman, 2001; Milne & James, 2002; Milne et al., 2012, 2013). There has also been a small-scale evaluation of two workshops (with $N=17$ multidisciplinary supervisors), which was based on the EBCS manual (Milne, 2007a), and which used the fidelity framework approach to evaluation (Culloty et al., 2010); and one large-scale evaluation, in which 22 trainers utilized at least one session from the same EBCS manual (Milne, 2007a) with nearly 300 supervisors (Milne, 2010). Additionally, maintaining the emphasis on intensive, small-scale and 'upstream' methodologies, there have been two qualitative evaluations of the tandem model (Milne et al., 2011a; Breese et al., 2012). Although the findings have consistently supported the tandem model, they were all conducted by proponents of the approach. It follows that there is a need for independent researchers to be engaged in large-sample, controlled evaluations of the tandem model. I agree with Hofmann et al. (2010) that we especially need mediational analyses (process and mechanism evaluations) in addition to effectiveness studies and component analyses (outcome and mediator evaluations).

The tandem model enhances CBT supervision

In relation to the 'focus' criterion (Warr, 1980), American colleague Robert Reiser and I have spent some time trying to differentiate the tandem model from CBT supervision (e.g. Milne et al., 2013; Reiser, 2014). In the first edition of this book I took the view that the application of the EBCS framework resulted in the tandem having distinctive features (e.g. a wider theoretical foundation; a more experiential approach), but that it was nonetheless entirely compatible with CBT supervision. As some colleagues pointed out at the time, the tandem model was 'CBT supervision done properly', straightforwardly enhancing features consistent with the theory and the practice of CBT supervision. This is detailed in Table 3.3, in terms of the core principles of CBT (drawn from Lomax *et al.*, 2005), which I translated for supervision, plus two principles from the EBCS framework. The underlined material alongside each principle in Table 3.3 represented the additional ideas that came from the tandem model, so it clarified where exactly it seemed to enhance CBT supervision.

To explain the differences noted in Table 3.3 a little further, within the tandem model all five modes are equally important (principle 2), so there is a greater emphasis on achieving a balance to the supervisee's experiential learning (as illustrated in Milne *et al.*, 2013). This emphasis includes greater affective awareness, and so may include work by the supervisor to improve the supervisee's ability to describe and identify different emotional accompaniments to the work they are describing (or reactions to what is happening within supervision: the 'experiencing' mode). By comparison, CBT supervision appears to privilege the 'conceptualization' mode, achieved through discussion (e.g. sharing information and reformulating a clinical case). This is noted in the definition of CBT supervision in Reiser (2014). The restorative function of supervision is regarded as a necessary focus within the tandem model, including social support in relation to

Table 3.3 General principles of CBT, showing the overlaps between the tandem model of supervision (EBCS) and CBT supervision, plus ways in which EBCS still augments CBT supervision (*italics*).

1. Specified problems identified collaboratively
2. Cognitive-behavioural mediation (*balanced experiential learning cycle, especially addressing affective and restorative aspects of supervision*)
3. Goal-directed (developmentally – informed; *address normative function*)
4. Theoretically driven (*draws on the applied psychology of learning literature*)
5. Cognitive and behavioural interventions (*techniques from neighbouring literatures*)
6. Self-control (supervisee a resourceful adult learner; cope with challenge)
7. Collaborative relationship
8. *Contextualized (e.g. address support system and other moderators of supervision)*
9. *Research and development orientation (apply EBP framework)*

EBP, evidence-based practice.
Source: Milne, D.L. (2009). Reproduced with permission of Derek Milne.

interpersonal stressors or the symptoms of burnout that supervisees may be experiencing. A chapter is dedicated to this topic in the CBT supervision manual (Milne & Reiser, 2017), including a guideline.

To illustrate this distinction between CBT supervision and the tandem model, consider the findings of surveys. For instance, the survey reported by Townend *et al.* (2002), indicated that less than 20 per cent of their 170 respondents (all qualified mental health practitioners) utilized 'experiential' methods (i.e. role-play; reviewing tapes; direct observation), leading them to conclude that adherence to a CBT approach was limited, indicating 'slippage' from the model (p.497). This is also borne out in the survey of CBT supervision reported by Liness *et al.* (2016), in that 76 per cent of the 196 respondents reported that the content of their supervision was 'mainly focused on case discussion' (p.9), whereas role-plays or reference to competency measures were rare (reported by only 4 and 1 per cent of respondents, respectively). Clinical outcome measures were discussed in less than one-quarter of supervision sessions, a finding that Liness *et al.* (2016) described as an 'alarming' (p.12) departure from the model, and as something likely to undermine patient improvement. A better picture was reported by Reiser and Milne (2016), who conducted an internet survey with a purposive sample of $N = 110$ accredited British Association for Behavioural and Cognitive Psychotherapies (BABCP) supervisors, directors of CBT training programmes and members of the BABCP supervision special interest group, who were selected for their assumed expertise (e.g. the mean experience as a CBT supervisor was over 12 years, and they were closely involved in supervisor development). In terms of content, the results of this survey were consistent with past surveys (e.g. Townend *et al.*, 2002), in that the most frequently reported supervision topics were case discussion and case formulation. However, the reported use of experiential methods (e.g. modelling skills and reviewing recordings) was much improved, with an average frequency approximating to their use in 88 per cent of supervisory sessions. Similarly, homework tasks, measuring supervisee competence and role-play were reportedly used in 82 per cent of sessions. Reiser and Milne (2016) concluded that the practice of this select sample of CBT supervisors matched recommendations, supervision competency frameworks and recognized best practice statements.

The normative function noted against principle 3 is also addressed in Milne and Reiser (2017, see chapter on 'support and guidance'), including the guidance that a supervisor can give in relation to coping with interpersonal stressors, grappling with employer requirements and standards, and so on. In relation to principles 4 ('the applied psychology of learning literature') and 5 ('cognitive and behavioural interventions'), this refers to assimilating relevant ideas and methods from within the fields of education (e.g. goal-setting research); psychotherapy (e.g. relationship theories); staff development/instructional design (e.g. training methods; adult learning models); the general literature on clinical supervision; general psychology (e.g. research on emotions); and the expertise material (e.g. feedback procedures; theories of skill acquisition). This eclectic approach to knowledge can be shown by comparing the reference list for this book with references cited in accounts of CBT supervision.

Turning to principle 7, both CBT supervision and EBCS recognize the important part played by a collaborative relationship, at least in terms of the value of a strong task alliance. But neither accords the relationship between supervisor and supervisee the same emphasis as those supervision models that treat the supervision alliance as a wide-ranging construct (embracing an emotional bond), granting the alliance a necessary or even sufficient basis for effective supervision. Therefore, in the CBT supervision manual (Milne & Reiser, 2017), we have devoted a chapter to clarifying this distinction, summarizing in a guideline what we understand to be good CBT supervision practice.

In terms of principle 8, Milne and Reiser (2017) also provides a substantial chapter regarding the role of the workplace context in CBT supervision, as we felt that this aspect, traditionally a strong feature of CBT, featured too rarely in accounts of CBT supervision. My summary of EBCS in the international handbook (Milne, 2014a) also noted the personal and situational barriers to EBP, whilst a special issue on CBT supervision in *The Cognitive Behaviour Therapist* (Newman *et al.*, 2016) provided a collection of papers acknowledging the different ways that the context of CBT supervision is influential in relation to the supervisee's functioning. Contextualization also relates to the supervisee's patients, as it means less emphasis on cognitive factors, and more attention to the environment as a determinant of patients' behaviour (e.g. including material deprivation and weak social support within case formulations).

Principle 9 (a research and development orientation) extends the empirical aspect of CBT, as this seems to have been neglected in CBT supervision. In particular, EBCS is distinctive in having been subjected to programmatic research (i.e. successive issues have been studied, starting with the empirical definition of clinical supervision and proceeding through $N = 1$ studies to larger scale dissemination efforts).

Is the tandem model the 'fourth wave' of CBT supervision?

It is timely to note that CBT supervision has developed through three stages (Reiser, 2014), gradually becoming more like the tandem model. The parallel with the development of CBT seems strong, in that successive 'waves' of development have also been distinguished for CBT. For example, according to Hofmann *et al.* (2010), CBT was the third developmental wave, building first on behaviour therapy and then on cognitive therapy. They described examples of the fourth wave (dialectical behaviour therapy (DBT) and acceptance and commitment therapy (ACT)), noting how the proponents of DBT and ACT argued that these new approaches were distinguishable and so represented a fourth wave of CBT (e.g. through being more contextual, and by emphasizing the reduction of experiential avoidance).

Applying the reasoning in Hofmann *et al.* (2010) to supervision, and building on the historical account in Reiser (2014), it seems equally possible to distinguish three waves of development in CBT supervision. The first was behavioural, and emphasized experiential supervision methods (role-play, modelling, rewards), addressing specific target behaviours until mastery was demonstrated in naturalistic contexts. Another distinguishing feature of behavioural supervision was direct observation, using purpose-made instruments to inform corrective feedback (e.g. Fleming & Sulzer-Azaroff, 1989). This was followed in the 1990s by the arrival of a cognitive emphasis, exemplified by two frequently cited theoretical accounts of CBT supervision (Padesky, 1996; Liese & Beck, 1997). This cognitive approach explicitly extended the methods used in cognitive therapy to supervision, reducing the behavioural emphasis on experiential learning, instead operating at a cognitive level (e.g. case formulation). The definition of CBT in the original Table 3.3 (Milne, 2009) was based on this second wave approach, which with hindsight should more accurately have been described as cognitive therapy supervision. As per therapy, one could say that the combining of the behavioural and cognitive models to form CBT supervision took place formally at the start of the twenty-first century, as exemplified by the endorsement of the competence approach (linked to direct observation and evaluation), the return of experiential and behavioural methods, plus a broader conception of the supervisor's role (e.g. embracing ethical and diversity issues; Newman, 2010). This CBT model was further developed in the account provided by Reiser (2014), which essentially integrated the tandem model as described in the first edition of this book (Milne, 2009).

This parallel with Hofmann *et al.* (2010) leaves me with the same question about the fourth wave that they faced. Phrased in terms of supervision, the question becomes: is the tandem model in this second edition distinguishable as a fourth wave of CBT supervision? In formulating their reply, Hofmann *et al.* (2010) applied three criteria: the assumptions made (theory), the specific interventions (techniques), and the research support. Although subtle but important differences in the respective theories and intervention techniques were recognized between CBT, DBT and ACT, they concluded that the research evidence was much stronger for the effectiveness of CBT. Overall, Hofmann *et al.* (2010) identified far more areas of overlap than difference (e.g. in the use of observable goals and behavioural techniques, such as exposure exercises). This led them to conclude that DBT and ACT did not constitute a fourth wave, and that it made more sense to think of there being a 'family' of CBT interventions, albeit including more than one approach within that generation of applications.

Is the answer the same for CBT supervision – is the present tandem model simply another member of the third wave CBT supervision family? Reasons to agree that it is simply another approach within the family are the many areas of overlap. Revisiting Table 3.3 for this second edition suggests to me that some of the differences identified in the first edition have been removed by the third wave of CBT supervision (i.e. the model outlined by Armstrong & Freeston, 2005; James *et al.*, 2006; Newman, 2010; and by Reiser, 2014). This includes the acceptance once more of behavioural methods; and the incorporation of concepts from the psychology of learning (e.g. developmental theory; experiential learning theory); and extending the supervisor's role to include cultural factors. But I still do not see in third wave CBT supervision an overlap with the tandem model in relation to the theoretical emphasis on experiencing (the emotional aspect of supervision, including supervisees' feeling reactions to their clinical work), nor the attention given in the tandem model to the restorative and normative functions of supervision, including attention to the environmental context (e.g. addressing moderators of the kind listed in Figure 3.1). In addition, perhaps the clearest distinction is that the tandem model is truly empirical, as it derives from a programme of research and development, including the routine evaluation of supervision (Figure 3.5). This has furnished more evidence of effectiveness than has the CBT model, evidence which is outlined in Chapter 8. By contrast, the third wave approach to CBT supervision described by Armstrong and Freeston (2005), James *et al.*

(2006), Newman (2010) and by Reiser (2014) consumes and utilizes rather than produces research (e.g. competence frameworks; guidelines; instruments), together with professional consensus work. Reiser (2014) actually uses the term 'integration', which I think is entirely accurate for this approach to research evidence. Table 3.3 has been suitably updated to reflect these developments. In summary, it strikes me that there are significant differences between third wave CBT supervision and the tandem model in relation to the respective theoretical assumptions, interventions and accumulated evidence.

Therefore, applying the three criteria used by Hofmann *et al.* (2010), there are reasons to disagree with the notion that the tandem model is simply another approach within the CBT family (part of the third wave), despite the growing areas of overlap. Further cross-referencing with Hofmann *et al.* (2010) leads me to the view that the tandem is sufficiently new and different to represent a fourth wave of CBT supervision. Interestingly, the tandem's claim to distinctiveness is close to that asserted for DBT and ACT: addressing experiential avoidance, enhancing emotion regulation strategies and giving more attention to context. In this sense, I find that I may be closer to the proponents of DBT and ACT than to Hofmann *et al.* (2010), although unlike one of them (Hayes *et al.*, 2006) I do not regard the difference as profound (not sufficient to designate the tandem as a unique supervision model), nor as indicating dramatic change (only some gentle enhancement of CBT supervision is indicated).

Assuming that the tandem model represents a fourth wave of CBT supervision carries implications about its status, amongst other things. As noted in Chapter 2, CBT supervision is a therapy-based model, whereas the tandem model is a supervision-specific model. Also, acceptance of the tandem model represents treating supervision as a professional specialization, in turn implying specialized training and proper recognition for supervisors within the workplace. It also suggests that supervision is a serious topic for attention, in terms of research and practice development. In short, the tandem model raises the status of CBT supervision and of those who practise supervision in this evidence-based way. Talking of practice, the tandem model also links smoothly to the CBT supervision manual (Milne & Reiser, 2017), so that supervisors and those who train and support them are properly resourced, addressing the need identified in a recent survey (Reiser & Milne, 2016). Similarly, it implies that this book is effectively the complete theoretical companion to that manual.

Kolb's (1984, 2014) account of experiential learning

A second major aspect uniting EBCS and CBT supervision that merits critical attention is their historical reliance on Kolb's (1984) account of experiential learning as a unifying concept. In EBCS, this account was placed at the centre of the circumplex model (Figure 3.3) and was similarly pivotal within the $N = 1$ studies and other associated work (Milne, 2009). In so far as CBT supervision addresses experiential learning explicitly, Kolb's (1984) account has also been incorporated (see Townend *et al.*, 2002; Armstrong & Freeston, 2005; Reiser, 2014; Rakovshik *et al.*, 2016). As this second edition is intended to update the evidence-base and review critically what was stated in the first edition, it becomes timely to shift from relying on Kolb's (1984) account, and to appeal to more recent evidence on experiential learning. This effectively buttresses and refines Kolb's learning cycle with the findings from more recent and more substantive research, and also helps to address some further significant problems with Kolb's account.

It should be borne in mind that Kolb (1984) was attempting to synthesize the ideas of some important pioneers in psychology, such as Bruner, Piaget, Dewey and Lewin. It is always difficult to reproduce faithfully the work of such prolific authors, and to do so without bias. Perhaps for these reasons, four main criticisms of Kolb (1984) seem to be warranted. I will now summarize these as criticisms from the perspective of those who train supervisors, and for researchers, supervisors and supervisees. In relation to trainers, there is a lack of attention to the system in which learning occurs, and to factors such as culture and history (i.e. inattention to moderators: a de-contextualized theory). Secondly, Kolb's approach is reductionistic, and can be seen as being too narrowly psychological, and, in particular, too cognitive. This yields implausibly neat sets of stages, which have then been described as 'intoxicatingly simply' (Kayes, 2002, p.142). Another issue for trainers is that Kolb's (1984) theory, like any other general theory, lacks widespread acceptance within academic circles; indeed, there is as yet no consensus on any one particular paradigm of adult learning.

Turning to criticisms related to the perspective of learners, Kolb places equal emphasis on all modes of learning, whereas reflection dominates in other influential accounts on how people learn from experience (e.g. Boud *et al.*, 1985; Schoen, 1987). A related criticism is that these modes may simply be different aspects of the same learning process: at one level 'reflection' may merge into 'experiencing' (for example). Kolb's account also ignores 'higher' (e.g. metacognitive) learning, for example how the super-visee might question their own learning style, and it assumes that all learning occurs through a fairly dramatic transaction between the different modes of knowing (as opposed to simple acquisition of declarative knowl-edge through lectures, or rote learning for exams).

Turning to the perspective of researchers, the empirical scrutiny of Kolb's (1984) account is remarkably minimal, and the studies that do exist do not provide clear-cut affirmation (see for example Holman *et al.*, 1997; Rey-nolds, 1997). To make matters worse, Kolb (1984) makes some rather grand claims, particularly for his learning styles inventory. But the research that does exist suggests that this 'theory of life and everything' is hard to substantiate (Reynolds, 1997). Also problematic for researchers are the vagueness of the essential constructs, particularly terms like 'experience', and again the absence of reference to more measurable, conventional forms of learning, such as habituation. An incisive and damming philosophical critique of the construct validity of Kolb's work has been provided by Webb (2006), in which she questions such fundamentals as the mechanism of 'dialectic tension' between the different modes of learning, which she describes as not being a viable mechanism.

Finally, from the perspective of supervisees, Kolb's model assumes that actions are rational, linear and quantifiable. It ignores, for example, the important power relations that can arise from things like differences in gender and status, and it also ignores pre- or unconscious processes (e.g. transference; Webb, 2006).

However, these are not necessarily fatal criticisms, as I attempted to show in Milne (2009, Chapter 9). In effect, my use of Kolb's (1984) account of experiential learning has been tempered by some of these criticisms, as reflected in the EBCS model (e.g. counter-balancing the cognitive emphasis with a behavioural and affective one). It now seems more straightforward to place Kolb's (1984) full account to one side, and to give the unifying, pivotal role to modern, evidence-based statements of experiential learning. Although Kolb (2014) has published a second edition of his classic, a book that includes in each chapter a lengthy section on 'updates and reflections', my impression is that this does not resolve some key criticisms, nor does it furnish significant new evidence on the experiential learning model. Indeed, as he notes, there appear to remain several philosophical tangles, which to my mind create insurmountable obstacles to his full model (e.g. regarding concepts like 'experience' and 'dialectical tensions'). There-fore, here I retain experiential learning as the main mechanism of change in

EBCS, as described above and as operationalized within the observational tool SAGE (Milne *et al.*, 2011a), but justify the refined learning cycle by reference to contemporary empirical analyses. Specifically, the evidence-base I rely on includes my own co-authored review of 24 research studies (Milne *et al.*, 2008a), which concluded that 20 of these studies described outcomes that were consistent with the experiential learning cycle. I also rely on other research studies (e.g. Bearman *et al.*, 2013; Rakovshik *et al.*, 2016), reviews of CBT training (Beidas & Kendall, 2010; Rakovshik & McManus, 2010), expert consensus statements (Falender *et al.*, 2004; Kaslow *et al.*, 2004; American Psychological Association, 2015), and neighbouring literatures, such as deliberate practice (Ericsson, 2009; Tracey *et al.*, 2014). A full review of this research literature also appears in Milne and Reiser (2017). I believe that such evidence provides a consistent and compelling case for the vital role of experiential learning, as defined and described in this book (e.g. Tables 3.1 and 3.2) and in Milne and Reiser (2014b).

Conclusions

The EBCS approach represents a case-study of how models of supervision can be researched and developed, resulting in a promising fourth wave enhancement of CBT supervision in particular. The tandem model of evidence-based CBT supervision offers an unusually integrative and detailed conceptualization, especially in relation to formative supervision. This model resulted from 20 years engagement with the successive stages of the EBCS framework. As part of this programmatic research, the tandem model was gradually bolstered by various resources and tools, including four supervision guidelines, a supervisor training manual and measurement instruments. Subsequent to that work, culminating in the first edition of this book (Milne, 2009), further stages of research and development have produced a newer and bigger manual (Milne & Reiser, 2017). These and other developments are described later in the present book. This development work built on the kind of careful reasoning advocated by Machado and Silva (2007), including clear concepts, acknowledged assumptions and proper arguments (e.g. about the boundaries with similar models).

Some criticize model-building as idle or academic, but I share the opinion that it 'represents a serious approach to science' (Watson, 1999, p.166), and it is hoped that, through maintaining this conceptualization effort, the

EBCS approach will eventually help us to better understand how supervision operates, leading to further refinements to (or replacement of) the tandem model. This developmental cycle was illustrated above in the careful scrutiny of experiential learning theory (Kolb, 1984; 2014), part of the tandem model, which I argued was now best replaced by an evidence-based account, depending on fewer philosophically problematic concepts.

Kolb's theory has consistently been incorporated in British models of CBT supervision (e.g. Armstrong & Freeston, 2005; James *et al.*, 2006), together with Vygotsky's (1978) concept of the 'zone of proximal development'. The tandem model has done likewise, but is perhaps distinguished by the much greater incorporation of a wider range of material from neighbouring literatures. These are the research findings and concepts in the staff training/instructional design, expertise, psychotherapy, human development, education and adult learning literatures. It is acknowledged that such analogies are not without their risks (as discussed in some detail in Milne & Reiser, 2017). However, this distinction is limited, as James (2014) has also made use of some of these literatures. What appears to better distinguish the tandem model is the extent to which it has been operationalized, implemented and evaluated as part of a coherent programme of applied research. Following some 20 years of this research and development activity, the tandem model can now be seen as an enhanced, fourth wave of CBT supervision, a stage at which supervision can be regarded as an evidence-based professional specialization, consistent with the era of evidence-based practice within health services.

Although this research programme has generated some promising findings, there are clearly some important caveats. Amongst these are the need to gather large-group and comparative data on the tandem model (preferably through independent researchers), and to clarify still further the fundamental concepts that underpin the approach, so that they have construct validity. But I do think that this enhancement effort should continue to be guided by the EBCS framework (Figure 3.3), or by a related programme of research and development. Thus far, qualitative and quantitative research of this kind has indicated clear differences between the tandem approach and (third wave) CBT supervision in practice (e.g. Milne *et al.*, 2011a, 2013), and also differences between CBT, systemic and psychodynamic supervision (Cliffe & Milne, 2012), proving the value of testing theoretical models in action. I return to these issues in Chapter 9.

4

Relating in Supervision

Introduction

Most accounts of what matters in clinical supervision treat the quality of the supervisory relationship as pivotal to success, and 'foundational to effective supervisory practice' (Inman *et al.*, 2014). In psychoanalysis, Freud referred to it as the 'vehicle of success' (Freud, 1912, p.105), while in cognitive-behaviour therapy (CBT) there is a prizing of relationship factors such as collaboration, a task alliance and attention to relevant interpersonal dynamics (Reiser, 2014). After more than half a century, it remains the single most prized variable within supervision generally: 'the supervisory alliance has increasingly come to be seen as the very heart and soul of supervision itself' (Watkins, 2014a, p.151). Watkins (2014a) reviewed how the supervisory alliance was treated in seven popular approaches (e.g. psychoanalytic and CBT supervision), concluding that all models regarded it as 'an accepted and incontrovertible pillar of good practice' (p.159). In his opinion, the alliance was also the most frequently cited ('supreme') common factor in the supervision literature.

Although strongly phrased, Watkins' view appears to be a unanimous one shared by all experts who have commented on the status of the supervision alliance. For example, Falender and Shafranske (2014, p.3) acknowledged that the alliance was 'a metatheoretical essential component of supervision. It is the central feature that influences...supervisory practices'. Similarly, the American Psychological Association (APA, 2015) guidelines on clinical supervision, developed by an expert Task Force,

Evidence-Based CBT Supervision: Principles and Practice, Second Edition. Derek L. Milne.
© 2018 John Wiley & Sons Ltd. Published in 2018 by the British Psychological Society and John Wiley & Sons Ltd.

included three alliance-specific guidelines, noting by way of introduction that 'The quality of the supervisory relationship is essential to effective clinical supervision' (p.37). The unanimous endorsement of the supervision alliance extends to the UK, where another expert group defined the 'ability to form and maintain a supervisory alliance' as a generic competence, 'crucial to the delivery of good supervision' (Pilling & Roth, 2014, p.28).

The vital role of the supervision alliance is reflected in the empirical definition provided in Chapter 1, which states that supervision is based on 'the formal provision, by senior/qualified health practitioners, of an intensive, *relationship-based* education and training'. In turn, the 'relationship-based' aspect is typically specified as something that is confidential and highly collaborative, founded on a learning alliance, featuring elements such as participative decision-making and shared agenda-setting, and entailing therapeutic qualities such as empathy and warmth. In this chapter I will describe this traditional emphasis on this pivotal role that is so unanimously ascribed to the supervision alliance, but I will also moderate and qualify the unreserved endorsement of the alliance by presenting and discussing the evidence behind these rather grand claims. In particular, I will note the surprisingly weak empirical support, together with growing recent evidence that some supervision relationships lack some of the supposedly critical features, yet still appear to be effective partnerships. This is consistent with the tandem model that guides evidence-based CBT supervision, in that collaboration is the natural and most desirable way of relating. It is also far more efficient than the alternative, but ultimately it is not essential, and we should anticipate many occasions when the relationship between the tandem riders is sorely tested.

Perhaps more so than any other factor, the alliance draws heavily on an analogy with the therapy literature. Broadly speaking, a therapeutic relationship can be defined as the 'feelings and attitudes that therapists and clients have toward one another and the manner in which these are expressed' (Norcross, 2002, p.7). In therapy, the relationship is thought to derive from various qualities and practices of the therapist (e.g. capacity to empathize), in conjunction with the characteristics and participation of the client (e.g. motivation to change). These facets of the relationship are brought together in the therapeutic work in what Norcross (2002) refers to as a 'complex reciprocal interaction . . . . a deep synergy' (p.8). The interaction is thought to be based on the different methods that are used by the therapist, the goals that are agreed and the specific techniques that are applied. Clinical outcomes are assumed to be based on this combination of factors.

The work of the APA Task Force, as reported by Norcross (2001), identified six variables in the therapeutic relationship that were 'demonstrably effective', based on a review of the research literature: the therapeutic alliance, empathy, goal consensus and collaboration (ingredients primarily provided by the therapist), and ways of customizing therapy on the basis of the client's behaviours or qualities (i.e. dealing with resistance and addressing functional impairments/distress). In addition, this Task Force noted a number of additional relationship variables that were considered to be 'promising and probably effective': positive regard, congruence/genuineness, feedback, repair of alliance ruptures, self-disclosure, management of counter-transference and the quality of relational interpretations. A subsequent APA Task Force drew on a series of meta-analyses, filtered by expert consensus, to define the features of evidence-based therapeutic relationships (Norcross & Wampold, 2011). It was again concluded that the alliance was demonstrably effective, as was empathy and collecting feedback from patients. The probably effective aspects of the relationship were thought to be goal consensus, collaboration and positive regard. Three other relationship elements were judged promising, but not yet demonstrated: congruence/genuineness, repairing alliance ruptures and managing counter-transference.

In summary, according to the 2001 Task Force, therapy outcomes are a product of the interaction between therapist factors and patient factors, both operating through a relationship likened to a diamond, in the sense that there are multiple facets. Whatever the metaphor, this basic logic has been applied since the work of Freud in the late nineteenth century, who advocated making a 'collaborator' of the client (for a summary see Safran & Muran, 2000). Freud's prime focus was on the transference phenomenon, but apparently he also recognized the importance of friendliness, affection and the 'analytic pact'. The idea gradually developed to the point where the therapeutic alliance was widely accepted, and defined in terms of an agreement about goals, the joint tackling of the tasks that are necessary to achieve those goals (mutual engagement in the tasks) and an emotional bond that develops between therapist and client (sometimes called rapport; Bordin, 1979). Bordin took the view that the bond developed as a result of either working together on the tasks (an emergent property) or on the basis of shared emotional experiences. These were thought to centre on the feelings of liking, caring and trusting that emerge from mutual engagement in the therapeutic tasks.

As this summary of the alliance indicates, in this chapter I will continue to draw on neighbouring literatures, particularly the fruitful field of psychotherapy. As a consequence, analogies between the phenomena of therapy and those of supervision will be made explicitly. In the case of relationships, this appears to be a widely accepted practice, a trend started by Bordin (1979; 1983) in relation to the alliance. Bernard and Goodyear (2014) are amongst those who agree that Bordin's (1979) reasoning on the therapeutic alliance applies equally well to supervision. Some rare empirical evidence to support the view that there are at least strong associations has been provided by Patton and Kivlighan (1997), who found a significant correlation between the supervisees' alliance in supervision and in their subsequent therapy (though the technical skills practised in supervision were not replicated in therapy). But this correlation was not replicated in a survey of 110 trainee therapists (Ybrandt *et al.*, 2016), as these trainees reported good therapeutic alliances despite some poor supervisory alliances. Such inconsistent findings are not unusual within research on the alliance, as I will describe below. But first I will provide a definition of the alliance in supervision, then go on to describe some of those facets of the relationship 'diamond' within supervision. Practical implications of these facets will then be specified, in terms of actions that supervisors can take to enhance their alliances. The next part of the chapter will be concerned with the conditions that are necessary for these facets of the alliance to operate successfully. This will draw on those 'probably effective' relationship variables noted above, in order to consider the process of relationship rupture and repair (and similar vital processes), within the evolving supervisory relationship. The final part of this chapter examines the kinds of results that can be expected if the conditions for a gem of an alliance are satisfied. Knowing about likely results helps supervisors by clarifying the kinds of micro-outcomes that they can expect to see within successful supervision.

Defining the Supervision Alliance

Although Bordin's initial work focused on the therapeutic alliance within psychoanalysis (Bordin, 1979), he subsequently extended this work to include supervision (Bordin, 1983), retaining the three-part approach in which the alliance was defined as an agreement about the goals, agreement and collaboration over the tasks of supervision, and an emotional bond (including mutual liking, caring and trusting). Shared goals refer to the specification of objectives within the supervision experience, and more broadly to ensuring that mutual expectations are clarified (Bernard & Goodyear, 2014). Whereas the specification of learning objectives for supervision is normally relatively concrete and straightforward, and recorded within a learning contract, the notion of 'expectations' is meant to cover the kinds of anticipatory beliefs that the supervisee (in particular) will have about the nature and outcomes of supervision. Therefore, Bernard and Goodyear (2014) encourage supervisors to be as clear about the mutual expectations about supervision as they are about the more familiar learning objectives.

In her review, Beinart (2014) noted that the alliance is a more theoretically driven term than the term 'relationship', because 'alliance' is associated with Bordin's work (1979; 1983) and with psychoanalysis. Beinart (2014) also detailed how the supervision alliance is a narrower construct (subsuming the three factors noted above) than that of the supervision relationship, which she and her collaborators in Oxford have shown through psychometric studies to consist of six factors (Table 4.1). Expert consensus has also indicated more than three factors within a supervision relationship. According to the APA (2015) guideline, the supervisory relationship includes a collaborative relationship that promotes competence in the supervisee, goal-setting and planning, and the regular review and repair of the relationship. Pilling and Roth (2014) defined the alliance in similar terms, overlapping with the APA (2015) guidelines on goal-setting and mutual feedback, whilst adding the aspects of helping the supervisees to present clinical information effectively and enabling critical reflection on their own experience. Therefore, the definition in Table 4.1 appears to subsume the alliance, but helpfully extends it to include three additional factors that are endorsed by experts and indicated by psychometric research. A further advantage is that the term 'supervision relationship' is common to all supervision models (pan-theoretical). For these reasons the definition in Table 4.1 forms the basis of the one used in this book, as described below. However, the term 'alliance' will be preferred, as it is now used generically in the clinical supervision literature (i.e. without the strict or delimited reference to the psychoanalytic relationship), and it is familiar and carries the right connotation.

The alliance can be measured by several of the instruments that are used to measure clinical supervision generally (i.e. in relation to multiple aspects). For example, the Manchester Clinical Supervision Scale (Winstanley, 2000) includes six items relevant to the alliance within the factor called 'support', part of the restorative function of supervision. This is

Table 4.1 The six factors in the Supervisory Relationship Questionnaire (SRQ; Palomo *et al.*, 2010), together with some action implications.

Components	Definitions and examples	Possible actions
A. Facilitative conditions (variance accounted for in SRQ scores)		
1. 'Safe base' (52%)	Supervisee feeling valued, respected and safe. Supervisor supportive, trustworthy and responsive	Empathize and connect emotionally (e.g. through self-disclosure); seek understanding and consensus (e.g. shared expectations); offer warmth and respond to learner's needs; avoid hostility, criticism and being judgemental
2. 'Structure' (4.5%)	Maintaining practical boundaries, like time	Be clear about duration and purpose (including shared goals/ joint agenda-setting); regular and structured supervision
3. 'Commitment' (2.9%)	Supervisor interested in supervision and supervisee	Show interest and enthusiasm; be approachable and attentive; offer constructive feedback; address and repair alliance ruptures
B. Goals and tasks		
4. 'Role model' (2.2%)	Supervisor perceived as skilled, knowledgeable and respectful	Draw on experience within system; provide practical support; demonstrate your approach and key skills, especially respect for patients and colleagues
5. 'Reflective education' (1.9%)	Facilitating learning through supervisee's reflection; sensitive to supervisee's anxieties	Draw on multiple models flexibly; encourage reflection; foster theory – practice integration; promote interesting discussions of techniques; focus on the process of supervision (including acknowledging the power differential)
6. 'Formative feedback' (1.8%)	Constructive and regular, including positive and negative feedback; tailored to stage of supervisee's development	Encourage interest in feedback from the supervisee, adapting it to fit his/her understanding and level of confidence; provide feedback regularly, including positive and negative comments, made in a balanced, constructive way

Source: Milne, D.L. (2009). Reproduced with permission of Derek Milne.

meant to measure the extent to which the supervisee feels socially supported by the supervisor. Items include: 'I can unload during my clinical supervision session'; 'my supervisor gives me support and encouragement'; and 'my supervisor is very open with me'. As these items indicate, there is almost complete reliance on self-report instruments within the alliance research literature (Watkins, 2014b), and so an evidence-based approach should complement such instruments with more objective alternatives, especially the use of direct observation. An example from therapy is the study by Andrusyna *et al.* (2001), in which four experienced CBT therapists were observed working with 94 adult patients, using an observational version of the Working Alliance Inventory (see Bahrick, 1990). Factor analysis of the observational data indicated that there were only two factors in this sample of CBT: agreed goals and tasks, and an emotional bond, featuring trust and confidence in the therapist. Similarly, the observational instrument for rating competence in supervision (SAGE; Milne *et al.*, 2011b, described in Chapter 8) includes four common factors relevant to the alliance: 'relating' (interpersonally effective); 'collaborating'; 'managing'; and 'facilitating'. That these observational tools do not yield the same factor solutions as the self-report tools underscores the value of employing multiple measures (Rossi *et al.*, 2004). It also questions the confidence that some have placed in self-report questionnaires as the basis for a definitive factor solution for the supervision alliance. To illustrate, Watkins (2014b, p.3) concluded that: 'Nearly 50 studies strong, the supervisory alliance has received a high degree of research support across varied samples and settings, and results have largely affirmed alliance theory and the bond–goals–tasks conceptualization.' It appears that not a single one of these studies utilized direct observation, and that almost all used correlational analyses, based on subjective ratings (mostly made by small samples of students), using psychometrically weak measures of the alliance. This represents a weak foundation for EBCS.

There are also instruments that focus exclusively on the supervision alliance, such as the Working Alliance Inventory (adapted for supervision by Bahrick, 1990; NB: a copy is appended to Falender & Shafranske, 2014). This Inventory was based on the Bordin model, so not surprisingly it includes the three elements of goals, agreement on tasks, and bond. The Supervisory Working Alliance Inventory (Efstation *et al.*, 1990) contains a 'rapport' factor (e.g. 'My supervisor stays in tune with me during supervision'), whilst one of the first such instruments, the Supervisory Styles Inventory (SSI; Friedlander & Ward, 1984), included an interpersonally sensitive 'counsellor' style of relating (NB: a copy of the unpublished SSI is appended to Bernard & Goodyear, 2014). A systematic review of 11 such alliance-focused instruments has been provided by Tangen and Borders (2016), together with recommendations for their use (e.g. as an aid to communication between supervisor and supervisee). The review by Wheeler and Barkham (2014) concluded the search for a core outcome battery of supervision instruments by recommending three alliance measures (the Supervisory Working Alliance Inventory; the Brief Supervisory Alliance Scale; and the Role Conflict and Role Ambiguity Inventory).

Beinart (2014) has reviewed the instruments associated with the more recent research activity of the Oxford group (including the Supervisory Relationship Questionnaire (SRQ); Palomo, 2004). An important observation arising from this research programme has been the recognition that 'although there are common elements, supervisors and the supervisees have somewhat different views and experiences of their relationships' (Beinart, 2014, p.266). Specifically, the Oxford group found that a supervisors' version of the SRQ, the Supervisory Relationship Measure (SRM) yielded five factors, only two of which overlapped strongly with the SRQ (i.e. 'safe base' and 'commitment'; Pearce *et al.*, 2013). For supervisors, the distinctive factors were 'trainee contribution', 'external influences' (e.g. work stress) and 'supervisor investment' (emotional investment in the supervisee and their alliance). As summarized in Table 4.1, six coherent factors were identified within the SRQ, following analysis of the replies of 284 trainee clinical psychologists. The SRQ has 67 items and good psychometric properties, including acceptable reliability and convergent validity. This analysis also supported the Bordin (1983) model, finding the essential emphasis on sharing expectations and clarifying objectives jointly, plus an emotional bond. However, the SRQ goes beyond these core elements to articulate additional facets of the supervisory alliance, including the 'safe base' stressed by Scaife (2001) and by many practitioners. The practical value of this six-component definition of alliance is illustrated by the third column of Table 4.1, as these facets help to suggest actions that supervisors might take to promote their supervisory alliance.

How close is the agreement between the supervisory and therapeutic alliances? Given the popular emphasis on drawing analogies between these two professional activities, it is appropriate to contrast these alliance instruments with examples published in the therapy literature. A case in point is the Agnew Relationship Measure (ARM; Agnew-Davies *et al.*,

1998). The ARM was developed explicitly to obtain clients' and therapists' views of CBT and an exploratory therapy alternative. A total of 95 clients and 5 therapists completed the ARM after every session within a comparative outcome evaluation (the second Sheffield psychotherapy project). As a result, five factors were extracted: 'bond' (client feeling friendly towards the therapist; the therapist being accepting, understanding, supporting and warm towards the client); 'partnership' (where the therapist and client agree on what to work on, and are willing to work hard to achieve these objectives); 'confidence' (where the client has confidence in the therapist, and is optimistic and finds the therapist's skills impressive); 'openness' (where the client feels free to express worries and embarrassment, does not keep things to him or herself and can express feelings and reveal things); and 'client initiative' (where the therapist empowers the client to take the lead and enables him or her to look for solutions and to take responsibility).

It can be seen that there is considerable overlap between the Agnew Relationship Measure and this SRQ in the areas of the emotional bond (touched on within the safe base and commitments parts of the SRQ), in the efforts to work jointly towards an agreed goal ('partnership' in the ARM; 'structure and commitment' within the SRQ) and in the third main area of the traditional Bordin (1983) definition of alliance, the capacity to work jointly to specify those objectives. However, clear differences are present in relation to two distinctive facets of supervision. Unlike therapy, supervision involves an explicit, formal evaluation function (covered by factor six within the SRQ, formative 'feedback'), participation is obligatory and there is a major educational function (covered by the 'reflective education' factor within the SRQ). These predicted differences between the two professional activities helps to show where alliance is continuous with therapy and where it is important to recognize a boundary to such analogies.

Definition of the Alliance in EBCS

If the alliance in supervision is different from that in therapy it requires a distinct definition. Partly in summary of this section, but also building on the definition of clinical supervision in general (Milne, 2007b), incorporating relevant aspects from SAGE (Milne *et al.*, 2011b), and drawing on the alliance guideline in the CBT supervision manual (Milne & Reiser, 2017), I regard the supervision alliance as:

> A highly collaborative, collegial and committed partnership, one that is task-focused and highly professional (e.g. interpersonally effective, confidential, empathic, and warm). It is intended to support (restorative function), guide (normative function), and primarily to develop the supervisee (formative function). The overall purpose is to maximize the supervisee's clinical effectiveness and ethical practice, and to promote patient safety. The CBT supervisor should act as a consistent role model (more like a scientist-practitioner than a teacher or therapist), providing leadership (e.g. structuring and managing sessions through a task alliance) and inspiring an evidence-based approach (e.g. taking a developmental perspective on the supervisee's learning). The leadership style also emphasizes participative decision-making (e.g. establishing an explicit learning agreement), educational activities (including challenging and the facilitation of reflection) and general professional guidance, in a context of mutual caring, trust and security (social support). The alliance should not become therapy, nor should it become focused on a relational experience (the goal of 'personal growth'). It can be measured subjectively for supervisees by the Supervisory Relationship Questionnaire (SRQ; Palomo *et al.*, 2010), and for supervisors by the SRM (Pearce *et al.*, 2013), and more objectively it can be measured with the observational tool SAGE (Milne *et al.*, 2011b).

This definition of the alliance is closer to a CBT approach (Milne & Reiser, 2017) than to the humanistic and psychodynamic approaches that tend to dominate this topic (for a comparison of several such models see Watkins, 2014a). In turn, there are some minor enhancements of CBT supervision that come from applying the EBCS framework. For instance, in EBCS the alliance emphasizes a more balanced approach to experiential learning (e.g. greater attention to the supervisee's affective experience than in third wave CBT). Also, the context is accorded greater weight in EBCS (environmental and developmental). The environmental context refers to factors outside the individual which influence behavior, such as peer support for supervisors, or the resources required for supervision. The developmental enhancement refers to lifespan development theory, and to associated principles and methods for measuring development. An example is the micro-analysis of the learning process (the 'microgenetic' study of developmental phases; Siegler, 2002). A supervision-specific example of

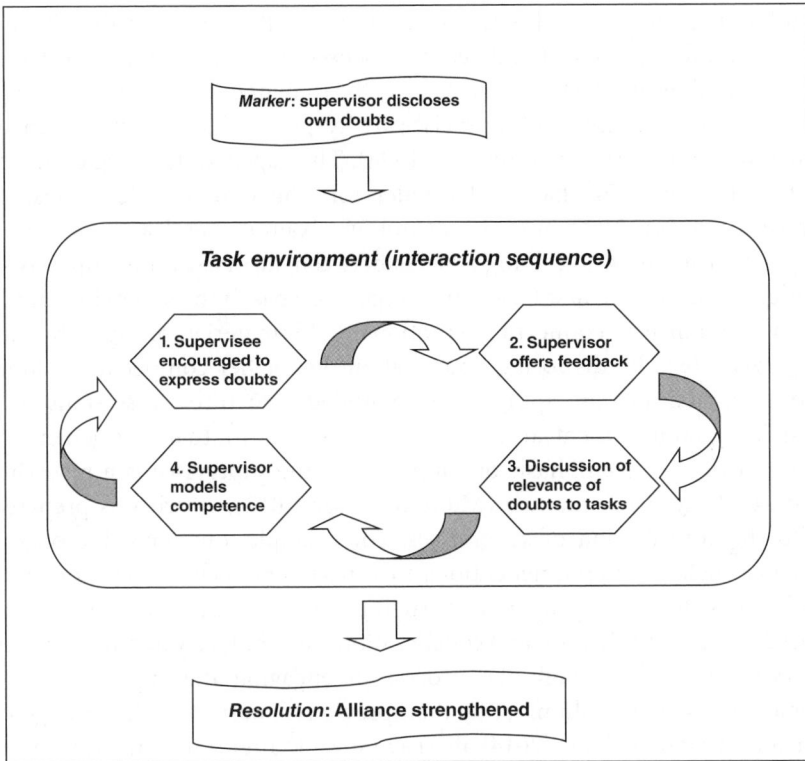

Figure 4.1   An episode analysis, illustrating how a CBT supervision alliance might develop.

Source: Milne, D.L. (2009). Reproduced with permission of Derek Milne.

microgenetic analysis is the study of supervision 'episodes' (Figure 4.1), where the terminology of episode analysis is used (Ladany *et al.*, 2005). However, the concepts are similar to CBT, particularly the idea of task analysis and the use of intensive ('dense') observation of rapid change processes, using qualitative and quantitative methods.

The Process of Alliance Development

As the above instruments hint, the APA Task Force's analogy (Norcross, 2001), likening the relationship to a multifaceted diamond, appears somewhat inadequate. This is because the so-called facets of the alliance (such as offering a collaborative, task-focused relationship) are not fixed, but rather they are the transient states within a dynamic process of relating, because the supervisor and supervisee are 'responsive' to one another in an emerging pattern (Stiles & Shapiro, 1994). This 'open system' logic was set out in the preceding chapter. To underscore this dynamic view, consider Table 4.1 again. Note how the definition, examples and actions are all dependent upon an unfolding process between supervisor and supervisee. For example, for the first factor to emerge ('safe base') the supervisor needs to be responsive, connecting emotionally to material brought by the supervisee (e.g. by disclosing doubts about his or her competence). Similarly, maintaining an appropriate, bounded structure to sessions and sustaining commitment and interest requires the mutual engagement of both parties. This emphasis on empowering the supervisee is a recurring feature of the EBCS manual (Milne & Reiser, 2017), which was prepared with the contribution of supervisees. For example, our guideline on the alliance includes recommendations to supervisors such as: 'Demonstrate early on your interest in both clarifying roles and expectations, and in ensuring full participation and collaboration. Generally, try to build a strong working alliance through the process of engaging the supervisee in a personal discussion, illuminating their previous experience, skills and goals for supervision.' Beinart (2014) also gave specific attention to the role of the supervisee, noting that one of her relationship questionnaires included a factor labelled 'trainee contribution'. She listed some relevant actions supervisees could take, such as taking responsibility, working hard, making a useful contribution and being organized. A further example of the importance of empowering supervisees concerns the need to address their issues, which may hamper such contributions. According to Falender and Shafranske (2004), one of the main ways in which the supervisory alliance may be threatened is by supervisees having negative reactions to their clients, because the client undermines the forming of an alliance (e.g. by having a narcissistic or antisocial personality). They take the view, consistent with the bulk of the relevant literature, that such strains within the supervisory alliance are not only common, but are actually a basis from which the alliance can develop.

Perhaps the clearest illustrations of the role of the alliance come from those unfortunate situations where the alliance breaks down. To illustrate, Bernard and Goodyear (2014) have summarized 'how to be a lousy supervisor'. This turns the preceding advice upside-down, and extends it by drawing out some of the lessons from research on the alliance. Lousy supervision includes: not revealing your own shortcomings; not providing a sense of safety wherein doubts and fears can be discussed; placing service needs above the supervisee's educational needs; ignoring the need for emotional support from the supervisee; ignoring the supervisee's strengths and interests; and not recognizing the need to share responsibility for any interpersonal conflicts that may arise. The survey of inadequate and harmful supervision by Ellis *et al.* (2014) elaborates and substantiates this list by enumerating the negative experiences reported by the majority of the 363 supervisees in their study (e.g. 'oblivious to interpersonal process' and 'relationship is cold and distant').

Fortunately, there are plenty of suggestions on how to ensure a productive alliance, some of which are listed in the right-hand column of Table 4.1. Bernard and Goodyear (2014) have also provided a helpful breakdown of some of the supervisor behaviours that contribute to the learning alliance: appropriate confidentiality (ethical behaviour); basing feedback and other evaluations on the agreed objectives of supervision (evaluative practices); a supervisory style that includes features such as an interpersonally sensitive and task-orientated approach (style); and moderate levels of supervisor self-disclosure (e.g. regarding personal experiences and struggles at work). Reflecting the relationship base to supervision, another helpful element was the supervisee's perception that the supervisor had expert knowledge to offer, but that the supervisee was recognized for his or her own input (use of power). Beinart (2014) drew on her psychometric research to suggest other ways that supervisors and supervisees can develop their alliances. She detailed specific actions alongside the relationship factors in her instruments, such as the 'trainee contribution' factor mentioned above, and a reciprocal factor termed 'supervisor investment', which covers actions like investing in the relationship by taking an interest in the supervisee by finding out about their learning needs, interests and culture. Scaife (2001) provided further suggestions, based on her experience and on the psychodynamic concept of developing a 'safe base' in supervision. She suggests that supervisors demonstrate things to the supervisee, before asking them to undertake a task; share work openly with trainees (e.g. showing tapes or encouraging the supervisee to sit in on their work); always take a respectful approach to clients and colleagues, so that the supervisee sees that the supervisor is unlikely to prove unreliable; keep confidences and be consistent in relation to what they say and do; ensure that any challenges are specific and work related, providing supervisees with clear guidance on how they can regulate the supervisor's challenges; and be prepared to take responsibility where difficult issues are at stake (e.g. client safety).

Even if one follows such suggestions, the process of alliance development may not go smoothly. Whatever their source, disagreements and misunderstandings in supervision (or therapy) can contribute to what Falender and Shafranske (2004) refer to as alliance 'ruptures and impasses'. With Safran and Muran (2000), they note that supervision is a particularly vital opportunity for supervisees to begin to repair ruptures to their therapeutic alliances. Given that the development of competence is one of the primary objectives of the supervisee, and that an uncooperative client is an impediment to demonstrating competence, addressing therapeutic ruptures is a pivotal topic. It is one in which the bond between the supervisor and supervisee is of particular significance, as there is reason to believe that the quality of the alliance in supervision will influence the quality of the supervisee's therapy alliances (Patton & Kivlighan, 1997). It is also an environment where the supervisees can feel safe to discuss such threatening material as their perceived incompetence, and can commence the repair work. The threat may arise from something that happened (e.g. angry allegations by the client), or from the absence of alliance-related behaviours (e.g. non-compliance with an assignment). It is easy for supervisees to perceive such events as implying their incompetence. However, it appears that supervisees who report receiving empathic supervision, and feel safe in expressing themselves, regard their clinical work as more effective (Kavanagh *et al.*, 2003). The same study, based on a survey of 272 multidisciplinary supervisors and supervisees in Australia's public health service (i.e. all qualified staff), also reported highly significant correlations between perceived clinical effectiveness and gaining skills and confidence through supervision, so there is some basis for assuming that establishing a good alliance promotes competence. A further reason for optimism is that supervisees reporting a good supervision alliance show adherence to the therapy approach addressed in supervision, where this adherence was observed directly from video recordings, and rated by judges (Patton & Kivlighan, 1997).

A micro-phase within the process of alliance development is illustrated in Figure 4.1 by means of an episode analysis (Ladany *et al.*, 2005). Some of the ideas outlined in the preceding text have been arranged within this figure, in the kind of chronological order that might typically occur within a supervision session. Actual examples drawn from a longitudinal study of EBCS can be found in Milne *et al.* (2011a).

In order to repair ruptures arising from things like a disagreement over the supervisee's competence, the procedure advocated by Safran and Muran (2000) for addressing therapy impasses can usefully be extended to supervision. According to this approach, the supervisor would explore with the supervisee the kinds of thoughts and feelings underpinning these events, while modelling an open, collaborative stance. Other contributions to the repair work, in both supervision and subsequent therapy, are appropriate disclosure by the supervisor of their own experiences of ruptures, processing reactions, discussing options, building understanding and re-engaging in a repair process with the supervisee and/or client. Helpful verbatim accounts of resolving alliance ruptures are provided by Ladany *et al.* (2005), who agree that this rupture–repair approach can be applied within supervision. Their account covers problems with counter-transference, parallel process and other common difficulties.

It is clear from this account of the responsive, dynamic process of relating effectively to the supervisee (in relation to ruptures) that the supervisor requires a measure of insight (e.g. to be able to self-disclose persuasively). Within the psychodynamic and humanistic traditions this is aided by the process of personal therapy. Latterly, a process of 'self-practice, self-reflection' has been advocated in relation to CBT (Bennett-Levy & Thwaites, 2007). Based on a cognitive model of how therapists develop competence, these authors outline a six-stage reflective process for heightening self-awareness, improving understanding and rehearsing possible solutions to relationship difficulties in supervision. This is 'self-practice' as some of the methods of CBT are applied reflexively to the CBT practitioner. Specifically, attention is focused on a problematic event (e.g. a relationship rupture), and imagery or role-play may be used to heighten awareness of relevant thoughts or feelings. This leads to cognitive clarification through reflection, and on to an enhanced conceptualization of that event. The final stages are behavioural rehearsal, so as to practise how to apply the new understanding (role-plays may be used again), and to test out the strategy in therapy.

The process of addressing alliance ruptures through processes such as 'self-practice, self-reflection' can also be construed in terms of a general process of assimilation, tackled by 'working through' the experience in supervision. According to the assimilation model (Stiles *et al.*, 1990), a problematic experience such as a rupture can be thought of as triggering a sequence of events. Most commonly, the supervisee will initially want to 'ward off' the problematic experience, to avoid unwanted thoughts and feelings that cause discomfort. At this initial stage there may be only a vague awareness of the precise nature of the difficulty, but as the process of working through commences (as per the accounts of repair work above), the supervisee may be helped to specify and gradually clarify aspects of the unpleasant experience. As progress is made in understanding the problem, greater insight may be achieved, initiating a process of applying oneself to solving the difficulty. This phase of working through would lead to some problem resolution and closure. This sequence of events is understood to involve increasingly positive affect and gradually decreasing attention (i.e. the discomfort is replaced by a sense of understanding or mastery, and a negative cognitive preoccupation with the problematic event is replaced with an ability to focus on other things).

A related account of the process of moving from upset to mastery is the 'resolution' model in therapy (Greenburg & Malcolm, 2002). This is similar in having six steps within the process, but draws on the gestalt approach to address how clients work through unresolved emotional experiences. In the first phase of emotional difficulty, the interaction may feature blame, complaint and/or hurt. Using the 'empty chair' dialogue technique from the gestalt approach, the supervisor may then take the role of the client, to re-enact these emotions. This may result in the expression of intense primary emotions, and the job of the therapist is to heighten awareness, encourage differentiation and clarify the associated emotions. In the next phase of successful resolution, these emotions are expressed more precisely, and the unmet interpersonal needs of the client are then identified and voiced. This heralds the penultimate phase in the resolution model, namely a shift in perspective. At this stage the client begins to develop a more complex and detached view of their antagonist. Finally, resolution occurs when the client is able to show increased understanding, empathy, compassion or forgiveness for the offending incident.

Textbooks on supervision contain numerous practical suggestions for enabling these processes of assimilation/resolution. For example, in CBT supervision, Liese and Beck (1997) suggest that the supervisor attend to the personal issues that the supervisee brings (e.g. passivity, avoidance), urging the supervisor to conceptualize them by raising the same kinds of questions as they would in therapy (e.g. 'What are the relevant prior experiences?'), and similarly to collaborate over problem-solving. Campbell (2006) also suggests sharing responsibility for solving problems; clarifying the factors that contribute to the problem (a variety of interesting questioning styles are suggested, including solution-focused questions); clarifying what efforts the supervisee has made to date to address the difficulty, noting anything that worked partially or for a brief time, and exploring the meaning that an event has for the supervisee (with questions such as 'What does it mean to you to be thought incompetent?' 'When this event happened how did you interpret it?). In this work it is important to focus on specifics, and to try to clarify the key details, through techniques like summarizing and paraphrasing.

In this work, Campbell (2006) rightly stresses the role of the supervisee, having sub-sections concerning working with 'perfectionistic', 'defensive' or 'resistant' supervisees. This emphasis on the supervisee's contribution is echoed in Bernard and Goodyear's textbook (2014), as they dedicate a whole chapter to such topics as their attachment styles, avoidance of shame or embarrassment, anxiety, need to feel competent and their transference towards the supervisor. Similarly, a survey of 176 counselling supervisors and supervisees identified ways that supervisees could facilitate supervision (Vespia *et al.*, 2002). The top three examples were thought to be demonstrating a willingness to grow (41 per cent of respondents endorsed this item), demonstrating respect and appreciation for individual differences (29 per cent) and demonstrating an understanding of one's own personal dynamics in relation to therapy and supervision (28 per cent). In these kinds of ways, it is important to give supervisees the opportunity to play their part in repairing the supervisory relationship. Careful, empathic discussion is appropriate, and care should be taken to engage supervisees with the appropriate support systems that exist within their system (as trainees or employees), and to abide by normal conventions of professional good practice (such as careful record-keeping). Ultimately, the supervisees should be given a realistic opportunity to make the appropriate changes, and should feel sufficiently supported. In their guidelines, Milne and Reiser (2017) have presented a recommendation specific to the rupture–repair situation: 'Build a collaborative bond: The aim is to build mutual commitment, through showing interest, being approachable and constructive, and by dealing with any difficulties (e.g. repairing relationship ruptures). A classic challenge is how you deal with power. Be aware of the built-in power differential and its impact on supervisee behaviour (e.g. non-disclosure)'. This recommendation is linked to video clips demonstrating how supervisors and supervisees can cooperate to deal with ruptures and to promote alliance development. In a small analysis of the 20 different contributions that supervisees felt they made to effective supervision, collaborating closely with the supervisor constituted 40 per cent of comments (Milne & Gracie, 2001). Figure 6.1 in Chapter 6 presents the full results.

Of course. supervisors and supervisees should collaborate in an effort to repair and strengthen their alliance. But what if this fails? In a novel section, Campbell (2006) recommends that the supervisor seeks consultation and guidance on how best to proceed, including approaching the director of the relevant training programme (if appropriate). If this is to no avail, it should be possible for supervisors to discontinue their rupture-repairing efforts (possibly by ceasing supervision), although it is obviously ideal for the supervisor to model the repair/assimilation/resolution process. Ultimately, all parties should be aware that the job of the supervisor is to ensure safe and effective clinical practice. If this cannot be ensured, then the supervisor is duty-bound to discontinue supervision and to alert the appropriate author-ities (e.g. a licensing body or manager).

'Games' that are played in supervision

At several points in the above account there is an implicit recognition of a power dimension within alliance-building (and indeed within supervision generally, as in the supervisor's formal authority to pass or fail a trainee). Power has been defined as 'the ability to influence others' behaviours and attitudes' (Bernard & Goodyear, 2004, p.173). This power is thought to derive from a variety of sources, including the formal authority invested in the supervisor by some training institution or professional organization, but also in relation to their expertness, attractiveness (i.e. being seen as an appealing professional model) and trustworthiness. These qualities gave the supervisor credibility and a basis for influencing the supervisee, without recourse to the more negative end of the power continuum, characterized by coercion. Again, however, it is important to keep the supervisee central, because power partly emerges from the interpersonal interaction between the supervisor and supervisee. On this logic, the supervisor's authority is simply the basis on which a process of negotiation concerning status unfolds. For instance, the process can be referred to as complementary (where there is an unequal amount of power), or symmetrical (where the parties have equal status). In the former process, the negotiation is straightforward and both parties accept the relative power of the supervisor, enabling a smooth and productive interactional process. By contrast, symmetrical interactions are thought to engender tension, and to be less productive (Tracey, 2002). Vivid illustrations of uncomfortable interactions are provided by two of the video clips in the Milne and Reiser (2017) supervisor training manual.

Kadushin (1968) provided an amusing account of some of the ways in which the supervisee may attempt to exert counter-control over the traditionally more powerful supervisor, couched in terms of inter-personal 'games'. The definition of games in supervision is 'an ongoing series of complementary ulterior transactions that are superficially plausible but have a concealed motivation to maximize pay-offs and minimize penalties for the initiator' (McIntosh *et al.*, 2006, p.225). According to Kadushin (1968), games that can be played by the supervisee to reduce the power disparity include 'BBC-manship', a game whereby the supervisee insists on a very high level of technical accomplishment before proceeding with an assignment. For example, the daunting requirement to produce a tape recording of his or her work may result in a series of conversations in which the anxious and avoidant supervisee plays the game of insisting that the technical quality of the recording equipment first be improved. This technical wizardry becomes the stalling tactic that ultimately avoids actually playing that tape to the more powerful supervisor. Other broad categories noted in this tradition are controlling the situation (e.g. 'heading the supervisor off at the pass' and 'one good question deserves another'); redefining the relationship, so that the supervisor comes to treat the supervisee more like a client ('treat me, don't beat me'), or a colleague ('evaluation is not for friends'); and manipulating demand (including 'two against the agency' and 'seduction by flattery').

Such light-hearted accounts provide some welcome respite from what can be a challenging business. Although it is tempting for generally democratic professionals to abdicate their supervisory power in favour of some kind of collegial collusion, this is ultimately misguided, because of their responsibility for the welfare of the client (and for the development of competence in the supervisee). Rather, the supervisor's task is to work closely and openly with the supervisee in order to find way of devolving the power appropriately: the objective is to reduce the imbalance, within the bounds of delivering the supervisory goods (e.g. as a supervisee in initial training reaches the final clinical experience episode). A case-study illustrated how collusion could emerge within CBT supervision (Milne *et al.*, 2009). Specifically, in this example supervision had drifted from the intended EBCS approach to passively listening to interminable clinical details, and the consequent avoidance of experiential effort. This was addressed within supervision-of-supervision, which followed the SP-SR six-stage process for reflecting on supervision difficulties outlined above (Bennett-Levy & Thwaites, 2007). The result was a supervisor-led formulation of the collusion, leading to schema re-appraisal, action-planning, and practising promising options.

Research on such power relationships in supervision include the work of Penman (1980), who created a recording system that allowed one to observe and analyse supervisory interaction in relation to the dimensions of power and involvement. This encouraged some research within the supervision field, which indicated, for example, that supervisors were more likely to reinforce high power statements when they were made by male supervisees than when these were uttered by their female counterparts (Nelson & Holloway, 1990). This demonstrated how gender affected the utilization of power within supervision.

McIntosh *et al.* (2006) conducted a survey of supervisors of genetic counsellors, concerning their encounters with destructive game-playing (games initiated by supervisor or supervisee that interfere with the super-visee's realization of training goals). This survey suggested that destructive games do occur in live supervision, and these were similar to the games that have been reported by other health professionals. Consistent with Kadush-in's (1968) summary, which is drawn from social work, McIntosh *et al.* (2006) found that the most common supervisee-initiated game reported in their survey was 'poor me'. They also described new games, such as 'make this little change'. This is a supervisor-initiated power game in which picky feedback (e.g. relating to letter-writing) is provided to the supervisee, in order to exert authority. These games highlight the great depth, breadth and subtlety of supervisory relationships, and their decidedly interactive nature.

Power struggles were also reported from an intensive qualitative inquiry with trainees (Nelson & Friedlander, 2001). The majority of the 13 participants reported impasses over roles, supervisors who seemed to feel threatened, and about the content of supervision. And, in the majority of cases, the supervisors were perceived by the supervisees to have denied responsibility or behaved irresponsibly. This had the effect of undermining the supervisees' trust and involvement, and contributing to their self-doubts and fears. For the majority of these trainees the struggle was never resolved, with avoidance, cynicism and distrust persisting. The authors conjectured that this ongoing conflict probably detracted from the supervisees' clinical work (mirroring the positive transfer in situations where the alliance is strong). In a similar qualitative study by Gray *et al.* (2001), the trainees were of the view that their 'counter-productive' experiences within supervision had negatively affected their clinical work. Understandably, most of them did not raise this concern in their supervision.

This parallels the ways that clients are thought to withdraw in therapy, when there is an alliance rupture (e.g. using 'story-telling', 'denial' and 'minimal responses'; Safran & Muran, 2000). These authors are also of the opinion that ruptures in supervision can affect therapy, and vice versa: 'impasses in the supervisory relationship . . . translate into impasses in the therapeutic relationship. A therapist who is feeling judged by his supervisor is more likely to feel self-critical with his patients . . . (which is) . . . likely to translate into negative therapeutic process' (p.215). This can further accentuate criticism from the supervisor, and contribute to a vicious cycle.

Outcomes of Successful Supervisory Alliances

Although some degree of game-playing and power-struggling may well characterize most supervision, it appears rarely to disrupt it seriously. I say this based on the extended experience of monitoring supervision within a training programme (i.e. based on personal experience of hundreds of supervision dyads), and because the evidence consistently indicates that supervision 'works', whether judged by the participants (e.g. Kavanagh *et al.*, 2003) or more objectively evaluated (e.g. Tharenou, 2001; Watkins & Milne, 2014). Therefore, I next want to consider how the alliance contributes to the general effectiveness of supervision.

The important outcomes that can follow from a strong alliance in supervision were indicated over 30 years ago by Bordin (1983), who listed eight anticipated benefits, such as enhanced competence in the supervisee. When an appropriate alliance is in place, we can expect to see some important outcomes within the supervisory relationship (what we might think of as the 'mini-outcomes', as in Figure 4.1), and in terms of subsequent outcomes, such as competence development in the supervisee. According to Bernard and Goodyear (2014), there are two empirically supported examples, based on research since 1983. These are the willingness of the supervisee to disclose material to the supervisor, and the subsequent quality of the alliance (which is associated with more significant outcomes, such as improved alliances within subsequent therapy; see e.g. Patton & Kivlighan, 1997). To underscore this dynamic pattern with a negative example, Bernard and Goodyear (2014) cited a study by Ladany *et al.* (1996), in which it was reported that 90 per cent of their respondents had omitted to disclose some negative feelings towards a supervisor, and 44 per cent had failed to disclose clinical mistakes or general observations of import (e.g. diagnoses). The main reasons cited for not disclosing were that the material was perceived as being too personal (73 per cent), too unimportant (62 per cent) or, in 50 per cent of cases, because of a poor alliance with the supervisor. Presumably a better alliance is associated with greater disclosure, an important mini-outcome in terms of allowing the supervisor access to potentially valuable information, not to mention the role it can have in enhancing the emotional bond. In turn, these should foster the supervisee's learning and clinical effectiveness.

An empirical example of the outcomes arising from the alliance is the national survey of counsellor trainees in the USA, conducted by Ladany *et al.* (1999). In an attempt to test Bordin's (1983) model, they asked 107 trainees to complete questionnaires measuring their confidence, their alliance with the supervisor (Bahrick's Working Alliance Inventory, 1990), and their satisfaction with supervision at two time points, approximately 2 months apart. According to Bordin (1983), a good alliance should be positively correlated with desired supervision outcomes, which in this study was assessed by the trainees' confidence and satisfaction. These researchers did find the expected association between the emotional bond aspect of the alliance and satisfaction, in that stronger bonds were positively correlated with satisfaction, while conversely trainees reporting weaker bonds reported less satisfaction. But none of the remaining correlations reached significance, leaving the authors wondering whether their methodology was the reason for their failure to verify the Bordin model, or whether the model itself was flawed.

Using different measures, more advanced trainees and only one data point, Efstation *et al.* (1990) did obtain a significant correlation between the alliance and confidence, so there is reason to suppose that the Ladany *et al.* (1999) methodology was the reason for their generally non-significant results. But Ladany *et al.* (1999) also highlighted difficulties with the model. Specifically, Bordin (1983) made the assumption that the supervisory and therapeutic alliances were equivalent, but (as noted elsewhere) there are fundamental differences between them. Amongst their recommendations, they urged that future research includes a more appropriate, supervision-specific alliance instrument (such as the SRQ). They also wondered about the appropriateness of assessing supervisee satisfaction, as they recognize that effective supervision, involving as it does some 'struggle' (p.454), may not be experienced as satisfying. Better options, they thought, included the clinical interactions of the supervisee. This measurement point will be picked up again in Chapter 8.

The review of the Oxford group's research by Beinart (2014) summarizes several associations between sound measurement of the alliance and a range of outcomes within the unfolding alliance (e.g. rapport; support; self-disclosure), and also a rare assessment of the link between the alliance and the supervisees' self-rated clinical effectiveness. A similar analysis was reported by Bambling *et al.* (2006), who studied the relationship between the 40 participating supervisors' characteristics (i.e. interpersonal skills and supervision alliances) and the supervision outcomes. Their 50 participating supervisees' completed self-report questionnaires indicated highly significant correlations between their supervision alliances and their learning (e.g. increased learning about their patients' therapies and general 'usefulness'). The longitudinal research design allowed Bambling *et al.* (2006) to infer that the alliance predicted these desirable outcomes, concluding that supervisors should prioritize their alliances, to maximize the supervisory experience and effectiveness.

Critical Review

To clinicians it must seem self-evident that the quality of the supervisory alliance influences the effectiveness of supervision, as reflected in the consensus-based identification of alliance-building as a core competence for the supervisor (Falender *et al.*, 2004). Similarly, the Association of Directors of Psychology Training Clinics in the USA produced a list of key competencies in the supervisee. This included the ability to interact collaboratively and respectfully with colleagues, including specifically 'the ability to use supervision', an ability defined as working collegially and responsively with supervisors (Hatcher & Lassiter, 2007). The APA (2015) supervision guidelines maintain this emphasis.

However, it needs to be acknowledged that there is surprisingly little evidence to support this assumption, and even some contrary evidence. An incredibly meticulous systematic review located only two rigorous studies of the alliance, and these reported only modest support for the assumption (Ellis & Ladany, 1997), consistent with the examples above. Specifically, they found some tentative support for the notion that the alliance may be related to both the supervisor's style and the supervisees' self-confidence.

They concluded that the studies they located and scrutinized presented only modest evidence that the supervisory relationship was related to a few specific processes and outcomes. However, the available data did not clarify adequately what constituted the studied relationships. There were also methodological weaknesses with much of the other research that they found, including the use of new measures with only preliminary psychometric data. They called for better, unique definitions of the supervisory alliance, and it is comforting to note (from the above account of instruments like the SRQ) that some progress is now being made on that score.

Has the situation improved since the first edition of the present book, in 2009? It has been estimated that there have been 46 new studies of the supervision alliance in the period from 1990 up to 2014 (Watkins, 2014b,c). In summarizing these 46 studies, Watkins (2014c) noted that 40 were conducted in university settings with multidisciplinary students, the rest occurring in the workplace. It appears that all of the 46 studies relied on self-report questionnaires, and that the majority (32) only considered the supervisees' perceptions. Thirty-five of the research designs were cross-sectional, with a few longitudinal analyses, and the dominant statistical analysis was correlational. As Watkins (2014c) concluded, it sadly appears that little progress has been made since the earlier research critiques (e.g., Ellis and Ladany, 1997; Bernard & Goodyear, 2009), or since the first edition of the present book. There remains a heavy reliance on correlational designs and self-report questionnaires, with only one controlled study (Livni *et al.*, 2012). Furthermore, only a small minority of these 46 studies address the fundamental assumptions regarding the alliance, such as whether a strong alliance influences supervisees' learning (competence acquisition) or clinical effectiveness. Instead, this body of literature studies correlations between the alliance and a wide range of theoretically insignificant variables (e.g. shame; emotional intelligence; cultural factors; disclosure). Consequently, this body of research does not permit any causal interpretations to be drawn about learning or effectiveness, and raises the question of why experts continue to affirm the alliance unanimously and without serious question. One possible explanation for the surprisingly high status of the alliance construct offered by Watkins (2014b) is that it has 'clinical validity' (i.e. a strong professional consensus that it is necessary for change, and its significant role in relation to professional practice arrangements).

In summary, it seems that little research progress has been made since 2009. Furthermore, before and since 2009 there are other studies that question whether the alliance is a necessary condition for effective supervision (defined as supervision that contributes significantly to the supervisees' learning or clinical effectiveness). In keeping with the sobering conclusions of Ellis and Ladany (1997), the reviews by Milne and James (2000) and Milne *et al.* (2008a) found few manipulations of the supervision alliance in their sample of successful supervision interventions. That is, it appears to be possible to provide effective supervision without an explicit emphasis on the alliance. Similarly, the account of the development of therapeutic expertise by Tracey *et al.* (2014) does not include a supervisory alliance, placing the emphasis instead on such factors as systematic feedback on patients' clinical progress and learning through deliberate practice. The text edited by Ericsson (2009) describes the successful use of deliberate practice in a wide range of occupations, including healthcare professions. But there is no chapter on the alliance, nor does it even appear in the index of a multi-authored text running to over 500 pages. It seems unlikely that the alliance was irrelevant or unnecessary, as the methods that were reported in these successful studies were consistent with traditional concepts of the important ingredients and processes in the supervision alliance (e.g. collaboration; modelling; constructive feedback). Rather, these substantive research studies and well-informed perspectives suggest that the role of the alliance may be significantly over-emphasized within the supervision literature, and that a basic task alliance may be sufficient for the acquisition of professional expertise in most cases. This view is consistent with research on inadequate and harmful supervision. Presumably the 36% of supervisees currently receiving 'inadequate' supervision in the sample surveyed by Ellis *et al.* (2014) were still able to demonstrate the competencies needed to complete their training successfully, despite the unfortunate and unacceptable personal discomfort that was entailed (74 per cent of the sample were second-year trainees). A further related observation from the expertise literature, based on case examples from various walks of life, is that some individuals have acquired very high levels of proficiency without the help of a supervisor figure. For instance, golfer Bubba Watson has won the Masters twice without the help of a coach or any form of learning alliance. Anecdotally, it seems that he developed his expertise through extensive solitary engagement in deliberate practice.

There is a third reason to question the current emphasis on the supervision alliance, arising from in-depth studies of alliance relationships. For instance, Rieck *et al.* (2015) correlated alliance variables with client outcomes and supervision. They were surprised to find that supervisor 'agreeableness' had a significant negative association with client change scores ('agreeableness' referred to trust, altruism, modesty and tender-mindedness). Rieck *et al.* (2015) suggested that this negative correlation was a result of the way that the participating supervisors were conceptually challenging and behaviourally direct with their supervisees. In practical terms, the supervisors did things like providing corrective feedback, intended to enhance the supervisees' effectiveness in therapy. Perhaps because this challenging style of supervision was clinically valuable and well-intentioned, congruent with the CBT approach being studied, there was no adverse effect on the supervisory alliance. In a related longitudinal study, examining Socratic questioning in CBT with 55 depressed adults (Braun *et al.*, 2015), the results indicated that it was this questioning style, rather than the therapeutic alliance, which explained the significant reductions in depression following CBT. These studies are also similar because care was taken to ensure that the assumed mechanism of change was correctly manipulated (i.e. feedback and Socratic questioning were observed and measured), methodological refinements that increase our confidence in the findings. A further fly in the alliance ointment comes from a survey of 110 trainee therapists (Ybrandt *et al.*, 2016), who reported good therapeutic alliances, despite some low ratings of their supervisory alliances. Ybrandt *et al.* (2016) thought that this negative perception of the supervision alliance may have been because it was challenging.

Where does all this leave the current status of the alliance? It may help us to gain perspective if we apply the benchmarks used by the APA Task Force in relation to therapy relationships (Norcross & Wampold, 2011). Three kinds of ratings of relationship elements were made by the five judges in the task force: 'demonstrably effective', 'probably effective' and 'promising but insufficient research to judge'. Criteria informing these ratings included internal and external validity. To be rated as 'demonstrably effective', each of the 12 relationship elements considered (such as the therapeutic alliance) required to be consistently demonstrated through the meta-analysis of approximately 50 controlled experimental studies, which reported significant results (and which had other features indicating high internal validity, such as utilizing therapy manuals). Additionally, these studies required to have high external (ecological) validity. If we apply these criteria to the studies reviewed above it is clear that the supervision alliance (unlike the therapeutic alliance) is decidedly not yet 'demonstrably effective', may have a few hits on the 'probably effective' rating, but overwhelmingly belongs in the category of 'promising but insufficient research to judge'. The examples reviewed above, where the alliance was absent or 'disagreeable', seem to me to make that category a fair if not a slightly generous assessment.

What should happen next? The long-standing difficulties in defining the alliance in a consistent, replicable fashion need to be addressed, as illustrated in the review of 11 alliance instruments by Tangen and Borders (2016). A combination of psychometrically sound self-report measures and observational instruments appears a more promising approach, drawing on multiple perspectives (supervisor, supervisee, patient), alongside other aspects of rigorous research (Rossi *et al.*, 2003). Secondly, as per supervision itself, in this era of accountability and evidence-based practice, research attention needs to shift to a focus on the outcomes that are achieved, in particular the learning and clinical outcomes identified by Beinart (2014). Furthermore, it would help if these outcomes were organized according to some logical, theoretical or practical framework, so that the assumed relationships were clarified. Contenders are listed in Chapter 8 (e.g. see an integrative approach in Table 8.1), which incidentally also outlines ways in which research might be strengthened. In this way, metaphors like 'diamond' or 'vehicle of success' (Freud, 1912, p.105) can be explicated and analysed scientifically. A helpful example is the review by Watkins (2014a), conducted in relation to the perspective taken by several popular approaches to supervision. In this way, Watkins (2014a) has carefully detailed how these approaches address the three alliance aspects within Bordin's (1983) definition (i.e. the alliance bond, goals and tasks). Additionally, he distinguished between the alliance medium and the alliance message. By 'medium' he referred to supervisory actions, such as modelling or challenging; while the 'message' referred to what was communicated to the supervisee by such action, for instance the importance of the relationship or of education. Watkins (2014a) concluded that the alliance was a common relational factor binding supervision together. He also argued that it was a 'transtheoretical' concept, being accepted by all popular supervision approaches. This kind of careful reasoning helps us to see the wood for the trees, facilitating research and practice.

However, the concepts Watkins (2014a) used are psychodynamic in origin, and so are not ideally suited to fostering the much-needed research. A transtheoretical translation might therefore help. Watkins (2014a) described what in evaluation research would be thought of as a classic structure–process–outcome analysis of the alliance (see Chapter 8, especially Donabedian, 1988). On this functional reformulation, 'structure' refers to the necessary resources, such as the participants and their joint effort to establish and maintain the supervision bond, including goal-setting and the collaboration over tasks. This creates the conditions for an effective alliance process, especially the actions taken by the supervisor, such as modelling. It is through the supervisee's engagement in such techniques that the desired outcomes are achieved. These outcomes are stepwise in nature, initial ones like experiential learning leading on to subsequent ones like competence enhancement and general professional development, then on to clinical effectiveness, and so on. Reframing the alliance in this way presents it in terms of a widely studied and productive research strategy (Rossi *et al.*, 2003). In effect, Figure 4.1 illustrates such a stepwise analysis, as the terms used within the figure (i.e. 'marker', 'interaction sequence' and 'resolution') can be thought of as the structure, process and outcome, respectively.

Conclusions

Although the professional consensus unanimously and emphatically affirms the importance of the supervisory alliance (e.g. Falender *et al.*, 2004; Hatcher & Lassiter, 2007; Roth & Pilling, 2007; Watkins, 2014a,b,c; APA, 2015), firm evidence to support the assumption continues to be surprisingly wanting. Not only are there very few studies that directly assess variation in the alliance in relation to the supervisees' learning or clinical effectiveness, but the studies that do exist continue to be methodologically weak and so are fundamentally not interpretable (Ellis & Ladany, 1997; Watkins, 2014b,c). Furthermore, the seeming effectiveness of weak/absent/ inadequate/disagreeable alliances raises important doubts about their assumed status and mechanisms. In short, the directly relevant research literature does not yet provide a firm evidence-base for the supervision alliance as traditionally conceived.

On the other hand, we cannot ignore or remove the alliance. This is partly as the social interactions that make up supervision represent the foundation of our professional practice arrangements. Therefore, we cannot remove relationship issues from supervision, even if we wanted to, without invent-ing a new arrangement. In addition to this 'practical validity', it would be difficult to discount the strong professional consensus favouring the alli-ance, what can be termed its 'clinical validity' in routine supervisory practice (e.g. we should address supervisees' support needs and time-honoured expectations). There is also the robust research evidence from the therapy literature (e.g. Norcross & Wampold, 2011), and the strong evidence for its importance within human development generally: 'relationship context strongly influences human behaviour and lifespan development' (Reis *et al.*, 2000, p.844). Therefore, all things considered, I believe that the structuring, task-focused (including demonstrations of competent practice) and collaborative aspects of the alliance are necessary ingredients within evidence-based CBT supervision. This is consistent with the tandem model, in that collaboration is the natural way of relating within professional practice.

5

Applying Supervision

Introduction

What are the main activities that supervisors should undertake within supervision? What goals or functions are they supposed to achieve? Which environmental factors are critical to these activities and functions? As these questions indicate, this chapter deals with what many would regard as the heart of supervision, the facilitation of the supervisee's learning and development ('formative' supervision). In order to address these questions, I will build on the reframing of supervision that was set out in Chapter 3, particularly the evidence-based cognitive-behaviour therapy (CBT) supervision model. Other relevant chapters will also be integrated, so that a coherent account of formative supervision can be developed. This creates a sound basis for the next chapter, which considers the supervisee's perspective.

There are a vast array of qualities and competencies attributed to the successful supervisor. In order to impose some sense of order, I will attempt to define the essential supervision tasks and activities, drawing on the staff development literature for guidance. Following the thinking presented in Chapter 3, it is proposed that these tasks are the conducting of an educational needs assessment, leading to the collaborative goal-setting (specification of the learning contract); empowering the supervisee to have a full role; the facilitation of the supervisee's learning through the application of different training and educational methods; and the use of evaluation in order to monitor and optimally direct this developmental cycle. Therefore it is

Evidence-Based CBT Supervision: Principles and Practice, Second Edition. Derek L. Milne.
© 2018 John Wiley & Sons Ltd. Published in 2018 by the British Psychological Society and John Wiley & Sons Ltd.

Contextual factors, including the learning alliance.

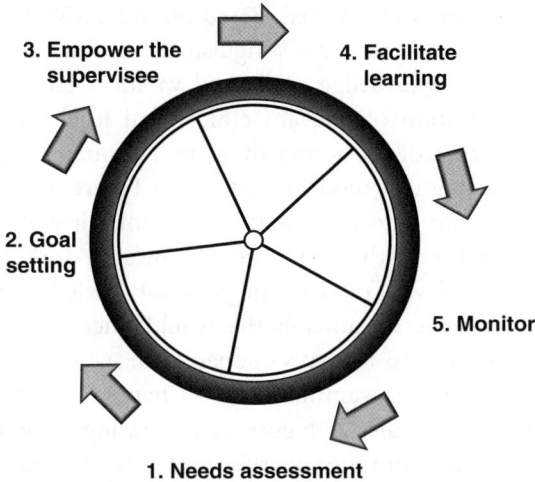

3. **Empower the supervisee**

4. **Facilitate learning**

2. **Goal setting**

5. **Monitor**

1. **Needs assessment**

Figure 5.1 The CBT supervision cycle, guiding formative supervision.
Source: Milne and Reiser (2017). Reproduced with permission of John Wiley & Sons Ltd.

proposed that supervision is basically a problem-solving cycle, within an organizational and relational context (the workplace environment, including technological advances, and the learning alliance). I refer to these tasks as the 'supervision cycle', as represented by the front wheel of the evidence-based CBT supervision tandem model. This cycle, as set out in Figure 5.1, is next tested against professional consensus (formal and informal), relevant theory and the latest research literature. I then consider some contextual considerations (the ethical and legal dimensions; cultural competence; technological advances), before addressing the five tasks set out within the supervision cycle.

Testing the Supervision Cycle

Expert consensus

Is this supervision cycle, drawn directly from the staff development literature, one that should be accepted within the supervision field? A significant test is provided by a consensus statement on supervision produced by a group of American experts (Falender *et al.*, 2004). They defined the competencies required of supervisors, alongside thoughts on how supervisors should be trained and assessed. Based on this activity, Falender *et al.* (2004) drew up a framework that distinguished between the domains of the supervisors' relevant knowledge, skills and values, related to their social context (e.g. recognition of relevant ethical and legal issues). Do these competencies (a total of 34 across these four domains) agree with the essential staff development model as set out in Figure 2.2? These competencies appear to map onto this essential account fairly well. Specifically, Falender *et al.* (2004) note that (within the knowledge domain) supervisors should know about relevant models, and possess knowledge of professional/ supervisee development. Presumably this would emerge from their understanding of approaches to formative supervision, which is dominated by developmental models (as summarized in Chapter 2). These are highly consistent with the outline in Figure 2.2, stressing such things as the importance of starting from the supervisees' developmental stage. Turning to the domain of skills, these authors go on to suggest that supervisors need to be competent in assessing the learning needs and developmental level of the supervisee. They also need to have relevant teaching skills, to draw on the scientific knowledge base and to have competencies in providing 'effective formative and summative feedback' (p.778; relevant to the evaluation part of the model). Connecting to my emphasis on the setting, they also note, within their 'social context' dimension, that the competent supervisor has knowledge of the immediate system, and the kinds of expectations that exist within that system in relation to supervision. Therefore, Falender *et al.* (2004) expect the competent supervisor to be aware of the 'socio-political context within which supervision is conducted' (p.778), and to create an appropriate climate within supervision (appropriately balancing support with challenge).

In summary, there appear to be direct parallels and no disagreements between these two accounts of what is essential in formative supervision, with the Falender *et al.* (2004) account helpfully providing a more detailed specification. Indeed, similarly consistent accounts of what formative supervision entails are provided in the main textbooks, such as Bernard and Goodyear (2014), and by the editor of the definitive *Handbook of Psychotherapy Supervision* (Watkins, 1997). Watkins (1997) stresses the importance of having a systematic, well-structured approach, featuring shared objectives, guided practice and constructive feedback. Within that handbook, Norcross and Halgin (1997) summarize some 'cardinal principles' of an integrative approach to supervision. These include customizing supervision to take due account of the individual characteristics of supervisees; conducting a needs assessment; constructing explicit learning contracts; using a blend of supervision methods (such as didactic instruction, reading assignments, discussion, modelling, experiential activities, video material and case examples); assessing the supervisee's emergent therapy competencies; and evaluating the outcomes of supervision. These methods are consistent with other consensus statements by American experts (Kaslow *et al.*, 2004; APA, 2015). Reflecting this marked consensus, professional organizations have adopted approaches to supervision that strongly resemble Figure 2.2 and the essential account provided above (e.g. British Psychological Society, 2003). More recent expert accounts continue to support this conclusion (e.g. Inman *et al.*, 2014).

Relevant theory

The supervision cycle is also highly consistent with other reviews of the supervision literature, and with the staff development and expertise literatures, closely parallel bodies of knowledge that speak directly to the business of formative supervision. For example, a major text in the staff development area, *Training in Organizations: Needs Assessment, Development, and Evaluation* (Goldstein & Ford, 2002), has a chapter entitled 'A systematic approach to training' which unpacks these essential elements of the formative enterprise. Drawing on the field of instructional technology, this approach is underpinned by the principles of continuous feedback; recognition of the complex interactions that occur between different parts of the system (including interactions between learner characteristics and teaching methods); specifying the objectives of training and facilitating appropriate planning; and recognizing that instruction is embedded within an organizational system.

A more recent and highly influential refinement of this reasoning appears in the expertise literature, under the banner of 'deliberate practice'. Deliberate practice (DP; Ericsson, 2009) is high-quality, intensive training, characterized by these features (Ericsson *et al.*, 1993; Ericsson, 1996; 2006; Lewandowsky & Thomas, 2009):

1. A highly structured context.
2. Task analysis.
3. Challenging tasks.

4. Systematic, ongoing, formal feedback.
5. Utilization of this feedback.
6. Repeated, intensive practice.
7. Receiving the help of experts, such as supervisors.

These seven elements represent the integration of well-established training methods, such as Vygotsky's (1978) Zone of Proximal Development, 'criterion-referenced instruction' (Mager, 1997), performance-related feedback (Locke & Latham, 2006), and mastery learning (McGaghie *et al.*, 2014). The five elements of DP are more detailed and so they helpfully elaborate Goldstein and Ford's (2002) account, which in turn is more contextual and systemic. Similarly, in modern reviews of staff development (e.g. Beidas & Kendall, 2010; Rakovshik & McManus, 2010) one finds somewhat different emphases (and terminology), but still the same fundamental approach to facilitating experiential learning. Because of this overlap, I will treat them as complementary approaches and integrate them with the tandem model, before combining this with the relevant supervision literature.

But DP also supplements an integrative approach with additional concepts from cognitive psychology, such as information-processing skills (decision-making, problem-solving, etc.), situational awareness, the processes behind biased judgement formation and the importance of a predictable environment in reaching valid causal inferences. For such reasons, DP challenges traditional approaches to training and many of our assumptions about professional experience, providing a stringent critique of some cherished beliefs about clinical expertise. Tracey *et al.* (2014) identified problems for therapists with each of these five elements of DP. For example, challenging tasks could be avoided once initial professional training was complete (i.e. post-qualification, post-licensure), partly because therapists form inaccurate judgements about their competence. Furthermore, feedback tends to become scarce or invalid: information that accurately defines the gap between actions and goals is absent or is distorted by the environment (e.g. social support has a greater impact than therapy). Additionally, formal training opportunities post-qualification/licensure can be rare, and even then such continuing professional development is often ineffective (see Chapter 1). Tracey *et al.* (2014) also argued that even when feedback exists, the capacity to learn from available feedback or training is significantly limited by human factors, as well as by unpredictable environments (i.e. providing invalid cues as to the true nature of the situation, as per the social support example). For instance, feedback can fail as a result of inadequate models of how therapy works or because of therapists' information-processing errors (e.g. a failure to notice patterns; biases), as a consequence of insufficient or inadequate training (i.e. failure to meet the DP criteria), or because we struggle to make valid inferences about the relationship between our actions and the results (because the environment clouds matters), resulting in limited expertise development.

To illustrate, Tracey *et al.* (2014) cited the study by Huppert *et al.* (2001). Huppert *et al.* (2001) reported a small positive correlation between general therapy experience and clinical outcomes (with panic disorder patients) following CBT. This association disappeared when these authors examined the 14 participating therapists' specific experience in CBT. It appeared to Tracey *et al.* (2014) that what had changed with experience, and so may have accounted for the positive correlation, was the therapists' confidence, rather than their enhanced expertise. To compound matters, such confidence may have been based on the erroneous therapists' belief that with experience they were growing in expertise. This creates what has been termed a 'double-burden': such therapists may be both unskilled and unaware of it (Dunning *et al.*, 2003). This double-burden makes them less likely to engage in DP, and generally less motivated to seek the training or feedback that could genuinely enhance their expertise. Therefore, according to Tracey *et al.* (2014), the best way to develop therapists' expertise (so as to help their clients achieve the best outcomes) is through career-long DP that addresses these barriers. The best-established method is clinical supervision (McMahan, 2014; Watkins & Milne, 2014); Table 5.1 suggests how the necessary conditions for developing expertise could be addressed in evidence-based CBT supervision.

Clinical supervision in general has much in common with DP, and can in theory readily address all seven elements (McMahan, 2014). However, DP has probably only occurred in an unsystematic fashion within clinical supervision. For example, although there are highly structured contexts and task analyses within CBT supervision, it is uncommon to find simulations, objective measurement and other core features of DP. Indeed, even the term 'deliberate practice' is rare within the supervision literature. To illustrate, the term does not appear in the 27-page subject index for the *Wiley International Handbook of Clinical Supervision* (Watkins & Milne, 2014), nor is there any mention of the term 'expertise' within this extensive index. This is not to say that many of the elements of DP are not employed within supervision implicitly, or referred to by other

Table 5.1 Applying the expertise literature to evidence-based CBT supervision.

Main features of deliberate practice (DP)	*Overlaps between DP and evidence-based CBT supervision*
Highly structured context Simulations and structured learning opportunities (e.g. carefully designed drills, concrete and real-life); performance objectives (competence standards); challenging, effortful tasks and high motivation in a supportive environment	Supervision is 'scaffolded' through a collaboratively agreed learning contract, and by standard procedures (e.g. agenda-setting each session; regular observation and feedback). 'Restorative' relationship. Supervisee treated as an 'adult learner'
Task analysis Specific elements of performance, reconstructed into realistic 'whole tasks', practised in carefully designed situations. Skills and their mediating mechanisms are considered together	Tasks specified through competencies. Material from the supervisee's clinical practice supplemented by experiential learning exercises within supervision
Hierarchical Progressively more difficult challenges (i.e. graded practice to mastery). Most difficult tasks practised most. Needs-led: activate prior learning and tackle identified weaknesses. 'Scaffolded', so that support and guidance diminish with expertise	Learning contract reflects an educational needs assessment, relating this to the required performance standards (e.g. competence goals). The developmental model guides increasing autonomy, with keen awareness of setbacks (e.g. 'deskilling') and the need to reframe and profit from such episodes
Repetition and sustained practice 10 000 hours (10 years) of deliberate practice for expertise. This is an intense, relentless, 'perfectionistic' pursuit of excellence, through refinements and the elimination of errors (learn from errors; mastery learning). Explicit advice; diagnosis of errors; leader demonstrates, follower repeatedly applies short chunks of complete performance	Supervisor at times acts like a sports coach, seeking to mobilize effort and commitment; also models expertise and an attitude of 'lifelong learning' (continuing professional development) Guidelines used to shape expertise, as are demonstrations and advice

Table 5.1 (*Continued*)

Main features of deliberate practice (DP)	Overlaps between DP and evidence-based CBT supervision
Feedback	
Performance immediately evaluated objectively by learner and trainer; attention given to critical aspects of aspects of performance (processes) and on standards/objectives (outcomes); followed by repetition and correction	Rating scales and performance standards used to evaluate tapes of supervisee's therapy, specifying strengths and areas for development. Feedback process itself is an art, requiring tact and skill. Corrections guided by demonstration
Problem-solving	
Learn from errors; train to think like expert: teach essential concepts, facts and procedural information (schema construction/elaboration). Conscious focus on highly structured mental representations of task (enabling rapid pattern recognition – typical problems and solutions); teach efficient problem-solving; increasing encouragement to function automatically (i.e. schema automation)	In addition to the above points on developing competence, through the use of educational techniques evidence-based supervisors also seek to foster 'capability'. This is the capacity to engage with issues with a critical mind, and to problem-solve in a systematic manner
Coaching	
Has a central and highly active role (e.g. structuring; managing; goal-setting; monitoring; feedback; motivating). Plentiful support and guidance	These and other coaching skills are captured within SAGE, an instrument for evaluating competence in evidence-based clinical supervision

names, or used partially. This claim is made on the basis of observations and surveys of CBT supervision (e.g. Milne, 2008b; Reiser & Milne, 2016), and on varied analyses of evidence-based clinical supervision (EBCS), the two related supervisory approaches that come closest to DP. For experts like supervisors to be effective, they need to address these DP factors more systematically. Table 5.1 outlines how each factor could be tackled within CBT supervision.

However, there appears to be at least one aspect of DP that is hard to reconcile with supervision, which is the role of individual differences in the learners (supervisees). These differences are minimized within DP, whereas they are a significant part of current accounts of supervision (e.g. APA, 2015) and of staff training (Colquitt *et al.*, 2000). A specific instance is that of the supervisees' contribution to supervision and to their acquisition of competence through their own learning expertise (Bransford & Schwartz, 2009). Although this term is not widely used within supervision, developmental models revolve around the supervisee. For instance, Falender and Shafranske (2012) provide examples of how supervisees can contribute to supervisory success, especially through self-assessment. Experiential learning theory also places learners at the heart of the developmental process (e.g. Kolb, 2014). The next chapter focuses on the supervisee's contribution, where I will return to learning expertise. In addition, scholars have challenged the minimal role of individual differences as asserted in DP (Hambrick *et al.*, 2014a,b). Consistent with EBCS and the general supervision literature (e.g. Watkins & Milne, 2014), it appears to me that DP is necessary but not sufficient to explain the development of competence. This is a significant perspective in relation to supervision, counter-balancing the helpful lessons from DP with the need to accord due attention to the supervisees' contribution, a strong feature of the tandem model and duly recorded as step 3 within Figure 5.1.

The tandem model offers an integrative account of formative supervision that can assimilate DP (with a suitable emphasis on individual differences), one that can be represented within a classic model of staff development, as set out in Chapter 2 (see Figure 2.2). This account is based on the work of Goldstein and Ford (2002) and other experts within the staff development field (see Milne & Reiser, 2017, for a summary of their work). As illustrated within Figure 2.2, the supervisor's initial task is to clarify the learner's status, with respect to the relevant supervisory experiences. In practice, this entails relating the learning opportunities within a supervision setting to the past experience of the supervisee, and to other important considerations (like the requirements of a professional body). Given this emphasis on the external considerations, Figure 2.2 proposes that evaluation measures are considered next, so that a clear idea is formed of the intended outcomes of supervision. Based on this initial work, the supervisor can begin to specify the content of the learning experience, conventionally recording this within a learning contract that is negotiated with the supervisee (and sometimes with other key stakeholders, such as the supervisee's line manager or a training programme). The content of this learning experience naturally implies the need to think about the methods and materials that will be required to enable the supervisee to address the content within the learning contract successfully. Following on from this planning work, the supervisee will be assisted by the supervisor in the development of the requisite competencies.

Although I have implied a 'top-down' approach thus far, I would wish to stress that effective supervision entails an appropriate balance between supervisor-led development and a more Socratic approach, one in which the supervisee is helped to acquire competence through his or her own initiative, in an adult learning, experiential approach to supervision (Safran & Muran, 2000). Supervisees can therefore develop as a result of problem-based learning (i.e. where the supervisor encourages independent educational activity designed around the solution of a problem, normally clinical work in the mental health field). Such development activity is preceded by the designation of the supervisor, as per the definition within Chapter 1. This essential model of staff development conventionally proposes that the final task for the supervisor is to ensure that some form of evaluation is built into the supervisory system. As in other areas of professional activity, evaluation is vital if we are to determine the extent to which objectives are being achieved, providing the basis for corrections or enhancements. Evaluation data also provide the basis for properly grounded feedback, namely feedback that is suitably linked to those prior learning objectives and to any external points of reference (e.g. competency checklists generated by the supervisees' training programme). The final dimension identified within the model presented in Figure 2.2 recognizes that these activities can only be understood properly within their context. This is apparent from the preceding sentences, as I have naturally chosen to give examples that imply the need to refer to the objectives that are set by the organizations that appoint supervisors, and so on. In addition, there are a myriad of factors within the workplace that will play a part in influencing the way that the supervisor facilitates learning (e.g. see Figure 3.1). Such 'situational variables' include the organizational climate and the degree to which managers, peers and others provide support (Colquitt *et al.*, 2000). These authors also drew attention to characteristics of the learner, such as their personality, cognitive ability and commitment to their development. In their meta-analysis, many of these factors were found to contribute to the learning outcomes that were obtained, and to the transfer of that learning to the workplace, as well as to the performance of the learner on the job.

Research

Is the expert consensus and relevant theory on the supervision cycle also consistent with the research literature? I would like to illustrate this with two systematic reviews to which I have contributed. In the first of these (Milne & James, 2000), a systematic review was conducted of 28 studies in which CBT supervision was manipulated. These studies were carefully selected, partly on the basis of there being hard evidence that these manipulations were educationally and clinically successful. We found that these studies featured a range of methods for facilitating learning, most common amongst them being the use of feedback and discussion, followed by more experiential methods such as educational role-play and behavioural rehearsal. Less frequently utilized were live and video-based models of competent practice. Subsequently, I participated in a review of 24 studies, about half of them being within the above review (Milne *et al.*, 2008a). We again found that these studies had utilized a wide range of methods (26 different methods in total), the most frequently used being different approaches to training and education (18 of the 24 studies used this method), feedback (16 studies) and observing/monitoring the supervisee (10 studies). On average, and consistent with the above consensus statements, each study used on average over six different methods to facilitate the supervisee's learning. A combined summary of the 'top 10' supervision methods within this literature is provided in Table 5.2.

Next, I discuss the Falender *et al.* (2004) competencies framework in detail, with reference to other relevant frameworks (e.g. Olds & Hawkins, 2014; Pilling & Roth, 2014). These competencies represent the 'road map' for supervision, the ground that needs to be covered for supervisees to be properly equipped for their clinical work and their careers. The first competence area that I want to examine concerns the contextual backdrop to formative supervision. As per Figure 3.1, there is an almost endless list of influences within the workplace that could be included within this review. Therefore, my strategy will be to select a few of the more frequently discussed competencies, ones that appear strongly within the consensus statements and the empirical literature, and examine the associated evidence, advice and implications. The aim is to help the supervisor to stay on track.

Table 5.2 Some distinctions between two fundamental ways of facilitating learning, education and training (based on Tate, 1997).

	Education	*Training*
1. Agenda	Learner dictates it	Someone else sets it (predetermined and imposed)
2. Objectives	Plural/divergent ('liberate the mind' to question and influence; divergent)	Raise proficiency in compliance with a standard (convergent)
3. Resources	Learners' unrealized potential	External view of best practice (e.g. professions)
4. Values	Challenge and change	Conformity and compliance
5. Learners outcomes	Wide-ranging response capability ('problem-solving')	Delimited scope and time-limited relevance
6. Consequences for facilitatiors	Unpredictability and discomfort/personal growth and development	Predictability and control/little stimulus to develop
7. Consequences for the organization	Increases its flexibility and adaptation and also the challenges it receives	Fosters conformity/loyalty but limited growth

Source: Milne, D.L. (2009). Reproduced with permission of Derek Milne.

Context for Facilitating Learning

Ethical supervision

The importance of ethical aspects of clinical supervision is a definite emphasis within the literature, appearing as a generic supervision competence in Pilling and Roth (2014) and as the first of nine broad themes in the integrative summary by Olds and Hawkins (2014). For example, the Falender *et al.* (2004) consensus statement pertaining to the value-base notes that competent supervisors should 'value ethical principles' (p.778), and additionally recognize the importance of 'ethical and legal issues' as part of the social context of supervision. There are a number of important dimensions to the ethical (i.e. proper conduct) of supervision, but these tend to revolve around three categories (Scaife, 2001): unethical practice (malpractice or professional misconduct); impairment (personal incapability); and incompetence (professional unsuitability). Unethical practice concerns breaching rules governing how one should work within an organization, or conduct oneself within a profession. This subsumes inappropriate romantic and sexual relationships with supervisees (or their clients) and emotional instability (including overt anger and deception).

An expert consensus (Ellis *et al.*, 2014) defined 37 examples ('descriptors') of unethical supervision, referred to as 'inadequate' or 'harmful' supervision. These were then rated for their accuracy as descriptors of their current supervision with a sample of 363 supervisees, drawn from a range of mental health disciplines. Overall, 25% of this sample rated their current supervision as inadequate, and 12% rated it as harmful. In terms of unethical practice (malpractice or professional misconduct) this included unsafe or exploitative dual relationships, including physical threats and engaging in a sexual relationship. Impairment consists of the diminished functioning of a supervisor, as in their inability to attend properly to their duties, perhaps due to stress, substance misuse or illness. Related difficulties include poor or absent self-awareness of personal incapability or an unwillingness to address any such problems. Examples from the survey reported by Ellis *et al.* (2014) included the omission or minimization of basic duties: 54% ($N = 197$) of the supervisees reported that their current supervisor did not use a supervision contract, while 40% ($N = 144$) reported that their therapy sessions were not observed, monitored or reviewed. Perhaps the most straightforward category is that of incompetence, namely inadequate (unskilled) or absent performance of supervisory duties (e.g. making repeated, unacceptable errors). Examples from the Ellis *et al.* (2014) survey included 'no feedback' and 'oblivious to cultural background'. Taken together, the findings from this survey 'suggested that the occurrence of inadequate and harmful clinical supervision were high...Fully 36% of supervisees in our sample were categorized as currently receiving harmful supervision, and over half were identified as receiving harmful clinical supervision at some point in their career' (Ellis *et al.*, 2014, p.28).

These alarming findings indicate that instances of unethical supervision are common.

It had been thought that serious ethical difficulties were rare. Falender and Shafranske (2004) reported that breaches of confidentiality and difficulties around maintaining appropriate relationship boundaries within professional practice generally were reported in 18 and 17 per cent (respectively) of incidents, but that only 2 per cent of these instances occurred within supervision. However, as the Ellis *et al.* (2014) survey suggests, minor examples may be far more common. Ladany (2002) surveyed supervisees in training and more than 50 per cent reported that they thought their supervisor had behaved unethically. A more recent survey suggests that the problem is common and international (Ellis *et al.*, 2015a).

Because of their seniority and status, supervisors should take the lead role in recognizing and rectifying unethical behaviour. By contrast, the power imbalance means that supervisees are inherently vulnerable (Ellis *et al.*, 2014) as they are not in a position to withhold consent for behaviours that make them feel uncomfortable, and may not even fully realize the relevant boundaries (Thomas, 2014). Indeed, the power differential may become exaggerated in situations featuring unethical practice, aggravating matters considerably. It is therefore appropriate that Ellis *et al.* (2014) note that 'adequate' supervision includes awareness of and attention to the power differential (and boundaries) between the supervisor and supervisee.

Arising from these three areas of difficulty are some recurring, more specific ethical issues. One of these is confidentiality. As all professionals know, this is not absolute and it follows that supervisees need to inform their clients of the limits to confidentiality, including advising the client that the supervisee is in receipt of supervision. Therefore supervisees should inform clients that the material discussed within therapy (or other kinds of work activity) is likely to be shared with a supervisor. It may also be disclosed to other parties too, in relation to the public interest (e.g. disclosing information about sexual abuse or terrorism). Similarly, it is important to be clear about the relative nature of confidentiality relating to material discussed within supervision, as in the degree to which information is shared with the relevant organization or professional body. Customary advice is to make these limits explicit and to record them within the learning contract. Thankfully, normal conventions regarding professional practice apply straightforwardly to supervision. Examples are the 'parsimony principle', which dictates that a professional should disclose only the information that is necessary to address a particular issue, and the primacy of protecting clients.

A second classic area of ethical difficulty concerns accountability. In keeping with my definition of supervision (see Chapter 1), supervisors are accountable to the organization that asks them to undertake supervision, as well as to their managers, professional body and other interested parties (there is always likely to be multiple accountability). Supervisors are accountable to these different people in relation to the performance of their duties, namely the specific responsibilities that they have agreed to undertake. In essence, these are as per Figure 2.2, such as negotiating an appropriate learning contract with the supervisee. Such accountability relationships include the right of bodies, such as the authorizing organization or employer, to hold the supervisor accountable when difficulties arise. This primarily includes responsibility for the supervisee's clinical practice, an area of particular difficulty for many supervisors (e.g. because they wish to empower and not oversee or take responsibility for the work of another professional). The 'cult of the positive' or of 'niceness' (Fleming *et al.*, 2007) makes most professionals feel decidedly awkward in exercising the authority that necessarily accompanies their accountability. But, strictly speaking, it is ethically and professionally appropriate for supervisors to make these formal relationships explicit with the supervisee, as in making it clear that ultimately the supervisor has the right to regulate the supervisee's work (e.g. to instruct a supervisee to discontinue a particular approach). In sum, supervisors who behave ethically need to exercise an appropriate level of authority (legitimate power), one that matches their level of accountability, which is managed in the conventional professional fashion. Problems can arise, and it is important that supervisors tackle these matters following 'due process'. This means that they should adhere closely to conventions and procedures that are set out within relevant organizations (e.g. the 'progress' regulations within a university training programme) or their professional body. In practice, this means that ethically informed supervisors know about relevant guidelines (e.g. regarding the treatment of lapses in confidentiality), and are aware of any codes or standards that may be relevant. This aids them in recognizing issues that arise, and assists them in reconciling any conflicts of interest or ambiguities, working to seek an appropriate solution. This can involve gathering key information, consulting with relevant parties and skilfully addressing issues within supervision. One helpful resource in tackling difficulties that may arise is to draw on problem-solving procedures that are relevant to ethical issues (see, for example, the five-step problem-solving cycle described by Knapp & VandeCreek, 2006). According to this procedure, the supervisor will:

1. Identify or scrutinize the problem.
2. Develop alternatives and hypotheses.
3. Evaluate or analyse the options.
4. Act or perform so as to minimize harm.
5. Evaluate the actions in relation to their success in minimizing harm.

This kind of procedure can helpfully be guided by some core ethical principles. One of these is 'autonomy', which recognizes that supervisees have certain rights to act freely and to exercise choice. This is perhaps most commonly recognized in the developmental progression of a supervisee through several years of pre-qualification training, during which they are gradually given greater autonomy. Secondly, there is the principle of 'benefi-cence', which emphasizes that actions should do good, and are designed to promote human welfare. In this sense one might judge a confidentiality issue arising from the supervisee's practice in terms of the degree to which it helps or harms a particular client. Thirdly, there is the principle of 'fidelity'. This requires professionals to be faithful to any commitments or promises that they have made, and generally to act in a right or proper way (e.g. as per the earlier illustration of informing clients about how confidentiality is relative). Fourthly, there is the principle of 'justice'. This draws attention to the obligation to treat all people equally and fairly, taking account of what is due to people in the particular situation. For instance, a supervisor may judge that a trainee who is well intentioned but has yet to demonstrate competence is accorded extra help in order to progress. Lastly, there is 'non-maleficence', which is the converse of beneficence, namely striving to prevent harm to the supervisee or the people with whom he or she works. Reflecting on these principles in relation to particular ethical issues can be most helpful, and in any case represents one part of ethical practice, the considered and informed reflection on issues that arise.

Legal awareness

If a supervisor is unethical, this may result in legal liability. This includes liability in law, liability to one's employer and liability to one's professional body. For instance, the latter may revoke the supervisor's licence or accredi-tation until such time as ethical supervision can be assured. As touched on earlier, this may include a lack of assertiveness in preventing a supervisee from engaging in work that is beyond their competence. In order to comply with this expectation, it follows that the supervisor needs to know how competent the supervisee is (i.e. the initial needs assessment function within Figure 2.2). Similarly, it implies the need for the supervisor actively to monitor the supervisee's performance, and to give any indicated direction. In legal terms, the supervisor needs to take responsibility for the supervisee, subsuming any appropriate control over their activities (as in giving directions or instructions). Ultimately, the supervisor can be held accountable for the actions of their supervisee, and the supervisor's employer can be held vicariously responsible in law. Whilst different countries and states have somewhat different guidance (Thomas, 2014), common liabilities are to:

1. Facilitate the professional development of the supervisee.
2. Inform clients in writing that therapy will be provided by a trainee, under the supervision of a suitably qualified person.
3. Inform the supervisee in writing (commonly through the learning contract) about the content and methods of supervision, particularly how monitoring and evaluation will occur.
4. Personally assess clients from time to time, in order to monitor treatment.
5. Document supervision (maintaining some kind of log or record, and requiring trainees to document what they are doing, with both parties signing off these records).

These liabilities have arisen through the harsh examination of the legal system. For example, the facilitation of professional development has been underscored by a case brought before the courts in Delaware. Referred to as the Masterson versus Board of Examiners of Psychologists (1995) case, the supervisor Masterson lost her licence because she allowed the supervisee to exploit social relationships (counselling a friend), amongst other things.

Ethical supervision is fortunately similar to ethical practice in other areas of professional life, and thankfully there are also detailed guidelines (e.g. BPS's Code of Ethics and Conduct, 2009) and detailed texts (e.g. Knapp & VandeCreek, 2006; Thomas, 2014). In addition, as professionals, supervisors will have access to colleagues, managers and others who can reflect on difficulties with them, drawing on the above principles to tackle ethical issues appropriately. These are ways in which the supervisor exercises due authority, though one hastens to add (in our cult of niceness) that these are bottom-line legal parameters; in practice, the supervisor would normally manage these issues in a low-key, sensitive and interpersonally effective fashion.

A solid value-base

The above underscores the view that one cannot function optimally as a supervisor without taking due account of the ethical and legal context.

Similarly, supervisors need to be explicit about their value-base, and how this affects supervision. According to Falender *et al.* (2004), the following values are part of competent supervision:

- Being respectful;
- Taking responsibility (e.g. for addressing diversity in all of its forms);
- Balancing support and challenge;
- Empowering the supervisee;
- Being committed to lifelong learning and professional growth;
- Balancing clinical and training needs;
- Valuing ethical principles;
- Being committed to drawing on the knowledge-base (including the scientific literature on supervision); and
- Being committed to recognizing one's own limitations.

Again, one is struck by the degree to which aspects of supervision overlap with many other aspects of professional practice. That is, one would expect professionals, well before they are sufficiently experienced to undertake supervision, to be already demonstrating many of these values (e.g. respect for their clients and a commitment to helping them change and grow). Because of this significant overlap, I will focus here on one key and potentially supervision-specific example, namely sensitivity to diversity. The other values listed are covered elsewhere within the book (e.g. balancing support and challenging being a theme within the next chapter), or are assumed to be as per general professional practice.

Cultural competence

Cultural competence is the 'ability to engage in actions or create conditions that maximize the optimal development of the client and client systems . . . the acquisition of awareness, knowledge and skills needed to function effectively in a pluralistic, democratic society . . . and on an organizational/ societal level, advocating effectively to develop new theories, practices . . . that are more responsive to all groups' (Sue & Torino, 2005, p.8). Implied in this definition is the ability to take different perspectives, to problem-solve flexibly and to recognize the influence of organizations or systems on our activities. It is therefore a dynamic process, carrying huge significance within our increasingly diverse societies (Whaley & Davis, 2007).

Culturally effective practice necessitates a rare degree of self-awareness and sensitivity, including the ability to respond appropriately to the individual characteristics of one's supervisees. This highlights the truth that competence in dealing with diversity entails both awareness and readiness on the part of the supervisor to address any issues that might arise, and to respond sensitively to any relevant characteristics of the supervisee. It is not apparent that supervisors are addressing issues fully, as indicated by a survey of cross-racial supervisees by Duan and Roehlke (2001). Their sample of 60 pairs of supervisors and supervisees provided views on cultural competence that suggested that the supervisors' perceptions of their efforts to address multi-cultural issues were exaggerated. More prominent, according to the super-visees, was the supervisors' positive attitudes to them. In reviewing a number of such studies, Bernard and Goodyear (2004, p.125) conclude that it is 'the willingness of the supervisor to open the cultural door and walk through it with the supervisee' that is of fundamental importance. Through an aware, caring and supportive approach, including self-disclosure and the provision of a 'safe space', this literature indicates that supervisors can manage cultural aspects to the satisfaction of their supervisees. Unfortunately, it appears that negative experiences are common amongst culturally diverse supervisees, whose supervisors may be oblivious to their own privileged status, and who may perpetuate cultural inequities (Thomas, 2014).

Culture is, of course, only one way in which we differ from one another. Hays (2001) has provided a handy summary of these characteristics in the form of the acronym ADDRESSING:

A: Age and generational influences
D: Developmental differences
D: Disabilities
R: Religion and spirituality
E: Ethnicity
S: Social economic status
S: Sexual orientation
I: Indigenous heritage
N: National origin
G: Gender.

As Hays (2001) noted, each of these areas may interact with another to create complex and unique individual characteristics. Authors tend to recommend that the uniqueness or diversity agenda is addressed openly and professionally within supervision, so that a collaborative approach can be taken to recognizing how such differences influence our interactions (including those between supervisee and clients). As per ethical practice, there are a number of guidelines and standards that can assist the clinical supervisor in being culturally competent (for further examples see Whaley & Davis, 2007). To illustrate, the American Psychological Association (APA, 2002) produced *Guidelines on multi-cultural education, training, research, practice, and organizational change for psychologists*. Of most relevance within the context of supervision is guideline 3. It states that, as educators, psychologists are encouraged to employ the constructs of multiculturalism and diversity in psychological education. In support of this guideline, the document notes that cultural competence should be part of educational practice: there should be a due emphasis within teaching programmes and clinical supervision settings, one that is able to promote the student's self-awareness and cultural competence, and to help reduce processes such as stereotyping and automatic prejudicial judgements. It is noted that addressing such competencies explicitly may engender some resistance and so a challenge is identified for supervisors in creating a safe, facilitating learning environment, and to manage any emotions that may emerge (including a non-judgemental demeanour and self-disclosure). The guideline also encourages educators to increase their understanding of how the different perspectives that accompany diversity influence the knowledge-base. The aim is to 'facilitate respectful discussion . . . positive modelling . . . (as part of an appropriate) posture when teaching about multicultural issues' (p.35).

Technological sophistication

In addition to the ethical and legal dimensions of supervision, it is worth noting some developments that build on the availability of new technology to create yet more contextual complexity. One example, already noted in Chapter 2, reflects our political context in the UK, with the advent of the case-based and outcome-orientated supervision that characterizes the Improving Access to Psychological Therapies (IAPT) initiative. This 'high volume' emphasis necessarily means that the essential tasks of supervision, as listed earlier, will need to be conducted with exceptional efficiency if the goal of routinely discussing all patients on the supervisee's caseload is to be achieved. Alternatively, complementary, 'two-tier' arrangements may prove necessary, in which normative or restorative functions are handled by different supervisors/individuals (e.g. managers or therapists; Schindler & Talen, 1994; Fleming *et al.*, 2007). More worrying, it creates a pressure that may limit the extent to which the more time-consuming but educationally valuable supervision methods are utilized (e.g. listening to therapy tapes, role-play). A survey of 196 IAPT high-intensity therapists indicated that such concerns were justified, as few of these therapists were listening to tapes in supervision (Liness *et al.*, 2016). Careful assessment of the supervisee's learning and clinical practice is therefore especially vital, to enable supervisors to monitor the effects of case-based supervision properly.

Another development is the availability of high-technology systems that can provide the basis for novel approaches to supervision. In Chapter 2, I summarized the different formats of traditional supervision, namely the one-to-one, group supervision, and related options. These are all based on the participants being physically located in the same place at the same time. This has been supplemented by the advent of internet-based resources (e.g. electronic textbooks, manuals and guidelines), as well as email communication (e.g. relevant chat rooms to foster discussion of this web-based material), and web-pages with resource material (e.g. access to slideshows, video or DVD recordings; Milne & Reiser, 2017). Novel formats include video-conferencing technologies and real-time feedback systems. The latter entail the supervisor offering written suggestions to the supervisee, providing a real-time graph-line to provide constant performance feedback, or highlighting current clinical issues. These are displayed on a screen positioned behind the patient, but readily visible to the supervisee ('tele-prompting'). For instance, Rosenberg (2006) drew on developments in cognitive science and expertise research to outline a computer-based approach in which the supervisee's therapy is taped through a one-way mirror and the supervisor can type and display, on the video monitor, real-time (concurrent) feedback whilst viewing the session. This feedback can also be provided to other supervisees who are behind the screen whilst they are watching the therapy (a variation on group supervision), and to the therapist, normally after the session. Providing feedback in a written form is an example of how the approach, Real-Time Training, draws on cognitive science, as research in that field suggests that the simultaneous presentation of visual and aural information (i.e. the typed feedback and the words spoken in therapy) decreases cognitive load and hence fosters learning.

Wood *et al.* (2005) have described a 'tele-supervision' system that utilized similar technologies, an approach that they felt pressured to develop because of working across vast rural areas. They noted advantages of the approach, such as a diminishing hierarchical relating, improved communication and the use of multiple instructional formats. For such reasons, Rousmaniere (2014) has suggested that 'Around the world, supervisors have been rapidly moving their services online; clinical supervision and training is no longer restricted by geography' (p.204). In addition to reviewing the latest advances in significant detail, Rousmaniere (2014) notes some of the ethical issues, laws and regulations regarding technology-assisted distance supervision and training (TAST), concluding with a best-practice model and a summary of the growing evidence on effectiveness. This evidence suggests that TAST is associated with high supervisee satisfaction, enhanced confidence and self-disclosure, comparable training effectiveness (in relation to in-person training) and no damage to the supervision alliance. However, he also notes risks, such as the lack of non-verbal communication, cross-cultural misunderstandings and heightened anxiety associated with video-conference-based supervision. Other disadvantages include the cost of the equipment, fears about confidentiality and adverse effects on the quality of supervision, but Rousmaniere (2014) offers suggestions on minimizing such problems.

Assessing the Supervisee's Learning Needs

Having described some important examples of the supervision context, we now focus on the core tasks of supervision. Following Figure 5.1, I begin with the supervisee's learning needs, alongside goal-setting.

By definition, a learning need is something that the supervisee ought to learn for his or her own good, for the good of the relevant organization or for the good of society (Cogswell & Stubblefield, 1988). Crucially, this definition distinguishes a need from a 'want' or 'demand' that a supervisee might express. But this is only the start of a needs assessment process. Additionally, a need is something judged by various participants as calling for some action due to some state of want or destitution, which, if it can be met, will remedy the situation (Bebbington *et al.*, 1997). As pointed out by Goldstein and Ford (2002), the circumstances that lead to the definition of need include an analysis of what the organization requires (specifying relevant supervision goals, clarifying the training climate and the available resources), linked to understanding details of the job and the tasks that it incorporates. As a result, an analysis can be conducted of the relevant knowledge, skills and attitudes, which provides the basis on which to define whether there is 'a state of want or destitution'. That is, an educational learning need is best understood within its context, based on the analysis that Goldstein and Ford (2002) describes, preferably (as he points out) utilizing quality instruments and other methods to assess the relevant parameters. Instruments can be particularly valuable in taking the first step, which is converting the supervisee's felt needs into expressed needs (i.e. those wants or demands). These should then be related to the expressed needs of others with a stake in the process (e.g. those who purchase the training programme within which the supervisee is registered: the employers, the service users). Ideally, these perspectives are then related to a normative perspective, that is, the judgements of professionals as to what is needed (e.g. consensus statements regarding competent supervision, such as Falender *et al.*, 2004). On a local basis, it would be more common for a particular training programme to have an agreed statement of what supervision should address or, in the case of continuing profession development (CPD) supervision, a professional body or employer may have similar specifications. Finally, in an ideal world, these three steps should then lead to a 'comparative' needs assessment, based on clarifying how the material derived through steps 1–3 relates to the standards and/or competencies expected by employers, and/or to any data regarding how others have specified learning objectives or demonstrated the 'fitness for practice' of any trained competencies. A recent illustration can be found in the specification of the competencies required to deliver effective CBT (Roth & Pilling, 2007). Based on these perspectives, and a negotiation process, these expressions of educational need should be specified in terms of the learning objectives for supervision, to which we will turn shortly. As Bransford *et al.* (2000) note, 'there is a good deal of evidence that learning is enhanced when teachers pay attention to the knowledge and beliefs that learners bring to a learning task, use this knowledge as a starting point for new instruction, and monitor students' changing conceptions as instructions proceeds' (p.11). They believe that this understanding has 'a solid research base' to support it (p.14).

Since the 2009 edition of this book the competence movement has grown in influence, with supervisory competence initiatives in Australia and the USA, following Roth and Pilling's (2007) work in the UK. A summary of these different approaches can be found in Milne and Watkins (2014), noting how they represent broadly similar blueprints for supervision (also noted by Olds & Hawkins, 2014), with appropriate national interpretations and specifications. Specifically, these competence statements embrace the nature of supervision, awareness of professional issues (including ethical and legal issues), the alliance, assessment and evaluation in supervision, difference and diversity, and the role of reflective practice (Milne & Watkins, 2014).

In summary, the purpose of an instructional needs assessment is to gain the information that is necessary to design supervision in such a way as to address the legitimate interests of all stakeholders and to clarify the extent of the supervisee's professional development. As Goldstein and Gilliam (1990) point out, 'many programmes are doomed to failure because trainers are more interested in conducting training than in assessing needs' (p.20). Sound supervision would dictate that this stage is treated with every bit as much care and attention as the other parts of the supervision cycle. Part of this emphasis is to consider sufficient areas of the supervisee's development to be able to produce a suitably wide-ranging account of their needs. As already suggested by Goldstein and Gilliam (1990), this would normally cover the areas of knowledge, skills and relevant attitudes. Additional areas that have been suggested include the motivational level of the supervisee and their preferred learning style (Milne & Noone, 1996).

However, the advent of competence frameworks, for supervisors and for supervisees, makes the task of educational needs assessment relatively straightforward and represents significant progress in this professional specialization. As discussed in Chapter 8, new instruments for measuring supervision and supervisee development have also emerged in the last few years. This welcome progress further enables us to specify learning goals, due to their complementary statements of competence (e.g. by providing more detailed specifications of broad competencies). However, there remain some key tasks for supervisors in arriving at a suitable assessment of the supervisee's educational needs, including the important process of discussing and agreeing the competencies and other goals that belong in the learning contract.

Negotiating the supervisee's learning needs

Collaborative goal-setting is one of the 'probably effective' elements of psychotherapy (Tryon & Winograd, 2011). Similarly, several studies in the field of professional education have suggested that active learning in a collaborative environment is a key to developing complex skills (Prince & Felder, 2006). Major competency frameworks for supervision (e.g. APA, 2015) also emphasize the value of collaboration, for example in maintaining the supervisory alliance. Collaboration is a mainstay of CBT supervision (Reiser, 2014). However, as stressed by Norcross and Halgin (1997), this process of collaborating in order to clarify what is needed in relation to a particular supervisee may not be straightforward. In addition to areas of blindness (lack of self-awareness), they note that supervisees may have wide-ranging or quite inappropriate expectations of supervision, as in seeking personal growth or therapy, or simply declaring that they have shown up because they were assigned to a particular supervisor. As they suggest, 'supervisees come with a panoply of preconceptions and needs, many unrecognized, and it is best to examine these at the outset and to modify them as the trainee obtains experience' (p.208). They recommend tactful enquiry and the careful negotiation of legitimate needs, to be counter-balanced against the needs of the supervisor and others.

An exceptionally sensitive and thoughtful treatment of this negotiation process can be found in Safran and Muran's (2000) account of negotiating within the development of a therapeutic alliance. Indeed, they suggest that the process of negotiation lies 'at the heart of the change process . . . a critical therapeutic mechanism' (p.15). They regard such negotiation in the context of therapy as more than a superficial consensus but rather referring to some fundamental dilemmas that we face, such as relating our own desires and wishes with those of another person, essentially a core struggle to identify with one's own reality at the same time as accommodating another person's reality. Essentially, there is an inevitable tension between 'the need for agency verses the need for relatedness' (p.15). Much of their book is dedicated to addressing ways in which ruptures in the relationship between therapist and client, pivoting around such negotiations, can be repaired. In CBT there is an emphasis on regular (albeit more superficial) negotiation, in the form of agenda-setting (Liese & Beck, 1997). Additionally, the emphasis is more on identifying and addressing the respective 'wants' of the respective parties, as opposed to actually negotiating a shared, needs-led agenda. However, it is clear that in the CBT model the supervisee is socialized into preparing carefully for supervision, which includes thinking of important agenda items ahead of each supervisory meeting. If a supervisee attends without any such preparation, then 'they're encouraged to do so, in order to use the time most productively' (p.121). The next chapter cites examples from IAPT services where the supervisees are trained to contribute in such ways, together with research suggesting that preparation and active collaboration enhance the associated effectiveness of both supervision and therapy. For their part, the CBT supervisors are meant to prepare by reviewing what the supervisee will need, based on the study of previous supervision sessions and the customary use of the supervisee's tape-recorded work. They give the example that a tape may indicate a comparable lack of focus in the supervisee's therapy, whereby this becomes an identified learning need, to be addressed within the next supervision session.

Such general statements of good practice inevitably have boundaries. I refer to exceptional circumstances, such as where a supervisee on a training programme is required to remediate or repeat a training experience, owing to the failure to demonstrate competence during a previous opportunity. In such circumstances the balance would tip strongly away from supervisee's wants to those dictated by the training programme, typically processed through the supervisor. By contrast, an exceptionally able supervisee in the final period of initial training might be treated in a far more collegial fashion, and given considerable scope to act on their wants and preferences.

Goal-setting (establishing the learning contract)

On the basis of the educational needs assessment process, a suitably individualized (needs-led) learning contract can be specified. The most familiar objectives within initial training are the competencies that the supervisee should demonstrate in order to graduate or practice, traditionally expressed in terms of knowledge, skills and attitudes (subsuming the value-base). Specifying objectives is another general area of professional practice that most supervisors will apply within their other duties, from therapy to staff training. Its application within supervision is fundamentally the same and the acronym SMARTER is a way of remembering the key criteria for the setting of sound objectives:

S: Specific
M: Measurable
A: Achievable
R: Realistic
T: Time-phased (scheduled)
E: Evaluated
R: Recorded (written down).

This acronym illustrates the bridge that should exist between the needs assessment phase and the final task in the supervision cycle, that of evaluating the extent to which objectives have been achieved. Classically, good behavioural objectives specify the 'performance' (state exactly what the learner/supervisee should be able to do); the 'conditions' under which this performance is expected to occur; and a 'criterion', being some description of what represents acceptable performance (Mager, 1997). Approximating to this degree of SMARTER objective goal-setting is extremely helpful. Amongst other things, it clarifies to the supervisee exactly what is expected of them and indicates priorities to the supervisor, suggesting too how they need to facilitate learning. Indeed, just as needs assessment tends to be under-emphasized yet critical, so good objective-setting can contribute hugely to the success of supervision. Research from schools indicates the empowering effect of good goal-setting, as classes with this degree of clarity of purpose have been found to proceed successfully without their teacher. In the case of able and motivated supervisees, there is surely good reason to believe that properly negotiated and communicated learning objectives are sufficient to motivate the supervisee towards self-directed learning. In some cases, this may be more productive than the learning that is managed in more traditional, supervisor-led ways, as in 'problem-based learning'. Indeed, in terms of the development of knowledge, it has been noted historically that 'everything that is actually known has been found out . . . by some person or other, without the aid of an instructor . . . there is no species of learning, therefore, which self-education may not overtake . . . all discoveries have been self-taught' (Craik, 1866, p.13, cited in Mithaug *et al.*, 2003).

Although a recognition and discussion of the educational needs assessment phase is rare in textbooks on clinical supervision, there is a clear and consistent recognition of the importance of establishing the learning contract, the way in which objectives are traditionally referred to and recorded within supervision. For example, Bernard and Goodyear (2014) and Safran and Muran (2000) have noted that the establishment of the supervision contract can be seen as an educational/relational intervention in its own right. However, surveys of the use of learning contracts indicate that they are often absent. For example, Kavanagh *et al.* (2003) asked 272 qualified practitioners receiving and providing CPD supervision across Queensland about various aspects of their supervision, finding that only 44 per cent of supervisors said that there was a learning contract (supervisees put the figure even lower, at 34 per cent). However, the existence of a properly specified contract was significantly correlated with the perceived impact of supervision on practice.

As regards the content of learning contracts, Hawkins and Shohet (2000) describe an exhaustive, 'seven-eyed' agenda of psychoanalytic origin. This consists of attention to:

1. Reflection on the content of therapy (to heighten awareness in the supervisee).
2. Exploration of the methods used by the supervisee (what was done and how it might be developed).
3. Exploration of the therapy process and relationship (studying the interaction as a whole, including the client's transference).
4. Focus on the therapist's internal processes (how counter-transference, etc., affects therapy).
5. Focus on the supervisory relationship (how client's dynamics affect supervision, e.g. parallel processes).
6. Focus on the supervisor's counter-transference (the internal experience of the supervisor).
7. Attention to the wider context (e.g. normative matters, like policies or work standards).

According to Hawkins and Shohet (2000), good supervision involves all seven topics (which they term 'modes') within a process model of supervision entailing 'moving effectively and appropriately from one mode to another' (p.86), which requires considerable awareness and timing. CBT supervision is more circumscribed, typically being concerned with case conceptualization, the effective application of CBT techniques and inter-personal strategies (Liese & Beck, 1997; Townend *et al.*, 2002).

Bernard and Goodyear (2004) listed some of the headings that typically appear within contracts. These include aspects of scheduling, such as the frequency and duration of supervision sessions; the methods that the supervisor will use, including the expectations that flow for the supervisee (e.g. making recordings of routine work for discussion in supervision; assigned reading); a statement of what is to happen in the event of the supervisor being absent (back-up arrangements – contact persons; lines of authority); reference to the organization's expectations (e.g. hours of work and dress code); the specific knowledge, skills and attitudes that make up the competencies to be demonstrated within the learning experience; communication issues (such as record-keeping and report-writing standards); and, of course, an understanding of the normal processes of review, feedback and evaluation. Other topics to consider for the learning contract include what might be termed 'professional matters', such as clarifying accountability arrangements; the legal framework; confidentiality arrangements; insurance; and ethical aspects of supervision (Falender & Shafranske, 2004). Returning to the Kavanagh *et al.* (2003) survey, respondents indicated that their most common topic was competence enhancement, as specific to each participating profession (reported by 56 per cent of supervisors). General practice skills (15 per cent) and personal issues (8 per cent) were also noted by these supervisors.

Given the widespread recognition of the importance of the learning contract, it should not be surprising to find that some approaches to clinical supervision give significant emphasis to the content and process of contracting. To illustrate, Gonsalvez *et al.* (2002) describe what they refer to as the 'objectives approach'. They argue that many current models of supervision are insufficiently specific to enable us to translate them into supervisory practice, as in failing to guide the setting of learning objectives. Therefore, the objectives approach (which coincidentally also derives from the educational and training literature) was applied to supervision. They define an objective as a 'specific statement of what trainees should be able to do as a result of a course of study' (p.69). Reiterating the convention that objectives cover knowledge, skills and attitudes, they underscore how these objectives should in turn inform the methods and resources that are applied to try to deliver them, as well as the implications they carry for evaluation. They helpfully provide some examples, as in the case of an objective concerning a CBT skill (e.g. 'trainee to demonstrate competence in identifying clients' automatic thoughts, cognitive distortions, and core beliefs'). In order to address this objective, they note that supervision needs to include individual sessions and video-taped interviews. In turn, when it comes to methods, they suggest that this particular skill can be developed through demonstrations by the supervisor, using prepared video material. The trainee is then expected to practise the competence, using audio and video-tape transcripts of therapist–client interactions. Finally, this can be evaluated, they suggest, by pre- and post-training assessment of the supervisee's competence using a test video. Although not providing any fundamentally new insights as to the importance of objectives in supervision, the Gonsalvez *et al.* (2002) paper does at least underscore the basic logic followed within this book. This is that general educational, therapeutic and other professional areas of practice can apply strongly to supervision.

Similarly, they also detail how a prior phase of needs assessment is crucial. Their account also furnishes detailed examples of how this approach can work in practice, at the level of the individual supervisor (and also in relation to what they refer to as the 'macro level' of supervisor training). In order to examine their objectives approach, Gonsalvez *et al.* (2002) surveyed the supervisees ($N=36$) and supervisors ($N=28$) associated with a clinical psychology training programme in Australia, using an ad hoc Supervision Experience Questionnaire. Amongst their findings, they reported significant differences between the supervisors' and trainees' ratings of the importance of various objectives. Specifically, supervisors gave significantly higher ratings to objectives related to professional issues, to enhancing interpersonal skills and to raising the supervisees' self-awareness. Both groups gave similarly high ratings to the importance of developing the requisite knowledge and skills.

Other studies have uniformly provided support for the value of clear objective-setting. For example, Methot *et al.* (1996) used a blend of participative and assigned goal-setting with their supervisors, finding that this led to improved specification of outcomes for supervisees and, in turn, for their clients. Fleming *et al.* (1996) also examined the value of participative and assigned goals, finding that, in combination with other methods such as modelling and feedback, their programme increased the maintenance of competencies in supervisees. Talen and Schindler (1993) studied the learning plans of 26 psychology trainees. Their results indicated that concrete, observable and theory-based goals were perceived as the most helpful by these supervisees, and were associated with positive improvements in their learning.

As regards the value of a learning contract itself, Solomon (1992) surveyed supervisors, finding that 90 per cent regarded the learning contract as a useful tool in both teaching and evaluation, fostering negotiation and self-directed learning. These examples from the supervision literature are consistent with findings within psychology more generally. As summarized by Bransford *et al.* (2000), 'there is a good deal of evidence that learning is enhanced when teachers pay attention to the knowledge and beliefs that learners bring to a learning task, use this knowledge as a starting point for new instruction, and monitor students' changing conceptions as instruction proceeds' (p.11).

Once more, research findings are consistent with the kinds of guidance provided by professional bodies. For instance, the British Association for Behavioural and Cognitive Psychotherapies (BABCP) produced a supervision supplement on the importance of both needs assessment and goal-setting (Townend, 2004), and the same expectation that suitably negotiated and individual learning contracts are established can be found in the guidance on training clinical psychologists in the UK (British Psychological Society, 2003). A CBT supervision guideline has been developed to summarize this research and guidance (Milne & Reiser, 2017). Although this section has only addressed examples from the pre-qualification field, it is to be hoped that those concerned with CPD supervision can draw out the relevant implications, as these tasks and processes are surely core to all variants of supervision. However, there are, naturally, some significant differences between supervisees when it comes to the learning objectives that result from this goal-setting process (for an approach to CBT supervision across diverse supervisees see Temple & Bowers, 1998).

The international development and widespread acceptance of competence statements and frameworks is an important professional milestone (Rodolfo *et al.*, 2013), providing supervisors with very helpful menus of supervision goals (Milne & Watkins, 2014), and breathing new life into supervision (Gonsalvez, 2014). These menus overlap with and complement the above account, which is more process-focused and therefore still relevant. By contrast, competencies are by nature outcome-focused, specifying what the supervisee requires to demonstrate to achieve success (e.g. a positive rating from a supervisor; course completion). Competence statements also have the benefit of clarifying transparently what is required of all supervisees, indicating the necessary learning opportunities, and suggesting how evaluation can occur, a veritable 'blueprint' for supervision (Gonsalvez, 2014). Competence is defined as the ability to perform a skill to the standard required in employment (a professional is 'qualified, capable, and able to understand and do certain things in an appropriate and effective manner'; Rodolfo *et al.*, 2005, p.348). By contrast, functional competencies are those observable elements that contribute to competence. In the competencies statement by Rodolfo *et al.* (2005) there are six functional competence domains, one of which was termed 'supervision–teaching'. This was defined as supervision and training of the professional knowledge-base and/or evaluation of the effectiveness of various professional activities.

Further levels of detail are sometimes provided within competence frameworks, through the listing of sub-competencies and the specification of 'behavioural anchors' or 'behavioural exemplars' for each sub-competency. For example, the Roth and Pilling (2007) supervisee competency of the general 'ability to make use of supervision' is defined through five sub-competencies, including 'an ability to work collaboratively with the supervisor' and 'capacity for self-appraisal and reflection'. In turn, these sub-competencies are defined by multiple behavioural anchors. For instance, the 'ability to work collaboratively with the supervisor' is defined by five such anchoring statements, such as 'an ability to present clinical material to the supervisor in a focused manner, selecting the most important and relevant material'. Roth and Pilling (2007) argue that this competence 'architecture' is user-friendly and intuitive, so aiding utility. By contrast, 'foundational' competencies are more general characteristics of supervisees, such as their professionalism and ethical stance, making them less amenable to observation (see 'context' section above). As the title implies, foundational competencies consist of the knowledge, skills and attitudes that professionals require in order to acquire functional competencies, usually as developed initially through pre-qualification education. For example, through a systematic process of expert consensus-building, Rodolfo *et al.* (2005) defined six foundational competencies, one of which was 'reflective practice–self-assessment'. This included 'engagement with scholarship, critical thinking, and a commitment to the development of the profession' (p.351).

Completing the competence architecture is a third category of competence that is frequently distinguished in the supervision literature: 'meta-competence'. This can be construed as the 'frontal lobe' of supervision, as it refers to one's capacity to actively monitor and adjust the use of competencies in order to maximize success, as in judging when to change tack or emphasis, a form of procedural knowledge or judgement that is based on factors such as self-awareness, reflection or responsivity.

Training versus education: supervision for competence or for capability?

So far, my emphasis has been on the relatively circumscribed and uncontroversial business of developing the supervisee's competence. However, professionals also need to develop capability if they are to be successful in grappling with complex and novel problems that naturally arise within their work. To quote Fraser and Greenhalgh (2001), 'in today's complex world, we must educate not merely for competence, but for capability (the ability to adapt to change, generate new knowledge and continuously improve performance) . . . education for capability must focus on process . . . supporting learners to construct their own learning goals . . . and avoid goals with rigid and prescriptive content' (p.799). To rephrase, we train supervisees in order to develop their competence, but we also need to educate them for capability. Training and education are associated with very different orientations and outcomes, as indicated in Table 5.2.

It seems to me that the preceding material on competence does not sufficiently articulate this vital distinction, although elements can be detected across some competence statements. For instance, Rodolfo *et al.* (2005) specified the functional competency cluster called 'reflective practice–self-assessment' (outlined above), and a second called 'research–evaluation', which referred to 'research that contributes to the professional knowledge base and/or evaluates the effectiveness of various professional activities' (p.351). The subsequent competence statement (Rodolfo *et al.*, 2013) also included competence in the modification of 'intervention/supervision/consultation' activities, defined in terms of using emerging information, outcome data and current research. These competencies would surely contribute to a supervisee's capability, but a stronger distinction seems warranted, given its importance. It follows that the effective supervisor will include educational goals within the learning contract and will alternate between training and educational methods in the pursuit of most or all of the objectives within the contract. An example from Fraser and Greenhalgh (2001) is that capability is likely to be enhanced through providing supervisees with unfamiliar contexts and non-linear methods (such as storytelling, and problem-based learning in small groups).

Empowering the Supervisee

The third task within the supervision cycle (Figure 5.1) is to empower the supervisee. There is much more on this topic in the next chapter, but I wish to include a brief note here. A review of research within clinical supervision indicated that 'one of the important facets of clinical training is the supervisee's ability to make use of his or her supervision experience... research suggests that supervisees with greater cognitive complexity and self-awareness or reflectivity more readily develop specific clinical skills and utilize supervision effectively' (Inman *et al.*, 2014, p.64). Conversely, they noted that supervisees may also have personal qualities that impede their development, such as unresolved personal issues, unwillingness to accept feedback or limited motivation. Another systematic review (Colquitt *et al.*, 2000) noted some of the main positive qualities, such as the supervisees' cognitive ability or motivation, which carried considerable weight within a path analysis. In an audit of 59 supervisees' supervision records within a training programme, 20 different contributions were identified (Milne & Gracie, 2001), leading the authors to conclude that 'the data portray the supervisee as an active participant in supervision, one who brings a range of seemingly helpful behaviours to bear within the supervision process' (p.14). A rare study of supervisee empowerment was conducted within six IAPT services in England by Green *et al.* (2014). They noted marked differences in the way the more effective therapists engaged in supervision, finding that they were more proactive (e.g. observing other clinicians), better prepared and more organized (e.g. stating what they sought from the supervisory discussion).

Expert consensus recognizes the importance of empowering supervisees to contribute to supervision in such ways. For instance, the APA (2015) supervision guidelines endorsed the value of supervisee self-assessment as a means of strengthening the supervisee's reflective practice and competence. Falender and Shafranske (2012) have written the first text devoted to empowering supervisees, providing tools, reflective exercises and an overview of the process of becoming a better supervisee (e.g. processing feedback; self-care; improving thinking). Their rationale is that 'supervision is dynamically co-constructed, and effective supervision is the responsibility of both the supervisor and the supervisee' (p.209).

Facilitating Learning

As already recognized, we start facilitating learning by conducting a needs assessment, collaboratively setting objectives and through creating a suitable learning context. For instance, supervisees are likely to be motivated by supervisors who are willing to identify and incorporate their needs within learning contracts. At the very least, they have created excellent preconditions for the successful use of the conventional methods of supervision.

Creating change as a result of a psychological intervention like supervision is at times a complex and exacting undertaking. Perhaps because of this challenge, there is a considerable range of intervention options. Some of these cohere naturally with particular theoretical models; others are developmentally based or derive from the unique models of supervision (see Chapter 2). As noted in Chapter 2, there are also pragmatic approaches which belong to no particular theoretical orientation, and are simply an extension of basic social science research, such as the outcome-orientated approach (Worthen & Lambert, 2007). Rather than attempt to list the various interventions in terms of each of these different supervision models, this chapter is organized in a more functional, integrative way, so as to clarify the main, evidence-based methods of supervision.

Have a coherent intervention plan

To begin with, supervisors are advised in many textbooks to adopt a frame-work or model to guide their approach, and to use a blend of supervision methods that are appropriate to the learning needs (e.g. the preferred learning style) of the supervisee. To illustrate, Bernard and Goodyear (2004) encourage supervisors to base their methods on what they understand to be the supervisee's needs, interests and experience of the material to be tackled through supervision. Importantly, they also lay stress on the need to monitor how the intervention process unfolds and to look carefully at outcome data to judge whether this needs-led, personalized blend of supervision methods is producing the intended outcomes. Norcross and Halgin (1997) agree with this broad strategy, adding emphasis to the importance of having a clear guiding model, and Watkins (1997) supports the notion of having a carefully structured approach. More recently, Gonsalvez (2014) has outlined the 'competency-based developmental plan', an integrated way of recording agreed learning goals and planned activities, alongside the supervision methods that are intended to achieve these goals, together with the intended assessment and evaluation approaches. This matches up nicely with the one provided by the APA (2015). Amongst the supervision methods, Gonsalvez (2014) lists and reviews case discussion, role-play, live observation, video review, plus recent technological options such as 'bug-in-the-ear/eye'.

Use multiple (blended) supervision methods

As this list illustrates, textbooks and professional consensus statements underline the necessity of using multiple, intelligently combined methods. For instance, in their consensus statement, Kaslow *et al.* (2004) recognized 'the value of modelling, role-plays, vignettes, in-vivo experiences, supervised experience, and other real-world experiences as critical instructional strategies' (p.706). The APA guidelines (2015) specify these methods: discussion; live observation (or review of tapes); performance monitoring; positive and corrective feedback that is sensitive to the supervisee's developmental level; supervisee self-monitoring (to foster reflective skills); developmentally appropriate challenge; and modelling professional skills. One reason for combining methods of this sort is to maximize the likelihood of building on the supervisee's prior learning. In addition to underscoring the importance of having a needs-led approach and of respecting and empowering the supervisee, there is a fundamental psychological principle involved in building on prior learning. This is the view that 'all learning involves transfer from previous experiences' (Bransford *et al.*, 2000, p.68). This is part of what these authors refer to as the new science of learning, an understanding of how humans engage actively with instructional material, as goal-directed agents seeking to develop: 'Humans are viewed as goal-directed agents who actively seek information. They come to formal education with a range of prior knowledge, skills, beliefs, and concepts that significantly influence what they notice about the environment and how they organize and interpret it. This in turn affects their abilities to remember, reason, solve problems, and acquire new knowledge' (p.10).

This understanding of how humans learn is based on a combination of expert consensus and their review (Bransford *et al.*, 2000) of the available scientific literature. It contrasts with a more passive version of how humans develop, often associated with the idea that learners come into situations like supervision as 'blank slates', just as newborn infants were once thought to enter a baffling world that is a 'booming, buzzing confusion' (James, 1890). This active account of learning from experience is helpfully synthesized within Kolb (2014). Implications of this active, goal-directed, account of how people learn has massive implications, including suggestions for how clinical supervision should be pursued. Professional organizations also endorse the importance of using a blend of supervision methods, although they may give a particular emphasis to something like the need to adopt an empirical approach within supervision, such as adopting such methods on a tentative footing, studying the effects with particular individuals closely and making any necessary adjustments as the learning experience unfolds (e.g. British Psychological Society, 2003).

Consistent with these consensus statements, general reviews and professional standards, systematic reviews of carefully selected studies in the clinical supervision field also indicate the value of utilizing a blend of methods to facilitate learning. The Milne and James (2000) and Milne *et al.* (2008a) reviews are typical in finding that a large number of methods are used within supervision manipulations, as summarized in Table 5.3. This combines the results of these two reviews to offer a summary of the top 10 supervisor methods (the Milne *et al.*, 2008a results alone were summarized in Table 3.1). This list is based on those methods that were used in at least two studies.

Table 5.3 indicates that the above views of experts are very much in step with this highly selected group of 52 research papers, studies that were

Table 5.3 Range and popularity of the different methods for facilitating supervisees' learning, as identified in two systematic reviews (including 52 studies of effective supervision).

Supervision method	*Frequency of use (% of studies)*
Feedback (including praise and constructive criticism)	42 (81)
Observation and outcome monitoring	41 (79)
Discussion (including providing a rationale; questions and answers; objective-setting; problem-solving; challenging supervisees' thinking)	39 (75)
Written/verbal prompts and instruction (including guidelines)	25 (48)
Encouraging autonomy (time management)	11 (21)
Formulation (including paper and pencil tasks to increase understanding)	7 (13)
Modelling skills (live/video; live supervision)	7 (13)
Behavioural rehearsal (including role-play)	5 (10)
Homework assignment (e.g. guided reading)	2 (4)
Other (e.g. alliance-building work) Total methods = 190, Mean number of methods per study = 3.7	11 (21)

Source: Milne, D.L. (2009). Reproduced with permission of Derek Milne.

included because their supervision methods produced successful outcomes (part of the evidence-based supervision rationale of working from a seam of high-quality, interpretable studies). In essence, Table 5.3 bears out the argument that a range of methods should be used. Of the 190 methods cited within the 52 studies, an average of 3.7 methods were manipulated within each study. These include methods that are primarily behavioural (sometimes referred to as 'enactive' methods: observation, modelling, rehearsal); methods that are more cognitive (traditionally referred to as 'symbolic': the various forms of discussion, verbal prompting and instruction); and then methods that are fundamentally working within the visual modality ('iconic': live and video modelling, live supervision). Therefore, the methods actually tap different modes through which individuals learn.

Perhaps two specific examples will help to bring these general figures to life. The example of Fleming *et al.* (1996) is fairly typical. Supervisors began supervision with a brief presentation of the relevant knowledge-base, then used a video to show the supervisee how a skill could be performed correctly, leading to the supervisee's rehearsal of the skill and corrective feedback. Similarly, supervisors in an analysis of training in short-term psychotherapy (Hilsenroth *et al.*, 2006) relied heavily on reviewing video-taped therapy sessions. However, in keeping with this orientation, the focus was on examining selected interactions in relation to the dynamics, including the supervisee's experiences and interventions. Alternatives were reviewed and rehearsed, with support, encouragement and praise provided to the supervisee (i.e. 'positive feedback'; p.297). This approach was found to increase significantly the 15 supervisees' use of appropriate techniques (e.g. exploring wishes, fantasies and dreams), whilst there was no concurrent change in their unsupervised CBT skills.

Before leaving Table 5.3, I should stress that this is meant to provide only an approximate summary of a particularly favourable sample of the research literature. In turn, within this literature – and within my attempt to capture it – there was at times a lack of precision. This is because it was frequently difficult to determine, from reading these reports, exactly where one method begins and another one ends (including the different terminology that I have summarized under one heading, as indicated by the qualifying terms in brackets within column 1 of Table 5.3). Also, several of the research papers appearing in the first review were again included within the second one. This will undoubtedly have biased the summary to some extent. For these reasons, I offer this table as a rough guide, helpful mainly because it does nonetheless provide greater specificity and quantification than is typically available.

Applying the methods

Of course, a general category or label like 'feedback' can subsume a diversity of educational practices. This is rarely spelt out within research papers, and indeed there is a striking lack of manuals, guidelines and other explicit statements of how these methods should be enacted, although the situation has improved latterly (Milne, 2016). Welcome examples of detailed best practice procedures include the 'supervision essentials' series published by the APA, being short but descriptive texts linked to illustrative DVDs, written for a range of supervision models. For instance, chapter 4 in the Newman and Kaplan (2016) text on CBT supervision lists the range of methods that are appropriate within this approach, supplemented by extensive sample dialogues between supervisor and supervisee and case illustrations. Sudak *et al.* (2016) is a more extensive text on CBT supervision, covering training and supervision methods in depth. There are online video clips accompanying much of the material, to be viewed in conjunction with learning exercises. To illustrate, the chapter by Milne and Reiser (2016a) links to a task involving viewing a brief video clip on agenda-setting, and the completion of a supervision competence rating scale (for later comparison with a scale completed by expert raters, as corrective feedback). The chapter by Milne and Reiser (2016a) also summarizes the manual for the rating instrument used in this learning exercise (SAGE: see Chapter 8). This provides an unusual degree of specificity, in relation to 17 methods of supervision, including what the supervisor should do (examples of specific questions and actions are included) and the kinds of mini-outcomes that should occur. The video clip on agenda-setting then demonstrates the competent execution of these skills. Milne and Reiser (2017) is a full-blown manual for CBT supervision, containing 18 video demonstrations covering all the relevant (observable) supervision competencies from the Roth and Pilling (2007) competence framework. This manual is also unusual in furnishing detailed guidelines that are carefully derived from the best-available evidence, guidelines that have been vetted by supervisors and supervisees for their clarity and relevance to practice. One of the six guidelines in Milne and Reiser (2017) addresses the topic of 'facilitating learning', so represents a manualized version of the present chapter. Since the first edition of the present book, such developments in specifying and modelling supervision supplement the competence movement in helping to promote evidence-based practice of an unprecedented standard. This is further supported by growing research on the nature

Table 5.4 A summary of some of the main functions and methods of feedback, based on Juwah *et al.* (2004).

Facilitates	Self-assessment/regulation/reflection
Engages	Prioritized/staff and students
Energizes	SMARTER objectives follow: specific; measurable; achievable; realistic; time-phased; evaluated; recorded
Dialogues	Mutual clarification
Backs	Consistent with system/support/reinforcement
Actions	Next steps specified – for all participants
Clarifies	Standards/expectations/gaps relative to possible standard
Knows	How to close gap/develop

Source: Milne, D.L. (2009). Reproduced with permission of Derek Milne.

and effectiveness of specific supervision methods (e.g. Bearman *et al.*, 2013).

In addition to manuals, supervisors can also gain guidance from relevant theories. Consider the most frequently used method recorded in Table 5.3, feedback. Based on a review within the educational literature, Table 5.4 summarizes some of the specifics that are supposed to compose feedback, in the form of an acronym. This can furnish the qualified practitioner with some helpful suggestions, ideas that they can apply because they require the same basic skills as other clinical duties. In the supervision literature, the practice of providing feedback to supervisees usually means informing them about their strengths and weaknesses (identifying some positives and negatives), followed by praise (positive reinforcement), related to the supervision contract (the learning objectives), based at least in part on direct observation. This summary is borne out by the fact that these items are the only ones mentioned in 'the evaluation process within supervision inventory' (Lehrman-Waterman & Ladany, 2001), one of the few available instruments for assessing feedback within supervision. Feedback is one of the most proven of all educational methods, and has quite rightly been deemed 'indispensable' to supervisees' learning (Goodyear, 2014, p.87). To illustrate, in a systematic review of 41 studies, Veloski *et al.* (2006), found that 74 per cent of these studies demonstrated a significant, positive effect. This was most pronounced when provided by an authoritative, credible source, and maintained over time. There are other suggestions on making feedback as effective as possible. To start with, explain the reason for any feedback to the supervisee (James, 2014), on the logic of collaborating with the supervisee (the 'interactive approach' to feedback).

This is in accord with the mentions of 'engages' and 'dialogues' in Table 5.3. In addition, reflecting the 'self-assessment' point in Table 5.4, engaging the supervisee can be highly informative, as self-evaluations are prone to significant bias (over-estimation by novices; under-estimation by experts: Kruger & Dunning, 1999). Also, any negative or critical feedback that a supervisor may be hesitant about providing to the supervisee may already have been anticipated, and facilitates a constructive discussion. Further suggestions come from the deliberate practice (DP; Ericsson, 2009) and educational literature (e.g. Hattie & Timperley, 2007), as the specification of the feedback procedure is notably more precise and detailed within DP, and there is much greater emphasis on the validity of the feedback data. Specifically, these literatures emphasize the need to specify the gap between current and desired competence; to draw on a variety of data collection methods (e.g. clinical outcomes, client satisfaction, direct observation); to demonstrate the correct performance of a competence; and to provide frequent feedback. The DP and education literatures also contain stronger evidence of effectiveness (i.e. more rigorous, larger-sample studies), increasing our confidence. In addition to a thorough review of the evidence, there is a guideline on feedback within the manual by Milne and Reiser (2017), covering the above procedural points in detail (also demonstrated through the linked video clips). For instance, there is this suggestion on demonstrating the required improvement:

> Having specified an improvement, describe in detail how the improvement could be made, or better still demonstrate how a competence can be performed at the required level. Feedback in the form of praise is popular, but look for evidence that the targeted skill is improving.
>
> *For example,* 'In relation to CTS(R) item 5 (interpersonal effectiveness), you might try listening more attentively before speaking. Let me demonstrate how I think it might work best, using a role-play. Basically, my thinking is to deepen listening through several non-verbal reactions and silence, before speaking.' Ask the supervisee to imitate your listening style.

This advice is consistent with the APA guidelines (2015), under the category of assessment and feedback, Guideline 3 stated that: 'Supervisors aspire to provide feedback that is direct, clear, and timely, behaviourally anchored, responsive to supervisees' reactions, and mindful of the impact on the supervisory relationship' (p.39). At a more concrete level, Table 5.5 offers a breakdown of another dominant method of supervision, the use of questions with the supervisee. These appear to feature significantly in all

Table 5.5   An elaboration of one popular supervision method, that of questioning the supervisee.

Function of question (related to the experiential learning cycle)	Illustrative *form* of questions	Main *focus*/purpose of this kind of question
1. *Heighten affective awareness (experiencing)*	*Open questions* (e.g. 'What were you feeling when the client wept?') *Awareness-raising questions* (e.g. 'Which negative reactions do you have to this event?')	• Recalling/describing • Information gathering • Supporting • Facilitating the alliance • Processing affect
2. *Facilitate cognitive reflection (reflection)*	*Generic questions* (e.g. 'How did that compare to the supervision you've had before?') *Exploratory Socratic questions* (e.g. 'Has this kind of interaction been a feature of your clinical work?')	• Challenging (e.g. creating a tension/dialectic) • Productive/solution generating • Formal reflection (e.g. assessing/appraising) • Meaning-making (e.g. reframing; induction; interpreting) • Classifying • Hypothesizing
3. *Connect to knowledge-base (conceptualization)*	*Closed question* (e.g. 'How do I know that this is the best approach?') *Critical engagement question* (e.g. 'Where can we find the best evidence?')	• Summarizing • Checking understanding • Informing/educating • Clarifying • Reasoning • Guiding discovery (improving grasp) • Critical thinking (e.g. analysing) • Defending viewpoint • Critiquing
4. *Apply to ongoing work (experimenting)*	*Task-specific questions* (e.g. 'Which goals are you trying to achieve?') *Miracle/imaginative questions* (e.g. 'If a miracle occurred, how would things be different?') *Transformational questions* (e.g. 'How could your understanding help to address this problem?')	• Eliciting feedback • Controlling (meta-cognition) • Monitoring • Evaluating • Extending knowledge (e.g. through analogies/deductions/generalizations/applications) • Demonstrating • Constructing • Practising

Source: Milne, D.L. (2009). Reproduced with permission of Derek Milne.

models of supervision, though taking on suitably different forms and functions. For example, in an evaluation of brief psychodynamic psycho-therapy, the supervisor who used specific questioning to adjust adherence (and who was generally more focused and active) achieved a much greater effect size than a colleague with a more general supervision style (i.e. 3.58 versus 0.46; Henry *et al.*, 1993). In CBT supervision, questions have a central role, as in gathering information pertinent to case conceptualization, and in facilitating effective dialogue (James & Morse, 2007; James *et al.*, 2008). It is hoped that the list of questions in Table 5.4 will give supervisors a way to reflect on their current methods, and to consider fresh options. The table is based on Bernard and Goodyear (2014); Campbell (2006); Ennis (1985); Follette and Batten (2000); James and Morse (2007); Moseley *et al.* (2005); Rigazio-DiGilio *et al.* (1997) and Siegler (1995).

Finally, in order to ensure that the preferred methods are used as effectively as possible, the supervisor might base their selection and application on an established theory. This is valuable as it encourages the supervisor to consider what mediates their supervisee's learning. For instance, the augmented CBT supervision account, as set out in Chapter 3 (Kolb, 1984), recognizes that one needs to create a certain amount of tension between different ways of understanding competence or capability. This tension can arise from the use of different methods (e.g. contrasting personal experience against textbook advice), from reflecting on experience (James *et al.*, 2004) or from challenging the supervisee's understanding (for an illustration, see James & Morse, 2007). A supervisor guided by this logic might alternate between asking the supervisee to describe something that happened, to recount some of the emotions that accompanied this event, to reflect on what possible understanding or meaning it might have within their frame of reference and then to provide some instruction from their understanding. This might then lead to a mutually agreed way of testing out an understanding, one that is now significantly improved because of applying this experiential learning theory. The specifics of exactly how to do this may be left to the preferred general approaches of the supervisor.

Monitoring (Evaluation)

The supervision cycle depicted in Figure 5.1 is concluded by 'monitoring', when the supervisor judges the extent to which these formative methods have contributed to meeting a learning objective, as specified in the learning contract or agreed at the start of the supervision session. There are almost as many ways of conducting an evaluation as there are ways of facilitating learning, so we are again faced with the challenge of finding some meaningful way to capture the essence of evaluation. I will attempt this in summary form here, but urge the reader to study Chapter 8, which is devoted to the topic.

Evaluation is normally defined as a judgement of the extent to which objectives are achieved, guided as far as possible by research methods (Rossi *et al.*, 2003). That is, it is good professional practice for this judgement to be aided by relatively objective sources of information, such as direct observation (ideally based on checklists or rating scales), or by the use of questionnaires and structured interviews. Supervisors may also use what are formally referred to as 'permanent products', such as the clinical reports or letters written by supervisees. Such information helps the supervisor to form a more objective judgement of whether an objective is being achieved by the supervisee.

In supervision, it is customary to distinguish 'formative' from 'summative' evaluation, the formative being concerned with corrective feedback, and the latter being focused on determining whether the supervisee's performance of a competence achieves some standard required for accreditation, approval or passing a course. This is why it is sometimes referred to as the 'gate-keeping' function of supervision. Backing up my observation that apparently discrete supervision methods (as listed in Table 5.2) sometimes merge into one another, note that feedback is also a form of evaluation, including as it does praise and constructive criticism. Psychologically, this appears inevitable, as in order to offer praise or suggestions the supervisor must have in mind some notion of the desired performance. In practice, guided by the feedback I myself have had from many supervisors and experts over the years, it is probably most sensible to treat feedback (i.e. the formative dimension of evaluation) as a method for facilitating learning, keeping the summative or gate-keeping version as a distinct competency.

Conclusions

In summary, in this chapter I have outlined a supervision cycle (Figure 5.1), based on the staff development literature. I have argued that this analogy is justified because it provides a well-established approach to facilitating the learning of professionals, one that is congruent with what we know about the supervision cycle from within the supervision literature, and from basic psychological research (Bransford *et al.*, 2000). Evidence was also provided from relevant theory, expert consensus and empirical research, following the evidence-based practice approach (Parry *et al.*, 1996). This approach to defining the best-available supervisory methods may also provide a common foundation for professionals who wish to develop expertise in more specialized approaches (e.g. psychodynamic or systemic methods).

As depicted in Figure 5.1, I have presented the featured supervision methods within a workplace and professional context, something that now appears essential given recent survey data on the worryingly high levels of unacceptable supervision (Ellis *et al.*, 2014; 2015a,b). These data are given extra credibility by the frequency of disciplinary action: improper or inadequate supervision is the seventh most reported reason for disciplinary actions taken by the APA's licensing boards (APA, 2015). Thankfully, there are many features of EBCS that help to replace unacceptable supervision with excellent supervision, such as its collaborative and empowering nature, and, reflecting this emphasis, the supervisees' ratings of EBCS have always been extremely positive (e.g. Milne & James, 2002). However, feedback is essential for the supervisor as well as for the supervisee, and so in following the EBCS approach we should monitor supervision too. Chapter 8 suggests how this can be done, indicating a number of ways in which we can test out the acceptability and effectiveness of our preferred supervision methods, particularly the ones that have been outlined above. In terms of the tandem model analogy, the 'supervision cycle' is represented by the front wheel of the tandem, which is the prime responsibility of the supervisor, who is the leader and there to guide the EBCS journey. The next chapter moves on to discuss the back wheel, the supervisees' cycle.

6

Learning from Supervision

Introduction

Now the plot thickens: having set out the subtle and dynamic ways in which we might understand supervision (see Chapter 3), I now outline how such a system operates. How does the supervision cycle (described in Chapter 5) link to the supervisory alliance (outlined in Chapter 4) to produce learning? To address this question we also need to know about the supervisee cycle. In order to make sense of this profound adaptive process, the chapter starts by setting out the basic stances to development currently taken by supervisors and supervisees. Of these relationship options, the emphasis is given to the 'constructivist' one, in which it is proposed that the supervisee is assisted by the supervisor to adopt an adult, active role in the co-construction of their own competence, an interpretation that presents the supervisee as an able and energized collaborator. After clarifying the role relationship between the two parties, the next section details the ways in which the supervisee can apply these skills, in effect the 'job description' of the supervisee. This leads to a more in-depth consideration of the process whereby this list of duties actually comes together to produce learning and professional development. I illustrate the process by considering two extremes, the uncomfortable experience of 'de-skilling' and the helpful art of 'responsivity' (the subtle moment-by-moment ways in which supervisor and supervisee adjust to one another, adaptively). The chapter finishes with some detailed description of the methods that appear to be primary in this adjustment process (especially the role of reflecting on experience). As a result of this in-depth

Evidence-Based CBT Supervision: Principles and Practice, Second Edition. Derek L. Milne.
© 2018 John Wiley & Sons Ltd. Published in 2018 by the British Psychological Society and John Wiley & Sons Ltd.

consideration of how the supervisee learns from supervision, we will be moving well beyond the ineffectual 'tyranny of niceness' (Fleming *et al.*, 2007) in order to characterize an industrious, goal-directed and mutually beneficial professional relationship between supervisor and supervisee. Many of these points are consistent with the tandem model analogy: the front wheel is like the supervision cycle, controlled by the supervisor, while the rear wheel is closest to the supervisee's experience. Like tandem cyclists, both are required to play an active part in fostering progress, adapting to the context so as to achieve their learning milestones, as they make progress down the developmental path.

Relationship Stances

The tradition in supervision is that of a rather paternalistic supervisory stance, the master–apprentice relationship. In his historical review of psychoanalytic supervision, DeBell (1963) noted that 'from the very beginning of psychoanalysis to the present there has been a strong tendency for both the student and the teacher of psychoanalysis to rely heavily upon the apprentice system of teaching' (p.546). This is not entirely surprising, because the dominant ideologies of the time emphasized 'top-down' relationships. Take the example of the classic bureaucracy, a system designed to ensure that people knew their place, and that the work got done with a minimum of friction. Key characteristics of bureaucracies were the clear division of labour, where the authority and responsibilities of the parties were clearly defined, so that the different positions were organized hierarchically, including a clear chain of command. Power was granted to those with the qualifications (based on training), and competitive appointment. Strict rules, discipline and controls regarding employees' duties were in place. In exchange, members of a bureaucracy were treated with kindness and justice, and remunerated fairly within a system providing stable employment (Morgan, 1997). These principles go back to the great leaders, such as Frederick the Great, and underpinned their military machines. In terms of analogy, the master–apprentice stance in supervision is akin to the potter, someone skilled who takes raw material and fashions it to a predetermined shape.

Within supervision, the bureaucratic model for organizing social behaviour has its clearest parallel in the work of Vygotsky (1978). He regarded culture (and the way it was expressed within the social environment) as crucial to development, providing the tools and models that supervisors engineered through carefully scaffolding their supervisees' learning opportunities. In addition, Vygotsky believed that within this structure there was a maturational process which allowed the individual's biological potential to be expressed. Learning is critical to this maturational process, and is regarded as highly embedded within social interactions within what Vygotsky (1978) famously referred to as the 'zone of proximal development' (ZPD). This zone describes the area between what the learner brings to the situation (their baseline status) and what it is possible to learn with the help of someone like a slightly more able peer or a supervisor (part of the scaffolding). Such social learning becomes privately internalized and represents new knowledge or skill. Wood *et al.* (1976) examined scaffolding within a school, noting that scaffolding (by a helper they termed a 'tutor') helps the learner. In particular, the tutor excludes what is beyond the learner's capacity, focusing concentration on what is achievable. Tutoring in their study also included:

- Allowing the learner to do as much as possible without assistance;
- When it is required, providing as little assistance as is needed to aid progress (e.g. a verbal prompt is used before progressing to a demonstration);
- Encouraging self-pacing by the learner;
- Highlighting critical features of the task;
- Demonstrating task completion, by modelling the best method;
- Motivating, by encouraging the learner to engage with the task (by offering general approval within a gentle, appreciative approach; and by easing frustrations); and
- Collaborating during an interactive experience.

The account of scaffolding in Wood *et al.* (1976) is dated and draws on a school context, but I detail it here as it has been influential within the supervision field, and offers helpful procedural detail to complement Vygotsky's (1978) more theoretical account. It also respects the fact that Bruner was the first to use the term in this context, in the 1960s.

Other ways of thinking about the relationship options in supervision are behaviourism, nativism and structuralism (Strauss, 1993). Structuralism is the most prominent of these options, at least within modern approaches to supervision. According to this view, we are born with reflexes and mental structures which have biological bases but which develop psychologically from experience. Development progresses from relatively weak to more sophisticated mental structures, as indicated classically by Piaget's account of successive, universal cognitive stages. These stages are reached by actively applying existing mental structures (logical abilities) to relevant material (tasks). These structures, usually referred to as 'schemata', were thought to constrain what can be understood by a learner at any one point in time, but ultimately enable learners to develop expertise. Structuralism is therefore intermediate between nativism and behaviourism, in terms of how we relate to our environment. The emphasis is on interaction, a give-and-take relationship between the individual and the environment, although the main emphasis is on the individual.

A topical version of the structuralist (Piagetian) approach is constructivism. Particularly emblematic of the constructivist school is problem-solving, because it motivates learners (when it is relevant to their needs and interests), is cognitive in nature and it draws on what they already know (Davies, 2000). Also, this problem-solving effort occurs within a context that is thought to further strengthen the learning process. This is therefore an adult learning paradigm, 'a cooperative venture in non-authoritarian, informal learning, the chief purpose of which is to discover the meaning of experience; a quest of the mind which digs down to the roots of the pre-conceptions which formulate our conduct; a technique of learning for adults which makes education co-terminus with life and hence elevates living itself to the level of adventurous experiment' (Lindeman, 1926, p.166, cited in Davies, 2000, p.15). The constructivist approach might be more familiar to some as an empowerment model (Triantafillou, 1997), entailing a shared responsibility between a supervisor and a supervisee to deal with problems within the supervisee's work, the job of the supervisor being to provide the resources and support so that the supervisee can resolve the problem successfully, with as little help as possible. Figure 5.1 incorporated this term in the previous chapter. This is consistent with cognitive-behaviour therapy (CBT) supervision (Padesky, 1996), in the sense that the supervisor should use procedures (such as guided discovery) to clarify what a supervisee already knows about a problem, then build on these strengths, drawing out the supervisee's understanding. Similarly, Reiser (2014) describes how the CBT supervision is active, pragmatic and problem-oriented. These are concrete illustrations of how supervisor and supervisee can collaborate within Vygotsky's zone, sometimes referred to appropriately as the 'construction zone' (Newman *et al.*, 1989). Related terms are noted by Davies

(2000), ones that convey the idea that the work environment and individual learner need to be brought together skilfully by some engineer-like supervisor figure. These include cognitive apprenticeship; guided participation; reciprocal teaching; assisted performance; and contingent learning.

The everyday analogy for the supervisee's stance within a constructivist approach is that of a traveller, a journeying metaphor. Related to this, the supervisor's stance towards the supervisee is that of the mountain guide. In this sense, their relationship is one in which the supervisee needs to exert sustained effort and collaborate effectively, thereby contributing significantly to what is undertaken and achieved. This works best alongside a supervisor who behaves like a guide, as in exercising leadership, based on expertise (e.g. drawing on past experiences of travelling the developmental path). By comparison, the behavioural analogy is that of the potter, like the master–apprentice stance, a relationship where the supervisee is judged to know nothing, and the supervisor therefore takes complete control, shaping the supervisee to a predetermined form. In turn, the nativism stance can be represented by the gardener, one based on supervisees' largely taking care of their own development, with their supervisors merely ensuring optimal growing conditions, to allow supervisees to develop their potential (e.g. providing learning opportunities and resources; encouraging 'self-scaffolding').

In practice, some of these more extreme stances (such as nativism) are not viable in their pure form, because the pressures of the modern workplace mean that initial or subsequent CPD supervision has to be accountable to third parties (e.g. training programmes, professional bodies, employers' requirements of supervisors). This is not to ignore the huge significance of prior learning, however, but rather to take that as an important launch-pad. That is, whilst we might not accept Plato's belief that 'there is nothing which our immortal soul does not know, prior to our birth', we might agree that 'the advance of knowledge consists, mainly, in the modification of earlier knowledge' (Popper, 1972, pp.10–11). Hence, supervisors will tend to adopt an integrative or eclectic stance, as in conducting a learning needs assessment (to clarify 'earlier knowledge') and through utilizing a range of methods. Also, supervisees will naturally draw on multiple ways to develop their competence, as illustrated within the developmental model (i.e. a behavioural stance is typically preferred initially, but is then overtaken by a constructivist one). Therefore, the idea that there can be one sole and successful stance is a hard one to defend. More realistically, supervisors will need to be flexible, occupying different stances as necessary to enable the supervisee to progress. Although stressing adult learning and problem-solving, even strong proponents like Knowles (1990) acknowledge that there is role for a range of techniques, including didactic instruction in a situation where learners have no experience of a content area, or cannot construe how material relates to their own tasks or problems. Thus, seemingly incompatible methods of facilitating the learning process may come to be seen as complementary (Davies, 2000). This is in keeping with the emphasis in this book on a structured learning format that utilizes a blend of instructional techniques, to target the supervisee's different modes of learning (as described in the preceding chapter and set out in Figure 6.2).

As exemplified in Table 6.1, a constructivist stance means that the supervisee is assumed to have a significant and essential role in supervision. This is consistent with the starting position of Falender and Shafranske (2012), who noted that 'supervision is dynamically co-constructed, and effective supervision is the responsibility of both the supervisor and the supervisee' (p.209). Similarly, Driscoll (1999) took the view that, 'the whole success of clinical supervision ultimately rests with the willingness and

Table 6.1   How dynamic skill theory defines the supervisee's contribution to experiential learning.

Experiential learning mode	Supervisee's role
Conceptualizing	Outline how you understand material at present, and what events or experiences have shaped your competencies. Help the supervisor to understand your current grasp and application of relevant theories, research and clinical methods. Think about your stepwise development plan, and how you have benefited most in the past from supervision. Consider how different competencies and assignments are different, and how some could usefully be combined
Planning	Contribute to the task analysis that profiles your skills in an individual way, and which underpins your learning contract, session agenda and learning experiences. Seek joint/social/collaborative learning arrangements, in transfer contexts (i.e. as similar as possible to your clinical practice situation). Look for help in finding the best focus for your momentary attention, and for your best way forward in the long term

Table 6.1 (*Continued*)

Experiential learning mode	Supervisee's role
Experimenting	Learning process: assume long periods of effortful, stepwise learning on diverse tasks. Seek scaffolding from your supervisor, in terms of emotional support and intellectual stimulation. It is also vital that your new learning translates into effective clinical practice, so get the supervisor to ensure early success (e.g. by modelling or through co-working). When specific supervision methods are used (e.g. modelling or feedback), apply them to your own personal experiences, events and contexts. This eases your grasp (internalizing) and application (generalizing) of new material
Experiencing	Be prepared to risk the discomfort that accompanies de-skilling and other learning phenomena. Be prepared to learn through trial and error, groping around in your incompetent areas. Communicate how you feel about your learning experiences, and how that influences you. Develop your ability to communicate about your affective world, and have faith that you can find a way forward. Compare how it feels doing things the old way versus the new way
Reflecting	Collaborate when considering what to make of your clinical and supervisory experiences, involving the supervisor and your peers. In particular, aim to consider things from different perspectives, seeking to combine, compare, contrast and differentiate. As a result you may find that you can find a better understanding, based on greater clarity or integration

commitment of clinical supervisees to engage in it and to learn from the experience' (p.29). Perhaps the most influential account of a broadly constructivist, experiential approach to the facilitation of learning is the integrative review provided by Kolb (1984, 2014). This has been credited with providing a helpful synthesis of these different stances, a simple but intuitively appealing account that has been 'very influential amongst adult educators and trainers' (Tight, 1996, p.99), as well as within clinical supervision (Milne *et al.*, 2008a).

Because of these factors, I next turn to Kolb's account, suitably modified to take account of the points made in the last chapter. In particular, I inject a neo-Piagetian emphasis, as Piaget's theory of human development has not withstood intact the more recent logical and scientific challenges. For example, according to Case (1992), Piaget's theory failed due largely to its inability to account for cross-cultural data, to explain intra-individual variability and to accommodate for dynamic discontinuities in learning, such as U-shaped learning (covered below). Of relevance to supervision, Piaget's theory gives little attention to situational factors and the role of direct instruction, or to social relationships and joint activity, such as tutoring and peer learning, as the basis for human development. At a more fundamental level, Piaget's theory failed because the assumed logical structures (the schemata) were never demonstrated objectively: 'In research extending over most of the twentieth century, these structures have proven forever elusive, with a long series of hypotheses and empirical efforts failing again and again to demonstrate consistency in terms of a broad structure for the mind' (Fischer & Immordino-Yang, 2002, p.3).

In particular, Fischer's neo-Piagetian 'dynamic skill theory' seems especially appropriate for the supervision context, as it explicitly considers the role of the environment (including tutors), incorporates skill development and emotions, and can explain the nature of development in real-world, social contexts (e.g. Fischer *et al.*, 2003). Fischer's dynamic skill theory is also compatible with the supervision methods and reasoning within evidence-based clinical supervision (EBCS; e.g. intensive analysis of individuals during the learning process, termed 'micro-developmental' analysis but seemingly identical to the $N = 1$ methodology). Fischer's new theory differs significantly from Piaget's theory – and hence from much in Kolb (1984) – in abandoning schemata for developmental webs, in replacing developmental stages with dynamic skill levels, in incorporating social support ('contextual support'), in analysing individuals not groups and by placing activity rather than cognition centre-stage (Fischer *et al.*, 2003).

However, the practical implications of dynamic skill theory for EBCS appear to be minimal, with the great majority of the theory underlining what is already within EBCS. The most novel aspects of dynamic skill theory for EBCS lie in the explanations that are offered for the learning process, such as 'co-occurrence' and 'coordination'. Table 6.1 draws out the implications for EBCS that I detect from dynamic skill theory, in relation to the supervisee's experiential learning (as introduced in Chapter 3 and developed below). For instance, to aid conceptualizing, supervisees might outline how they understand material at present, and what events or experiences have shaped their competencies.

Role of the Supervisee

Driscoll (1999) and Falender and Shafranske (2012) offer a number of tips on how supervisees' can play their part. For example, in relation to feedback from the supervisor, Driscoll (1999) suggests the following supervisee actions:

- Ask for feedback in a way that reassures the supervisor that you are unlikely to be offended;
- Listen carefully to what is being said; even if it feels uncomfortable, resist the temptation or argue, explain or disagree;
- Clarify what the supervisor is saying to you by asking questions;
- Ask for suggestions about ways of taking the issue forward;
- Ask for some time to ponder any implied actions; and
- Thank the supervisor for responding openly to your request for feedback, acknowledging that it may not have been easy for the supervisor.

Similar lists of how the supervisee can enable supervision have been offered by Inskipp and Proctor (1993), Pearson (2004) and Hatcher and Lassiter (2007). Their suggestions overlap with those in Table 6.1, and the audit data in Figure 6.1. The recurring themes include preparing a plan for supervision (including provisional agenda items); being aware of the dynamics that can arise (trying to anticipate ways to manage these should they occur); generally having an active, collaborative role (as in helping to negotiate the agenda once supervision commences); providing information and updates on ongoing work in a structured fashion; responding to the supervisor's efforts and initiating your own (e.g. requesting guidance on procedures); seeking and offering specific feedback; initiating discussions; and accepting the discomfort and anxiety that goes with some of these activities. In this context, Pearson (2004) helpfully goes on to outline some anxiety-management strategies that supervisees might wish to use (such as positive self-statements, reframing the struggle as an opportunity for growth; drawing on social support within the peer group; openly discussing the discomfort; and asking the supervisor for suggestions). Carroll and Gilbert (2005) extend this emphasis by producing a virtual manual on how

Learning from Supervision

Hierarchical structure of the third order theme 'role of supervisee'.
[Figure in brackets = number of mentions; there were 27 other/unclassified meaning units = 11%]

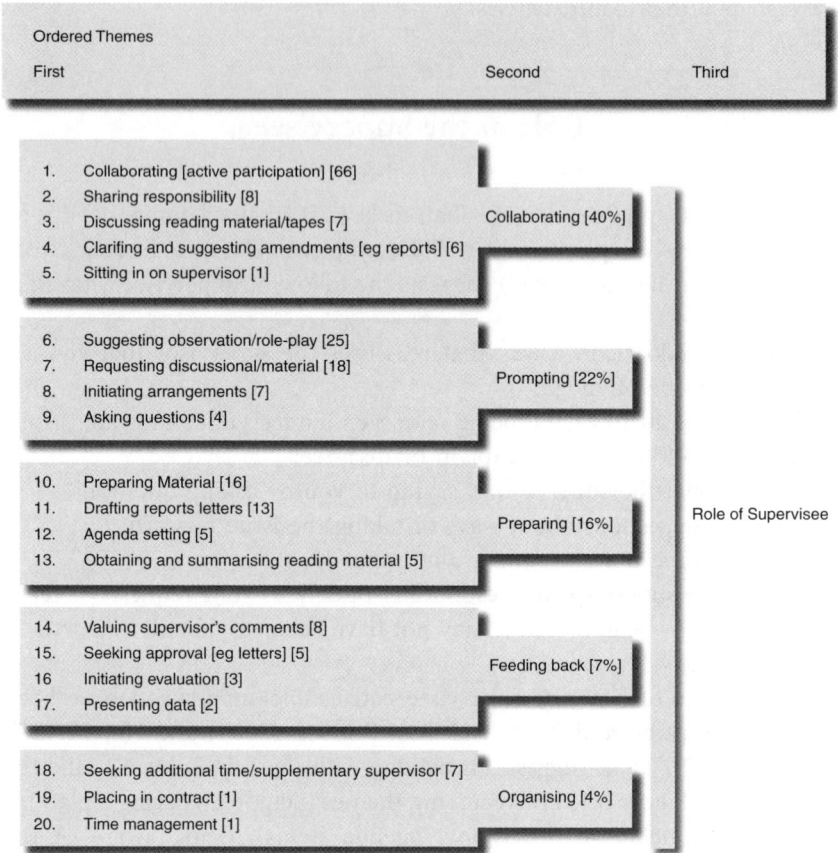

Ordered Themes

First | Second | Third

1. Collaborating [active participation] [66]
2. Sharing responsibility [8]
3. Discussing reading material/tapes [7] — Collaborating [40%]
4. Clarifing and suggesting amendments [eg reports] [6]
5. Sitting in on supervisor [1]

6. Suggesting observation/role-play [25]
7. Requesting discussional/material [18]
8. Initiating arrangements [7] — Prompting [22%]
9. Asking questions [4]

10. Preparing Material [16]
11. Drafting reports letters [13]
12. Agenda setting [5] — Preparing [16%]
13. Obtaining and summarising reading material [5]

14. Valuing supervisor's comments [8]
15. Seeking approval [eg letters] [5]
16 Initiating evaluation [3] — Feeding back [7%]
17. Presenting data [2]

18. Seeking additional time/supplementary supervisor [7]
19. Placing in contract [1] — Organising [4%]
20. Time management [1]

Role of Supervisee

Figure 6.1 A summary of the 20 ways that supervisees reported contributing to supervision, based on an audit of one year of their training experience.
Source: Milne, D.L. (2009). Reproduced with permission of Derek Milne.

to engage effectively in such activities as mutual feedback, collaborative goal-setting and reflecting on experience. Inskipp and Proctor (1993) have also written a practical handbook, detailing the respective responsibilities of the supervisor and supervisee. Again, the emphasis is on the supervisee preparing thoroughly and then engaging freely within supervision, so that they are open to feedback and prepared to try out new ideas in practice. A more recent account of the supervisee's role merits a mention because it appears to be the only book dedicated to the topic. Falender and Shafranske (2012) wrote a guide to trainees (practicum students) to 'jump-start' their experience of being a supervisee, with a strong foundation in the competence approach. Consistent with the present chapter, they encouraged supervisees to orientate their supervisors to their developmental needs, to seek and to offer feedback, to engage in reflective practice, to foster their learning alliances, to prepare and plan, and to aspire to ethical practice and personal effectiveness (e.g. self-regulation when experiencing challenging emotions).

It is worth pausing to note that these recommendations also provide detail on how the alliance ruptures (described in Chapter 4) can be repaired jointly. Even if the supervisor is understood to shoulder lead responsibility for tackling impasses, it is evident that the supervisee can sometimes make the difference and make the repair. This might arise from their personality, their motivation to make supervision a useful experience or from the technical qualities noted above.

Learning expertise

Another central resource that a supervisee can draw on is their prior experience, in particular their capacity to learn from their experiences of coping and adapting ('learning expertise'). The field of 'deliberate practice' (Ericsson, 2009) offers some insights into this rather distinctive and priceless type of proactive, metacognitive involvement by supervisees. In an expertise-based account of co-construction, Bransford and Schwartz (2009, p.432) asserted that 'it takes expertise to make expertise'. They meant that trainers should use their expertise in the facilitation of learning to prioritize the learners' expertise as a learner. They reasoned that both forms of expertise are necessary, and hence that both parties have complementary roles. Bransford and Schwartz (2009, p.433) stated that: 'Learning expertise involved the degree to which would-be experts continually attempt to refine their skills and attitudes to learning – skills and attitudes that include practicing, self-monitoring and finding ways to avoid plateaus and move to the next level.' They cited deliberate practice (see Chapter 2) as a 'powerful example' of such skill refinement. Bransford and Schwartz (2009) were discussing the development of expertise across different professions and activities, as per the tradition within the expertise literature. For example, they explicitly referred to medical physicians, musicians, golfers and chess-players to indicate that their observations on expertise were of general relevance. Similarly, they readily interchanged the terms 'coach' and 'teacher'. As they noted, learners (like supervisees) can read books, seek help from others, experiment with their environment and generally draw on the learning resources of their culture.

Although Bransford and Schwartz (2009) argued that the teacher was necessary for the development of 'routine' expertise, the very notion of learning expertise raises the possibility that some learners may at times be able to dispense with a teacher, what has been termed 'self-scaffolding'. However, they also acknowledged that other forms of 'contextual supports' might at times replace the leader, such as books, learning opportunities, self-monitoring, experimentation and information from peers (sometimes termed 'adaptive' expertise: the self-taught expert). I would imagine that most supervisees would be able to recall an example of acquiring a specific competency without any help from their supervisor, for example by learning from their patients or peers. There are also case-studies in sport where top athletes reportedly never received any coaching, and then there are the inventors and scientists who have by definition pushed boundaries beyond their teachers' guidance (although a teacher could still facilitate learning expertise or provide social support). Indeed, this self-scaffolding phenomenon is described in relation to the process of self-directed learning that Charles Darwin pursued in arriving at his theory of natural selection (Fischer *et al.*, 2003). Such self-directed learning or adaptive expertise goes beyond problem-based learning and other forms of 'discovery' learning in professional education, as the learner is assuming responsibility for the tutor's role, while using performance outcomes as feedback (Tracey *et al.*, 2014). Such case-studies draw our attention to the part played by individual differences in supervisees, something that is rather down-played within the deliberate practice literature (Hambrick *et al.*, 2014a,b).

As Bransford and Schwartz (2009) stated, patterns of adaptive and routine expertise development are not incompatible, and presumably the best approach within supervision combines both, in what they termed 'bi-directional cycles': 'Ideally, learners learn from teachers and teachers learn from learners' (p.436). For instance, both can provide one another with feedback, and work symbiotically in terms of the learning contract. Some rare examples from supervision of self-scaffolding and a generally symbiotic approach are described below (e.g. Green *et al.*, 2014).

Where are the data?

As is often the case within a developing field, suggestions and guidelines tend to dominate, whereas data regarding what actually happens tend to be scarce. In this context, the Ellis and Ladany (1997) review is of particular relevance, noting as it does the role that the supervisee must have in enabling the alliance to be successful. However, their conclusions about the overall significance of the alliance were muted, and no specific data on supervisee input were reported. Analyses of the supervision alliance do, however, bear out the significant role of the supervisee. The Supervisory Working Alliance Inventory (Efstation *et al.*, 1990) has a supervisee version which includes two factors: 'rapport' and 'client focus'. Relevant items include 'My supervisor encourages me to formulate my own interventions with the client' and 'My supervisor helps me work within a specific treatment plan', respectively.

There are also some data from an audit, undertaken within a training programme for clinical psychologists (Milne & Gracie, 2001). In that study we took a one-year sample of the material recorded in the trainees' 'supervision record' (a standard form maintained by all traineeswithin the programme). Their replies to the question about how they had contributed to supervision were summarized inductively, to produce a content analysis of their input to the supervision that they had received. Figure 6.1 displays their replies, in the form of a dendrogram.

Of the possible sample of 73 trainees, 59 supervision records were available for analyses. Of these, 51 (86 per cent) had at least one entry about the supervisee's role or contribution to supervision, and a total of 239 meaning units were extracted. These were then categorized into 20 first-order themes, as set out in Figure 6.1. It can be seen that by far the most common theme was collaborating with the supervisor, which was noted on 40 per cent of occasions. This mainly took the form of actively participating in supervision, which we bracketed with sharing responsibility, discussing material, clarifying, suggesting amendments and sitting in on the supervisor. This is highly consistent with the opinions and consensus statement above, as are the remaining first-order themes in Figure 6.1. It is heartening to see that 'prompting' is the second most frequently reported supervisee activity, backing up the idea that the supervisee co-constructs supervision.

This kind of general summary can be brought to life by personal descriptions of the experience of collaborating. For instance, Brown and Ash (2001) provided a 'supervisee's tale', which noted the experience of progressing from a time when supervision dragged on and was dreaded, to it becoming something that was engaging and tiring (because of the amount of effort the supervisee was investing). In a notably candid fashion, the supervisee noted how the relationship that was established played a crucial part in facilitating the expression of difficult thoughts and feelings. A further way to enliven general pronouncements or audit data is by detailed observation of the interactions between supervisor and supervisee. James *et al.* (2004) captured their own brand of difficult thoughts and feelings by examining the phenomenology of the supervisory process. They accomplished this by means of video recordings of five consecutive weeks of CBT supervision, focusing on one index patient. Following each supervision session, both supervisor and supervisee kept independent audio-taped commentaries of the session, based on viewing the recording. The instructions to the supervisor and supervisee were: 'while watching the recording, please describe your experiences of the supervision using the Dictaphone provided. Please give specific details about your feelings, physical sensations and thoughts' (p.509). The supervisor and supervisee then met to discuss the resulting data, so as to reflect on the dynamic processes associated with their supervision. The most frequent emotion reported for the supervisee was anxiety, which was reported on 38 occasions within four supervision sessions (i.e. meetings with the supervisor falling in between the clinical work with this patient). The supervisee's transcript in relation to feeling anxious included examples such as: 'I felt put on the spot'; 'I thought: "Oh no"'; 'I was worried because . . . '; 'I did not feel comfortable.' The other emotions were those of feeling contained (27 occasions; included the supervisee feeling safe and pleased with himself or herself); feeling relieved (13 occasions); feeling confused (9 occasions); feeling interested and intrigued (2 occasions); and feeling angry (2 occasions). One can also bring to life the role of the supervisee within a quantitative approach. Examples are provided in the next section, based on observing the micro-processors and outcomes of routine clinical supervision.

More recent examples of research on the supervisee's contribution include a survey of 363 trainees conducted by Ellis *et al.* (2014) to assess self-reported instances of inadequate or harmful supervision. In terms of one indicator (developing a clear agreement regarding the ongoing roles, responsibilities and tasks of supervision), Ellis *et al.* (2014) found that a majority of the supervisors involved (54 per cent) were reported to not use a written consent or a supervision contract. A contributory factor may be that the trainees were too anxious to play their full part in establishing a learning contract, and in this regard Ellis *et al.* (2015b) examined the effects of a two-hour workshop to clarify expectations regarding supervision, and to provide information about roles and responsibilities. This role induction appeared to reduce anxiety in beginner or novice trainees. The review of recent research provided by Inman *et al.* (2014) noted that supervisees are not usually trained in the optimal use of supervision. This is paradoxical, as 'one of the important facets of clinical training is the supervisee's ability to make use of his or her supervision experience . . . research suggests that supervisees with greater cognitive complexity and self-awareness or reflectivity more readily develop specific clinical skills and utilize supervision effectively' (Inman *et al.*, 2014, p.64). Conversely, they noted that supervisees may also have personal qualities that impede their development, such as unresolved personal issues, unwillingness to accept feedback or limited motivation. One of the rare studies of supervisee empowerment was by Green *et al.* (2014), within six Improving Access to Psychological Therapies (IAPT) services in England. Using interviews, supervisees' self-ratings and supervisors' ratings, Green *et al.* (2014) clarified that the more effective supervisees were more proactive (e.g. observing other clinicians), better prepared and more organized (e.g. assembling key material in advance). Similarly, Edmunds *et al.* (2013) reported from a study involving 99 supervisees that their active engagement in experiential learning affected their skill development. Those 'who were more involved in consultation benefitted more from behavioural rehearsal conducted during consultation sessions' (p.462: the consultation was remotely provided supervision).

Additional to research on the role of the supervisee, it is important to consider expert consensus statements. For example, a report on practicum (i.e. training placement) competencies was developed in the USA by the Association of Directors of Psychology Training Clinics (Hatcher & Lassiter, 2007). There is a comforting degree of overlap between this consensus statement and the earlier material, as both stress how the supervisee needs to be aware of local issues regarding feedback, and so on. This statement goes on to detail 'professional developmental competencies' such as critical thinking, reflection and awareness of how one's own personal identity may influence what goes on in supervision. But perhaps the clearest illustration of how this consensus statement acknowledges the vital role of the supervisee is in the final section, on metacognition. It is recognized there that the training programme needs to help the supervisee to develop this particularly powerful form of reflective understanding, as it is concerned with how they know what they know, and come to discover what they do not know. The emphasis on metacognition clearly articulates how the learner can reflect in order to draw on their available skills, and thereby solve problems. More recently, a competence statement has been generated in the UK, partly based on seeking input from experts throughout the country (Roth & Pilling, 2007). In this document, concerned with the core competencies of CBT, the main contributions made by the supervisee are thought to be:

- An ability to work collaboratively with the supervisor (e.g. clarifying respective roles; presenting an honest and open account of work undertaken; discussing work in an active and engaged manner – i.e. without become passive, avoidant, defensive or aggressive);
- Capacity for self-appraisal and reflection (being open and realistic about their capabilities, and sharing this self-appraisal with the supervisors; using their feedback to develop the capacity for accurate self-appraisal);
- Contributing to active learning (taking up suggestions regarding relevant reading and applying this material; taking the initiative in searching for and drawing on relevant literature);
- Ability to use supervision to reflect on developing a personal and professional role (using supervision to discuss the personal impact of one's work, especially related to one's effectiveness); and
- Capacity to reflect on the quality of supervision (seeking advice and guidance where there is concern about the quality of supervision or where the supervisor's actions are unacceptable, breaching professional guidelines).

A specific approach identified more recently by Pilling and Roth (2014) is to encourage the supervisees to engage in 'self-practice, self-reflection' (SP/SR; Bennett-Levy *et al.*, 2001), the use of CBT techniques by supervisees in order to promote their own CBT learning (e.g. by completing thought records).This forms part of the aim of ensuring 'that supervisees are active participants' (Pilling & Roth, 2014, p.30). This is consistent with the APA (2015) guidelines on supervision, which recognized supervisee self-assessment as a means of strengthening the supervisee's reflective practice and competence. The expert group convened by Falender *et al.* (2004) also noted the importance of empowering the supervisee. Table 6.2 and the surrounding section below provide examples of how the supervisee can contribute to the success of supervision through managing the emotional aspects of experiential learning.

Table 6.2 Examples of the supervisee managing emotional aspects of de-skilling in supervision.

Experiential learning mode	Supervisee actions that support experiential learning
'Experiencing'	Prompt the supervisor to self-disclose the emotions he or she feels during difficult or satisfying clinical work
'Reflecting'	In preparation for casework supervision, draw a formulation that crystallizes your current grasp of a client's difficulties. Engage fully with the task, concentrating hard
'Conceptualizing'	Ask for guided reading from your supervisor, making a point of agreeing an objective (e.g. two ideas for a reformulation) and discussing the outcome next time, to judge your understanding
'Experimenting'	Contribute to enactive learning by providing tapes of challenging aspects of your current work, and by engaging in educational role-plays while managing the associated anxiety
'Planning'	Engage the supervisor in generating and appraising some options for an action plan, based on presenting a plan that flopped

Source: Milne, D.L. (2009). Reproduced with permission of Derek Milne.

The process of learning from supervision

Whether it is the supervisee or the supervisor who initiates an episode of experiential learning (through activities like giving feedback), a critical issue is how such learning unfolds. The better we understand this process, the more efficient we can be in facilitating and benefiting from learning opportunities. The expert consensus guidelines and research findings noted above refer to how various aspects of the supervisee's learning contribute to the learning process, such as reflection on feedback. This process will now be clarified and formulated, as depicted in Figure 6.2. Figure 6.2 represents the supervisee cycle, which is analogous to the back wheel of the tandem model of supervision (see Chapter 3). Although depicted as a circular wheel, to continue the analogy with the tandem, it is more accurate to think of experiential learning as a succession of developmental cycles, in the form of a rather uneven spiral (Vec *et al.*, 2014). This is why Kolb (1984) termed this learning process the 'spiral curriculum', with setbacks such as de-skilling and alliance ruptures causing the uneven progress.

Contextual factors

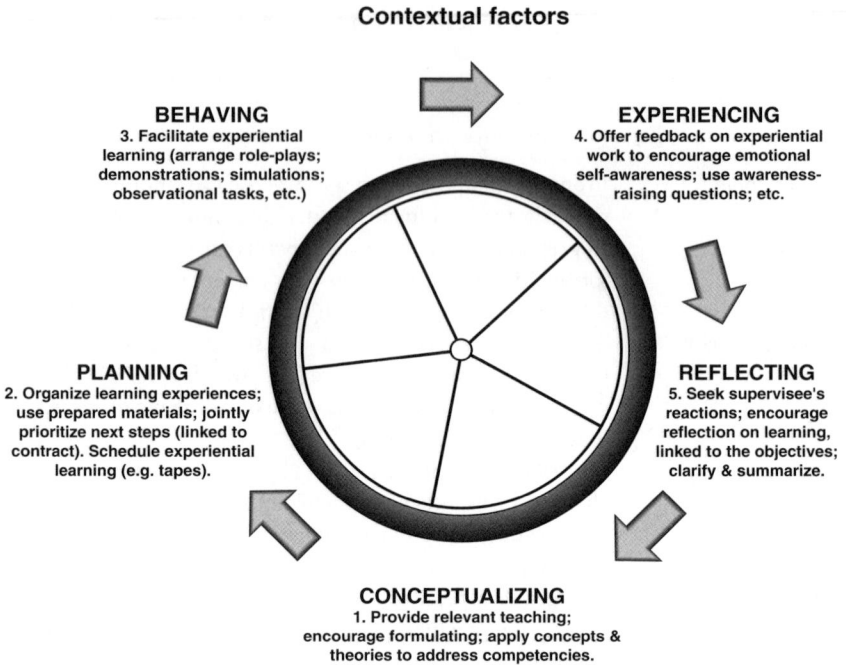

BEHAVING
3. Facilitate experiential learning (arrange role-plays; demonstrations; simulations; observational tasks, etc.)

EXPERIENCING
4. Offer feedback on experiential work to encourage emotional self-awareness; use awareness-raising questions; etc.

PLANNING
2. Organize learning experiences; use prepared materials; jointly prioritize next steps (linked to contract). Schedule experiential learning (e.g. tapes).

REFLECTING
5. Seek supervisee's reactions; encourage reflection on learning, linked to the objectives; clarify & summarize.

CONCEPTUALIZING
1. Provide relevant teaching; encourage formulating; apply concepts & theories to address competencies.

Figure 6.2 The supervisee cycle, depicting an idealized process of experiential learning (capitals), facilitated by supervision (the numbered points).
Source: Milne, D.L. (2009). Reproduced with permission of Derek Milne.

Figure 6.2, from the evidence-based CBT supervision manual (Milne & Reiser, 2017), is a simplified version of Kolb's (2014) experiential learning cycle, itself based on earlier versions by prominent theorists (including Piaget, Dewey, Vygotsky and Lewin; see Chapter 3). The supervisee's cycle combines the five learning modes described in Chapter 3 (i.e. conceptualizing, planning, behaving/experimenting, experiencing and reflecting), setting them out in a simpler, more accessible form than in the circumplex figure within that chapter (see Figure 3.3). However, the logic remains the same, and so Figure 6.2 is in effect a fresh representation of the experiential learning process, suggesting what is required for learning to occur. The wheel is intended to capture the idea that learning is a complex cyclical process, combining thoughts, feelings and behaviours (Vec *et al.*, 2014). Although set out as a neat, idealized sequence of five learning modes (with associated supervisor activities, drawn from Chapter 5), this formulation is

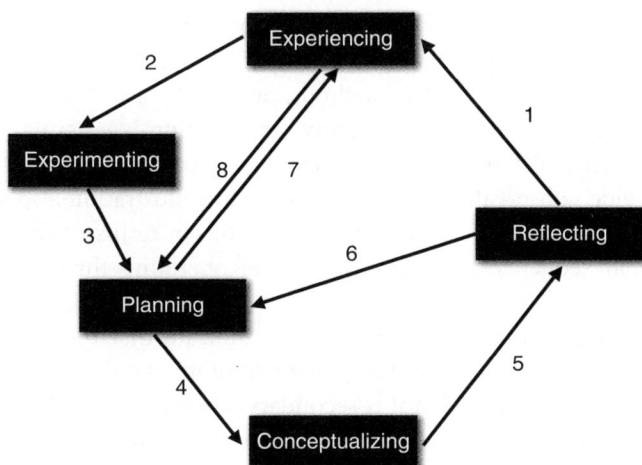

Figure 6.3 An illustration of how one supervisee actually engaged in the supervisee cycle.

purely to aid understanding, rather than to suggest that learning will only occur if this precise sequence is followed. In practice, supervision can start with any of these modes of learning, and can be initiated by the supervisee or the supervisor. For example, in Figure 4.1 the hypothetical experiential learning episode that is depicted is started by the supervisor disclosing some doubts, which initiates a process that involves the supervisee also sharing doubts, leading to a stronger supervision alliance. Actual examples drawn from an 11-month long study of EBCS can be found in Milne *et al.* (2013). Complementary ways of depicting the process of experiential learning have been provided by James *et al.* (2004) and by Johnston and Milne (2012), both based on empirical research. Figure 6.3 provides an illustration of how one supervisee proceeded to learn during a successful supervision episode, drawn from the Milne and James (2002) study, as observed and recorded by Haines (2006). Prompted by a question from the supervisor, Figure 6.3 shows the supervisee starting to reflect on something ('I think I revert back to . . . '), and how, within the 12.5-minute duration of this episode (guided by the supervisor), the supervisee went from one learning mode to another (and sometimes back again), ultimately using all five modes. This balanced or 'integrated' (Kolb, 1984) cycle is clearly not as neat as depicted in the supervisee cycle (Figure 6.2), but it is functionally equivalent. This is because all five modes are engaged, which is logically why an episode occurred (defined in terms of a supervision interaction that has a successful resolution). Across this whole study (Milne & James, 2002), the supervisor also utilized up to 14 different methods, and in the six observed maintenance phase sessions he most frequently used 'guiding experiential learning' (106 instances), 'listening' (89), 'informing/educating' (57), 'supporting' (24) and 'video observation' (21). Therefore, this illustration also serves to indicate the complexity of effective supervision, in terms of the dynamic interactional sequence between two people operating through multiple methods.

These examples of the learning process indicate that the five learning modes mediate experiential learning, singly or more often in various combinations, and also indicate that it is secondary whether the supervisor or the supervisee initiates the process. What matters is that the supervisee has the opportunity to engage sufficiently in the learning cycle, engaging enough to grasp and transform their understanding. 'Grasping' is defined as 'seizing and holding firmly . . . understanding and comprehending fully . . . a person's capacity to attain something' (*Concise Oxford English Dictionary*, 2004, p.621). Dewey (1938, p.83) gives the example of how a child grasps something: 'when a child of two . . . learns not to approach a flame too closely and yet to draw near enough to a stove to get its warmth . . . it is grasping and using the causal relation'. The same dictionary defines transformation as: 'marked change in nature; converting or transferring material'. According to Kolb (1984, p.38), it is a 'process of continually creating and recreating knowledge, through transactions between opposed ways of knowing (including personal versus public)'. This process involves operating within the dialectic tensions between two fundamentally different ways of knowing about our world: grasping our experience through apprehension, versus grasping it through comprehension. Apprehension ('experiencing' in Figure 6.2) is primarily a private, emotional way of knowing, including the awareness of sensations, and intuitive, 'right brain' awareness. This is thought to be opposed to (i.e. in tension with) the way that we understand the world cognitively, through what is termed in Figure 6.2 as 'conceptualization' (the remaining modes are discussed below). This latter way of grasping our experience is based on public knowledge, epitomized by what is known through the scientific method, and through the supervisor's understanding. A recent theoretical review by Veilleaux *et al.* (2013) revived the notion of opposing forces ('dialectical tensions'). Examples that they cited included the tension between the supervisor and the supervisee over support and challenge, and the question of taking the lead during supervision (a tension for the supervisor between taking and giving responsibility). This kind of tension arises naturally because the supervisee's experiential learning will tend to foster professional development, and with it a growing sense that the supervisee requires greater autonomy and responsibility in order to thrive.

As a result of the contrast between these two structural components (akin to the traditional contrast between knowing in one's heart and knowing in one's head, respectively), there is a dynamic process or 'rhythm' that moves from a rather de-stabilized and uncomfortable lack of knowing or incompetence (e.g. de-skilling), to a point where something is ultimately grasped. In this sense, the heart and the head find a mutually acceptable way of making sense of material, mental balance is restored and some experiential learning has taken place. This can therefore be thought of as the 'internal' transformation of material, a private, largely cognitive episode. The notion of stability or balance is used to convey the conclusion of a learning episode ('equilibration'), whereas opposite terms are used to refer to the unstable and uncomfortable experience during engagement in learning (imbalance, destablization or 'dis-equilibration'). This turbulence should be managed by the supervisor, to create optimal challenge to the supervisee's existing understanding (e.g. through Socratic questioning). When the challenge is excessive the supervisee may disengage (e.g. avoidance or escape behaviours, such as not providing tapes of therapy), or may experience de-skilling (see next section), but when there is too little challenge the supervisee is likely to become bored and disengaged.

The functions of transformation are to give personal meaning to material, and to enable the individual to applying the new meaning to solve problems. Examples include making associations or analogies; creating metaphors; making initial inductions; understanding and applying information or a method/principle/law (e.g. constructing a framework, taxonomy or graph); and abstraction (e.g. classified, generalized and transfer). A useful guide to understanding these concepts can be found in Moseley *et al.* (2005). In this sense, then, 'Learning is the process whereby knowledge is created through the transformation of experience' (Kolb, 1984, p.38).

Lastly, we should note that we need to consider experiential learning alongside the contextual factors noted in Figure 6.2. Veilleaux *et al.* (2013) also emphasized the context for supervision, taking the view that the 'current context...pervades and informs all aspects of the supervisory endeavour. Each individual player (the supervisor, the supervisee and the client) has his or her own cultural background, and the therapy sessions as well as supervision sessions take place at a particular point in time, in a clinical setting embedded in a larger community, each imbued with a myriad of cultural norms and processes' (p.5).

Although still popular (e.g. Vec *et al.*, 2014), this account of how we learn from experience has ancient roots. To quote Popper (1972):

> Neither observation nor reason are authorities. Intellectual intuition and imagination are most important, but they are not reliable: they show us things very clearly, and yet they may mislead us. They are indispensable as the main sources of our theories; but most of our theories are wrong anyway. The most important function of observation and reasoning, and even of intuition and imagination, is to help us in the critical examination of those bold conjectures which are the means by which we probe into the unknown (p.28).

To place this section in context, it is also salutary to note that trying to comprehend the learning process has proved extremely challenging for researchers, making it the dominant issue in the study of cognitive development (Siegler, 1995).

De-skilling

Concepts like imbalance and destablization, which are used in explaining experiential learning, recognize the inherent discomfort that may arise for the supervisee during experiential learning, referred to by Kolb (1984) as a 'tension and conflict-filled process' (p.30). He thought that successfully resolving these tensions and conflicts resulted in either assimilation (the connection of new material to existing schema: the learning process) or accommodation (where new schemata are required to understand our world: the development process). Unsuccessful learning experiences are naturally aversive to the supervisee, as in the example of de-skilling. De-skilling is something that most people will have experienced and not forgotten quickly. It refers to feeling confused, helpless and incompetent during an unsuccessful period of training. It is incorporated most clearly in the writing of developmental theorists (e.g. Friedman & Kaslow, 1986; Skovholt & Ronnestad, 1992), but is little discussed within the supervision literature. A rare example is the developmental angle on de-skilling that has been provided by Stoltenberg and McNeill (1997), who assume that a supervisee's competence will fluctuate, possibly as a result of excess complexity, which shakes confidence and leads to 'confusion, despair, vacillation' (p.190). This is consistent with the findings from rigorous experimental research within the field of cognitive science, where developmental paths (growth curves) show how new, challenging skills develop through repeated rebuilding, in a robust wave-like pattern of construction, deconstruction and reconstruction stages (rather than a linear, steadily progressive trend; Fischer *et al.*, 2003). Formally, this has been termed 'backward progression', better known colloquially as 'two steps forward, one back', or as the 'back to scratch' phenomenon. Interestingly, these authors suggest that this backward progression pattern follows the basic form of growth in biology, which includes periods of turbulence leading to rapid growth. This growth is so rapid that it 'overshoots' the natural limits of the system, like the cognitive overload hypothesis in supervision (i.e. too much to think about at once).

It is the subsequent correction of this overshoot that is thought to produce the turbulence within de-skilling episodes. Fischer *et al.* (2003) believe that cognitive science provides a strong foundation for educational research and practice, indicated by intensive ('microdevelopmental') analysis of how individual students learn in school classrooms. By means of technological sophistication, including computer modelling of the learning process as it unfolds, students' learning of a new task has been commonly found to follow a pattern of initial regression (de-skilling), before gradually recovering and mastering the skill (at least for new, challenging tasks). By contrast, less challenging tasks (defined as tasks within the learner's functional scope) are learnt following a smooth progression. In turn, this information is considered to provide a powerful tool for improving educational practice, for example through the feedback of the students' learning processes to inform the teachers' classroom practices.

Supervisors and supervisees need to address these uncomfortable, seemingly paradoxical experiences, as they are widely viewed as a natural and necessary phase in human development. For instance, recognition of this pattern of discomfort, destabilization and ultimate development is also part of the psychodynamic view. Learning, by its very nature, is thought to challenge our current understanding and 'thus invariably involves uncertainty, some degree of frustration and disappointment. This experience is a painful one' (Salzberger-Wittenberg *et al.*, 1983, p.54). In this sense, it has recently been argued that there should be 'desirable difficulties' within experiences such as supervision, such as providing contextual interference or reducing feedback during learning, as this promotes long-term retention and transfer (Bjork, 2006). The term 'perplexity' has also been used to capture the idea of the desirable but initially discomforting process of gentle de-skilling (Dewey, 1910).

Such theories are also borne out by a large body of research within the field of developmental psychology, where this pattern of de-skilling is referred to as 'U-shaped' development (Pauls *et al.*, 2013). There is also support from the limited research that is available within the supervision literature. For instance, in-depth interviews with family therapy trainees indicated that a number of these trainees had found the training experience to be 'overwhelming and de-skilling' (Nel, 2006, p.307). An integrative theoretical account of this de-skilling process has been provided by Zorga (2002), who appealed to Piaget's notion of 'equilibration' (i.e. balance between schema). When this balance is disturbed (dis-equilibration) we feel de-skilled and material we are dealing with cannot be readily assimi-lated and hence appeals for a new schema, the act of accommodation within Piagetian thinking. This means that new ways of thinking about the stimulus material are developed, so that future responses are qualitatively different (e.g. occur at a higher level of processing). Successive episodes of dis-equilibration and adjustment yield the classic spiral of upward devel-opment, the process through which balance is temporarily re-established and our special human talent for learning and adaptation takes place. In this sense, as pointed out by Dewey (1955), it follows that the supervisee cycle in Figure 6.2 should actually be conceived of as a spiral rather than as a circle. According to Kolb (1984), this upward spiral is cone-like in shape, as it culminates in increased integration of the different modes of knowing, and in a progression to a more unified and sophisticated relationship to our world. Expressed differently, three developmental stages make up this conical process: initial acquisition, growing specialization and ultimately integration. Although these are described classically in terms of the whole lifespan (e.g. 'acquisition' occurring between birth and adolescence), one can also think of these in relation to a supervisee's development of competence in one particular area over a relatively short period of time.

Although a number of authors appear to accept this account of how learning occurs, and there are experimental demonstrations (Bjork, 2006), there is surprisingly little advice or research on de-skilling within the professional development literature (Lombardo *et al.*, 2009). In one study, James *et al.* (2001) studied how qualified mental health staff attending a training programme in CBT varied in their learning trajectory over the nine-month period of this part-time course. A multidisciplinary group of 20 professionals were assessed at three time points, using the Cognitive Therapy Scale. The authors reported a mid-training dip in the competence levels of these professionals, which was attributed to a destabilizing of their understanding, specifically because of systematic reflection and questioning (James *et al.*, 2006). In fact, this dip was only observed for the 11 females within the study sample, and did not reach significance. Rather, it stood out because it was discrepant from the significant overall increase in competence by the end of training for the whole group. In a related study, Lovell (2002) studied the development of 67 counsellors attending a Masters course. Using the Supervisee Levels Questionnaire, Lovell reported a 'discontinuous pattern' (p.235) in the students' development. He also appealed to the notion of dis-equilibration to explain how their competence fluctuated. Gonsalvez *et al.* (2015a) also noted a faltering progression in a sample of 204 trainee clinical psychologists in Australia: large initial improvements in competence were followed by small and non-significant variations. This de-skilling pattern can be obvious to the supervisee and supervisor alike, as illustrated by a longitudinal study of 24 cognitive therapy trainees undergoing a one-year part-time course (Bennett-Levy & Beedie, 2007). The six self-ratings completed during the course were similar to their supervisors' ratings of their competence, including setbacks and a loss of confidence during this period, which the authors considered normal. These fluctuations in the supervisees were attributed to the process of acquiring competence, including self-reflection on their performance, increased awareness of the required standards and emotional state (e.g. current life stress).

Another way of capturing this de-skilling process is to study critical incidents within supervision. These are episodes or events that are perceived as being a catalyst for change. Furr and Carroll (2003) adopted this research approach with 84 Masters-level counselling students by means of an end-of-term questionnaire, made up of open-ended questions eliciting their experiences of 'positive or negative experiences recognized as significant' (p.485). They found that the most frequently reported critical incidents were those related to experiences within clinical supervision that affected their development as professionals, and that involved emotional obstacles and personal growth. Students also acknowledged that events beyond the training programme had also contributed significant critical events to their development (e.g. personal growth arising from interpersonal involvement with partners and friends, and the private counselling that they received).

Furr and Carroll (2003) concluded that critical incidents were frequent, arising from a wide range of influences, but that the dominant influence was experiential learning. 'It seemed that experiential learning activities had a greater emotional impact than did courses based on cognitive learning strategies' (p.487).

Although little-researched in relation to supervision, this de-skilling phenomenon is well established within the clinical practice of CBT. For example, in CBT clinical practice it is recognized that the patient has to endure unpleasant emotions in order to better understand and cope with clinical problems. Wells (1997), for instance, describes how 'affect shifts' (changes in emotion during therapy) should be monitored, in order to access the patient's negative automatic thoughts (he even advocates using role-play, to manipulate affect therapeutically). In general, it has been noted from a review of research in CBT that minimizing affect shifts can render the approach ineffective (e.g. through allowing safety behaviours, such as compulsive washing rituals, to regulate anxiety; Roth & Fonagy, 1996). In summary, although supervisees might naturally seek to minimize de-skilling experiences, it is important to reframe these as a necessary part of the undulating path of development. But the accompanying emotions are still distressing at times, making it useful to understand more about the way that our emotions operate during experiential learning.

The role of emotions in the learning process

Phenomena such as de-skilling are potentially problematic, as strongly aversive experiences of incompetence or discomfort may very well cause the supervisee to withdraw from experiential learning. A case-study by Milne *et al.* (2009) illustrates how the supervisor can end up colluding in the avoidance of experiential learning. Therefore, such emotions need to be managed carefully, which is fundamentally the job of the supervisor (because they are the formal leader), whilst it falls on the supervisee to process them constructively (as in reframing them). In terms of the tandem model, this means working within the supervisee's zone of affective toler-ance or comfort. As noted by Bennett-Levy (2006), a state of 'inner discomfort' (p.67) can helpfully focus attention and mobilize the super-visee's adjustment, for example through reformulating the experience as potentially beneficial, or by construing it as a fascinating or perplexing business. By one means or another, the effective supervisee, aided by a containing and responsive supervisor, will work through this challenge to engage constructively in their professional learning and adaptation. Table 6.1 illustrates how this might be done in relation to the five modes of learning from experience (Figure 6.3).

The examples in Table 6.2 represent self-regulation by the individual (Warr & Downing, 2000), involving emotional control (ways of warding off excess anxiety and ensuring good concentration), motivation control (ways of staying activated when disinterested) and comprehension monitoring (procedures that allow the supervisee to assess progress towards learning goals and to modify their learning experience as necessary). This kind of self-regulation has been found to directly influence learning outcomes (Vermunt & Verloop, 1999). This is consistent with theory, in that emotional and cognitive development can be understood to influence one another. This happens through processes such as the emotions generated through event appraisal and the on-going emotional accompaniments to thinking and behaving (e.g. emotion-based self-control through approach and avoidance behaviours). According to dynamic skill theory, emotions organize behaviour whenever they are activated, profoundly shaping learning and development (Fischer *et al.*, 1989). To be concrete, using examples from her own experience, Reilly (2000) argues that CBT practitioners and supervisors should not only identify, experience and normalize emotions, but that they should also use their feelings as a guide to more effective practice.

Vermunt and Verloop (1999) provide a helpful list of coping strategies applicable to supervisees. For instance, in relation to remaining motivated, supervisees might develop appropriate expectations about supervision and about its processes. This may include self-reinforcement for attaining sub-goals, thinking of the negative consequences of failing and generally trying to generate interest in a topic. In order to concentrate and exert due effort, they recommend focusing attention on the task-relevant aspects. When it comes to judging oneself (attributing), the authors suggest ascribing success in achieving sub-goals to internal causal factors (i.e. under the control of the supervisee). Conversely, negative experiences should be attributed to a lack of effort, or some variable that is beyond their control. When it comes to dealing with emotions, Vermunt and Verloop (1999) suggest coping with negative emotions by talking to oneself in a reassuring way and by setting realistic learning goals.

Although plausible, it appears that the relationship between these coping strategies and learning is far from straightforward (Hook & Bunce, 2001).

For instance, in an empirical analysis of a training situation, Warr and Downing (2000) found an interaction between these seemingly adaptive coping strategies and learning. For example, the coping strategy of emotional control had a significant negative correlation with learning, but only for those with high levels of learning anxiety. Part of this complex relationship may also be a result of the supervisor's approach. For example, consider the findings from interviews conducted with psychotherapy trainees about a counter-productive event in supervision (an experience that they perceived as hindering, unhelpful or harmful in relation to their learning and development; Gray *et al.*, 2001). A typical example was the supervisor's dismissal of the trainee's thoughts and feelings, so lacking empathy or denying a trainee's request. All of the trainees reported such events but, more interestingly, they reported that this led to subsequent counter-productive interactions, such as the trainee trying hard to be agreeable, but finding the supervisor was not responding or disputed and challenged the trainee. This sequence was perceived by all 13 interviewees as weakening the supervisory alliance, to the point where most did not raise their experience of negative events with the supervisors concerned. This indicates how a vicious cycle or downward developmental spiral may arise, arguably because the supervisees did not utilize adaptive coping strategies. The case-study reported by Milne *et al.* (2009) is another illustration.

By contrast, as indicated in Table 6.2, they may help to engineer a virtuous cycle by working with the supervisor to try to repair such relationship ruptures (Safran & Muran, 2000). An empirical assessment of such effort has been conducted by Zorga (2002), who analysed how clinical reports were treated within supervision. There was a general feeling amongst the professionals in this study that supervision had helped them to become more confident and self-respecting, resulting in them looking to their own resources for answers, rather than relying on the supervisor. As they developed strengths and this constructive attitude to problem-solving, they were reportedly better able to recognize emergent feelings and to express these clearly and effectively. This account is akin to the gestalt therapy process described by Greenberg and Malcolm (2002), who examined how individuals resolved 'unfinished business' (e.g. childhood mistreatment) by having them express their feelings about the issue constructively. This led to 'adopting a more self-affirming stance' (p.407).

These kinds of relationship interactions are addressed more thoroughly in Chapter 4. The main point that I am making here is that the supervisee is inevitably involved in shaping the effectiveness of supervision. With appropriate coping skills, supervisees can significantly co-construct supervision. Supervisors are ideally placed to enable the development of such skills.

Responsivity

An example of a more comfortable transactional process is one involving the supervisor's responsivity to de-skilling or challenging episodes within supervision. The Zorga (2002) illustration points to this fascinating and vital aspect of the supervisory process. The concept of responsivity, like many within this book, is borrowed from the psychotherapy literature, in order to develop the idea of co-construction. According to the responsivity logic, both supervisor and supervisee make appropriate adjustments in their behaviour as a result of the context and the moment-to-moment changes in each other's requirements (Stiles & Shapiro, 1994). Their interaction is governed by a set of complementary roles, and results in joint participation in the supervisory process. This should be contrasted with the dominant drug metaphor concept in psychotherapy (Stiles & Shapiro, 1994), which would lead us to assume that the right 'recipe' of supervision ingredients (e.g. goal-setting and feedback) would explain the link between process and outcome. This metaphor ignores processes like responsiveness, which is thought to be made up of responsive speech acts, and which might better explain how people learn and change. Responsive speech acts include enquiring, exploring, reframing and interpreting. As these categories imply, in therapy the patient is an active contributor to this responsive process (Stiles & Shapiro, 1994). Similarly, as illustrated by some of the examples in Table 6.2, the supervisee also needs to be responsive to the supervisor.

In a subsequent analysis of the therapeutic alliance, Stiles *et al.* (2004) studied different alliance setback profiles in brief therapies, such as the 'U-shaped' and 'V-shaped' development slopes. They only found support for the 'V-shaped' pattern. This is the 'rupture–repair' pattern, where a stormy relationship with an initially strong alliance (large sessional fluctuations) subsequently deteriorates. Consistent with Bennett-Levy (2006) and the rupture–repair logic (Safran *et al.*, 2007), those in the stormy relationships actually achieved similar or better clinical outcomes than the clients with different profiles, attributed by the authors to the therapists' responsivity. Specifically, therapists responded effectively to fluctuations by encouraging emotional experiencing, by enhancing insight and through providing structure. As a result, instead of a therapy rupture, the clients with a V-shaped profile appeared to learn from their setbacks, as a result of their therapists addressing them effectively as they occurred.

Methods of Learning from Supervision

Most of the competencies outlined above, from self-regulation to their own responsivity, are part of the general skills that supervisees bring to supervision. After all, they are part of the repertoire that probably enabled them to obtain a place on a competitive training programme (where such personal and interpersonal qualities tend to be prized), and are in any case part of being an effective professional. Appropriately, this emphasis mirrors the rest of this book, in that I have similarly assumed the transferability of supervisors' general professional competencies in relation to supervision (see, for example, Chapter 1). If supervisors can 'hit the ground running' because of these general skills when it comes to supervision, so can the supervisee. And to make this empowering assumption not only enables the process of supervision, it also recognizes the supervisees' learning histories, providing the proper baseline for defining the lower reaches of their zones of proximal development.

However, both parties should also add additional, supervision-specific, competencies. The one I wish to focus on here is reflection, probably the single most discussed goal of supervision. As illustrated in Figure 6.2, reflection is one of the modes of learning from experience, as described by Kolb (1984). However, in the supervision (and training) literatures, reflection is prized above the other modes. The dictionary defines reflection in two complementary ways: 'deliberation' (the action of fixing one's thoughts, of giving something deep or serious consideration) and 'metacognition' (the faculty by which the mind has knowledge of itself and its operations; thinking about thinking). The intended functions of reflection are to enable:

- Heightened awareness (e.g. reflecting on the feelings accompanying supervisor feedback);
- Consolidation (e.g. recognizing patterns in one's therapy);
- Discrimination (being aware of relationships, synthesizing and connecting new information to previously learned material);

- Interpretation (the analysis and reconstruction of material in a form that enables assimilation);
- Extrapolation (the extension of concepts to their action implications); and
- Evaluation (awareness of the value judgements accompanying actions).

This summary is based on the work of Boud *et al.* (1985) and Dewey (1933). It is comforting to note how similar these activities are to the transformational processes described in dynamic skill theory (Fischer *et al.*, 2003), as partly noted in Table 6.1. In order to achieve these outcomes, Boud *et al.* (1985) advocate allocating time and effort for reflection, including the maintenance of a reflective diary. Within supervision, the supervisee should be making efforts to recapture experiences accurately (e.g. returning to salient events and recounting experiences); viewing experiences from different perspectives in order to gain distance and an orientation to how others may see an event; attending to feelings that accompany the event (as in expressing feelings); re-evaluating experiences (including associating it to prior learning); integrating experiences with other material and placing it on a conceptual map; validating the experience (through reality testing or guided imagery); and appropriation (making the new version of the experience one's own).

According to Dewey (1910), reflection can occur privately, be provoked by a problem or be triggered by something that created perplexity, hesitation, doubt or some kind of challenge to the individual (i.e. which caused them to question their beliefs). This is viewed as sufficiently motivating to cause the individual to search actively for facts (e.g. from memory or observation), to investigate and to think about the available evidence and to consider ways that the experience may best be understood. 'Demand for the solution of perplexity is the steadying and guiding factor in the entire process of reflection' (Dewey, 1910, p.11). Consistent with the above account of de-skilling, Dewey (1910) saw reflection as 'always more or less troublesome because it involves overcoming the inertia that inclines one to accept suggestions at their face value; it involves the willingness to endure a condition of mental unrest and disturbance . . .(reflection) . . . in short, means suspense . . . which is likely to be somewhat painful' (p.13). The conclusion he drew is that what is most troublesome is actually ultimately what is most essential to effective thinking. This is something professionals know well from experiential learning experiences within workshops, in that they may initially be avoided, but these experiences (e.g. educational role-play) are ultimately rated the most valuable part of the workshop.

An interesting example of facilitating reflection is to be found in the 'self-practice and self-reflection' (SP/SR) approach within CBT. According to Laireiter and Willutzki (2003), self-reflection can be used to attend to the supervisee, focusing on relevant themes in their lives, such as their learning history and family background. This work typically occurs within group sessions lasting two hours, led by two experienced supervisors who have no other role within the training system. These leaders encourage the supervisees to analyse central cognitive–affective schemas by self-observation and through the observation of other members of the group. This is expected to enable the supervisees to define problematic patterns or themes, and to work on changing these to more adaptive alternatives. Methods used within the self-reflection process include self-observation, guided imagery, role-plays, analysis of group processes and cognitive techniques (including confrontation). Summarizing the available literature at the time, Laireiter and Willutzki (2003) acknowledged that there was no study that had examined the effects of SP/SR on the clinical effectiveness of the supervisees, and that is still the case at the time of writing (October 2016). However, there is some evidence that participation in the groups improves inter-personal functioning, and participants tend to perceive the group as effective in developing their empathy and ability to cope with emotional material. To illustrate, Bennett-Levy *et al.* (2003) engaged 14 cognitive therapists in a programme designed to encourage them to utilize SR/SP. One group of six engaged in a co-therapy approach with their partner, while the eight remaining therapists practised applying cognitive therapy techniques to themselves in private. Reflective diaries maintained by both groups indicated that there were improvements in their ability to communicate about CBT, and enhanced attention to the therapeutic relationship. They also felt better able to reflect on their practice, and were more inclined to use self-reflection spontaneously following the group. Subsequently, Bennett-Levy (2006) has constructed an information-processing model to account for how therapists develop competence, placing reflection at its heart. SP/SR has also been increasingly incorporated into supervision, though not yet researched in that context. For instance, the SP/SR workbook (Bennett-Levy *et al.*, 2015) encourages supervisors to include SP/SR as a regular agenda item. This can help the supervisees to review their SP/SR in supervision, to target understanding (alliance ruptures are mentioned), enhance competence or simply to gain support).

Outcomes of Learning from Experience

Based on successfully negotiating the challenging processes of supervision, what kinds of outcomes should we anticipate? What are the milestones that a supervisor could observe along the supervisee's developmental journey? How can supervisees tell whether they are progressing satisfactorily, particularly as the journey is undulating and even distressing at times? Taking a micro-development perspective once more, the first kind of positive outcome is engagement in experiential learning. Table 6.3 collates the views of a number of authors who have written about the initial effects of experiential learning: Bloom *et al.* (1956); Krathwohl *et al.* (1964); Kolb (1984); Boud *et al.* (1985); and Klein *et al.* (1986). Of course, it is also possible to have initially negative outcomes, such as the anxiety, confusion

Table 6.3   Examples of supervisees' developmental milestones during episodes of learning from experience.

If I experience, I will . . .
- be more aware of my current emotions/sensations
- recognize/define my own feelings
- develop my intuition
- have had a 'here and now' moment
- be more aware of the emotional or sensory accompaniments to my activity
- recognize my own attitudes or motivation better (e.g. concerns, barriers, uplifts)
- discriminate amongst the emotions/sensations I experience at work
- better regulate or manage my emotions (positive or negative ones)
- recognize patterns that arise in my work
- interpret my emotions/patterns
- draw out the action implications of my patterns/emotions
- evaluate how I feel
- process some of my affect/sensations

If I reflect I will . . .
- integrate my material with other material (e.g. prior learning experiences)
- assimilate things into a personal, reasoned understanding
- ground my experience (etc.) in my own understanding (particularly through personal images, metaphors, etc.)
- tell my story, recalling and summarizing recent events
- prioritize things (e.g. work objectives)
- clarify things (e.g. a formulation)
- reconcile conflicting pressures/beliefs
- develop and define my own belief system or personal 'stance'

Table 6.3 *(Continued)*

If I conceptualize, I will . . .

- access new material (e.g. compare what I know with supervisor's grasp of a topic)
- comprehend something better (improve my grasp of a knowledge-base)
- integrate new material with my own understanding (including theories, data, literature, drawing on knowledge-base)
- analyse material (e.g. try to figure out what maintains a clinical problem)
- synthesize new material with my old ideas (e.g. from reflection)
- evaluate my comprehension (e.g. reviewing work/idea critically, to define my strengths and weaknesses)
- explore ideas
- develop a new understanding (e.g. re-formulation)

If I experiment, I will . . .

- want to test things out
- address a puzzle/concern/worry (e.g. rehearse a new skill in order to see what happens, gain competence or to get feedback)
- engage in educational role-play, learning exercises
- assign myself a task (like conducting an 'experiment')

If I plan, I will . . .

- come prepared
- set myself a goal during agenda-setting
- agree a 'homework' assignment
- decide/summarize what I want to do next

Source: Milne, D.L. (2009). Reproduced with permission of Derek Milne.

and anger reported with high frequency by the supervisee during CBT supervision (James *et al.*, 2004). James *et al.* (2004) regarded these emotions as being responsive to the supervisor's conscious attempts to facilitate desirable emotional arousal. From the supervisor's perspective, Watkins (2014d) similarly recognized the supervisee's negative reactions in the first supervision session, such as feeling overwhelmed by the complexity and responsibility, and being uncertain or ambivalent. Again, these emotions are perceived as being necessary for learning, termed 'growth tensions' by Watkins.

According to Table 6.3, supervisees can infer that they are making progress when engaged in the experiencing mode of learning from experience if they find (for example) that they are more aware of their current emotions (e.g. they are better able to list and articulate their feeling states). Similarly, the reflecting supervisees who are able to integrate this experience with existing material will have grounds for believing that they are progressing. Milestones whilst conceptualizing include accessing new material, or comprehending existing material better. Lastly, productive engagement with the 'experimenting' mode is indicated by creating plans, and so on. In keeping with the travelling metaphor, these milestones can be placed in order, corresponding to how readily they can be achieved. Bloom *et al.*'s taxonomies are a classic example of this approach (e.g. 1956). To illustrate, the Experiencing Scale (Klein *et al.*, 1986) recognizes the early stages as simply entailing talking about events with an emotional tone, whereas at 'higher stages' these are explored and result in heightened awareness and meaning-making. This kind of engagement has been found to predict beneficial change in therapy (Castonguay *et al.*, 1996), and is one of the recognized 'change processes' in therapy (e.g. based on the opportunity for catharsis/ventilation; affective experiencing; assimilation of problematic experiences: Grencavage & Norcross, 1990; Lambert & Bergin, 1994). It is also accepted as an 'essential' part of productive supervision, though CBT approaches to supervision seem to place somewhat less emphasis on processing experiencing within supervision than most other approaches (Follette & Batten, 2000; Lombardo *et al.*, 2009). This is surprising given the vital role of emotions within CBT, where clinical progress (e.g. new learning) relies on increasing emotional awareness, encouraging repeated practice and providing opportunities for corrective experiences (Reilly, 2000; Boswell, 2013).

Beyond the initial phase of engaging in experiential learning (within or between supervision sessions), there should be stepwise gains towards competence and clinical effectiveness. The well-established training taxonomy of Kirkpatrick (1967) is detailed in Chapter 8 (see Table 8.3), commencing with satisfaction and progressing through learning to clinical and systemic outcomes. Using this taxonomy, Table 8.3 also reported the relative frequency with which the different outcomes had been reported in a sample of 24 supervision studies. In reviewing the methods used to assess competence in 64 CBT studies, Muse and McManus (2013) adopted a similar four-step taxonomy, starting with the assessment of declarative knowledge, then proceeding to procedural knowledge ('knowing how'), skill acquisition (competence) and lastly to an assessment of the transfer of that skill into proficient clinical practice. This taxonomy was sufficient to capture the assessments used in the 64 studies they reviewed. However, in their discussion they also recognized a role for assessing clinical outcomes, as an indirect measure of competence. By contrast, a systematic review of 18 supervision studies by Wheeler and Richards (2007) categorized the impacts of supervision inductively, that is, without imposing an existing framework or taxonomy. Perhaps because they also sampled more broadly (including studies with any outcome evaluation), they found a slightly different set of outcomes. This included the supervisees' self-awareness, skill development, self-efficacy, theoretical orientation, experience of support and clinical outcomes.

All of these diverse outcomes are usually deemed desirable, but many regard the definitive or 'acid test' to be clinical effectiveness: 'The impact of clinical supervision on client outcome is considered by many to be the acid test of the efficacy of supervision' (Ellis & Ladany, 1997, p.485). Consistent with the view expressed in Muse and McManus (2013), I have challenged this perspective (Milne, 2014a) by means of the fidelity framework, a clinical outcome taxonomy (Borrelli *et al.*, 2005). According to this framework there are five equally important stepwise outcomes, and privileging any one risks missing information that is necessary to form a balanced understanding. In terms of the supervisees' learning outcomes, the fidelity framework evaluates whether the 'right' initial impacts occur with the supervisee. This is termed 'receipt' and asks: 'Is supervision resulting in the right (mini) outcomes?' The next step in the fidelity framework is 'enactment', an assessment of whether supervisees apply what they have learned in supervision when they provide therapy. This is the fifth and final step in the fidelity framework as described by Borrelli *et al.* (2005). To these I have suggested four further steps, including evaluation of the clinical outcomes obtained by the supervisee (therapist) with clients (the 'acid test'), but also including generalization to the system within which the supervisee is working (e.g. reactions of clients' social supporters to therapy outcomes; Milne, 2014a). This paper was a logical review of the evaluation options, intended to discourage a misguided onus on one step. Consistent with the logic of service evaluation (Rossi *et al.*, 2004), I also wished to draw out an appropriately complex view of the possible links between supervision and clinical effectiveness, reflecting the multifaceted roles of supervisor and trainee, together with their reciprocal influences. When we examined a sample of 12 interpretable studies of the clinical outcomes of supervision in terms of the studies' attention to the five fidelity framework dimensions (Borrelli *et al.*, 2005), we found that all five steps had been evaluated in three of these 12 studies (Reiser & Milne, 2014). Overall there was 67 per cent adherence to the fidelity framework, suggesting that other supervision researchers shared our emphasis on stepwise evaluation. We concluded that an over-emphasis on clinical outcomes alone carries unnecessary risks (e.g. encouraging weak causal reasoning and failing to identify mechanisms of change), while minimizing the benefits of a more inclusive, stepwise approach (e.g. increasing outcome research and improving supervision). On this logic, our evaluation efforts should also include the possibility that supervision has negative impacts (Ellis *et al.*, 2014; 2015a). I return to these themes in Chapter 8.

Conclusions

Until recently, the contributions made by the supervisee to clinical supervision were surprisingly neglected (e.g. Falender & Shafranske, 2012). To illustrate, when we counted the number of references to the supervisee's contribution within the *Handbook of Psychotherapy Supervision* (Watkins, 1997), we estimated that only about 9 of its 613 pages (1.5 per cent) were concerned with the supervisee's input (Milne & Gracie, 2001). This is a perverse state of affairs for therapy-based professions and a relationship-based enterprise such as supervision. As every health practitioner knows, whether in therapy or supervision, the process and outcomes are influenced greatly by the other person. Who would question that 'it takes two'? Indeed, in one of the chapters in the Watkins' handbook, Dewald (1997) stated that: 'The nature of the patient and his or her aptitude and capacities to use the analytical procedure effectively have a major impact on the entire supervisory situation. A naturally good patient can make a poor student look competent, and a difficult or un-analysable case can make a good student seem to have major difficulties' (p.33). In this context, I feel justified in having given a whole chapter to the supervisee's role within supervision. However, I should also acknowledge that a whole book could readily be devoted to the subject, as there are many fascinating and important ways in which the supervisee contributes to the profoundly important business of supervision, surely as many and varied as there are in relation to the supervisor (see, for example, Carroll & Gilbert, 2005; Falender & Shafranske, 2012).

To summarize, in this chapter I have covered the basic stances or role-relationships that the supervisee and supervisor may take to the enterprise, concluding that the traveller–guide relationship (i.e. the constructivist–structuralist combination) is generally most appropriate within evidence-based CBT supervision, though there will surely be times when other stances are at least fleetingly appropriate. This logic is part of the reason for adopting a tandem analogy, alongside the recognition of the co-constructed nature of supervision (the tandem bicycle only really works when both riders play their part equally). Like the supervisor, the person at the front of the tandem is a leader and a guide, but will at times swap leadership roles with the person at the back of the tandem (the 'stoker'). Both depend on each other for efficient progress. I then looked at the micro-processes of interacting effectively, including the notions of de-skilling and of responsivity, critical processes underpinning the most commonly acknowledged supervisee duty, reflection. These '3Rs' of successful supervisee-hood (roles, responsivity and reflection) are intended to deepen our appreciation of complex contribution made by the supervisee, but are recognized as being only a sample. Arguably, they are themselves only milestones on the supervisee's developmental path. In closing, I suggested that to better understand how supervisees learn from supervision, especially as a result of their own efforts, we need to adopt stepwise evaluation strategies.

7

Supporting and Guiding Supervision

Introduction

Within professional circles the emphasis on clinical supervision is marked, but attention to how supervisors themselves might best be supported and guided is minimal: who supervises the supervisors? There is scant sign of an answer in the supervision literature. Organizational systems have 'rarely been investigated or discussed' (Holloway, 2014, p.612). Although supervisors may account for 16 per cent of the variance in clinical outcomes (Callahan *et al.*, 2009), the majority of dissemination programmes for evidence-based treatments in community care have omitted ongoing support for supervisors (Dorsey *et al.*, 2013). There is, however, an awareness of the problem. In the UK's National Health Service there is recognition that staff should be 'trained, organized and managed properly' (Department of Health, 1998, pp.46–47); that they need to be 'supported' (p.36), and that an infrastructure is required to enable them to be 'skilled', drawing on 'multiple knowledge and learning sources, technical and other resources' (Department of Health, 2001, p.ix). However, it appears that no practical assistance is available (e.g. guidelines or toolkits). To re-quote Watkins (1997), 'something does not compute' (p.604). This recognition that supervisors require a variety of supports to enable them to do their work effectively is also echoed by practitioners working within the health and social services. For example, Stallard *et al.* (2007) noted that, in order to

Evidence-Based CBT Supervision: Principles and Practice, Second Edition. Derek L. Milne.
© 2018 John Wiley & Sons Ltd. Published in 2018 by the British Psychological Society and John Wiley & Sons Ltd.

extend the availability of cognitive-behaviour therapy (CBT), their survey indicated 'an urgent need to develop a training and supervisory infrastructure' (p.504) for therapists. In social work, a survey by Harmse (2001) concluded that the participants did not receive support in their work, but that systems like peer support groups and a supportive work culture could be effective. In clinical psychology, only 17 of 127 respondents to a UK survey (i.e. 18 per cent) were satisfied with their supervision (Gabbay *et al.*, 1999). A more recent survey of 110 senior CBT supervisors in the UK indicated that there continued to be a pressing need for training resources (Reiser & Milne, 2016).

A special issue of the journal *The Cognitive Behaviour Therapist* finally addressed these issues thoroughly in 2016. A model of an appropriate organizational infrastructure was proposed in relation to CBT supervision (Milne & Reiser, 2016b), and a series of accompanying papers provided examples of how this kind of infrastructure could be implemented successfully (e.g. Schoenwald, 2016), particularly with respect to the training of supervisors (including the supervision of supervision). These papers were summarized in Newman *et al.* (2016), but the most relevant points are noted here. The starting point was that there had been a continued 'failure to systematize support for supervisors, an unacceptable strategic and moral oversight, leading to burnout and to dissatisfaction over arrangements' (Milne & Reiser, 2016b, pp.7–8). There are two infrastructure aspects within this assertion: the normative and restorative functions of supervision (Kadushin, 1976; Proctor, 1992). Those two functions are the focus of this chapter. As touched on in earlier chapters, and summarized within Figure 7.1, supervisors are tackling the normative function of supervision when they seek to embed the supervisee's work within the relevant organizational context, in order to ensure that workplace arrangements are effective and satisfactory. This is the 'guiding' role. Examples are managing the supervisee's workload, seeking to ensure quality control, discussing policy issues and encouraging outcome monitoring. When addressing the restorative function, supervisors are more concerned with 'supporting' the supervisee's personal coping efforts at work, as in offering debriefing, encouraging emotional processing and through providing or enabling social support. The aims are to boost personal coping strategies and job satisfaction, encourage awareness of the environmental origins of stressors, whilst reducing the threat of occupational burnout. In terms of the tandem model (see Chapter 2), the normative and restorative aspects of supervision are part of the organizational and professional context, by

Normative

Management

Policy issues; organizational logistics and planning; ground rules; quality of care and quality control; supervisor's role: Evaluation/feedback/ outcome monitoring

Supervision functions

Formative

Competence development

Problem-solving; identifying training needs; education and training; reviewing/formulating case work; understanding other perspectives

Restorative

Support

Debriefing; emotional processing; understanding personalities/workplace stressors; mutual support /validation; improving communication; ensuring group membership

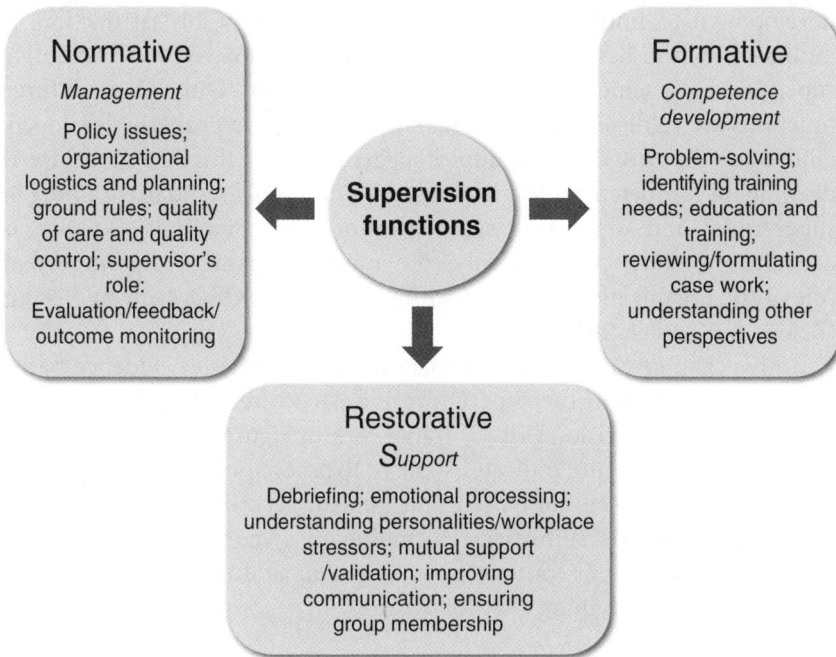

Figure 7.1 The three main functions of clinical supervision (Kadushin, 1976; Proctor, 1992).

analogy the climate and horizons that represent a backdrop or point of reference. These aspects should also be agenda items within supervision, in order to stay on track and to ensure that the supervisee is fit and able to proceed.

The model proposed in relation to CBT supervision by Milne and Reiser (2016b), incorporating the normative and restorative functions, has the supervisee at its heart, embedded in the supervisee's cycle of experiential learning, a formative function to reflect how supervision can foster safe and effective therapy. Surrounding the supervisee's cycle is a supervision cycle, as described in the preceding two chapters (i.e. a process of needs assessment, goal-setting, supervision methods and evaluation). The outer ring of this model is the 'support our supervisors' (SOS) cycle, essentially a problem-solving cycle that indicates the tasks that need to be completed to support supervisors within a sound organizational infrastructure. The SOS model is an evidence-based, systematic, organizational process that shows how supervisors can receive the necessary leadership, support and development to fulfil their role effectively, and enjoy job satisfaction. It outlines how the basic functions of normative, formative and restorative supervision are achieved by evidence-based methods. Only when all three functions are fulfilled can we expect supervisors to be properly developed, guided and supported. The examples suggested within this SOS model were: drawing on competencies frameworks; providing 'gold standard' training in supervision; and organizing supervision-of-supervision (also known as consultancy), respectively. Lastly, the model recognizes the important role of the organizational context within which the SOS cycle would occur (Beidas & Kendall, 2010).

In this chapter I describe the best-available examples of evidence-based practice in relation to the supervisory infrastructure, using the evidence-based clinical supervision (EBCS) framework in Figure 7.2 to organize this information. This figure indicates some of the more popular ways in which supervisors have been supported and guided, according to the research literature and experts' summaries (including my own experience). I start by considering the overall context for supervision, as this sets the scene and makes sense of everything that follows.

Context

Frequently cited contextual factors include staff shortages and turnover, high clinical caseloads, limited access to support or supervision and poor management relationships. In our review of 24 studies of supervision (Milne *et al.*, 2008a) we defined 36 moderating influences, 11 of which we termed general contextual factors (see Figure 3.1). The most commonly mentioned of these was administrative support, which was reported by the study authors as being a positive influence on supervision. By contrast, insufficient organizational support, high staff turnover, scheduling difficulties and problems in residential care settings were amongst the barriers to supervision. Similarly, Moran *et al.* (2014) reviewed 43 studies where training and support had been introduced to overcome such barriers. Their analysis suggested that the successful provision of supervision depended on role clarification, training in supervision, improvements in competence following supervision, good leadership and adequate resources. This account by Moran *et al.* (2014) is consistent with a consensus statement on supervision (Falender *et al.*, 2004), which considered context in terms of

12. Context
Effective leadership and proximal workplace factors (including local policies and practices; stress); distal system factors (e.g. course accreditation/professional registration); social support

8. Research & development
(appreciative enquiry: survey local arrangements; $n = 1$ studies;

9. Consensus work
(supervision workshop design, including learning objectives)

10. CPD
(supervision workshops)

11. Guidelines
(evidence-based manuals and guidelines)

1. Judging what to do with the supervisee
(reflexive thinking; consultancy; use of 7–11)

2. Supervision
(personal coping strategies; preferred methods of supervision; mentors; groups)

4. Outcomes
(client outcome tracking)

3. Supervisee development

7. Theory development
(fidelity framework)

5. Patient care
(outcome measures)

6. Audit

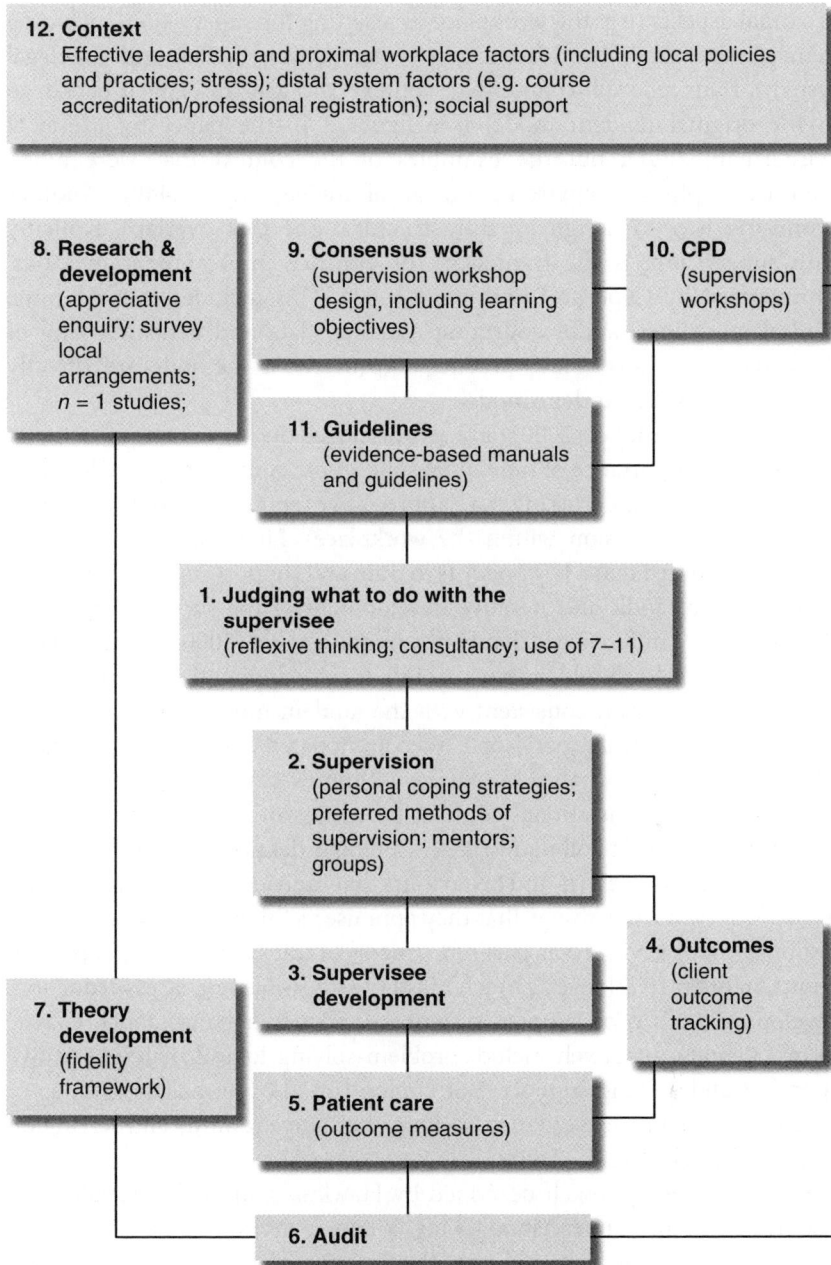

Figure 7.2 Supporting and guiding evidence-based clinical supervision: examples of the necessary organizational infrastructure. Source: Parry *et al.* (1996). Reproduced with permission of Guilford Press.

proximal aspects (e.g. the workplace as a setting for supervision, including management) and distal aspects (e.g. accrediting bodies and the legal system). I am relieved to note that 'context' was also an explicit backdrop to the original tandem model (see figure 2 in the paper by Milne & Westerman, 2001), but the examples of the context that were noted then were 'physical environment; social milieu, etc.' (p.448). Another promising way to design an infrastructure, one that overlaps explicitly with supervision, is the framework of 'practice improvement methods' summarized by Cape and Barkham (2002). This includes staff training, clinical guidelines, audit, collecting outcome data and benchmarking of these data. In short, these practice improvement methods are directly comparable to the tandem model.

Hawkins and Shohet (2000) have also discussed the organizational context, stressing the importance of individual supervisors contributing to a learning culture (e.g. by undertaking an 'appreciative enquiry' into the current strengths of supervision within the workplace). Like Cape and Barkham (2002), they noted that a key policy is to train and support supervisors, linked to a system of audit and iterative development of the surrounding infrastructure. But a difference is that Hawkins and Shohet (2000) urged supervisors themselves to shoulder responsibility for developing their own support systems. This is again consistent with the tandem model, but places more onus on the individual supervisor. To accommodate this suggestion, the panel labelled 'supervision' (panel 2 in Figure 7.2) notes ways that supervisors can adapt to their organizational context, by means of their personal coping strategies (Lazarus & Folkman, 1984). Coping is defined in terms of a broad range of thoughts, feelings and behaviours that individuals utilize in response to stressful events (i.e. things that they appraise as threatening or requiring a response). This is viewed as part of a process of transacting with people and events, in order to achieve as much mastery as possible (e.g. stress reduction; developing one's own support system; confidence enhancement). Classic forms of coping adaptively include problem-solving, logical analysis, positive appraisal and seeking support. But coping can also be maladaptive, as in engaging in cognitive avoidance, seeking alternative rewards and relying on emotional discharge.

Following the approach described by Hawkins and Shohet (2000) may also result in the supervisors taking a more environmentalist or even political stance in order to promote the functioning of their host organizations, or to at least raise awareness of the powerful influences of the wider environment on themselves and others within their system (e.g. Smail,

1991). In practice, this may take the form of mental health professionals forming action groups or working parties. They can become champions of particular approaches, joining forces to try to enhance the local supervision policies and practices, perhaps in close collaboration with a service manager. For instance, resources such as supervision guidelines and other training resources can be developed through local project groups, and such groups may also address barriers to the use of such materials, promoting innovation and experimentation through an action research approach (e.g. Milne & Dunkerley, 2010). However, this environmental level of activity is rare, reflecting more of an ecological, empowerment or community psychology orientation (Orford, 2008). If nothing else, such a perspective heightens awareness of how the wider or 'distal' environment may influence supervision, with implications for the way that we formulate and seek to address barriers. To be concrete, in terms of social justice it is reasonable to regard some workplaces as being so toxic as to represent the appropriate focus for change, rather than expecting supervisors to develop the kind of superhuman resilience required to avoid burnout in such aversive settings.

In terms of adapting to or tackling challenging workplaces, an empowerment process can be offered to supervisors (or consultants who support supervisors), and Newman (2013) has described a graduate training course in CBT supervision for new supervisors, also termed 'metasupervision'. This was defined as 'situations in which a highly experienced clinician serves as a consultant to a clinical supervisor' (Newman, 2013, p.13). However, Newman's (2013) version is focused purely on formative aspects of supervision. By contrast, Ogren and Boethius (2014), and the group supervision described by Vec *et al.* (2014), helped supervisors to cultivate organizational support and innovation. The term metasupervision has also been used for work intended to empower supervisees (Buus *et al.*, 2016), to encourage their sense of ownership through reflecting on the personal and organizational barriers to their supervision. Group discussion, facilitated by a consultant, encourages supervisees to consider and implement strategies to tackle these barriers (such as high workloads or disruptive shift patterns). A randomized controlled trial indicated that metasupervision increased participation in supervision, and subsequent work has detailed how supervisees have collaborated with managers, supervisors and each other to address barriers (summarized in Buus *et al.*, 2016).

A rare systematic study of the organizational barriers to the implementation of supervision within a healthcare organization involved the help of outside consultants. Lynch and Happell (2008) applied Lewin's (1951) 'force-field analysis' in order to study the organizational culture and so guide the implementation process. In applying this method, they adopted a qualitative approach, so were able to describe the 'pushing and resisting' forces that are at the heart of this analysis. For example, a pushing quote stated 'I had sought out and received clinical supervision during the change process so I knew on a personal level how beneficial it was', but Lynch and Happell (2008, p.76) countered this with a resisting quote: 'angry, hostile . . . demoralized and anti-management . . . evidence of horizontal violence and cannibalism'. This qualitative information from the force-field analysis provided a baseline and guided a formulation regarding the organization's preparedness, indicating the kind of support that was necessary from the host organization. Lynch and Happell (2008, p.79) summarized this support requirement in this way: 'Given the level of mistrust, paranoia and the lack of knowledge about clinical supervision at all levels of the organization, commitment was needed from the organization to provide resources for external facilitators. The main resource would include funding for the training, including accommodation and backfill.' At the end of this process, the participants judged that clinical supervision had been successfully implemented in this Australian service, based on the number of supervisors (22) and supervisees (110) who had been trained for their respective roles, together with the improved morale and culture of the organization.

It is reassuring to note how these various approaches overlap with one another and with the SOS model, suggesting a promising, integrative infrastructure for supervisor support and development. Figure 7.2 captures the main points, using the evidence-based practice (EBP) framework (Parry *et al.*, 1996). I have retained this EBP figure because the emphasis in the present book is on EBP, but the contents and implications of the EBP figure and the SOS one are the same. In summary, Figure 7.2 details how supervisors could be supported and developed, incorporating the SOS model (Milne & Reiser, 2016b) and similar approaches. The remainder of this chapter is used to identify the different theoretical options and research findings for supervisor support and development, as indicated by the bold headings in each of the 11 panels (boxes) in Figure 7.2. As you will notice, these headings are linked to some specific practical examples, showing how the tandem model can be applied to the task of supporting and guiding supervisors. The lower part and left-hand side of the figure note the research and development activities (panels 4, 6 and 8), to be discussed primarily in Chapter 8. However, in this chapter I will note briefly some relevant ways that supervisors have engaged in research, viewing them as professional coping strategies (part of 'experimentation', through action research). Also, I will assume that Chapter 6 addresses panel 3, 'supervisee development'. I will shortly describe these and other practical examples, starting at the heart of the model, with the moment-to-moment demands that tend to be placed on supervisors, and the critical role of their personal coping strategies. Note that these strategies naturally address other panels, providing the important interactions between the panels in Figure 7.2, as signified by the connecting lines. But first I will describe how the social support within the supervision context can support and guide supervisors in vital ways.

Social support

Although supervisors should receive support and guidance from formal sources, such as their line managers, others can have a crucial informal role. The term 'social support' refers to how people aid our coping efforts by buffering us against stressors, by suggesting better ways of coping and by providing information, practical assistance, emotional sustenance and companionship (Cowen, 1982). As a result of these forms of support some vital functions are served. These include a sense of attachment, in the sense of feeling close to others (thereby allowing nurturance and unconditional assistance to be provided); social integration or belonging-ness; social validation (the recognition of one's identity and competence); and guidance (the availability of advice and information). As these functions indicate, our social supporters are a vital and rather neglected aid to our coping strategies. Therefore, a suitable context for supervision will include opportunities for individual and group-based social support (e.g. informal gatherings and encouragement for support), and will also be embedded within formal arrangements, such as mentoring and peer discussion. A systematic review of burnout and stress management interventions for mental health professionals indicated the significance of such support, as the most frequently reported coping strategies included drawing on social support (the other strategies were recognizing one's own limitations, dealing with problems when they occur, developing skills and accessing supervision: Edwards *et al.*, 2006).

The survey of social supporters (bartenders, stylists and others) reported by Cowen (1982) provided startling evidence of the degree to which something approximating to therapy was being offered on the high street. As he put it, 'help is where you find it', rather than being the preserve of mental health professionals. Could the same be true of supervision: do social supporters also supervise? Based on a survey reported by Farber and Hazanov (2014), they do! They had their survey respondents rate the extent to which they 'share clinical information' with each of 10 potential informal supervisors, including friends and siblings, based on a 7-point scale, ranging from 1 (not at all) to 7 (to a great extent). The three most frequently approached social supporters were peers within the same training programme (mean rating of 4.9), followed by a significant other (mean = 4.1) and one's own therapist ($M = 3.8$). Other prominent supporters were parents ($M = 2.6$), siblings ($M = 1.7$) and a religious or spiritual leader ($M = 1.7$). Also consistent with the degree of helpfulness reported by Cowen (1982), these supervisees rated the help that they had received from their wide range of supporters favourably. The most helpful source of support was a peer on the same programme ($M = 5.4$), followed by a colleague in the mental health field in a different programme ($M = 4.6$). By comparison, the sample rated their formal supervisor rated slightly more favourably ($M = 6.4$), indicating that supervision was satisfactory and that social support complemented supervision. Among the lowest rated sources of helpful advice were friends ($M = 2.6$), siblings ($M = 2.2$) and a religious/ spiritual leader ($M = 1.7$).

According to Bennett-Levy and Thwaites (2007), these opportunities afford 'a sense of safeness, non-judgemental acceptance, affirmation, empathy, care, warmth and encouragement to explore' (p.264). They add important considerations, like providing a rationale for the supportive approach that is adopted, and providing appropriate models. Bennett-Levy and Thwaites (2007) quote Ladany *et al.* (2005), whose suggestion concerning supervision is to 'do unto others as you would have them do unto others' (p.215). That is, there is a good case for treating the support of the supervisor as per the support provided to the supervisee, on the assumption that this will cascade down to the client. This restorative component of supervision includes the provision of a 'safe-base', appropriate structure and commitment. Palomo *et al.* (2010) defined the safe-base in terms of making the supervisee feel valued, respected and secure. The implication is that a leader (e.g. a metasupervisor) who supports the supervisor should also be trustworthy, empathic and responsive, able to maintain practical boundaries, interested in the supervisor and enthusiastic about supervision itself. Table 4.1 spells out these qualities more fully.

Therefore, activities like peer discussion, mentoring and consultancy can all be understood as formal devices for promoting one or more of the functions of social support. This general observation is borne out by the available research within supervision. For example, Barrow and Domingo (1997) noted, from their study of supervisor training, that those supervisors who were more supportive and exhibited more facilitating of interpersonal conditions created more change in the supervisee. Their programme explicitly included research on the role of interpersonal relationships, and so they encouraged the recognition of a supportive atmosphere. The opposite also seems to be true: Deery (2004) explored the need for support amongst midwives, recognizing that significant negative emotion was generated but was difficult to regulate, resulting in them expending energy needlessly. She noted that maladaptive coping strategies were employed by the midwives in response to the emotions (such as 'pseudo cohesion' and 'resistance to change'). Deery (2004) concluded that more effective methods of support were needed, such as supervision. Indeed, supervision does appear to ameliorate the kinds of stress reported by healthcare staff. In one study, burnout (i.e. emotional exhaustion, de-personalization and low levels of personal accomplishment) were reported by a sample of 189 community mental health nurses (Edwards *et al.*, 2006), but those staff receiving effective supervision (measured by higher scores on the Manchester Clinical Supervision Scale, MCSS: Winstanley, 2000) reported lower levels of burnout. Similarly, Greenspan *et al.* (1991) surveyed 198 social workers, finding a significant association between supervision that was perceived as supportive and effectiveness (e.g. a better focus on the clinical work). These findings are consistent with studies of problematic supervisory relationships, where support from peers comes through as a major coping strategy (Nelson & Friedlander, 2001).

Note that this summary does not include much mention of issues of authority or responsibility, and indeed the content is pretty much the opposite of supervision in other respects too (e.g. not explicitly educative). Whilst this informal context is probably a necessary condition for social support to occur, boundary issues can arise, raising ethical and other concerns. This was indicated by a survey of 146 novice supervisees, where confidentiality was compromised through informal discussion of their provision of therapy. Drawing also on individual interviews with three of these respondents, the authors stated that: 'many supervisees are routinely acting in an unethical fashion by sharing clinical information outside the boundaries of formal supervision or practica classes without the knowledge or permission of their client' (Farber & Hazanov, 2014, p.1070). These authors acknowledge that supervisees need social support (especially early in their careers), but suggest that supervisors and others who are involved in training should be more aware of the extent and nature of social support, and should offer advice regarding ethical and other boundary issues. Farber and Hazanov (2014) also recommended that supervisors make themselves more available to novices, to reduce reliance on social support. These suggestions make good sense, but I think that it makes every bit as much sense to 'formalize the informal', creating well-bounded opportunities for social support to flourish (e.g. mentoring arrangements, social opportunities, encouragement and guidance). Social support overlaps with our personal coping strategies, informing and nurturing them. I will discuss some of these overlaps shortly, as part of moving on to panel 2 in Figure 7.2: providing supervision. But following downwards through Figure 7.2, I will now turn to consensus-building work, and its role in supporting supervisors through guidelines. As this indicates, here and elsewhere I combine two or more panels from Figure 7.2, to give due weight to the topics of most relevance to this chapter.

Consensus Work and Guidelines

Guidelines are an example of consensus work amongst a group of stake-holders, including professional peers, and can be regarded as addressing several of the headings in Table 7.2, leading to 'problem-solving'. An expert consensus may serve as a substitute for an adequate evidence-base, or interpret it in acceptable, practical ways. The individual supervisor can draw on such considered views of experts, representing a source of guidance and collegiality. An example of the use of consensus-building in the absence of adequate research knowledge is the derivation of a training programme for supervision workshops (Green, 2004). The Delphi technique is one of a group of consensus-building methods (Jones & Hunter, 1995), and Green used it to enable a panel of 50 experts to define a supervisor training curriculum through the completion of a succession of increasingly refined questionnaires, together with feedback on how their individual replies compared with those of the other experts. The technique succeeded in building consensus, and a number of possible topics were rank ordered by the group (which included those 'clinical tutors' who trained supervisors,

supervisors themselves and the directors of the training programmes of which they were all part). The most popular topics were 'considering when and how to fail a placement', which received a mean rating of 6.8 out of a possible 7. Closely behind were the topics of addressing the legal responsibilities of the supervisor, ensuring that the client receives appropriate care, and knowing how to negotiate a placement contract (all rated above 6.5). Least supported were 'requiring supervisors to provide recordings of their supervision' and other topics carrying high threat.

An illustration of a consensus that is based on an adequate knowledgebase is the definition of supervision competencies (Falender *et al.*, 2004). This consensus was achieved by forming workgroups from amongst the experts attending a conference, and having them engage in three days of discussion. The participants drew on their knowledge of the literature to agree a list of competencies, as well as how they should be trained and assessed. Their competencies framework included knowledge, skills and values, such as 'knowledge of ethics and legal issues specific to supervision', 'relationship skills – ability to build supervisory alliance' and the values of respect and empowerment. They considered that supervisor training should include didactic coursework and experiential methods (e.g. 'observation of supervision, with critical feedback'). This should be assessed in a variety of ways, including evidence from this direct observation, supervisee feedbac, and the assessment of the outcomes of supervision (including supervisees' learning and their clinical results with clients).

One of the most common results of consensus work is a guideline. Although manuals and guidelines are amongst the least popular of the influences on the practice of healthcare staff (Lucock *et al.*, 2006), they nonetheless have the potential to support the coping repertoires of supervisors. This is reflected in the ratings given to professional guidelines by this sample of 96 qualified therapists, as (on average) they rated professional guidelines at 3.9 on a 6-point scale, equating to 'slightly helpful'. By contrast, supervision obtained a mean rating of 4.8. Treatment manuals were less well regarded, except in the case of those practitioners who came from a CBT background (they rated treatment manuals at 4 on the rating scale). Whilst manuals have become essential within psychotherapy efficacy studies (Nathan *et al.*, 2000), these modest ratings probably reflect numerous objections that many practitioners have to manuals. Amongst these objections is the view that manuals do not deal with the specific idiosyncrasies of specific patients; that they give little or no scope for clinical judgement; that there is inflexibility in the scheduling of the different elements within the manual; and that fundamentally therapy is more of an art than a science. On the other hand, manuals provide explicit information that can help supervisors to know what the main options are, and they do seem to contribute to improved outcomes (Neufeldt, 1994). However, manuals for supervisor training and development are extremely thin on the ground, Neufeldt's (1994) being one of the first. It was designed to foster 26 discrete supervisory skills, drawn from Bernard's discrimination model, plus ideas regarding reflective practice. The manual defines these skills and offers step-by-step procedures (including a transcript to provide illustrations). It was designed to support weekly supervision seminars, which utilized role-plays and reflections on the participating supervisors' video-presented material. Examples of these skills are: 'Assist trainee to conceptualize case' and 'Present a developmental challenge'.

More recently, Fall and Sutton (2004) have designed a workshop to accompany Bernard and Goodyear's (2004) textbook. This provides learning exercises, examples, case-studies and illustrative transcripts to enable the supervisor to develop. There are also self-assessment questionnaires and checklists. However, this is primarily intended to be used by a workshop facilitator and is therefore of limited value to the individual supervisor. The most sophisticated manual is the one developed by Baltimore and Crutchfield (2003), who provided an interactive, CD-rom-based training programme. This covers 16 modules, from definitions and models, to ethical and legal issues. The manual contains learning objectives, reflective exercises, experiential activities and references, whilst the CD has video and audio clips. Henggeler *et al.* (2002) also described the use of a supervisory protocol to support their supervisor training efforts in multisystemic therapy. This was linked to annual workshops for supervisors, and to measures of the supervisor's adherence to the therapy. Like Bernard and Goodyear (2004), there was a manual accompanying the first edition of the present text, which can still be accessed at the website (www.wiley.com/go/milne). This includes four guidelines on clinical supervision and DVD clips of naturalistic supervision. All items reflect the tandem model. However, a more recent and comprehensive manual is now available for those interested in CBT supervision (Milne & Reiser, 2017).

In a recent review of supervision guidelines and manuals (Milne, 2016), I located and discussed a handful of more recent written materials, concluding that they had proved effective in improving supervision, but only when used within local implementation studies (i.e. as part of action research programmes). Yet more recent guidelines and manuals have appeared since

I wrote that review, including the relatively descriptive series on 'supervision essentials' published by the American Psychological Association (e.g. Newman & Kaplan, 2016) and the text by Sudak *et al.* (2016). My own co-authored manual on EBCS and CBT supervision (Milne & Reiser, 2017) is another instance, perhaps being more directive than these other examples. Returning to the conclusions from my 2016 review of guidelines and manuals, several steps appeared to be essential for their successful dissemination or implementation:

- Formulate the service system, to identify the barriers and boosters to implementing guidance material;
- Ensure that supervisor training is of sufficiently high quality (e.g. that supervision competencies are acquired through 'gold-standard' training; that 'supervision-of-supervision' is provided);
- Work collaboratively with participating professional groups (e.g. to ensure shared ownership); and
- Adopt a collaborative, action research approach (e.g. to monitor adherence to the guidance materials, and the transfer of supervisor training).

Continuing Professional Development

Developing supervision skills in groups

By far the most popular approach to supporting and guiding supervisors is to provide them with relevant training, the 'continuing professional development' part of the EBCS framework (continuing profession development, CPD: see Figure 7.2, panel 10). Training will often include supervision guidelines and itself be influenced by a training manual. However, such CPD may not reach everyone: a survey of CBT practitioners indicated that only 108 of 170 respondents in the UK (i.e. 64 per cent) had received some form of training in supervision (Townend *et al.*, 2002). A follow-up survey indicated that training remained relatively unsatisfactory (Reiser & Milne, 2016). Also, there appears to be a huge gulf between the complex, stressful role of the supervisor and the kind of training that is usually provided within healthcare systems. In this vein, Watkins (1997) concludes the *Handbook of Psychotherapy Supervision* in exasperation, noting that: 'Something does not compute. We would never dream of turning untrained therapists loose on needy patients, so why would we turn untrained supervisors loose on those untrained therapists who help those needy patients?' (p.604). He is of the view that supervisor training should be given the same degree of importance as initial training. Surveys of practitioners tend to support this negative view, and it is widely thought that 'most psychologists have never received formal training and supervision in supervision' (Falender & Shafranske, 2004, p.19). They go on to add that 'many, if not most, supervisors practise without the benefit of education, training or supervision . . . It is likely . . . that supervisors' behaviours are based on implicit models of supervision, culled from their experiences as a supervisee, from their identification with past supervisors, or from skills derived from psychotherapy or teaching' (Falender & Shafranske, 2004, p.7). This appears to have been the case for years, regardless of theoretical orientation (Perris, 1994).

In response to this unacceptable situation, these authors and others have produced a consensus statement regarding competent supervision (Falender *et al.*, 2004). Similarly, professional organizations are increasingly requiring that supervisors receive training in order to practice within initial training programmes. For example, the British Psychological Society (2007, p.65) states that training programmes in clinical psychology 'must organize regular supervision workshops to train supervisors in methods of supervision'. Similarly, all of the other nine NHS professions within a review of supervision arrangements conducted at the turn of the century (Milne, 1998) expected their supervisors to attend some form of training in supervision, with workshops lasting between one and five days. However, at that stage none of these 10 professional bodies required supervisors to be trained in supervision, with the onus placed instead on the relevant professional training programmes, which were expected to offer this training in order to be accredited by their professional bodies. Alongside the workshops provided by local programmes of initial professional training, independent, university-accredited courses in clinical supervision began to emerge, such that Wheeler (2004) was able to note that training courses for supervisors were becoming common, ranging from brief one-day workshops to two-year, part-time Masters courses. She surveyed 10 expert supervisors in the field of counselling and psychotherapy and concluded that supervisor training should vary from a minimum of 45 hours of theory and 45 hours of practice to a maximum of 200 hours in total. These experts were optimistic about the effectiveness of this supervisor training, particularly where this took account of organizational factors that impinge on effective supervision.

In the same book, Fleming (2004) recounts the history of supervisor training within clinical psychology. Fleming surveyed the Doctoral training programmes in the UK and Ireland in 2001, obtaining an 87 per cent response rate. All respondents reported providing training for supervisors, averaging 4.6 training events per annum. However, most of these workshops were only of one day's duration, and there was little attention to evaluating the effectiveness of the workshops or of seeking any form of accreditation. On the other hand, there was a significant consensus on the content of these workshops, the great majority emphasizing the need to cover learning processes, different theoretical models and the vexatious issue of failing those trainees who are not making satisfactory progress. Fleming (2004) concluded that the situation regarding supervisor training was improving, as it was being provided on 'an increasingly systematic basis within an enactive framework. There is a good uptake of training by supervisors generally' (p.91). In a second survey (involving 95 qualified psychotherapists of various orientations), training was perceived as the third most influential factor in their development (Lucock *et al.*, 2006). A mapping exercise conducted by Docchar (2007) suggested that there were by then 85 supervisor training courses in the UK, split equally between university and independent-sector providers, and ranging from Diploma to Masters programmes (though about one-third of these were not accredited at all). These courses also varied significantly (e.g. in cost, supervision methods addressed, delivery, etc.). Against this apparent progress, it should, however, be recognized that supervisor training courses are rarely accredited by professional organizations, that regulation of individual professionals may only require them to 'recognize the role and value of clinical supervision' and that there is no scheme, within the largest UK organization, to regulate supervisors (Health Professions Council, 2007, p.39). However, some professional groups do accredit supervisors (e.g. British Association for Behavioural and Cognitive Psychotherapies, BABCP).

Latterly, the situation has begun to improve, in that some countries now have credentialling systems in place, and one (Australia) now has a mandatory system of supervisor training and accreditation (Watkins & Wang, 2014). In other countries progress is also being made. For instance, in the USA, guidelines for clinical supervisors have been published and there is recognition that supervision 'is a distinct professional competency that requires formal education and training' (APA, 2015, p.35). For such reasons, these authors concluded their review by noting that a sea-change had taken place, with growing international recognition of the need to train supervisors, enabled by the emergence of the competence movement. But as Watkins and Wang (2014) noted, research on supervisor training remains in its infancy. Although it is pleasing that there are now at least 11 controlled evaluations that indicate that supervisor training can be effective (Milne *et al.*, 2011c), we need 'more consistent, sustained, and systematic attention across researchers and educators...if the evidence-based challenge of supervisor training is to be most fully realized' (Watkins & Milne, 2014, p.688). For example, a systematic review by Gosselin *et al.* (2015) identified 52 papers reporting supervisor training in the prior 20 years, but only 12 of these were deemed original and interpretable research. These 12 studies reported positive impacts of the training, but only five of these studies measured learning through performance on a specific task or through ratings by a supervisor or a supervisee (the majority only assessed attendance, workshop satisfaction or attitudes). None evaluated the effects of the training on the supervisees' patients.

However, slow progress is being made on the practicalities of training, partly through the development of the educational components used within supervisor training, such as the use of video materials (Gonsalvez *et al.*, 2016) and supervision guidelines (Milne, 2016). Another important development has been the emergence of computer-based technologies to deliver and strengthen supervisor training, such as web-based video-conferencing and virtual reality software, as extensively reviewed by Rousmaniere (2014), and as illustrated by the blend of e-learning and traditional workshops as described by Ferguson *et al.* (2016). This e-learning involved supervisors reviewing summarized information on the training topics, with links to supporting documents (such as supervision guidelines) and to further references. There were also interactive exercises (including video material) and 'pause and reflect' exercises, to promote experiential learning. There has also been progress through the complementary effort to develop comprehensive training manuals and quality-control systems (e.g. Schoenwald, 2016; Sudak *et al.*, 2016).

According to our work on developing an evidence-based CBT supervision manual (Milne & Reiser, 2017), supervisor training needs to address four tasks:

1. Specify the training goals: clear training objectives and learning outcomes should be stated at the start of training, the outcomes being clarified in the form of supervision competencies (e.g. Roth & Pilling, 2007).

2. Provide structure and support (e.g. leadership; effective time-management and communication; materials and learning resources).
3. Facilitate experiential learning, using a blend of training methods in a responsive way, including demonstrations and feedback, so that the supervisors can readily understand what is required to demonstrate competence.
4. Evaluate the workshop's effectiveness, to assess goal-attainment and to identify improvements.

I next briefly illustrate each of these tasks with recent research. In terms of training goals and evaluation, Newman-Taylor *et al.* (2013) had their workshop participants twice self-rate their competence in relation to the 18 competencies within the Roth and Pilling (2007) framework. The first self-rating was at the outset and so defined their baseline proficiency (affording an educational needs assessment), while the second self-rating concluded the workshop (providing an evaluation of learning). In terms of structure and support, Bagnall and Sloan (2014) described how innovative supervisor training in Scotland's NHS was based on a blend of traditional workshops and set readings (including questions), interactive online activities, online discussion forums (critical debate with peers) and collaborative learning online, in small groups. As just noted, an updated account has been provided by Ferguson *et al.* (2016). Task 3 requires trainers to use a blend of training methods in a responsive way. Practical methods for such training were identified as a result of the systematic review of 11 controlled evaluations by Milne *et al.* (2011c). In all, 15 methods were used within these workshops. All studies used feedback, and 8 of the 11 used educational role-play and modelling (live/video demonstration). Less frequently used methods were teaching, written assignments, behavioural rehearsal, providing a rationale, guided reading, discussion, educational needs assessment, direct observation, questions and answers, agenda-setting, homework assignments and a quiz. This is consistent with current best practice in staff and supervisor training (Rakovshik & McManus, 2010; Roth *et al.*, 2010), and is associated with successful supervisor training (Milne & Reiser, 2017).

Although significant progress has been made in developing training methods, problems remain. For example, a survey of 110 CBT supervisors and supervisor trainers (Reiser & Milne, 2017) indicated that satisfaction with the training received in supervision was modest (only 66 per cent reporting that they were 'satisfied' or 'very satisfied'), and only 36 per cent of these respondents reported that they were 'satisfied' or 'very satisfied' with the available training resources. This contrasts strongly with the respondents' mean rating of their own supervision, which reached 93 per cent satisfaction. Supervisor training also takes place individually, and support and guidance can take place through various arrangements. I will next describe the main options.

Supervision-of-supervision ('metasupervision')

Research on supervision frequently involves a senior supervisor or subject expert who supports and guides the supervisors within the study, representing a more individualized approach to training. For example, in the review I conducted with Ian James (Milne & James, 2000) we scrutinized 28 studies, which included 28 consultants who participated in nine of these studies. The consultants were reported to observe the supervisors (four studies), to provide active assistance (two), to provide feedback (three) and to hold meetings and discuss progress with the supervisors (five studies). Very little information was provided about the consultants themselves, or about how they applied these methods.

I have continued to use supervision-of-supervision, regarding it as an ideal way to train supervisors on account of the capacity for individualized and intensive learning experiences, guided by ongoing evaluation (it is basically easier to address the four tasks noted above within supervision-of-supervision). A recent example followed the supervision manual that is linked to the present text (Milne, 2007a), explicitly extending this evidence-based approach to the supervision-of-supervision that was provided over an 11-month period (Milne *et al.*, 2013). This represents a detailed and structured account of supervision-of-supervision, because it included all the behaviours listed within the observational tool SAGE that was used within the study (Milne *et al.*, 2011b). For example, there was sessional feedback to the supervisor, including quantitative ratings and qualitative remarks. Examples are provided within Milne and Reiser (2014), including notes to explain the extreme competence ratings, and suggestions for next time (e.g. 'Please always end by asking the supervisee for feedback'). Supervision-of-supervision in this study was effective in developing the supervisor's competence and adherence, particularly for the tandem model (Milne *et al.*, 2013).

Supervision-of-supervision can also take place within a group, and a helpfully detailed summary of a group for novice counselling supervisors in a training context was provided by Ellis and Douce (1994). The topics raised were eight recurring issues, which appeared to be addressed productively (there was no formal evaluation). These issues included the anxieties experienced by supervisors, group cohesion, and intervention choices. Remarkably similar issues were found in a UK survey, also of counsellors (Wheeler & King, 2000). In the Ellis and Douce groups, five to eight supervisors meet for two hours weekly to work through these issues, and each week a different supervisor presents a supervision case. This is supposed to start with the supervisor explaining what they want from the group, then include review and discussion of taped segments of the selected session. The group also allocates 30–60 minutes to consider pressing concerns of the others present. A 'trainer' provides supervision to the supervisors, using established methods (e.g. role-plays, role reversals, discussion, interpersonal process recall: IPR). IPR (Kagan & Kagan, 1997) is an effective yet relatively non-threatening way to present taped material, as the supervisor is given the power to select which sections to replay, and the group's reactions are meant to be enquiring (about underlying thoughts and feelings present during the segment) and generally facilitating and supportive. Although the methods used in the groups encountered by the respondents in the Wheeler and King (2000) survey were not specified, they did find them very helpful in their own supervisory work (accorded a mean rating of 80 per cent).

Supervision-of-supervision also takes place in routine practice (i.e. not for research purposes), and in place of a senior supervisor (licensed or post-registration) there may be trainee supervisors involved (pre-qualification trainees, unlicensed graduate students). For instance, Keenan-Miller and Corbett (2015) described how, within a Doctoral training programme, trainees in their fourth or fifth year of training (with at least two years of training as a therapist) provided supervision to less experienced trainees within the same programme. The experienced trainees' provision of supervision is in turn supervised, according to the metasupervision approach described by Newman (2013). The authors indicate that this kind of arrangement for indirect training in supervision as common in the USA. This training in supervision consists of weekly metasupervision meetings, which are small group meetings ('clinics'), including didactic and experiential components. That is, meetings include discussion of assigned reading of several major supervision texts, and develop practical supervision skills through verbal and video-based review of the supervision that has been provided. Based on the analysis of 11 years of archival clinical outcome data for 255 patients, Keenan-Miller and Corbett (2015) compared the effectiveness of metasupervision (related to 76 of these clients) with supervision as usual (i.e. as provided to trainees by the senior supervisor directly, related to the remaining 179 patients). They argued that there were few significant differences between the outcomes achieved by these two groups (e.g. no differences in the perceived therapeutic alliances or the therapists' skill; no differences in patients' distress levels, retention or satisfaction), and so judged metasupervision to be a reasonably effective and hence an ethical approach. However, they did report clear and categorical differences between the two groups, in that the patients of the therapists receiving supervision as usual achieved the more statistically reliable and substantial improvement (achieving 'recovered' status), indicating that this supervision was definitely more effective.

These different approaches to the training of supervisors represent ways of enhancing their competence, but to be useful competence needs to be transferred to supervision. A critical influence on such transfer is the way that supervisors draw on their personal coping strategies, alongside other resources, as noted in panel 2 of Figure 7.2.

Providing Supervision

The definition of coping, presented in the 'context' section above, notes the inseparable link to stressors. The range of potential stressors is huge and hard to capture fully, but examples include poor management, destabilizing shift work, excessive workloads and psychological conflicts between staff members (Buus *et al.*, 2016). These authors also listed stressors reported within supervision, such as interruptions, group dynamics (making participants feel unsafe and vulnerable) and poor supervision. Key parameters of stressors are their perceived predictability and controllability, though several other factors are important, such as whether the stressor is a result of something one did, or was something done to one. At a more general (distal) level of the system, there appears to be an unrelenting increase in social, economic and professional practice developments. These include re-engineering, downsizing, job and budget cuts, and reductions in technological and other resources, all of which have been related to supervision (Bhanthumnavin, 2000). To illustrate, Deery (2004) noted how midwives had been given new powers and greater influence, while at the same time being asked to increase the number of people they see, to improve the care that they provide to clients, to reach out and help previously under-served groups in deprived areas and to introduce new antenatal screening programmes. As a result, 'the climate of continual change often brought about by various policy directives has become a potential health hazard for midwives, leading to stress-related disease' (p.162). In their effort to cope, Deery (2004) reported that midwives worked longer hours, but still experienced emotional exhaustion. This is substantiated by a survey of multidisciplinary staff within mental health services. Kavanagh *et al.* (2003) found that 55 per cent of their supervisors had issues concerning a high clinical workload, one-quarter of them felt there were insufficient guidelines to support their supervision, and one-fifth of these respondents felt there was lack of support from their line manager. Similarly, the supervisees in this sample thought that the amount of clinical work that they had to undertake was an issue (41 per cent of respondents cited this as a difficulty). Cleary and Freeman (2006) also noted additional 'realities' affecting supervision, such as inadequate facilities (lack of distraction-free, quiet rooms) and token committees.

Supervision may not only be inadequate, it can also be harmful, and in a surprisingly high proportion of instances (Ellis *et al.*, 2014, 2015a). This is consistent with the high prevalence of burnout amongst mental health professionals, averaging about 40 per cent of survey respondents (Paris & Hoge, 2010). However, according to the transactional stress model, we need to understand that distressing outcomes such as burnout are the result of the transactions between stressors, coping and the other variables within the coping model. That is, burnout does not follow automatically from exposure to stressors, as the outcome of transactional coping may convert a stressor into a stimulating challenge.

Part of coping effectively is recognizing that supervision is an intrinsically stressful activity. Within the transactional stress model, this recognition is termed 'appraisal', and includes judging whether an event requires a reaction, and deciding whether one is able to respond effectively. For example, group dynamics may be perceived as a problem (as implied by Buus *et al.*, 2016), or viewed as a rare opportunity to work on something that is making the workplace toxic. Similarly, the probing questions and guided discovery process described in James *et al.* (2004) are perceived by the supervisee as stressful and she reports anxiety, but she responds adaptively by appraising the questions as 'making me think hard' and copes by drawing on her relevant experience, ending up feeling pleased with herself. From the supervisors' perspective, a supervisee who has a rather predictable and non-threatening way of using supervision, and who responds readily to guidance, will tend to be appraised as presenting few stressors. However, supervision is typically dominated by a more stressful profile of events, which I will now describe. The important implication is that supervision, if conducted properly, is intrinsically stressful and should be regarded as a challenge to our coping repertoire (and our support and guidance resources), rather than being viewed as a personal weakness of the supervisor.

As indicated by the notion of the 'seven-eyed supervisor' (Hawkins & Shohet, 2000), supervisors need to attend to complex information, on several concurrent channels. They not only have to deal with their supervisees' therapy (and other work activities), but also how this is being presented in supervision, and other related topics. It is stressful in other respects, because the supervisor is charged with integrating formative, normative and restorative functions (Figure 7.1). As Holloway and Wolleat (1994) put it, 'because the goal of supervision is to connect science and practice, supervision is among the most complex of all activities associated with the practice of psychology' (p.30). Indeed, it is arguably the most complex of all the 'complex interventions' in the mental health field.

Another stressor is the growing requirements of supervisees. As they become better trained and more knowledgeable about what it is reasonable to expect from supervisors, they are likely to put increasing pressure on supervisors for more opportunities and relevant experiences, as indicated in the work of Buus *et al.* (2016). Schindler and Talen (1994) underscored this trend, recounting how 'trainees were more articulate in identifying their developmental training needs, better equipped to define the goals of supervision, and more informed about the styles or strategies of supervision that would help them meet their goals (e.g. video tape, co-therapy, live supervision). In essence, now that they know more, they want more' (p.304). They also noted that supervisors were facing more complex demands within the workplace, becoming responsible for administrative supervision and the monitoring of complex ethical, legal and policy issues. Furthermore, theories of both clinical practice and supervision have been developing, placing supervisors under pressure to understand and apply new clinical ideas, as well as to undertake accreditation as a supervisor (Greenspan *et al.*, 1991). Other pressures intrinsic to supervision listed by Bernard and Goodyear (2004) include the following:

1. *Additional responsibilities.* Alongside a reduction in direct client contact (with the attendant reduced ability to directly influence quality of care), supervisors also have to accept responsibility for their supervisees' cases.
2. *Parallel processes.* It is not unusual for supervisors to experience some of the complex and uncomfortable emotions that are encountered by their supervisees in therapy. This means that the supervisors need to deal with clinical practicalities, whilst also attending to process phenomena.
3. *Maintaining control.* There is often a complex dynamic around the exercise of power within supervision, and it is not uncommon for struggles to occur between the supervisor and the supervisee (e.g. striking a balance between behaving as a colleague, and exercising some form of influence over the supervisee).
4. *Needs-led supervision.* Whilst it is of course highly desirable to tailor supervision to the individual characteristics of the supervisee (including aspects of race, culture, gender, sexual orientation and religion), this represents a further burden on the supervisor's coping strategies.
5. *Interpersonal effectiveness.* In addition to these various pressures on the supervisor's ability to function, there may also be some sexual attraction between supervisor and supervisee, which may add further challenges.

In short, such stressors are a formally recognized and inescapable part of supervision, alongside whatever else the supervisee brings to supervision. This aspect refers to panel 1 in Figure 7.2 ('judgements about what to do with the supervisee'). As recognized by the Department of Health in the UK, the workforce needs the opportunity to learn and develop within a system that provides support. In the absence of these factors there can be 'a downward spiral that manifests itself . . . in poor morale in the workforce, an increase in complaints, and dissatisfaction for everybody' (Department of Health, 2007, p.3). In this stressful context, supervisors require a supportive work environment, allied to effective personal coping strategies. In the above, I have tried to suggest that the first of these strategies is accurate appraisal, namely recognizing that supervision inevitably comes with some complex stressors. This appraisal is a preferable way of coping as it is grounded in reality and should minimize the alternative appraisal, in which difficulties are attributed to oneself as a supervisor.

A rare and helpful study of how supervisors cope was reported by Grant *et al.* (2012), who interviewed 16 'wise' supervisors regarding their difficulties and coping strategies in providing supervision. These supervisors reported a wide range of difficulties, including supervisee incompetence and unethical behaviour (e.g., inappropriate interventions); negative supervisee characteristics (e.g., arrogance, defensiveness, validation-seeking); supervisor counter-transference (e.g. anger, criticalness, boredom); and specific problems in the supervisory relationship (e.g. parallel processes, romantic attraction). In interview, these supervisors described their preferred coping strategies in relation to these difficulties, as summarized in Table 7.1. All supervisors reported using the 'relational' and 'reflective' strategies, but only using confrontational strategies if necessary. Half of the supervisors reported using the 'avoidance' approach. Overall, these coping strategies helped the supervisors to resolve most difficulties. These strategies apply to supporting supervisors too, so they can serve as ideas for enhancing effective coping in the context of methods such as supervision-of-supervision.

I will now describe examples of adaptive coping that build on the appraisal process and complement the strategies noted in Table 7.1. In clinical work, adaptive (effective) coping has repeatedly been found to be approach-based, that is, concerned with tackling stressors rather than avoiding them. In addition, I will utilize the distinction between behaviours, thoughts and feeling reactions, three established parameters of coping.

Table 7.1 How wise supervisors reported coping in supervision.

Supervisors' coping strategies	*Specific techniques reported*
Relational (for alliance difficulties)	Naming; validating; attuning; supporting; anticipating; exploring; acknowledging mistakes; modelling
Reflective (for clinical/ competence problems)	Facilitating reflection; remaining mindful; monitoring; remaining patient and transparent; processing counter-transference; seeking supervision; formulation
Confrontative (for supervisee characteristics)	Tentative and direct confrontation; refusing or terminating supervision; taking formal action; referring supervisee for personal therapy; becoming directive
Avoidant (for ethical concerns)	Struggling on; withholding and managing difficulties

Source: Grant *et al.* (2012). Reproduced with permission of the American Psychological Association.

Specifically, I will outline how supervisor training can strengthen supervision skills; summarize ways of developing supervision-linked thinking; and note how groups (and other arrangements) allow supervisors to process the emotionally loaded aspects of their work.

Self-supervision

Sometimes referred to as the coping or self-regulation approach, self-supervision has been defined as 'a systematic process in which a professional works independently, directing his or her own professional development . . . in the context of counselling . . . It involves assessing and modifying . . . ineffective patterns and improving clinical skills' (Dennin & Ellis, 2003). Self-supervision can therefore be viewed as a specific example of the coping strategy enhancement approach outlined in broad terms above. Dennin and Ellis (2003) used a small-n design to evaluate self-supervision in four novice trainees, finding no effect on the main outcome of improved empathy. However, the authors were more sanguine about its value in the hands of competent counsellors, concluding that, once staff are trained to use self-supervision, 'it shows promise as a means by which they can maintain or enhance counselling skills and competence' (p.81). Presumably, self-supervision could be applied by supervisors to themselves.

The work of Safran and Muran (2000) includes discussion of self-exploration, in which they describe the importance of helping the supervisor to attend to their own moment-by-moment experiences, and trusting these as a basis for intervening. They believe that addressing self-exploration requires an explicit discussion about the role this can have in training, contributing to the careful establishment of a working alliance around agreed objectives. They also emphasize the need to acknowledge that this process may not feel comfortable to some supervisors, but encourage them to enter into a trial period. Concerns that may be felt by supervisors about feeling safe enough to explore feelings, conflicts and other work issues are acknowledged, and they are given permission to keep selected observations private.

In CBT, the example of 'self-practice, self-reflection' (SP/SR) also illustrates a reflexive approach, applicable to supervisors. Bennett-Levy and Thwaites (2007) described it as the use of CBT techniques on the CBT practitioners, especially effective in relation to interpersonal skills, which are tackled within supervision and self-supervision. The self-practice method is based either on homework (a workbook of structured assignments) or through 'co-therapy' (i.e. four to six sessions of providing CBT to one another). Self-reflection is viewed as addressing otherwise tacit, automated interpersonal processes. It involves focusing on the personal self within a safe, non-judgemental supervisory environment. Six stages of the reflective process are proposed: focusing attention on an interpersonal problem (e.g. therapist avoiding emotionally laden material); heightened awareness of the relevant thoughts, feelings and behaviours (e.g. through a reverse role-play, in which the therapist played the client, and the supervisor the therapist); clarifying this experience (reflecting on how hurtful it felt to have a therapist avoid the client's feelings); conceptualizing the problem more objectively (formulating why this pattern occurred); developing new skills (practising within role-plays); and finally testing out the new skills in therapy (apply in the next clinical session). Bennett-Levy and Thwaites (2007) report some evidence that these approaches can facilitate therapists' development.

Newman (2013) has also endorsed the use of SP/SR within a simulation approach he termed 'self-supervision', although this was in relation to supervisees. Specifically, he suggested that supervisees should role-play evaluating their own therapy tapes as if they were the supervisor, including attending to relationship factors (he suggested being nurturing and constructive). The SP/SR aspect was for supervisees to also monitor their own thinking while studying their recordings, working on questioning negative thinking as in CBT and as a supervisor might do. Although addressed to supervisees, this method could also work with supervisors, in relation to supervision-of-supervision or other similar arrangements, as per Ellis and Douce (1994).

Peer groups for supervisors

Groups are noted in Figure 7.2 as an example of the ways that supervisors are helped to cope with demands of the role. Bernard and Goodyear (2004) believe that the peer group is the most frequently used method for supporting supervisors, serving formative and supportive functions. A popular version of groups for clinicians is 'peer supervision'. Note that this is technically an oxymoron, in that supervision is by definition hierarchical and hence cannot logically or practically be provided within a peer relationship (see Chapter 1). Similarly, 'self-supervision' is an illogical use of the concept of supervision (self-regulation would appear to be a better term for what is being described). Bernard and Goodyear (2004) suggest that it actually sits somewhere between consultation and supervision proper, and may be better labelled as 'peer consultation', because these groups also tend to be voluntary, and they rarely involve the explicit exercise of differential power (e.g. evaluation or feedback: Campbell, 2006). Perhaps this is why Bernard and Goodyear (2004) were able to cite evidence for the popularity of peer supervision from a survey. This suggested that 24 per cent of psychologists in private practice had belonged to a peer supervision group, and a further 61 per cent expressed a desire to belong to such a group. A more recent survey suggests that peer group supervision (PGS) has continued to be popular, with over 50% of a sample of clinical psychologists (practicing both in private and in a public health service) reporting using PGS (McMahon & Errity, 2013). According to Bernard and Goodyear (2004) and Campbell (2006), the popularity of peer supervision groups is due to a number of perceived benefits:

- Provides insight into novel approaches;
- Allows reflection to occur, aiding problem-solving;
- Suitable throughout the career span;
- Offers peer review;
- Provides a source of continuing professional development;
- Offers reassurance, validation and other products of effective groups, reducing the likelihood of burnout;
- Combats loneliness and isolation; and
- More collegial and less affected by evaluation or other power issues.

There is much to be said for peer group discussion or consultation, as long as it does not masquerade as supervision or replace it. Indeed, the progressive Psychology Board of Australia now requires a minimum of 10 hours of peer consultation a year as part of psychologists' mandatory CPD, in order to maintain their registration. This value is especially evident for mutual support groups, as they tend to be formed amongst colleagues with some sense of compatibility, including similarities in their activities and methods. They may also be individuals who know and respect one another, perhaps as they are part of the same profession or clinical service. These circumstances may foster greater empathy and fewer criticisms and challenges, encouraging more genuine discussion than occurs in supervision, in terms of issues like the disclosure of difficulties or errors (Ladany *et al.*, 1996). From the perspective of the clinical manager or health service, PGS also appeals because it is relatively inexpensive and easy to arrange, which is especially valuable in remote contexts. There are various PGS formats, including the 'supervisory peer consultation group'. In one example, the four participating supervisors were selected because they were assumed to hold very different perspectives, something that was expected to develop their cognitive complexity (Granello *et al.*, 2008). Cognitive complexity refers to the use of multiple perspectives, aided by actions such as admitting uncertainty, examining one's beliefs, tolerating ambiguity, suspending judgments and adjusting opinions. According to the review by Borders (2012, p.69), 'Although there is enthusiastic support for peer models and high satisfaction anecdotally, few models have been investigated empirically, and published studies provide weak support for the few models that have been investigated, often due to study design.' The lack of evidence and the illogical notion of PGS are not the only problems. If professionals only receive PGS (or peer supervision in any other format) then they are not receiving supervision from a trained and properly authorized supervisor. As a result, their competence is unlikely to develop as it would be expected to do with a proper supervisor, and so patients may receive poor care. This threat is especially real as in PGS it is not customary to monitor or observe what the 'supervisee' is actually doing, to guide therapy, or to evaluate clinical outcomes. Furthermore, case discussion is the dominant method used in PGS, and this is unlikely to develop safe and effective practice. In addition, employing organizations that rely on PGS neglect their responsibility to support and guide their staff, and may at the same time deceive interested parties into believing that supervision is in place, when it is not (that is, there exists a risk of fraudulence). The absence of proper supervision may also jeopardize the status of PGS participants, with respect to their professional body, or in relation to their registration to practice. Not least, participants in PGS may be held vicariously liable in Law for the clinical work of their peers (Saccuzzo, 1997). PGS is therefore a highly dubious arrangement, and can be rightly perceived as part of the swampy lowlands of professional life (Schoen, 1987).

Despite these serious concerns, PGS remains popular, and indeed there may be some circumstances where PGS is just about acceptable as a temporary arrangement. These circumstances include the supervision of senior colleagues, and coping with the absence of suitable supervisors in remote locations. It is therefore appropriate to continue to consider PGS. Although by definition formally leaderless, peer discussion groups tend to require some structure, and so a convention is for the Chair to rotate around the group members. The normal content is case presentations and discussion. The procedure used within peer group supervision can simply be followed within peer group discussion amongst supervisors. As described by Lakeman and Glasgow (2009), but adapted here to refer to a group for supervisors, this procedure would entail that group members take turns presenting supervision material, such as a critical incident or stressful experience. They also select a relevant function to be served by the discussion, such as restorative (e.g. seeking validation or sharing a difficult experience) or normative (e.g. through seeking advice). The facilitator's role should be rotated among the members, and involves ensuring that the process is followed, and through soliciting comments, observations or feedback in 'rounds', and ensuring that participants had the opportunity to speak uninterrupted. Again, an exception was the group for supervisors (Granello *et al.*, 2008), in that there was a 'convenor', someone who not only arranged several meetings a year, but also chaired the group. Otherwise the procedure was as per Lakeman and Glasgow (2009), though group members presented the cases initially in a written format, and the group decided which cases to discuss. The convener ensured that all voices were heard equally, with no interruptions, disrespect or criticism.

Again, there is good reason to assume that a discussion group for supervisors will also yield similar benefits, as indicated by the outcomes reported by Granello *et al.* (2008). However, this relatively cosy relationship can bring its disadvantages, as noted by Proctor and Inskipp (2001). They conjectured that supervisors in such groups can become rather too relaxed, failing to accept challenges or take risks. The lack of formal leadership may also compromise the sense of safety, promoting destructive group processes. There may then be a pressure on those present to exercise facilitation skills in lieu of a formal leader, in a context where senior members exercise poor group 'manners'. Not surprisingly, the focus of the group may then become contentious, or hard to maintain. Campbell (2006) offers some tips to make them 'more meaningful' (p.260), such as adding some mutual feedback through utilizing rating scales occasionally, or by inviting someone of suitable experience and stature to offer feedback. Other tips that she offers are to establish a group purpose, to agree expectations and to appoint an observer to monitor the group process and keep it productive.

Mentors

Mentors are also mentioned in panel 2 of Figure 7.2, and mentoring has been defined as 'a personal and reciprocal relationship in which a more experienced (person) acts as a guide, role model, teacher, and sponsor of a less experienced (person). A mentor provides the protégé with knowledge, advice, counsel, challenge and support in the protégé's pursuit of becoming a full member of a particular profession' (Johnson, 2007, p.20). Clearly, as discussed at length in Chapter 1 in relation to the definition of clinical supervision, mentoring overlaps with supervision both in its forms and in its functions. According to Johnson (2007), the mentor functions actually complement supervision, emphasizing an enduring personal relationship and emotional support. Extrapolating from Johnson's (2007) account of 'transformational leadership', mentoring for supervisors would include: a partnership stance with their mentors, so that the mentor could shepherd them safely through vulnerable transitions and other stressors; showing concern for the supervisor's welfare and development; and attempting to offer wisdom, empathy and compassion.

An example of a mentoring relationship is provided within arrangements for 'personal professional development' (PPD) for trainees (Gillmer & Marckus, 2003). This can be achieved through group activities, like Balint groups, or individually, through buddy systems and mentoring arrangements involving slightly more experienced colleagues. Although focusing on supervisees, there is reason to believe that supervisors could also benefit from PPD, including mentoring. Since a mentor could be a more experienced peer, this represents another way in which supervisors could support one another, consistent with Vygotsky's (1978) reasoning about the zone of proximal development.

Consultancy

The term 'consultancy' is sometimes used interchangeably with supervision-of-supervision (I have done so myself), but there are important differences between these terms, as well as grounds for international misunderstanding, so I now believe that they should be distinguished. A further source of confusion is that the term consultation may be used to refer to a supervision technique. An example is the use of consultation breaks within live supervision. According to this procedure, the supervisor will interrupt therapy so as to guide the supervisee (e.g. by making a phone call, or by co-working within therapy). Numerous variations on the phone-in are described in a review by Goodyear and Nelson (1997). They also cite an in-depth study by Heppner *et al.* (1994), which helps to characterize phone-ins and other forms of live supervision. As with my own approach to supervision-of-supervision (Milne *et al.*, 2013), the methods used within supervision and during supervision-of-supervision may be the same. For instance, Heppner *et al.* (1994) found that consultation breaks included suggested actions, offering clarification and providing emotional encouragement. However, consultation breaks are clearly a technical aspect of live supervision, and not a way of supporting and developing supervisors.

For present purposes, consultancy is understood to differ from supervision-of-supervision in terms of the basic relationship and responsibility issues. That is, the consultant is typically an optional adviser to the supervisor, having no necessary role or formal authority over the supervisor. The supervisor retains responsibility, and may take or leave advice from a consultant. Indeed, they may also take or leave consultancy itself. By contrast, I take supervision-of-supervision to be a direct extension of supervision, and hence regard the relationship as a formal one in which the supervisor of a supervisor has the authority to direct the work of the supervisor, and will assume corresponding responsibility for that work. Therefore, consultancy is an opportunity for the supervisor to seek guidance and support from a suitably qualified peer, or simply an opportunity to discuss and reflect on issues. In the latter sense, a consultant may at times have limited experience of specific activities (like supervision), but be a valuable resource to a supervisor because of other types of expertise (e.g. about leadership or experiential learning).

According to this definition, a consultant will tend to primarily facilitate supervisors' reflection, and other aspects of their cognitive functioning. Table 7.2 summarizes some examples of this role, based on the functions of

Table 7.2   Cognitive functions of consultancy for supervisors, with illustrative methods (page numbers refer to sources in Kilburg & Diedrich, 2007).

Cognitive functions	Methods used by consultants
Heightening self-awareness	Expressive writing (p.312)
	360° feedback (gaining views of a wide range of significant others on the supervisor)
	Assessment centres/techniques (e.g. in-basket task and prioritization of work) (p.6)
Improving self-care	'Ventilation' – encouraging emotional expression to reduce tension (p.312)
	'Deep interpersonal communication' (e.g. acknowledging concerns conflicts and the 'loneliness of leadership' (p.314)
Greater self-confidence	Affirmation of strengths to promote avidities understanding (e.g. of conflicts in team: p.300)
	Rational–emotive therapy to foster personal growth (p.7) (e.g. 'should be perfect')

Table 7.2 (*Continued*)

Cognitive functions	Methods used by consultants
Science-informed practice	Discussing personally relevant research
	Considering local applications of research (e.g. use of instruments)
	Guiding supervisors research activity
Educational	Hearing about the organizational system by providing technical information
	Opportunities to experiment and practice in a safe, respectful, confidential environment ('gentle but honest': p.264)
Critical understanding	Questioning contentional accounts (intensive analysis of critical event/situation)
	Examining different types of data; different explanations
	Synthesizing a fresh formulation
	Evaluating the strengths and weaknesses of this formulation
Decision-making	Emphasizing cooperation and identification with others (including empathy and compassion and their link to helping others: p.294)
	Seeking 'win–win' solutions
	Encouraging tolerance
Problem-solving	Clarifying problems (aiming for operational definitions perceptions)
	Generating options (e.g. modify; substitute; rearrange; combine; copy: p.306)
	Appraising options
	Judging results
	Drawing out implications for future practice (e.g. by facilitating reflection)
Supporting self-monitoring	Facilitating reflection on key events
	Considering sources of information (e.g. 'helpful aspects of supervision questionnaire')
	Interpreting results and informal information

Source: Milne, D.L. (2009). Reproduced with permission of Derek Milne.

supervision cited in Figure 2.1. These examples are meant to be illustrative rather than exhaustive, and I imagine most readers will be able to think of additional ways in which supervisors are able to think more effectively through the process of reflecting on their work with a suitably senior colleague. The methods cited within Table 7.2 are drawn from a major textbook on consultation (Kilburg & Diedrich, 2007), supplemented by material from my own experience. Drawing on the therapist training literature, there is good reason to believe that consultancy is necessary to maintain the effects of training (Stirman *et al.*, 2015).

To take an example from Table 7.2, self-awareness is widely recognized as an important professional skill, particularly so within the complex business of supervision (e.g. consider its implication in transference and parallel process phenomena). Self-awareness depends on a combination of meta-cognitive skills, such as the ability to self-monitor. Not only will these skills foster more effective supervision, they also help us to understand incompetence (Kruger & Dunning, 1999). One of the examples of imperfect self-assessments cited by these authors is the tendency for most people to view themselves as 'above average', resulting in what can be a serious overestimate of one's performance. The literature on expertise bears out the relationship between metacognitive skills and proficiency, in that novices are much poorer at judging their own performance than experts. Kruger and Dunning (1999) evaluated what they referred to as a dual burden: the observation that the unaware individual is poor at self-monitoring (burden 1), hence making unfortunate choices which their incompetence robs them of realizing (burden 2). They are 'unskilled and unaware of it' (p.1121). In one of their studies, they examined this double burden in terms of a logical reasoning task. Forty-five psychology undergraduates completed a 20-item logical reasoning test, then they compared their ability with that of their peers, as well as estimating their own score. The authors found that the less able participants over-estimated their ability to reason relative to their peers, placing themselves in the 66th percentile (i.e. significantly higher than the actual mean of 50). In a sub-analysis, Kruger and Dunning (1999) were able to attribute this gross miscalibration to those participants with the least reasoning ability: it was the participants from the bottom quartile ($N = 11$) whose estimates of their reasoning differed most from their actual performance. Even though these individuals averaged scores that placed them at the 12th percentile, they believed that their reasoning ability placed them at the 68th percentile. Not surprisingly, their estimates as to how many items they answered correctly were significantly below the actual score. The authors were able to show that a short training programme, which taught unskilled participants how to test the accuracy of logical syllogisms, improved their ability to monitor their success (and to become significantly more self-aware than their untrained peers).

Interestingly, it was not just the relatively incompetent individuals who miscalibrated, showing this lack of self-awareness. The work of Kruger and Dunning (1999) also indicated that the relatively expert students under-estimated their ability, which the authors attributed to these participants believing that, because they had done well, their peers must have done likewise. Once these better-performing participants were given information to the contrary, they raised their self-appraisals to a more accurate point. There are thus burdens on both the relatively incompetent and the relatively competent. They conclude by suggesting that one of the key explanations for these burdens is the failure of individuals to act on corrective feedback. A number of other ways in which the supervisors' cognitive functioning can be enhanced are defined within Table 7.2. For each of these, some ideas are listed in terms of methods that might be used in consultancy to achieve these goals. However, it should be realized that these are simply illustrative examples, as opposed to evidence-based interventions (and indeed this literature tends to be pitched at the level of anecdotes and case-study material). Therefore, supervisors would be wise to engage in consultation rather cautiously. In conclusion, I suggest that we treat these ways of strengthening supervisors' thinking as relevant to the panel of the infra-structure model that focuses on 'judging what to do with the supervisee' (see Figure 7.2, panel 1), linked to an evaluation of whether the supervisee is learning the kinds of competencies outlined in Falender *et al.*'s (2004) consensus statement. If these are shown to be present, then one can also look for stepwise results, in terms of the supervisee's provision of clinical care (e.g. as assessed by adherence to local audit standards), and by the clinical outcomes (e.g. improved health). An appealing and coherent way to think about these linked indicators is the 'fidelity framework' (Borelli *et al.*, 2005). This will be addressed more fully in the next chapter. However, there are some aspects of feedback and performance monitoring that are best addressed here, because they represent coping strategies that supervisors might utilize in order to adapt to a challenging role.

Three arguments for measuring one's supervision have been noted by Campbell (2006). The first is that it can help to set limits on the personal and other resources that are invested in supervision. Secondly, it can help one to feel more effective and useful. Another is to address one's natural inquisi-tiveness. A method that satisfies at least two of these needs is 'systematic client tracking' (Worthen & Lambert, 2007). Their example is with adult outpatients, and entails weekly completion of a standard symptom/well-being questionnaire. Scores from the individual supervisee's clients can then be compared with normative data from hundreds of other clients, allowing judgements to be formed about whether the client is progressing as well as would be expected. Real-time feedback is provided against this national clinical outcome benchmark, which indicates whether clients are progressing satisfactorily or where there is a risk of a negative outcome. A written feedback message is provided, suggesting evidence-based ways of rectifying problems (e.g. client drop-out from therapy might be addressed by reviewing progress collaboratively and by considering the client's readiness to change). Four clinical trials of this feedback system have indicated that it could improve therapy significantly (overall effect size of 0.34). As the authors note, this kind of routine clinical evaluation could enable supervisors to identify problems and potential solutions more rapidly. A related approach, Continuous Quality Improvement, has been applied to the supervision of nursing teams within residential care (Hyrkas & Lehti, 2003).

Another example is to audit one's supervision, which can also be aided by using published instruments and by comparing one's profile with that of others. To illustrate, Edwards *et al.* (2006) surveyed 260 community mental health nurses in Wales with the MCSS (Winstanley, 2000). The MCSS contains seven sub-scales (e.g. 'trust/rapport'; 'support/advice' and 'improving care/skills'), providing the basis for a supervision profile. In the Edwards *et al.* (2006) sample, these three factors were equal to or better than the normative data published with the MCSS. An individual supervisor could use the MCSS in a similar way, by asking supervisees to complete it in relation to his or her supervision, then comparing the resultant profile with these norms.

A further topical example concerns case-based supervision, in which the focus is upon the supervisees' clinical effectiveness with their caseload, guided through routine clinical outcome monitoring (Richards, 2008). This is relevant here as one can regard the monitoring data as feedback on the supervision, as well as on the therapy that the supervisee is providing to these patients. However, this feedback on the supervision is indirect, being mediated by the independent functioning of both the supervisee and the patient, so is two steps removed and hence potentially insensitive to the quality of the supervision (Sharpless & Barber, 2009). Therefore, it has to be treated with caution, but logically there is still some potential value in it, particularly where stepwise links can be demonstrated or reasonably assumed (e.g. the treatment goals of all three parties are agreed and communicated regularly, so that clinical goal attainment could serve as a common thread). I return to clinical outcome monitoring in the next chapter, providing a summary of the more recent research. A further issue that this case-based approach implies is that the organizational context of supervision needs to include effective leadership (e.g. managers who can secure the technical resources to build and maintain the feedback system), and an innovation culture (e.g. creative planning and addressing resistance collectively). These kinds of factors have been identified as necessary for the implementation of outcome-monitoring systems (Lyons *et al.*, 1997), and are well illustrated in the introduction of the clinical instruments HoNOS and CORE in the UK (Barkham *et al.*, 1998; Milne *et al.*, 2001). In short, to paraphrase Machiavelli, innovations like routine outcome monitoring are devilishly difficult to achieve.

How Support and Guidance Work: A Formulation

In this chapter I have noted a wide range of contextual factors, intervention techniques, guidance methods and nurturing processes through which supervisor support and guidance might operate. How might this information be integrated, to explain how in essence supervisors (and their supervisees) benefit from these wide-ranging factors? How do they come to feel understood and validated, encouraged and skilled, motivated and effective? Since many of the examples I have cited are reflexive approaches, drawing on the methods that supervisors use in supervision to address the needs of supervisors (e.g. SP/SR, self-supervision and metasupervision), it seems appropriate to continue to be reflexive now. Therefore, I will use the well-established idea of the zone of proximal development (ZPD: see Chapter 6) to capture the essential factors that appear to explain how support and guidance operate. Like this chapter, the formulation in Figure 7.3 emphasizes positive cycles, but the formulation could equally well be used to explain negative cycles, leading to supervisor burnout.

Step 1 in this formulation is to clarify the context, which effectively explains the situation in which supervision occurs, and why it happens the way that it does. The context was discussed at the start of this chapter, and I emphasized how organizational infrastructure and culture, including social support, represented highly influential factors. Following the ZPD logic (Vygotsky, 1978), to help supervisors through support and guidance we require to provide suitable 'scaffolding', which is indicated in Figure 7.3 by the methods of adaptation (training; peer support groups; etc.). One of the tasks that such methods should address are the stressors perceived by supervisors (step 2), both situational (e.g. poor management) and personal

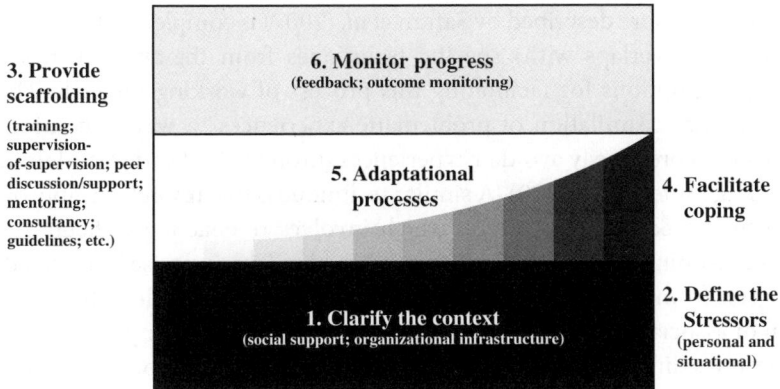

Figure 7.3 A reflexive formulation of how support and guidance operate.

(e.g. challenging supervisees). Based on the nature of these stressors, step 3 is to ensure that supervisors receive the scaffolding necessary to adapt, which is represented by the different interventions discussed within this chapter (training, peer support, etc.)

Step 4 is to work with supervisors to bolster their personal coping strategies, and to offer support. In particular, healthy organizations will ensure that their supervisors are enabled to process or 'work-through' troubling experiences, so that they can have a 'corrective emotional experience' and adapt successfully. For example, stressors such as alliance ruptures might be tackled through what Safran and Muran (2000) term the 'preliminaries to therapy', such as empathic clarification, openness to working through and relationship work (e.g. understand the core relational themes that underpin the rupture, and reframe experiences). Later these authors developed a procedure for dealing with alliance ruptures (Safran *et al.*, 2007). This starts with identifying the triggering or activating event that appears to have caused the rupture, then reflecting on the interactional problem using perspective-taking and trying to 'not take it personally' or 'jump to conclusions' about what has happened. The third task is to gently and collaboratively encourage and invite exploration of what happened, trying to understand the problem together, from a non-blaming perspective (using a systemic point of view to understand both sides of the problematic interaction). Fourthly, supervisors should be helped to work on a plan to resolve the problem, including addressing the underlying feelings (typically anxiety, vulnerability or anger). The final step is carefully monitoring efforts to resolve the rupture.

The procedure described by Safran *et al.* (2007) is complementary to (and sometimes overlaps with) specific techniques from therapy which seem promising options for facilitating this process of working-through. These include the 'assimilation of problematic experiences', a way of coming to terms with previously avoided experiences through clarification and under-standing (Stiles *et al.*, 1990). A similar technique is the 'resolution' approach (Greenberg & Malcolm, 2002), which involves re-enacting difficult expe-riences within an emotionally charged role-play. This exercise is intended to progress from blaming/complaining to re-enacting the incident, the expres-sion of associated and intense emotions, the specifying of any unmet needs and proceeding to trying to shift perspective, then resolution (e.g. through self-affirmation or compassion). Some empirical support for the resolution model has come from survey data, involving 81 counselling supervisees (Bertsch *et al.*, 2014). Drawing on experiential learning rather than therapy, Lombardo *et al.* (2009) suggested how 'experiencing' can be facilitated by highlighting emotional aspects of the work, so as to encourage acceptance, accurate labelling, differentiation or heightened awareness. 'Reflecting' could focus on identifying recurring patterns or helpful precedents in the supervisors' coping repertoires. 'Conceptualizing' might be aided through drawing on the supervisor's understanding (e.g. case reformulation) or knowledge of the literature. Finally, Lombardo *et al.* (2009) suggested that 'experimenting' could be enabled through joint action-planning and role-play rehearsal.

Step 5 in Figure 7.3 is the process of adaptation that takes place in supervisors, closing the gaps between the stressors and the personal coping strategies and support arrangements. As this gap closes, supervisors should become more positive about their role and further removed from occupa-tional burnout. They may become strong advocates of supervision, or work to improve the infrastructure through action research or supervising other supervisors. Finally, in step 6 there needs to be a system to ensure that supervisors receive feedback, as a basis for guiding further steps towards successful adaptation.

Conclusions

This chapter has considered the widely recognized but little-addressed challenge of supporting and guiding supervisors in undertaking an intrinsically stressful role (Hawkins & Shohet, 2000; Milne & Reiser, 2016). In terms of the tandem model that underpins this book, the normative and restorative aspects of supervision are part of the organizational and professional context, by analogy the climate and horizons that represent a backdrop or point of reference for the supervisory enterprise. These aspects should also be agenda items within supervision, in order to stay on track and to ensure that the supervisee is fit and able to proceed.

While there is an explicit and widely accepted way of thinking about the educational framework within which the supervisee operates (i.e. Vygotsky's scaffold around the ZPD, as illustrated in Figure 7.3), there is less consensus regarding the organizational framework that should aid the supervisor. Although formal governmental policy recognizes that there needs to be an infrastructure of this kind, including effective leadership from managers, there appears to be few suitable frameworks available. Therefore, in this chapter I have assimilated to the tandem model insights from the 'whole system' or 'systems-contextual' approach (Beidas & Kendall, 2010), as well as the SOS model outlined by Milne and Reiser (2016). This integrative model is set out in Figure 7.2, using the same panels and variables as the original EBCS framework (see Chapter 3), but with these insights noted in the text, together with some practical examples of supervisor support and guidance.

A major part of the tandem model is the incorporation of the transactional stress or 'coping' model, in order to place the individual supervisor at the centre of the EBCS framework, as well as to make more systematic sense of how we might support supervisors. In particular, we recognized the unrelentingly stressful nature of modern healthcare systems, compounded by the complex intervention that is supervision. It is not surprising, then, that many surveys of health practitioners indicate that significant numbers are complaining of burnout. But the tandem model does not accept that such stressors necessarily lead to burnout or other forms of distress. In theory, such stressors might equally well be transformed into a sense of job satisfaction and even mastery, through adaptive coping and support arrangements. This means that it is important to attend at least as much to the ways that we cope with these stressors as to the support arrangements if we are to create a restorative and normative system that helps supervisors to feel that they are supported, guided, accepted, nurtured, acknowledged and validated. Formal arrangements, like peer discussion groups and mentoring, have been found to be helpful. In addition, I noted how informal processes were vital to well-being (social support). Supervisors also require a normative system of support, and I have presented some arrangements that can help them to come to terms with the demands that their host organizations place on them (e.g. through peer and individual consultation).

Using the coping model also helps us to understand how a supervisor can enter a vicious cycle, as a result of an unfortunate combination of excessive work demands, maladaptive coping (including faulty appraisals of the stressors that are experienced) and absent social support. In this kind of cycle, supervisors will readily perceive themselves as failing, and hence will risk spiralling downwards to professional burnout. By contrast, effective coping strategies that are well supported within a healthy organization are likely to lead to the supervisor feeling positive about the role, and to enhanced effectiveness and to higher levels of job satisfaction. The major study of therapist development by Orlinsky and Ronnestad (2005) elaborates this kind of coping analysis. I have formulated coping, support and the other main factors identified within this chapter in Figure 7.3, as a way to organize the essential variables and adaptational processes.

Although we can be reasonably confident about this formulation, it has to be acknowledged that the literature that I have been able to harness within this chapter (and within our recent journal special issue: Newman *et al.*, 2016) lacks the degree of scientific rigour that has been found within the literature used in previous chapters. That is, the material in this chapter is rich in qualitative detail but not yet convincing as an evidence-base for modern mental health services. The absence of a strong literature in this area reflects the continuing limited attention accorded to the much-needed supervision infrastructure. It is appropriate, then, for supervisors (and others) to treat this material with particular caution, seeking opportunities to evaluate any applications of this literature review. Some suggestions for evaluating one's work were noted above, and the next chapter suggests more formal ways of improving what we know about supporting and guiding supervisors.

In conclusion, the practical support and guidance provided to supervisors is unsystematic and unsatisfactory, and the available evidence is the weakest in the whole enterprise of clinical supervision. The emergence of infrastructure frameworks (as per Figure 7.2), and the growing emphasis on evidence-based supervisor training, together with other methods, heralds some long-overdue progress.

8

Developing Supervision

Introduction

In the last chapter I discussed how the organizational system needs to support and guide supervisors, individually and in groups. In general terms, support and guidance can be regarded as maintaining the supervisory system, but systems also require development. I now address this vital aspect of an effective system, the capacity to adapt and improve through development activities, focusing on a complementary set of service evaluation and research tasks. In terms of the tandem model analogy, evaluation provides information on essential concerns, such as where we are now, the progress we have made, what seems to be working best and the amount of effort and resource that will be needed to progress smoothly down the development path.

Within the evidence-based clinical supervision (EBCS) framework (see Figure 7.2), there are four panels that are particularly related to evaluation: 'supervisee development' (covering feedback and gate-keeping), 'outcomes' (client outcome tracking or 'clinical outcome monitoring'), 'improved patient care' and 'audit'. These panels suggest that evaluation should focus on the supervisees' learning and development (panel 3), relating this to patient care (panel 5) and in turn to the clinical outcomes that they achieve (panel 4). This information should be supplemented by audit (panel 6), which relates patient care to organizational and/or professional standards. For example, quality standards (or 'statements') are published by the NHS to encourage care providers to identify gaps in their services, to specify areas

Evidence-Based CBT Supervision: Principles and Practice, Second Edition. Derek L. Milne.
© 2018 John Wiley & Sons Ltd. Published in 2018 by the British Psychological Society and John Wiley & Sons Ltd.

for improvement, to measure and demonstrate the quality of care and to guide the commissioning of services (Department of Health, 2012).

The difference between patient care and clinical outcomes is essentially the difference between process and outcome, which, alongside the available resources for care ('structure'), represent the three most fundamental criteria for evaluating healthcare (Donabedian, 1988, 2005), criteria that are still used explicitly by the NHS as the main measures of care quality. For example, within the NHS outcomes framework (Department of Health, 2012), structure includes a safe environment (protection from adverse incidents and avoidable harm; emotional support), the process of patient care is defined in terms of positive patient experiences (e.g. respectful, personalized, comfortable), while outcomes should be benchmarked against international comparators, including cost-effective interventions, to detect under-performance. Translated into the context of clinical supervision, patient care is the caring and competent provision, by the supervisee, of evidence-based therapy. This should be based on an individual formulation, and on collaborative decision-making with the patient about the goals and methods of therapy (or other professional activity). In terms of translating 'process', competent supervision is defined in Table 8.1 in terms of the

Table 8.1 The augmented fidelity framework, a stepwise, integrative approach to evaluating supervision.

Steps	Objectives (functions)	Evaluation questions and criteria
1. Designing supervision	a. *Conceptualization*: justifies and specifies the model, guiding supervision	Addresses the questions: *What is the right way to supervise? Which resources are required?*
	b. *Implementation planning*	Frequency, duration and content of supervision (accessibility); supervisors' and supervisees' 'credentials' (selection); supervision model and guidelines that are relevant to the need (involve service-users)
2. Training supervisors	c. *Implementation integrity*	*Is the right supervision being done?* Describing and standardizing supervisor training (manual); assessing attendance, participation and competence acquisition and auditing maintenance, in terms of adherence to model

Table 8.1 (*Continued*)

Steps	Objectives (functions)	Evaluation questions and criteria
3. Delivering supervision	d. *Faithful implementation* (performance monitoring)	*Has supervision been done right?* Assessing and enhancing the supervision contents, processes (alliance), procedures (method fidelity) and proficiency (skilful adjustments – e.g. 'dosage'/ timing)
4. Receiving supervision	e. *Supervisee development*	*Did supervision lead to the right learning?* Effectiveness evaluation (plus acceptability, participation, reactions, knowledge gain, skill acquisition, attitude development)
5. Transferring supervision	f. *Outcome benchmarking* g. *Generalization* h. *Formulating*	*Did supervision produce results/ did it work?* Clinical outcome evaluation, based on transfer of learning, related to performance standards/norms/barriers and boosters in workplace (e.g. patients' characteristics; social support)
6. Developing supervision	i. *Create feedback loops* j. *Economy and efficiency* (continuous quality improvement)	*Are we getting good value? Have we got our system right? Is there a better way?* 'Cost–benefit' analysis (including 'summative' decisions about 'blacklisting'/ accrediting supervisors and 'gate keeping'/promoting supervisees: reduce 'wastage' and retain/ develop talent); dismantling and coordinating/streamlining supervision; enhancing (e.g. clinical outcome monitoring and supportive feedback); improving environmental factors (e.g. leadership/equipment) or any of 1–5 above (e.g. supervisee socialization/induction)

Source: Milne, D.L. (2009). Reproduced with permission of Derek Milne.

contents (e.g. agenda), processes (e.g. alliance), procedures (e.g. fidelity) and proficiency (skillfulness) of supervision. All of these variables are thought to influence the outcomes.

In addition, panel 8 (research and development) is also relevant to developing the supervision system. Research and evaluation are major fields of professional activity, each meriting dedicated texts. Therefore, within this chapter my aims need to be suitably focused, so I primarily describe and illustrate how the tandem model and its implementation can be developed through research and evaluation. Also, to make the task yet more feasible, I essentially combine research and evaluation, through an emphasis on 'effectiveness' or evaluative research to foster local development (rather than addressing 'efficacy' or basic research issues). In particular, I aim to discuss evaluative research in relation to an evaluation taxonomy, the fidelity framework. As a result, the reader will be informed of a range of complementary options for developing their own supervision system. This includes a summary of measurement instruments and methods, and suggestions on using the feedback from such instruments.

Evaluation

Evaluative research is 'the use of social research methods to systematically investigate the effectiveness of social intervention programmes in ways that are adapted to their political and organizational environments, and are designed to inform social action to improve social conditions' (Rossi *et al.*, 2004). Put more concretely, evaluative research entails a data-based judgement about the extent to which supervision objectives are achieved. This information provides feedback that can be used to develop supervision (e.g. guiding future training activities). In Chapter 5 I described 'deliberate practice' (Ericsson, 2006), which included two phases of feedback: systematic, ongoing, formal feedback (e.g. data from clinical outcome monitoring), and the utilization of this feedback (e.g. learning from errors made, by developing and executing an improvement plan). Both are discussed below, in relation to supervision.

Evaluation is an integral, indispensable part of all systematic models of clinical supervision, although formal evaluation (and evaluative research) is perhaps   most   prominent   in   cognitive-behaviour   therapy   (CBT) supervision, as indicated in Chapters 1 and 3. Indeed, evaluation is fundamental to any basic problem-solving process, as reflected in modern healthcare. The following factors have been thought important in the rise of evaluation (Knapp, 1997):

- The purchasers' requirement to assure themselves that they are getting the best value for their money;
- Sharply increased healthcare costs (e.g. new, expensive medication);
- The emergence of a business culture in the UK, following on from the establishment of managed care in the USA;
- New treatments that imply the need for fresh, comparative evaluations, including new treatment environments and new interventions, not to mention new providers of health services;
- Greater fiscal stringency; and
- The arrival of the era of evidence-based practice, in which healthcare resources are allocated on the basis of compelling evidence of cost-effective interventions.

These factors remain highly influential, as reflected in the NHS outcomes framework (Department of Health, 2012). As noted by Fonagy *et al.* (2002), the consequence of these growing public demands on health service providers has been to create an environment in which health professionals now shoulder much greater accountability for their services to clients, and to those who purchase the services. This makes service evaluation an essential activity, as it can furnish persuasive evidence that these various responsibilities have been addressed effectively. Although not included as a specific example, we can think about these various pressures as part of the context for supervision, as set out in Figure 3.3, and part of increasing the emphasis on evaluation.

Although the healthcare context has increasingly emphasized evaluation, it has always had a pivotal role within supervision, being intrinsic to its definition, function and development. To illustrate, Bernard and Goodyear (2004) have referred to evaluation as the 'nucleus' of supervision (p.19). It appears reliably in all textbook definitions of supervision, such as the one in Falender and Shafranske (2004). They wrote that: 'supervision . . . involves observation, evaluation, feedback, the facilitation of supervisee self-assessment . . . and mutual problem-solving' (p.3). This is similar to the definition provided in Chapter 1, underlining the link between formative evaluation (corrective feedback, intended to develop competence) and the summative function of evaluation, in which a judgement is made about fitness for practice or award ('gate-keeping'). Whilst these are the two dominant purposes of evaluation, as many as 10 such functions or objectives of evaluation have been articulated within the supervision literature. Table 8.1 lists these 10 objectives, in the context of a stepwise, 'fidelity framework' approach to evaluation. It can be seen that these objectives combine the healthcare context (e.g. continuous quality improvement and leadership) with objectives related to the process of supervision performance (contents, processes, fidelity and proficiency), and in turn to resource considerations (economy and efficiency). We need such a comprehensive, integrated framework if we are to develop supervision efficiently.

Although it is unusual for more than one or two of these objectives to be evaluated within any one supervision study, this is a seriously flawed approach when it comes to developing a supervision system. There are some long-established and persuasive reasons to seek to evaluate at least three elements of this fidelity framework: the structure, process and outcome of supervision (rows 1, 2 and 5 in Table 8.1, respectively). I will discuss these reasons shortly. A commendable example of the full fidelity framework in use is the evaluation of Multisystemic Therapy (MST), an intensive family and community-based treatment originally developed for delinquent youths that addresses aspects of the youths' family, peers, school, neighbourhood and community systems (summarized in Schoenwald, 2016). MST evaluation is based on the logic of continuous quality improvement, so there are feedback loops that include data about MST implementation at the level of the family, therapist, supervisor, expert consultant and the organization operating the MST programme. In terms of supervision, this evaluation system includes:

- Assessment of the suitability of the host organization;
- An orientation for therapists and clinical supervisors;
- Clinical supervision within the host organization, guided by a supervision protocol;
- Consultation with an MST expert;
- Quarterly booster training; and
- Valid and reliable measures of adherence for the therapist, supervisor and expert consultant.

Therefore, although not explicitly an application of the fidelity framework, this continuous quality improvement strategy is nonetheless an outstanding example of stepwise evaluation that fits the fidelity framework, with the effectiveness of MST being judged ultimately by its effects on client outcomes. Schoenwald (2016) summarized the favourable clinical outcomes achieved by MST, noting reductions in the participating youths' antisocial or delinquent behaviour, and their decreased association with deviant peers (consistent with the systemic logic). Importantly, these reductions were mediated by high therapist adherence to the MST manual, indicating how the steps in evaluation are linked.

Reasons to be Systematic about Evaluating Supervision

Schoenwald (2016) and her MST colleagues are wise to include multiple measures of MST, because this will tend to enhance the validity and utility of the evaluation. Also, in prizing the clinical outcomes obtained with patients, they are in a position to respond to the growing demand for accountable services that are cost-effective and evidence-based. In particular, purchasers, clients and others will welcome the primacy accorded to outcome data in Schoenwald's (2016) approach to evaluation. Indeed, within the field of supervision research the clinical outcomes obtained with patients has often been judged the acid test: 'The impact of clinical supervision on client outcome is considered by many to be the acid test of the efficacy of supervision' (Ellis & Ladany, 1997, p.485). This is consistent with the best-established approach to healthcare evaluation, in which the clinical outcomes are judged to be the 'ultimate validators of the effectiveness and quality of care' (Donabedian, 2005, p.694). In effect, clinical outcomes have also become the common-sense criterion for evaluating healthcare interventions such as supervision and therapy. However, as already hinted, there are some significant problems with prizing this criterion. Failure to address these problems will probably result in a failure to develop supervision optimally, ironically leading to poorer clinical outcomes.

The most fundamental problem with prizing clinical outcomes as the focus for the evaluating supervision is that it may well provide invalid and misleading information, and this will seriously impair attempts to develop supervision. There are additional reasons to be concerned about 'the acid test', and some of these are listed in Milne (2014b), and in a special issue of *Training and Education in Professional Psychology* (e.g. Olds & Hawkins, 2014; Reiser & Milne, 2014), but, because my interest in this chapter is on developing supervision, I will focus on the problems and solutions related to invalid and misleading information as feedback.

The validity of information on clinical outcomes is threatened by the various alternative explanations for an outcome, a serious and long-standing methodological problem (Holloway & Neufeldt, 1995; Ellis & Ladany, 1997; Wampold & Holloway, 1997). Considering that the outcomes of therapy have continued to prove difficult to demonstrate definitively (Borkevic & Bauer, 2010), it follows that adding supervision of the therapist as a further level of evaluation represents a significant methodological challenge. Additionally, and perhaps even more so than in therapy, we are dealing with complex interactions between variables (e.g. recursive processes and co-construction; Rigazio-DiGilio *et al.*, 1997), carrying a real risk that causal inferences become attenuated (Donabedian, 2005).

The essence of this problem of internal validity is that supervision outcomes may not in fact be due to supervision. Instead, they may be the result of various alternative explanations. Prizing clinical outcomes may blind us to these reasons and encourage us to make the appealing inference that supervision works, leading to invalid feedback and mistaken developments. To illustrate, Rousmaniere *et al.* (2014) listed 10 variables that have been shown to obscure the relationship between supervision and client outcome, including endogenous client factors (e.g. symptom severity); supervisee/therapist factors (e.g. the influence of peers within group supervision); and supervisor factors (e.g. the quality of the alliance or the methods used). To these one should add contextual or environmental (exogenous) factors, such as the social support available to the patient from friends, changes in medication prescribed by physicians, stressful life events within the family or workplace, and so on. Given such threats to validity, it is not surprising that there appear to be only six rigorous (interpretable) studies of the acid test (Reiser & Milne, 2014), again including Schoenwald's work (Schoenwald *et al.*, 2009). These six sound studies are not interpretable because they do not clarify the causal mechanisms (i.e. which aspects of supervision actually contributed to client outcomes), but we considered that they did indicate that supervision that improved adherence to an empirically supported protocol appeared likely to improve client outcomes. Secondly, we concluded that supervision was likely to outperform no supervision in terms of client outcomes. However, any conclusions should be highly tentative, not least because of the inconsistent or weak links between supervision and clinical outcome (e.g. Rousmaniere *et al.*, 2014). The most convincing demonstrations to date come from meta-analyses of dozens of controlled clinical outcome studies, analyses that examined the effectiveness of collaborative care for depressed patients in primary care (Bower *et al.*, 2006; Gilbody *et al.*, 2006). Utilizing regression analyses, these authors were able to demonstrate that 'the use of regular and planned supervision of the case manager, usually by a psychiatrist, was related to a more positive clinical outcome' (Gilbody *et al.*, 2006, p.2317). The finding that the case managers with a mental health background and regular specialist supervision contributed significantly to the outcomes suggested to the authors that expertise was important. These good clinical outcomes appeared to be mediated by the effect that this supervision had on the therapeutic alliance, and on adherence to the biopsychosocial treatment model.

Turning to the problem of clinical outcomes providing misleading information, even if the clinical outcomes of supervision are valid, the outcomes alone do not indicate how to explain or improve them. To develop supervision, we need to know why it is achieving its effects, in order to be able to make informed decisions (e.g. is it good adherence to a supervision guideline?). That is, the acid test has limited feedback utility. But if we at least gather information on the associated structures and processes we are in a position to understand the basic cause and effect variables, and so develop supervision. If that fails, we would be wise to extend our evaluation to include the fidelity framework, as set out in Table 8.1 and described below. There are many sound reasons for providing supervision (e.g. Figure 2.1 notes 17 such reasons, and Table 8.1 suggests more). Each of these has a valid outcome, particularly as it could indicate the presence or absence of an expected link to clinical outcomes (i.e. such information would have high feedback utility). It would be unhelpful and illogical if these were devalued by an over-emphasis on the acid test. Therefore, perhaps the most compelling reason for questioning a reliance on the acid test is that it may encourage us to turn a blind eye to the mediating variables and to the mechanisms of change that make up the causal chain, as these could illuminate how supervision can be developed most effectively, and hence lead to enhanced clinical effectiveness.

Ways to be Systematic about Evaluating Supervision

There are a large number of possible solutions to the methodological problems associated with the acid test (Ellis & Ladany, 1997; Inman *et al.*, 2014) but, as just mentioned, the minimum is to ensure that an evaluation links outcomes to the resources (structure) and processes that are thought to cause them (Donabedian, 1988; Rossi *et al.*, 2004). This 'structure–process–outcome' approach to service evaluation allows us to better understand the outcomes that supervision achieves. The 'structure' or resources that are allocated to supervision are essentially 'the tools needed to do the job', including competent supervisors and facilities with the necessary equipment (e.g. tape players). For example, Roth *et al.* (2010) reviewed 27 controlled evaluations of CBT in order to clarify the resources that were reported for training and supervising the therapists in these studies. They found information on nine factors related to supervision: the experience and qualifications of the supervisors; the use of a therapy manual, linked to observation, monitoring and if necessary further supervision; the format, frequency and duration of supervision; and the provision of additional group supervision or meetings, concerned with adherence to the therapy manual. Roth *et al.* (2010) found that this information was reported inconsistently and only in outline form in these 27 studies, which led them to advocate that study authors ensure that sufficient information is available in future.

As an illustration of the problem, in the Rousmaniere *et al.* (2014) study, all we are told about supervision is that it lasted two hours per week and was in group supervision format. Although the participating supervisors had all had some training in supervision (at least one 'academic' course), there was no information concerning the nature of this training, nor were there data on their competence as supervisors. By comparison, an illustration of the solution can be found in Bambling *et al.* (2006), who provided useful information on the structure behind their evaluation: the participants were 40 supervisors, selected on the basis of a supervision competence rating (and paid by being given free training in supervision); all were qualified and experienced mental health practitioners; the training consisted of two 1-day supervision workshops for a total of 127 therapists, also selected based on therapeutic competence, also repaid with free training; also, there were six trainers, who rated all therapists' and supervisors' competence. Another resource was the 127 adult clients (one per therapist), who presented with anxiety or depression and were given 8 hours of therapy; manuals supported the training and guided the evaluation. All therapists and supervisors were provided with information packs, including manuals, measures, audio tapes and a procedural booklet. As Roth *et al.* (2010) pointed out, knowing about such structural features helps to ensure that the resources needed to achieve similar clinical outcomes within routine services are well-defined, and also helps to protect client welfare.

Process variables link to information on structure and outcome, as in the mediators (e.g. the use of specific techniques within supervision, such as goal-setting) and mechanisms (e.g. experiential learning) of supervision. Part of a stepwise approach to evaluation is to clarify these links in the causal chain, as suggested by Holloway and Neufeldt (1995). The summary in Table 8.1 adds the desirability of also assessing and enhancing the content of supervision (e.g. the use of awareness-raising questions), plus the supervisor's proficiency (e.g. ability to be responsive, by making skilful adjustments or by careful timing). Later in this chapter I outline some instruments for measuring the process of supervision along such dimensions. This can be especially informative when the links to outcome are unclear. For instance, Wampold and Holloway (1997) highlighted the need to examine contingent patterns of activities (as in a sequential analysis of supervision interactions; for an example see James *et al.*, 2004). They noted that some of these links have proved difficult to demonstrate, so encouraged a focus on more 'micro' connections between supervision and the consecutive mini-outcomes, focusing on mediators in the causal process, rather than trying to show causal relations between supervision and more distal elements, such as clinical outcomes. In essence, they concluded that researchers should simplify the phenomena of supervision to make research realistic and feasible. This gels with reviews of the psychotherapy outcome literature, in that different levels of analysis, treated collectively and seen as responsive to one another (Norcross, 2002), including micro-analysis of content, impact and outcome, are advocated as ways of resolving traditional problems in the evaluation of psychotherapy (Shapiro, 1995). Table 8.1 lists a variety of examples that suggest how this kind of stepwise, in-depth, micro-analysis of process and outcome might be undertaken. Such analyses are similar to the microgenetic method advocated by Fischer *et al.* (2003), in relation to the dynamic skill model (described in Chapter 6).

Outcome variables studied in relation to supervision have also been varied and numerous (Wheeler & Richards, 2007; Wheeler & Barkham, 2014). To bring some order to these multiple outcome criteria, Holloway and Neufeldt (1995) argued for four consecutive levels of evaluation, together with the linkages between these factors. Specifically, they saw outcome evaluation as embracing:

1. The supervisee's acquisition of attitudes, beliefs and skills relevant to treatment.
2. The supervisee's performance in therapy, related to supervision.

3. The interactional processes in therapy, as related to processes in supervision.
4. Clients' changes, related to supervision.

Wampold and Holloway (1997, p.23) agreed, commenting that research may make surer progress 'by studies focusing on various pieces of the mediated causal process'. Similarly, Donabedian (2005) endorsed the logic of a stepwise approach, noting how each link in the chain 'has a kind of conditional or interim validity which may be more relevant to the purposes of assessment in specific instances' (p.711). A more recent review of the evaluation of supervision similarly recommended a stepwise approach, indicating its durability and appeal (Lewis & Hendricks, 2014). In arguing this point myself, and offering a supervision-specific reformulation of outcome evaluation (Milne, 2014b), I noted these advantages to a stepwise approach to evaluation, as per the fidelity framework (Table 8.1):

- Increasing the likelihood that causal inferences are valid;
- Encouraging study-specific outcomes, fostering focused research;
- Ensuring adherence, so improving outcomes;
- Attending to proficiency (competence), so we can logically interpret outcomes;
- Illuminating the explanatory processes and mechanisms, improving the utility of feedback;
- Encouraging a well-founded, cumulative research agenda; and
- Thinking systemically, in order to identify any side-effects and recognize the complex determinants of ineffective and effective supervision.

This is not to question the need for evidence of a link between supervision and clinical outcomes (Watkins, 2011), but rather to encourage a systematic approach to developing supervision. Therefore, in this chapter I will describe an integrative, stepwise approach to outcome evaluation that includes clinical outcomes, applies the fidelity framework to supervision and which augments the framework with a sixth and final step ('developing clinical supervision'). This final step reflects the need to also study how interventions generalize across time, place, people and behaviour. Befiting the EBCS approach to evidence, this augmented framework derives from the neighbouring literatures in applied psychology, education, medicine and research methodology.

Although not yet used explicitly within clinical supervision, the fidelity framework is consistent with the ways that some supervision researchers have conducted evaluation. For example, a review of 12 studies of the acid test (Reiser & Milne, 2014) indicated moderately good adherence overall to the fidelity framework (0.67). The weakest areas of adherence were 'receipt' (the supervisees' learning: 0.33) and 'supervisor training' (0.50), followed by the 'delivery' (provision of supervision: 0.67) of supervision. We concluded that, although there was a general improvement over time, only three of these 12 studies met all five evaluation criteria within the fidelity framework: Triantafillou (1997); Bambling *et al.* (2006) and Schoenwald *et al.* (2009). On the other hand, this suggests that all five evaluation criteria within the original fidelity framework (Borelli *et al.*, 2005) are accepted by this sample of supervision researchers.

As set out in Table 8.1, I have expanded the original five-step approach to six steps, also elaborating the steps by drawing on a range of relevant literature, including Wheeler and Richards (2007); Milne (2007b; 2008a); Bruce and Paxton (2002); Oakley *et al.* (2006); Watkins (1997); Godfrey *et al.* (2007); Harmon *et al.* (2007); Beutler (2001); and Wilkes and Bligh (1999). This extended framework is consistent with accounts of evaluation in supervision texts and reviews (e.g. Lewis & Hendricks, 2014), but significantly extends them in what I believe to be a novel fashion that can greatly help us to develop supervision.

The Fidelity Framework

According to Borelli *et al.* (2005), there are five successive steps in a systematic evaluation of an intervention such as supervision. The six-step, augmented fidelity framework is supervision-specific, as summarized in Table 8.1. I next describe each step, alongside an example from supervision research (as far as possible drawn from the work on developing EBCS).

Intervention design

The first aspect of the fidelity framework concerns specifying and justifying a model for the intervention, alongside providing information on its structure (including how long the intervention takes; how frequently it should be applied; what its content or constituent parts are; the qualifications or background of supervisors or others involved in the intervention; and any other resources that are required). In essence, then, step 1 of the fidelity framework is to offer a theory-based conceptualization of the supervision intervention and to specify its implementation. A theory contributes to a cumulative and cohesive evidence-base, and helps to guide an intervention (Barker & Hunsley, 2013). Working towards these objectives allows us to address two fundamental research questions: 'what is the right thing to do?' and 'which resources are required to do it?' Table 8.1 sets out these facets of the design aspect, alongside the subsequent five steps.

Example: Using a systematic review approach to design supervision
As noted in Chapter 2, a powerful influence on the designing of the tandem model was a systematic review of 24 empirical studies (Milne *et al.*, 2008a). To recap, these studies were selected partly because the reported supervision had been effective (i.e. they provided evidence in support of their supervision interventions, including clinical effectiveness). The basic model that emerged from this review included contextual factors (moderating influences within the supervision system, such as administrative support); supervisory techniques (mediators like goal-setting and feedback); supervision outcomes (mechanisms of change in the supervisees, such as reflection and experimenting); and the associated therapeutic interventions. Supervision emerged as a highly complex phenomenon, in that these studies had manipulated a total of 26 supervision techniques, typically used in combinations within each study (e.g. goal-setting plus modelling plus observation plus feedback). However, there appeared to be a clear common pathway, in that 82 per cent of these studies reported that such structured supervision formats led to experiential learning in the supervisees, indicating that this was the best-supported concept underpinning the supervisees' successful therapy. This evidence lent support to the tandem model (e.g. the back wheel, being the supervisee's cycle, should represent the experiential learning cycle). Systematic reviews have also been used as a tool to clarify and develop other aspects of EBCS (e.g. Milne & Reiser, 2010).

Training supervisors

The second step in the fidelity framework is to train supervisors in ways that ensure that the right thing is being done ('adherence'). This entails carefully describing and attempting to standardize the way that supervisors are trained, usually achieved through the development and application of a training manual, including supervision guidelines. Evaluation of this step should also include demonstrating that competence has been acquired and can be maintained in a form that is faithful to the model in step 1. As noted in the previous chapter, although there are many published studies of supervisor training, there appear to be few recent examples where this training has been based on a manual, and fewer still where a clear conceptual framework has been justified and specified as the basis for any such manual. Exceptions include the MST work already noted (Schoenwald, 2016), and my own efforts (Milne, 2010; Milne *et al.*, 2013). These and other examples of supervisor training manuals are reviewed in Milne (2016), as summarized briefly in Chapter 5.

Example: Supervision-of-supervision

We again started our EBCS work on supervisor training by conducting a systematic review, though this time we struggled to locate many empirical studies of traditional training workshops or seminars. Ultimately, we found 11 controlled studies of supervisor training within traditional (i.e. face-to-face) workshops (Milne *et al.*, 2011c), which, like the design review, indicated strong support for many well-established methods (especially educational role-play, observational learning and corrective feedback). We also studied EBCS training within a workshop, using repeated measures (Culloty *et al.*, 2010), and undertook a larger scale but weak cross-sectional research design to evaluate the national dissemination of the training manual linked to this book (Milne, 2010).

In the first of these two studies, direct observation indicated that the trainer ('workshop leader') conducted the workshop competently and with good fidelity to the manual. Six of the 17 workshop participants subsequently reported transferring (i.e. 'enacting') the training in their supervision sessions, by such means as a greater goal-orientation, more experiential learning and increasing the emphasis on reflection. Within the national dissemination study (Milne, 2010), 256 clinical supervisors received workshops, from a variety of leaders, at least partly based on the same EBCS manual. Consultancy provided to the trainers appeared to enhance adherence to the workshop manual, and also the supervisors' high satisfaction with the workshop. But the main approach that we have taken to training within EBCS is supervision-of-supervision, again utilizing $N = 1$ designs. In a series of studies (e.g. Milne & Westerman, 2001; Milne & James, 2002;

Milne *et al.*, 2008b; 2013), the effectiveness of training has been measured largely through direct observation, using direct observation, primarily the instrument SAGE (Supervision: Adherence and Guidance Evaluation; Milne *et al.*, 2011b: SAGE is described below). The findings consistently indicated that training was effective in improving the supervisor's adherence and the supervisee's engagement in experiential learning. Demonstrating this link with high internal validity (i.e. under rigorous experimental conditions) permits us to proceed to the next link.

Delivering supervision

Having designed and delivered a programme for training supervisors, the next step in the fidelity framework is to evaluate whether the supervision has actually been conducted correctly. This addresses the objective of faithful implementation, usually through the monitoring of how supervision is performed. It typically concerns an evaluation of key aspects of adherence and skillfulness, embracing what is covered within supervision (content evaluation), the processes or procedures that are followed and the skill with which they are administered. The supervision alliance is a popular aspect of the way that supervision is delivered (e.g. the Supervision Relationship Questionnaire; Palomo *et al.*, 2010). As set out in Table 8.1, this step subsumes a number of exacting and vital analyses. Specifically, the different models of supervision will each have their own distinctive contents, processes and procedures, although all will require that supervisors are appropriately skillful, including the use of the right amount of the relevant ingredients, applied in a timely, responsive fashion. An example of the contents of supervision is the material covered in Chapter 5 about the tandem model and the use of questions (see Table 5.4). These questions are faithful (adhere) to this model of supervision, and so an evaluation that demonstrated their presence would help to show that it is being performed with fidelity. By contrast, a psychodynamic approach might use rather different questions, timing their use differently and expecting them to serve rather different functions (e.g. fostering insight, rather than information-gathering).

Example: Observing supervisees

As a result of well-designed training, do EBCS supervisors 'deliver' the goods? Do they provide supervision that adheres to their training, or do they 'drift'? In one observation-based case-study, there was reason to believe that an EBCS supervisor had drifted into a collusive relationship with her supervisee, by engaging in 'safety behaviours'. For example, the supervisor allowed the supervisee to provide extensive and unnecessary details of his casework, thereby avoiding difficult topics or cases, and also minimizing his exposure to experiential supervisory methods (Milne *et al.*, 2009). In an earlier study (Milne & James, 2002) we actually found the opposite: an improvement in the delivery of EBCS during the follow-up period, attributed to a lag in the supervisor's socialization to the approach. In a third study we found the third possibility: adherence was maintained over a two-month follow-up period at the level achieved during training (Milne *et al.*, 2013). In summary, we have evidence that supervisors do 'deliver', but there is also reason to be cautious, making ongoing evaluation vital.

In the earlier of these $N = 1$ studies we used an observational instrument called Teachers' PETS to undertake these evaluations (described in Chapter 3), involving coding tape recordings of supervision by counting the frequency of some well-established elements of supervision, such as setting an agenda collaboratively and providing corrective feedback (Milne *et al.*, 2002). In the later examples we moved on to a more user-friendly instrument, SAGE (described below).

Receiving supervision

Having designed a system for training supervisors and ensured that it is being delivered faithfully, the next step in the fidelity framework is to evaluate whether or not this results in the 'right' initial impacts on the supervisee. Logically, if the prior steps are implemented correctly, then we would expect to see clear evidence that the supervision is being received and is having the intended effect. This corresponds to the mini-outcomes illustrated by the SAGE instrument. It is the first fidelity step that involves outcome evaluation (or 'impact') as normally construed and asks: is supervision resulting in the right (mini) outcomes? Outcomes refer to improvements that are targeted through an intervention, and they have traditionally been regarded as the paramount measure of various forms of healthcare (as in the structure–process–outcome logic dating from Donabedian, 1988). As far as the NHS is concerned, activities such as staff development and clinical supervision are regarded as instrumental and pragmatic ways to foster changes in professionals' practice that are designed ultimately to improve patients' health outcomes (National Health Service, 1998). The most popular approach to measuring outcomes in relation to staff development within the mental health field is probably the Kirkpatrick (1967) taxonomy. This consists of four successive levels of outcome, ranging from simple reactions (e.g. supervisees' satisfaction with their supervision) to impacts on a service system (including health outcomes for the service users). This taxonomy is embedded in Table 8.1, including the augmented taxonomy suggested by Kraiger *et al.* (1993); Alliger *et al.* (1997) and Belfield *et al.* (2001). As a result, changes in knowledge, skills and attitudes as a result of learning have been added, and a fifth level of evaluation inserted: a new initial step of 'participation or completion'. An example of a supervisee satisfaction measure is provided in Figure 8.1 (REACTS).

Example: In-depth qualitative analysis
We have used the observational tool SAGE to study the supervisees' engagement in experiential learning, which provided longitudinal evidence that EBCS encouraged receipt, and to a significantly greater extent than CBT supervision (Milne *et al.*, 2013). But qualitative methods are also an important approach within EBCS, and in particular we have valued the 'episode' approach, as advocated by Ladany *et al.* (2005). This is essentially a supervision application of functional analysis, so sits comfortably with CBT and an evidence-based perspective. Figure 4.1 details and illustrates the episode approach. Additional episode diagrams are provided in Breese *et al.* (2012) and in Milne *et al.* (2011a). Both of these studies were essentially concerned with capturing excellent supervision through the episode method. We have also used grounded theory to zoom in on the 'receipt' phenomenon (Johnston & Milne, 2012). Following individual interviews with seven trainee clinical psychologists, a conceptual model was developed, depicting the learning process from the supervisees' perspective. We concluded that 'the receipt of supervision was experienced against a developmental backdrop involving a progression along two continua: competency and awareness. A set of core processes (Reflection, Socratic Information Exchange, Scaffolding, Supervisory Alliance) were thought to interact, enabling appropriate learning across developmental stages. This was thought to facilitate movement through individualized Zones of Proximal Development (ZPD)' (p.1). While this finding represented support for core aspects of the tandem model, this searching grounded theory method also indicated that 'receipt' is complex, and so does not lend itself to a quantitative approach.

Personal Identifier:_____ Date of supervision: _____

Please rate the following aspects of the supervision session you have just received. Use the scale below:

1	2	3	4	5	N/A
Strongly disagree	Disagree	Neither agree nor disagree	Agree	Strongly agree	Not applicable

1. I am satisfied that the duration of the supervision session was appropriate (i.e. it lasted as long as it was should have).	1 2 3 4 5 N/A
2. I am satisfied with the frequency of supervision sessions (i.e. this supervision session occurred when it should have).	1 2 3 4 5 N/A
3. *Management;* The supervisor helped me with planning, managing, evaluating and problem-solving issues.	1 2 3 4 5 N/A
4. *Support;* I felt supported through the supervisor's use of 'core' relationship conditions (e.g. feeling accepted, receiving recognition).	1 2 3 4 5 N/A
5. *Learning*	
a) I was able to recognise relevant feelings, becoming more self-aware, (e.g. role-play helped me to express emotion).	1 2 3 4 5 N/A
b) I was able to reflect on events and perceive things more clearly (e.g. draw on my own experience to give events more personal meaning).	1 2 3 4 5 N/A
c) My understanding of my work was improved (i.e. analyzing cases to gain more insight and a better grasp).	1 2 3 4 5 N/A
d) We agreed action/s based on this supervision session (e.g. made a plan, agreed steps, set a goal).	1 2 3 4 5 N/A
e) The supervisor helped me to try things out and to solve problems/practise skills, (e.g. gave me corrective feedback that improved my competence).	1 2 3 4 5 N/A
6. Of the events which occurred in this supervision session, which one do you feel was the most helpful for you personally? It might be something you said or did, or something the supervisor said or did. (continue over the page if necessary)	
7. Any other comments (e.g. unhelpful events, unresolved problems: continue over the page if necessary)?	

Figure 8.1 REACTS: An example of measuring a supervisee's feedback by questionnaire.
Source: Milne *et al.* (2012).

Transferring supervision

According to the fidelity framework, the clinical outcomes obtained with clients represents 'transferring' supervision, to the benefit of others (see Table 8.1, row 5). A breakdown of the evaluation methods used within the

Milne (2007b) review of 24 successful studies indicated that 42 per cent of these studies utilized some measure of clinical outcome, most commonly measures of clinical functioning (such as self-injurious behaviour). Measures of distress (such as low mood) were measured in one-quarter of the studies, whereas clients' quality of life or satisfaction with the service that they received was measured in 17 per cent of instances (in both cases). Such assessments create the possibility for comparing different models of supervision in terms of their relative clinical outcomes (see, for example, Bambling *et al.*, 2006, summarized below). It also allows auditing to occur in terms of achieving a benchmark standard.

Example: Client satisfaction and clinical outcome
Bambling *et al.* (2006) conducted a randomized controlled trial in which 127 depressed clients were allocated randomly to therapists who were either receiving supervision or who were unsupervised, and who provided eight sessions of a problem-solving therapy. The Beck Depression Inventory (BDI; Beck *et al.*, 1987) was utilized as the clinical outcome measure. There were two conditions of the supervised therapy, one focusing on processes (i.e. psychodynamic group) and the other on skills (i.e. CBT group). In the process supervision condition, the discussion of patients focused on helping the supervisees to understand the interpersonal dynamics occurring within therapy (e.g. implicit feedback from the client, resistance, or the flow of exchanges). In the skill-focused group, attention was given to specific therapist behaviours, and advice and guidance was provided on optimal ways of treating the patients. Eight sessions of supervision were provided, one before treatment commenced, the remainder taking place after each of the first seven therapy sessions. A total of 60 patients were treated by therapists in the unsupervised condition, with 33 therapists in the skill-focused supervision group, and 34 in the process-focused supervision group. Supervisors were qualified mental health practitioners with at least two years' experience in providing supervision. They received a one-day workshop to try to ensure their competence within the different approaches, which were both manualized. The results indicated that the BDI scores for the full sample of patients reduced significantly by the end of the eight-session treatment period. Supervision had a significant main effect on the average BDI score, which indicated that therapists receiving supervision obtained the best clinical outcomes. However, no difference was obtained between the process and skill approaches to supervision. Measures of client satisfaction with therapy and rates of client completion also favoured the

two supervision conditions significantly. The mean BDI scores for clients seen by the supervised therapists corresponded to remitted depression by the end of the study, and indicated that in 44 of the 65 clients depression was no longer clinically evident. Bambling *et al.* (2006) concluded that the study provided initial evidence that supervision can enhance treatment outcome.

Developing supervision

Finally, the augmented fidelity framework implies the need to have a system of monitoring the supervision arrangements so that feedback is available, in order that decisions can be made that promote the effectiveness and efficiency of the supervision system. Suggestions are made below for optimizing such feedback (e.g. Table 8.2). This systemic level of evaluation

Table 8.2 Suggestions for effective feedback in evaluations of supervision.

Feedback about the success in undertaking supervision (e.g. learning *outcome* evaluation), which specifies the distance between the current and the expected success (the benchmark, expected standard or normative data), and indicates how any gap can be bridged (e.g. through a guideline or via demonstrations in supervision). Feedback should be timely, factual, clear and precise. Supervisors should comment on and ideally verify the accuracy and interpret the relevance of the information

Feedback on how supervision skills were applied (*performance*); should be ongoing and regular, focused on current and desired competencies, rather than remarks about the personal features of the supervisor (e.g. body language, personality). Try to include information of special interest to the participating supervisors (e.g. qualitative data), and consider jointly what actions are implied by the feedback

Feedback on how tackling supervision was managed subjectively (*process*, such as self-regulation skills). Feedback should also be tailored (e.g. responsive to objectives agreed with individual supervisors) and reinforce progress (cumulative). Supervisors should help to illuminate the information (e.g. recounting their more effective coping strategies)

Feedback should adhere to the normal standards of professional practice (e.g. respectful and considerate), and should address the formative (supervisor development) and summative objectives (standards for supervision and its outcomes). Acknowledge and seek to tackle structural/resource barriers (*structure*) that impede or limit supervision; seek to strengthen boosters (e.g. peer support) addresses the following questions. Are we are getting good value for the resources that are invested in supervision? Have we got our system right? Or is there is a better way? The previous chapter discussed various aspects of a supportive infrastructure for supervision. To those aspects we can add cost–benefit and other economic analyses, which might feed into summative decision-making (e.g. a judgement that a given form of supervision provides minimal benefits at excessive costs, and so should be replaced by a better alternative). An illustration is the comparison of individual versus group supervision, as the group format is much less expensive and any weaknesses may be compensated by the benefits of peer discussion. For example, Stirman *et al.* (2015) compared individual and group supervision (which they termed 'consultation') of CBT for 85 community mental health clinic therapists, reporting equivalent outcomes (competence gains, which were observed directly) over a two-year follow-up period for a fraction of the supervision time: 2 hours per week for a group of eight therapists, compared to 17 hours for individual supervision. This suggests that group supervision has the greatest cost–benefit.

In routine practice, cost–benefit analysis might also involve decisions about discontinuing the use of low-fidelity supervisors, and setting up systems of accreditation and monitoring so that appropriately trained and effective supervisors are engaged properly, and are duly rewarded for their high-fidelity work. Other related activities that are identified in Table 8.1 include reducing the loss of good supervisors (whilst identifying and developing talented supervisors); dismantling supervision, and the methods used to train supervisors, so as to better identify the most effective ingredients; and creating feedback loops that allow us to monitor and support supervisors (e.g. to help identify and remediate environmental factors that may help or hinder supervision). The lines that connect the panels in Figure 7.2 represent these feedback loops. In essence, service evaluation in the various forms discussed can be used to develop supervision methods and systems, through a process of feedback and action research.

Example: Clinical outcome monitoring
A promising extension of outcome or transfer evaluation is a system whereby client outcomes can be monitored on a routine basis using norm-referenced, standardized measures, and then feedback of the results from such instruments can be provided regularly to the supervisor and/or supervisee. This feedback is intended to provide the supervisor and

supervisee (therapist) with supplementary data on the clinical progress of the patients on the therapist's caseload, in order to illuminate reflection on the need to alter or refine the selection or implementation of therapy, or to consider alternative explanations about progress. The data include alerts that 'flag' patients who are not responding as expected (relative to the normative data), alongside specific advice or guidelines. It should be contrasted with traditional clinical supervision, in which the supervisee selects which patients to discuss in supervision, and is unlikely ever to discuss all patients on the caseload, or to present any evaluation data, keeping the supervisor somewhat in the dark. A review of clinical outcome monitoring indicated that it has consistently resulted in significant improvements in therapy results (and reduced drop-outs: Swift *et al.*, 2014). These authors offered suggestions for incorporating clinical outcome monitoring into supervision, including illustrative vignettes.

An early example of linking clinical outcome monitoring to supervision was reported by Worthen and Lambert (2007), who outlined a system for tracking the client's response to treatment longitudinally, and comparing the data with norms for treatment response. When there is a discrepancy between the results from the local provision of therapy and the outcomes achieved within the normative sample, then a system is in place to alert therapists and their supervisors to this relatively poor progress. This includes providing therapists with a problem-solving decision tree, together with recommendations for possible interventions to boost progress. An even earlier variation on this approach is to define limits to the variation in outcome data statistically (statistical process control), which is fed back to staff and supervisors in graphic form. This information indicates whether the outcomes are 'in control' (i.e. are as expected), or are 'out of control' (i.e. require attention). These data, which were derived from weekly staff and patient satisfaction questionnaires, were tabled and discussed at monthly meetings, resulting in significantly higher patient satisfaction (Hyrkas & Lehti, 2003).

Within the UK's Improving Access to Psychological Therapies (IAPT) initiative, an even more sophisticated patient case management information system (PC-MIS) has been developed (York University, 2007; Richards, 2014). This provides real-time information on structure (therapist/patient contacts; demographic data), process (nature of contact activity) and outcome (clinical functioning). In addition, PC-MIS has many other potential uses, including prompting therapists about next steps (e.g. assertive follow-up of a patient), allowing them to prompt their supervisor for help at any stage or access the supervision notes from the last session. In turn, the supervisors can readily access all of these data, enabling outcome monitoring in relation to their own supervisees, and in relation to the whole service (outcome benchmarking). This allows one supervisor to monitor dozens of cases (in treatment or on a waiting list, partly aided by graphically presented data), as well as several supervisees' clinical effectiveness.

Evaluations of clinical outcome monitoring linked to supervision have also appeared latterly. For instance, Callahan *et al.* (2009) examined the effects of supervision on the outcomes of 76 adult psychotherapy clients, by means of a regression analysis of the archival data from a training clinic. This clinic tracked client outcome as part of routine practice, through the use of two self-report symptom measures, administered at the start and end of therapy (an average of 18 sessions of CBT). These supervisors were found to have a significant effect on client treatment outcome, accounting for 16 per cent of the variance, although the study design did not link this to outcome monitoring in supervision. This is a greater effect than typically reported for specific therapies. Supervision was provided individually (one hour per week) and in groups (two hours per week) by the experienced academic staff of the training clinic, though there was no information on the nature of this supervision, nor on the use of the intake (baseline) data in supervision. However, a second regression study using a much larger sample found that less than 1 per cent of the clinical outcome variance was attributable to supervision (Rousmaniere *et al.*, 2014), possibly due to methodological differences (e.g. the statistical tests used; the sample size, the relative competence of the supervisors). More intriguingly, this difference may have been attributable to the role of regular joint outcome monitoring. Specifically, the session-by-session use of outcome monitoring data by supervisees and supervisors may have made all supervisors equally effective.

A more precise and controlled study by Reese *et al.* (2009) compared the outcomes of trainees receiving supervision that included regular outcome feedback ($N = 9$) with the outcomes of trainees receiving supervision without regular outcome feedback ($N = 10$). Data were drawn from one year of a clinical service ($N = 115$), and it was reported that the trainees in the supervision-with-feedback condition had significantly better clinical out-comes than trainees receiving supervision without feedback. Notably, no significant differences were found between supervisors within the treatment conditions. However, Reese *et al.* (2009) did not study how outcome mon-itoring was actually processed within supervision. According to the under-lying theory, feedback will work best when it is utilized to provide information that suggests a specific improvement to the therapy provided by the supervisee, which is duly processed in supervision (e.g. learning from errors made; developing and executing an improvement plan: Tracey *et al.*, 2014).

In turn, a review by Macdonald and Mellor-Clark (2014) suggested that outcome monitoring that facilitates clinical outcomes may be effective because it raises awareness and corrects biases in therapists' assessment of their work (e.g. being unaware of client deterioration), and can then be integrated with action-planning and ongoing discussion between supervisor and supervisee.

Feedback approaches

These studies indicate large differences in the way that clinical outcome monitoring is used within supervision, and raise important questions about the best feedback practices. One way forward is to evaluate supervisees' reactions. Grossl *et al.* (2014) compared the effects of trainees assigned to a continuous client feedback condition in supervision versus supervision as usual. Supervisors in the feedback condition were trained to discuss the outcome data in every weekly supervision session, including an assessment of the client's status (i.e. progressing as usual, above the clinical cut-off score, not improving, or deteriorating). The results indicated that trainees who discussed client outcome data in supervision reported greater satisfaction with their supervisor, and tended to report more positive feelings about use of outcome monitoring instruments. Lucock *et al.* (2015) also took care to design the feedback to therapists so that it was as acceptable and effective as possible. In addition to the usual outcome monitoring, they evaluated the addition of client data considered relevant by the participating therapists (e.g. alliance, social support and stressful life events information). The authors also undertook a force-field analysis, seeking the therapists' perceptions of the barriers and boosters to outcome monitoring. They found that 64 per cent of the participating therapists regarded the feedback as helpful, but barriers included insufficient administrative support and problems with the information technology. Perhaps for these reasons, only around 20 per cent of therapists discussed the feedback information with their clients, or took the information to their supervision. A similar emphasis on maximizing the acceptability of feedback was reported in a study that involved providing competence feedback to therapists (Weck *et al.*, 2016, p.4):

Feedback providers were instructed to formulate the qualitative feedback respectfully; the feedback was to be based on observable therapeutic behaviours, to be formulated concretely and to include specific information. Competent behaviours were to be reinforced, and qualitative feedback was to be phrased in descriptive, common, and non-judgmental language. For each of the 14 items of the Cognitive Therapy Scale, brief qualitative feedback was given, which also included suggestions for improvements. For example, qualitative feedback regarding Item 1 (agenda) might be as follows: 'The patient could benefit from a jointly-developed agenda, including a time schedule. Furthermore, he/she should be asked about their own concerns at the beginning of the session.'

Many of these points are equally valid in relation to providing feedback to supervisors based on various evaluations of their supervision (i.e. not just clinical outcome data), and they align with traditions within service evaluation, such as the 'stakeholder-collaborative' model (Ayers, 1987). The more detailed sequencing of problem-solving activities and relational tasks, explicated helpfully by Bouwen and Taillieu (2004), indicate how intelligent approaches to ensuring effective evaluation such as the stakeholder-collaborative model might best be pursued. These participatory and collaborative approaches to evaluation make good motivational sense (in terms of engaging key parties in the evaluation process), are consistent with the collaborative style of most therapies and probably lead to the best outcomes (Rossi *et al.*, 2004). Therefore, so as offer some suggestions for feedback in relation to evaluating supervision generally, Table 8.2 incorporates these useful points with those made by Hattie and Timperley (2007) and Lyons *et al.* (1997). Table 8.2 is adapted from the EBCS manual, which includes a guideline on the provision of feedback within supervision (Milne & Reiser, 2017). Note that the earlier emphasis on structure–process–outcome evaluation (Donabedian, 1988; 2015) is embedded within Table 8.2, with a distinction added between 'process' (as subjective experience) and 'performance' (as observable actions), based on the feedback literature (Hattie & Timperley, 2007).

Measuring Clinical Supervision

The material above pivots on the use of instruments or qualitative approaches for data collection. Measurement in supervision is a further area where a multitude of models and methods have been used within research. I next describe some of these approaches, noting key issues and suggesting promising strategies.

As per Kirkpatrick's (1967) taxonomy, the first step in outcome evaluation is to assess the reactions of the learner, typically couched in terms of their satisfaction with an intervention like supervision. To this day, satisfaction appears to be the most widely accepted and widely utilized of the evaluation options, at least under naturalistic training and supervision conditions. This is because satisfaction is seen as a precondition for participation in supervision, as well as reflecting the importance of capturing the supervisee's perceptions, usually attempted through qualitative means. A case in point is the events paradigm (Ladany *et al.*, 2005), in which the supervisee is asked to identify something that occurred within supervision that was helpful. This is described in the supervisee's own language, linked to a simple quantitative rating of helpfulness. For another example, see the Helpful Aspects of Supervision Questionnaire (HASQ; reproduced in appendix B, Milne, 2008a, p.245). Further examples of satisfaction instruments (alongside other tools) are described and reviewed in O'Donovan and Kavanagh (2014).

REACTS (Rating of Experiential learning And Components of Teaching and Supervision) is an instrument specifically designed to measure supervisee satisfaction with the tandem model of supervision (Wilson, 2007). REACTS is an 11-item, supervisee-completed, paper-and-pencil rating of supervision (as reproduced in Figure 8.1). It is intended to assess 'normative', 'restorative' and primarily the 'formative' aspects of supervision (through the listed experiential learning modes). The five-point rating scale ranges from 'strongly agree' to 'strongly disagree' (with a 'not applicable' option), giving a score range of 8–40 (there are eight rated items), where higher scores represent greater supervisee satisfaction and self-reported learning. REACTS also includes a 'helpful aspects' item (Llewellyn, 1988) to collect qualitative data, and a final item inviting any further comments. It can be completed by the supervisee within five minutes. REACTS has good test–retest reliability ($r = 0.96$) and internal consistency (alpha $= 0.94$). Additional psychometric information can be found in Milne *et al.* (2012).

However, whether it measures satisfaction, affective reactions, enjoyment, usefulness or the acceptability of an approach, the relation between reactions and outcomes is far from straightforward (Hook & Bunce, 2001). For example, Alliger *et al.* (1997) found the correlation between affective reactions (including the degree to which a training session was enjoyed) and immediate learning to approximate to zero. Interpreting these findings, Hook and Bunce (2001) suggested that there are no theoretical or empirical reasons to expect variables such as the pleasure or enjoyment of learning to be associated significantly with things like knowledge gain. However, in their study of 57 telesales staff receiving training in relation to a new computer system, they obtained findings that clearly indicated an important role for affective reactions on the training outcomes. Interestingly, their sub-analysis indicated that the more empathy the trainers provided, the less the group learnt. They speculated that the inconsistent pattern of relations between reactions and learning may be explained by the relative amount of challenge provided: insufficient challenge and excess empathy may produce limited outcomes. This is consistent with the tandem model, which posits that a moderate degree of destabilization is necessary for competence enhancement (see Chapter 3), and with the results reported by Rieck *et al.* (2015). Challenge may not be appreciated by the supervisee, at least in the short term (e.g. James *et al.*, 2004), resulting in lower satisfaction ratings when the supervisor is actually doing a great job (as judged by other criteria or as rated by observers). Conversely, there is good reason to believe that a non-threatening, relaxed approach leads to higher satisfaction, as a review of some old studies in education have found that students who learnt the most rated their instructors least favourably (e.g. Parker & Thomas, 1980).

This kind of relationship between challenge and satisfaction helps us to understand the more recent finding that relaxed ('degraded', largely conversational) CBT supervision was associated with high satisfaction (Townend *et al.*, 2002). However, 'being challenged' has also been rated as valuable by supervisees, although not regarded as being as important as a trusting and supportive relationship (McMahon & Errity, 2013). Harkness (1987) argued that supervisees based their satisfaction ratings on the degree to which supervision helps to promote clinical benefits (i.e. it is actually a proxy measure of outcome). This agrees with an attempt to formulate these findings: Radcliffe and Milne (2010) used a qualitative, grounded theory approach, based on semi-structured interviews. The results indicated that supervisee satisfaction was based primarily on the supervisor addressing the subjective needs of the supervisee, in an alliance in which the supervisor is available and empathic. Supervisees also believed that supervisors should demonstrate adequate expertise in their field, create a secure space and contribute to clinical solutions. In conclusion, there are theoretical and practical reasons for treating the measurement of supervisee satisfaction with considerable caution, as it appears quite possible that 'effective supervision is not always the most satisfying supervision (i.e. the struggle inherent in learning may not always be experienced as the most satisfying)' (Ladany *et al.*, 1999, p.454).

The review by O'Donovan and Kavanagh (2014) reached the same cautious conclusion. These authors therefore recommended that researchers also include other outcomes of supervision. The range and frequency with which the different types of evaluation measures were used within rigorous research on supervision was indicated by a sample of 24 supervision studies (Milne, 2007b). Supervisees' reactions to supervision were actually infrequently measured (14 per cent of these studies), whereas measures of learning (cognitive and behavioural) were applied in 29 per cent of studies. Similarly, evaluations of the transfer of learning to the workplace were reported in nearly half of the included studies, most commonly in terms of the transfer of supervision to therapy (48 per cent of studies). Note that on average 3.7 different kinds of supervision outcomes were evaluated for each of the 24 studies (a 'multiple measures' strategy), suggesting that these evaluations have been conducted thoroughly. Therefore, consistent with the preceding material, in these 24 studies satisfaction was little emphasized, whereas learning and transfer represent around half of all assessments made. In terms of the types of measures used in this sample, most studies included direct observation (47 per cent of studies), followed by self-report questionnaires (34 per cent), ratings (13 per cent), and interviews (3 per cent). Very few studies used focus groups or archival data. This differs from a more recent review, presumably because of different sampling methods: Watkins (2011) reported that most studies that explored the impact of supervision on clinical outcomes relied on supervisors' or supervisees' perceptions, rather than on clients' self-reports. Wheeler and Richards (2007) reviewed 25 carefully selected studies and found the impact of supervision had been measured by means of 32 diverse instruments and qualitative approaches, only one of which had been used more than once. Not surprisingly, Wheeler and Richards (2007) concluded that there needed to be a more clearly defined research agenda, akin to the efforts made within the therapy literature to develop and apply core outcome measures.

Such a battery was duly developed and presented (Wheeler & Barkham, 2014), with the goal that a practitioner research network might start to use the same instruments to measure supervision, alongside the clinical outcomes that were measured routinely in hundreds of services in the UK. The supervision instruments selected should also maintain the user-friendly emphasis of the clinical outcome tool, CORE (Barkham *et al.*, 1998). The literature search by Wheeler and Barkham (2014) revealed 150 instruments used in supervision research since 1980, which they whittled down to 49 for evaluation against seven criteria (e.g. short, face valid and free to use). As a result, a 'toolkit' or core battery of five of these instruments was recommended for practitioner research. These five instruments measured the supervision alliance (two tools), supervisee/supervisor characteristics, HASQ and role conflict. Preliminary use by one of the authors suggested that the HASQ (supervisee and supervisor versions) was the most useful in tracking the success of supervision.

Further aids to those who are interested in implementing some form of evaluation system are the toolkits that have helpfully been appended to textbooks on clinical supervision. For example, the 'supervisor's toolbox' in Bernard and Goodyear (2014) includes a simple, eight-point Supervision Satisfaction Questionnaire, a more detailed, 29-item breakdown of the supervisee's perceptions of their supervision (e.g. 'I was not comfortable using the technique recommended by my supervisor'); and even a measure dedicated to assessing the evaluation processes within supervision itself. This latter instrument, Evaluation Process Within Supervision Inventory (Lehrman-Waterman & Ladany, 2001), includes items such as: 'The objectives that my supervisor and I created were specific'; and 'My supervisor balanced his or her feedback between positive and negative statements.' Falender and Shafranske (2004) also appended a toolkit, which includes the Supervision Outcomes Survey (Worthen & Isakson, 2000). This has 20 items, and is designed to assess the supervisee's perception of the learning outcomes achieved through supervision. Items are rated on a seven-point scale and include: 'Supervision helps me improve my ability to conceptualize my cases' and 'My supervisor's feedback encourages me to keep trying to improve.' There is also a scale for measuring the supervisee's competence, the Therapist Evaluation Checklist (Hall-Marley, 2000). The supervisee's proficiency is rated in terms of competence, either being a 'strength', being 'commensurate with the level of training' or 'needing improvement'. Items include the contribution made to team-working and general therapy skills. Within the latter category are assessment skills, such as establishing an alliance and demonstrating objectivity; within the intervention category are skills in developing a working alliance and in addressing interpersonal issues. Finally, a variety of supervision-specific instruments are described and presented within Part IV of the *Wiley International Handbook of Clinical Supervision* (Watkins & Milne, 2014). One of these chapters was devoted to SAGE, the main instrument used to measure the tandem model (Milne & Reiser, 2014). I next describe SAGE (Milne *et al.*, 2011b), an instrument for rating competence in supervision through direct observation.

SAGE ratings are made on a seven-point competence rating scale, which ranges from 'incompetent' to 'expert', based on the popular Dreyfus definitions (1989). Following Blackburn *et al.* (2001), in developing the revised Cognitive Therapy Scale, we added more extreme ratings (i.e. a lower level of 'incompetent' performance; and a seventh rating point to capture expert functioning under difficult/adverse circumstances). Competence was defined in terms of 22 items, as set out in Table 8.3. Note that this tool operationalizes the essence of this present book, including the importance of leadership (items 1–4, the common factors), a range of supervision methods (items 5–18, the supervision cycle), and finally the supervisee's cycle of experiential learning (items 19–22). Therefore, SAGE is ideal as a measure of EBCS, including the tandem and CBT models of clinical supervision.

To illustrate, SAGE was used in the 11-month long evaluation of the tandem model (Milne *et al.*, 2013), and provided excellent information that aided fortnightly discussions in supervision-of-supervision. An account of that process can be found in that chapter by Milne and Reiser (2014). SAGE also fares well in terms of the seven criteria used by Wheeler and Barkham (2014). Specifically, we know that SAGE is face valid, has high utility for developing supervision, captures supervisor and supervisee behaviours, has acceptable psychometric qualities, can be used longitudinally and is accessible and free to use (for a copy, contact derek.milne@ncl.ac.uk; or robert.reiser@gmail.com). On the other hand, it is not especially short (completing the ratings takes a few minutes longer than the session being observed, typically amounting to a total of 70 minutes). But, as far as we know, it is fairly pan-theoretical, being most sensitive to CBT and systemic supervision models, but also detecting key features of psychodynamic supervision (Cliffe & Milne, 2012). Therefore, SAGE is a serviceable, free, high utility measure, particularly worth considering given the scarcity of competence instruments within supervision, and we think that it merits further development (we invite readers with an interest in collaborating on this psychometric development effort to get in touch). To date we have provided copies of the SAGE manual to dozens of researchers, supervisors

Table 8.3   SAGE (Supervision: Adherence and Guidance Evaluation): an observational measure.

SAGE items	Brief definition
COMMON FACTORS	
1. Relating	Core conditions; 'restorative'
2. Collaborating	Alliance
3. Managing	Scaffolded; optimal challenge; 'normative'
4. Facilitating	Improving group (inc. perplexity)
SUPERVISION CYCLE	
5. Agenda-setting	Needs-led/developmental objectives
6. Demonstrating	Modelling
7. Discussing	Reviewing; challenging; problem-solving
8. Evaluating	Closely monitoring (e.g. clinical data)
9. Experiencing	Expressing and processing affective aspects
10. Feeding back (giving)	Highlight gaps and demonstrate improvements
11. Feeding back (receiving)	Elicit reactions (e.g. helpful events in supervision)
12. Formulating	Analysis, synthesis, explanation
13. Listening	Attending & summarising
14. Observing	Live/taped therapy
15. Prompting	Reminders & cues
16. Questioning	Gather information; raise awareness
17. Teaching	Informing/educating (symbolic)
18. Training	Experiential learning (e.g. role-play)
SUPERVISEE'S CYCLE	
19. Experiencing	Awareness; identification & processing of affect (assimilation)
20. Reflecting	Summarising & integrating subjective material
21. Conceptualising	Integrating objective material (e.g. theories/findings)
22. Planning	Decision-making about actions
23. Experimenting	Enacting plans (in and out of supervision, e.g. trial and error learning through role-play/reality-checking)

Source: Milne *et al.* (2011b). Reproduced with permission from Cambridge University Press.

and clinicians internationally, and we know that it is used routinely within many IAPT services in England, following one-day workshops. In the USA, the Felton Institute of San Francisco has incorporated SAGE into its training programmes (oriented to helping supervisors with non-traditional providers or case managers using CBT), and EBCS (including SAGE) is now part of the training and ongoing consultation process within several county mental health systems in California.

Evaluation Designs

The design of research studies in supervision is yet another aspect of the field where a multitude of approaches have been used. I again describe some of these approaches, noting key issues and suggesting promising strategies, especially the relatively straightforward research designs that can encourage participation in evaluation. I will once more focus on designs of relevance to EBCS, encouraging the interested reader to study one of the many research textbooks, particularly those concerned with quasi-experimental designs (e.g. Kazdin, 1998; Shadish *et al.*, 2000; Rossi *et al.*, 2004). These texts helpfully set out the core requirements of a sound research design, utilizing the kinds of instruments just described, designs that allow one to draw inferences about the effectiveness of supervision.

A particularly appealing design for CBT supervisors to consider is the 'small-n' or $N = 1$ methodology (Hayes *et al.*, 1999; Hersen, 2010), as this is congruent with CBT and it allows the supervisor to evaluate key parts of the augmented fidelity framework with relatively minimal effort, whilst gaining maximum ability to interpret findings. Thus, instead of the considerable work entailed in recruiting many participants to experimental groups and then trying to match them with control participants, the small-n study can be conducted rigorously with just one supervisee. This is achieved through making the supervisee his or her own control, and by using a number of different experimental conditions in a sequential, systematic manner. The classic example is the multiple baseline design, in which a baseline condition is followed by some kind of intervention, which is followed by a mainte-nance or a reversal phase. This might involve supervision as usual, which is measured in terms of the supervisee's experiential learning alongside a suitable measure of supervisee satisfaction. In the experimental (intervention) phase, a specific form of supervision is introduced, ideally based on a manual, while the same form of measurement continues. It might be predicted that this will result in a greater receipt of supervision, as measured through the supervisee's enhanced learning (i.e. step 4 in Table 8.1).

SAGE has been used in such a design (Milne *et al.*, 2013). The reversal design entails reverting to the baseline condition (supervision as usual). If the learning outcomes revert to the initial baseline level, following a clear, significant and stepwise increase during the intervention phase, then it is reasonable to infer that the manipulation was the reason for the improved learning. There are many variations on this $N = 1$ theme, but sticking with the option of looking at only one supervisee's development one can also consider the design in which there is a multiple baseline across different supervisee behaviours (Hersen, 2010). This would identify three or more competencies that the supervisee should develop over time, and each of these is tackled in turn, in such a way that, ideally, a stepwise pattern of the intended changes occurs. The $N = 1$ design is an example of a broader class of designs sometimes called 'microgenetic' (Siegler, 2002). These furnish a feasible yet fascinating approach to the study of learning and development. For instance, Siegler (1995) studied how five-year-old schoolchildren acquired number conservation.

A different but complementary option is to adopt qualitative methods, such as grounded theory (Johnstone & Milne, 2012), episode analysis (Breese *et al.*, 2012) and force-field analyses (Lynch & Happell, 2008). As touched on earlier, such descriptive and case-study approaches have the advantage of considering multi-strand, non-linear causal pathways, which appear to fit well with the complex nature of supervision. The examples of complex causal analyses in management and public health seem to closely parallel supervision, and the evaluation methods are also similar (e.g. case studies and causal diagrams akin to clinical formulations: Bennett & Elman, 2006; Joffe & Mindell, 2006). Of course, as these authors note, there are also disadvantages to such qualitative methods, but the similarity of these methods to some supervision research, and the relative success of these methods in other social science fields, suggests that we may improve our evaluation efforts by adopting some of the concepts (e.g. multifinality) and methods (e.g. causal diagrams).

These small-n and qualitative options afford a way of bypassing (or at least postponing) the long-standing challenges of large-N group designs, which have largely failed to deliver cumulative progress in relation to understanding how therapy works: 'basic difficulties continue to exist in the very approach we take to the business of determining therapy outcome relationships' (Borkovec & Bauer, 2010, p.140).

Conclusions

In this chapter I have recommended a stepwise, integrative framework for evaluating clinical supervision. As set out in Table 8.1, this augmented fidelity framework consists of six successive and equally important evaluation steps, in contrast to the emphasis on the 'acid test', which prizes clinical outcomes. There is no question about the importance of the clinical outcomes associated with supervision, especially within a political context for healthcare that is dominated by demands for cost-effective, evidence-based practice. However, it needs to be supplemented by other intermediate outcomes if the acid test is to be passed convincingly, and if supervision is to be developed efficiently (Barker & Hunsley, 2013). The augmented fidelity framework provides a suitable approach, and also has advantages because of its firm foundations in the well-established structure–process–outcome approach to health service evaluation (Donabedian, 1988; 2015). I share Donabedian's view that the structure–process–outcome evaluation is the minimum interpretable evaluation: we need to know whether something works (outcome evaluation), how the outcome was achieved (process evaluation) and the input or resource (structure or effort evaluation) on which this was based. But the biggest argument for the augmented fidelity framework is that it is sufficiently precise and detailed to provide us with the kind of information that can help us to develop supervision (feedback utility). Being made up of some discrete, potentially straightforward steps, I believe that the framework is also empowering, in the sense that it enables supervisors (and others) to engage with the evaluation agenda in ways that are relatively straightforward, as per the example of the instrument SAGE (Table 8.3). However, a comprehensive evaluation, in which all six fidelity framework steps are measured, provides us with additional information, which may be particularly informative. For example, as in step 2 of Table 8.1, it allows us to audit whether supervisors are adhering properly to a training manual, and whether supervision is having the intended effect on the supervisee.

In relation to all of the fidelity steps, I have urged that self-report instruments, especially when used to assess the supervisee's satisfaction with supervision, are treated with caution, requiring the addition of more objective instruments to afford a balanced evaluation. Examples of two instruments used within the research on the tandem model were provided in Figure 8.1 (REACTS, as a subjective measure of supervisee satisfaction) and in Table 8.3 (SAGE, an observational measure of supervisory competence). Also, I suggested that there is a further challenging aspect to evaluation, namely the business of implementation. As with other kinds of service development, the introduction and maintenance of a system of evaluation is no trivial matter. Respecting this challenge, some key factors were identified, such as using instruments that have high yield (feedback utility), and closely collaborating with the stakeholders in an evaluation.

Although the chapter has covered a significant amount of material, including some attention to the kinds of evaluation designs that one might consider (such as the small-n approach), it is important to acknowledge that there are many other aspects of evaluation that it has not been possible to address. However, these are covered fully in other texts on supervision (see, for example, Wampold & Holloway, 1997) and in general textbooks on service evaluation (Shadish *et al.*, 2000; Rossi *et al.*, 2004). For these reasons, I have chosen to emphasize what I believe to be a fresh, feasible and promising avenue to the evaluation of clinical supervision (especially applications of the tandem model). In terms of this model, evaluation provides essential information on where we are, the progress we have made, what seems to be working best, and the amount of effort and resource that will be needed to complete the journey down the developmental path. In general, evaluative research provides the basis for developing supervision systems (Milne & Reiser, 2016b).

9

Concluding Supervision

Clinical supervision is an 'essential' ingredient in modern mental healthcare (Department of Health, 2008, p.29), essential in order to foster competence, professionalism and effective self-care amongst the professionals providing that care (Care Quality Commission, 2013). It is also essential in terms of achieving adherence to evidence-based practices and obtaining good clinical outcomes (Layard, 2005). Yet we know surprisingly little about supervision: something does not 'compute' (Watkins, 1997). Therefore, this book was written to clarify the best available evidence on supervision, in order to aid our understanding of what it is and how it works, and to enhance the practice and study of supervision (especially CBT supervision). In terms of the continuing analogy with the tandem model, this chapter deals with the end of a developmental journey, a time to reflect on the progress that has been made, and to learn lessons about supervision, but first I consider the practicalities of concluding supervision.

Concluding Supervision

It is surprising to find that the business of bringing supervision sessions to an end is virtually ignored in research (Baum, 2011), given its prominence in the therapy literature and its obvious potential significance as the end of what may have been an important professional relationship. Ending therapy can leave patients feeling abandoned, hopeless and betrayed, whilst their

Evidence-Based CBT Supervision: Principles and Practice, Second Edition. Derek L. Milne.
© 2018 John Wiley & Sons Ltd. Published in 2018 by the British Psychological Society and John Wiley & Sons Ltd.

therapists may feel frustrated, sad, guilty and unsure about their competence (including the very task of how best to address endings: for a case study see Anthony & Pagano, 1998; and for the results of a survey see Baum, 2006). It is also surprising that it is ignored within supervision given the widespread adoption of a developmental perspective, which naturally includes tricky transitions to different roles and relationships, an important task that is frequently discussed in relation to therapy (e.g. Newman & Kaplan, 2016).

Similarly, such issues are rarely addressed empirically within the supervision literature. This is also surprising in the light of attention to endings in an early text (Mueller & Kell, 1972), where a 'terminating phase' of supervision was emphasized as much as the prior phases of 'developing' and 'maturing'. These authors suggested that the terminating phase (including the period prior to the end of supervision) should embrace consolidation of knowledge gain, decreasing need for direction, increasing reflection and developing skills in ending relationships. This thinking has been influential, as indicated by more recent statements, including inclusion in a current text (Holloway, 2016). There is also a somewhat surprising contrast with the end of individual supervision sessions, which are frequently mentioned, albeit in a brief and pragmatic fashion. For instance, the '10-step' procedure described by Gordon (2012) in relation to cognitive-behaviour therapy (CBT) supervision includes checking if the session's question has been answered (to encourage reflection and consolidate learning), action-planning (formalizing the task of transferring learning), homework-setting (addressing the supervisee's developmental needs) and seeking feedback on the session (e.g. learning points). Within the Improving Access to Psychological Therapies (IAPT) system, it has been suggested that each session should end with a summary of the points discussed, leading to shared decision-making about the clinical action plan (Richards, 2014). Illustrative examples and practical suggestions on some of these steps are also provided within Newman and Kaplan (2016).

However, research on how best to conclude an extended period of supervision (lasting months or years), or how to address the task of termination is rare (where a contract is cancelled, and supervision discontinued prematurely). For instance, the events (episodes) approach excludes endings from its list of seven 'critical events', the 'most common and challenging incidents that arise in psychotherapy supervision' (Ladany *et al.*, 2005, p.19). Similarly, when Chambers and Cutcliffe (2001) searched the literature, they found that not one of the 275 papers they located dealt with issues of endings in their titles or key words. Issues of ending supervision (concluding or terminating) are also little discussed in texts or consensus statements.

Thankfully, this oversight is corrected in the Bernard and Goodyear (2014) text, where the lack of attention to endings is again noted. They opined that some form of mutual debriefing was missing in most routine supervision, despite being a natural stage in the process. They note that it is recognized as such in group supervision, where it is referred to as 'adjourning'. This tends to cover farewells, the handing over of unfinished cases or work (often including incomplete reports and paperwork), recognition of successes and some direction about addressing weaknesses subsequently (e.g. an improvement plan). If appropriate, it would also subsume mutual evaluation. Lomax *et al.* (2005) agree with this agenda, adding that the concluding phase should include clarification of the supervisor's future availability, recognition of achievements and disappointments, a special 'celebratory' final session and a suitable closure event (they advocate an informal lunch meeting). Consensus statements say little about endings, either being absent (Pilling & Roth, 2014) or subsumed under the general management and structuring of sessions (Olds & Hawkins, 2014).

Given that one possible part of such endings is that a trainee is informed that they have failed to demonstrate the requisite competencies to receive a pass mark (or may have their placement or internship terminated early, or may even be advised to leave the profession), it seems evident that the conclusion of supervision can be a highly challenging event for all concerned. Korinek and Kimball (2003) review a number of such tense 'conflicts', drawing on the marital and family therapy literature for ways to resolve them effectively (e.g. conflict over the goals of supervision, as in the supervisor's tendency to insist on the supervisee's personal and professional growth, versus the supervisee's focus on passing, and on gaining the qualification with the minimum of effort or risk). They urge supervisors to work preventively, as in specifying relevant objectives within the contract, the regular provision of mutual feedback, and they also add some ways of resolving conflicts when these cannot be prevented (e.g. access to a consultant).

More commonly, supervision ends affirmatively, with a dominant sense of achievement and partnership. Based on a survey of 55 experienced social worker supervisors in Israel, Baum (2007) reported positive feelings such as satisfaction with their trainees' progress, pride in their contribution to this development, and a sense of gratification and fulfillment. Although the slight majority ($N = 28$) recounted such affirmative feelings, 24 also reported more uncomfortable feelings (including sadness over ending a productive relationship; frustration over the incompleteness of the experience; relief from the supervisees' demands). Echoing the reports immediately above, 39 of these supervisors also expressed concerns about their own ability and performance, and half reported concerns over professional issues (e.g. 22 were unhappy about not knowing how best to end supervision). These reports are especially remarkable because these supervisors appeared to be carefully selected, exceptionally well prepared and supported in this role.

In a similar study with 80 social work supervisees, Baum (2011) posed some questions about ending supervision, inviting open-ended written comments (to preserve confidentiality). Two raters then conducted a thematic content analysis on the comments, achieving 95 per cent agreement. The 58 supervisees who described having had good relationships (73 per cent) reported ambivalent feelings about the ending, because of their feelings of attachment on the one hand (the supervisor had become a significant person for them), but also sadness at parting (alongside relief that the placement obligations were now over, especially report writing). By contrast, those supervisees who reported poor or fair relationships had no feelings of sadness or loss, but reported discomfort. For example, one wrote: 'I'm quite overwhelmed with negative feelings and especially concerned with how it will end . . . I'm occupied with what exactly to say to her. Is it my place to criticize her? And how much was I at fault for not saying anything till now? . . . I don't know yet how I'll talk to her about it, or if I will at all' (p.90). Baum (2011) noted that this is consistent with observations and research findings indicating that supervisees who have had a poor alliance tend to remain silent during endings, continuing to avoid dealing with the unsatisfactory relationship. In her sample, this silence included saying nothing about such supervision despite various arrangements for students to provide feedback within the training programme. These findings indicate the need for proper closure of the supervisory relationship, especially when it was not good. Baum (2011) offered these suggestions: supervisees should be helped to become aware of how alliance difficulties can affect their ending experience; address the quality of the supervisory relationship with supervisees; and offer supervisees the opportunity to switch supervisors (where the alliance cannot be improved). For their part, supervisors should acknowledge when their alliance has been problematic, attempting to have an honest and open conversation with the supervisee about what went wrong (support, guidance or counselling should be offered, if necessary); and they should receive training in achieving satisfactory endings (especially dealing with conflicts and dilemmas).

These suggestions are similar to some of those offered by Chambers and Cutcliffe (2001) who proposed that healthy endings can be promoted by having supported, negotiated and gradual endings (no wrench of sudden loss), where the supervisee retains some control, and where both work towards a sense of closure. The latter should, they propose, include the supervisors being genuine about their feelings, thereby modelling a healthy response (e.g. reviewing the journey; celebrating success; recognizing loose ends). As a result, the participants should feel a sense that this stage of the professional journey is complete, and are ready to get on with the next one.

These ideas also suggest how I might best go about concluding this book, starting with a review of the main points that have been covered. To give weight to this book's subtitle ('principles and practice'), I list the 10 main principles that have been emphasized within the book, based on the theory, research and expert consensus that have been reviewed. To enhance the practice of evidence-based CBT supervision, I also summarize the essential practice implications that have been suggested in relation to each principle. Appropriately, this kind of pause to take stock represents the basis of reflection, an essential part of learning from experience. As well as being central to supervision, it is also part of critical thinking, a cognitive process 'that is focused on deciding what to believe or do' (Ennis, 1985, p.45). This seems especially fitting at the close of this book. Finally, I offer a commentary on the main strengths and weaknesses that have been noted, suggesting suitable actions to address the unfinished work, before concluding with my farewell.

Review of the Main Principles and Practices of Evidence-Based CBT Supervision

1. Be context-conscious

Just as in clinical work, professional activities can only be understood in their wider context. Research reviewed in this book has indicated the surprisingly large number and hugely diverse nature of contextual factors that influence supervision (Milne *et al.*, 2008a). Sometimes these are obvious, but sometimes contextual factors operate in subtle ways. These factors are an explicit part of the context for the tandem model, as set out in Figure 3.3. This principle is consistent with a review of training for mental health professionals (Beidas & Kendall, 2010), which concluded that we should adopt a systems-contextual model: 'Influencing one variable (e.g. therapist training) within a system is unlikely to result in effective implementation without addressing contextual factors. It is unlikely that training, dissemination and implementation will succeed without the understanding that therapists' function within a context and that multiple variables (i.e., organizational support, client factors, and therapist factors) affect this context' (p.26).

The implication for our practice is that we need to clarify which factors are relevant in our own supervision, and work with others to harness the boosters and minimize the barriers, as per the different approaches to metasupervision. At worst, we need to be aware of how the relevant contextual factors are moderating our supervision efforts, so that we can draw balanced conclusions and gain satisfaction from our work. The long-standing formula to bear in mind is that the behaviours of the supervisor and supervisee are a function of their personal characteristics, in the context that they operate, and of the interaction between the two (Lewin, 1951).

2. Utilize a problem-solving cycle

Whether within an individual supervision session or as part of the process of delivering a training programme, it is important to have a clear and shared sense of direction, based on collaborative goal-setting. This should be linked systematically to the methods that are deployed in pursuit of these goals, and to regular measurement, so that there is corrective feedback and an opportunity to reflect on and revise our approach. These are the basic elements of a problem-solving cycle. This principle encourages a vigorous, developmental perspective that is guided by effective leadership, as in IAPT and other healthcare systems that make routine use of outcome monitoring data. The evidence-based clinical supervision (EBCS) framework (see Figure 7.1) embodies this problem-solving logic, and in this book has been applied successively to the supervision system (e.g. supervisor training and outcome monitoring arrangements), and to the supervision and supervisee cycles.

While it might be natural to utilize a problem-solving cycle to consider issues within the supervision system, the same emphasis on evidence-based practice (EBP) should also influence individual supervision sessions (in the sense that discussions of the supervisee's work can equally well be considered in terms of the same headings).

3. Draw critically on the best available evidence

There are some damning reviews of supervision, but I fear that they may have failed 'to see the wood for the trees', obscuring sound material by combining it with uninterpretable material. By adopting more selective approaches, such as the best evidence synthesis approach to the systematic review, we can define a clear and helpful seam of rigorous research. If this is sensitively wedded to what professionals believe (especially through carefully developed expert consensus statements) and linked to relevant theory, then evidence-based approaches become viable. Of course, in time we should benefit from better research, and this may well suggest better approaches, but to my mind these principles afford an intelligent professional coping strategy. An example of my critical engagement with the research literature can be found in Chapter 4, where I challenged the rather casual acceptance within the supervision literature of the supervision alliance as a major explanatory factor.

Individual supervisors also need to be critically engaged in their consumption of the knowledge-base in supervision, as in questioning the adequacy of the methodology of key studies, and in generating alternative interpretations of the findings (Ellis, 1991). Ideally, supervisors also contribute to research, at least through evaluating their own local applications of research. The EBCS framework specifies outcome monitoring, audit and a range of research and development activities. Supervisors need to understand what is worthy of their belief, through exercising their critical faculties. Table 7.2 illustrated how a variety of reflective questions, raised within consultancy, could foster a questioning perspective (see especially the 'critical understanding' section). Critical engagement is also vital within supervision, as in educating supervisees to become capable practitioners. A further benefit of critical engagement is that it places us in a good position to integrate relevant theory with our practice (cf. Table 9.1).

Table 9.1　Evidence of poor theory–practice integration in CBT supervision.

Supervision dimensions	Assumptions and beliefs	Examples of observational evidence related to these beliefs (i.e. data as a reality check)
A. The Model	1. CT supervision parallels the therapy (Padesky, 1996)	'Outcomes of grounded theory analysis (10 consecutive supervision tapes from 1 supervisor receiving consultancy) mapped on very closely to the revised CT scale' (Milne *et al.*, 2003, p.198). CT supervision 'less structured and active than therapy' (Townend *et al.*, 2002, p.485)
B. The Objectives	2. Mastering cognitive therapy (Padesky, 1996)	Extensive use of questioning (Milne & James, 2002, pp.32–33). No data in other studies
C. The Content	3. Prevent 'drift' away from standard cognitive therapy (Liese & Beck, 1997, p.114)	'Cognitive Therapy was appropriate' (Milne *et al.*, 2003, p.200). No data in other studies
D. The Methods	4. Structure should be as per cognitive therapy (Liese & Beck, 1997, p.120)	'Managing' (including agenda setting) observed on only 1% of baseline occasions (Milne & James, 2002, p.64; 3% frequency observed in Milne & Westerman, 2001, p.457)
	5. Review case conceptualizations, utilize basic counselling skills, use CBT techniques (this one, and beliefs/assertions 6–7, 9–10, from Liese & Beck, 1997) 6. Weekly supervision (60 minutes)	Formulation (including re-formulation) the most frequent focus in supervision (94% of respondents affirmed this topic, in Townend *et al.*, 2002, p.491) 60 minutes per fortnight (Milne & Westerman, 2001, p.447); by contrast, mean duration of 136 minutes per month was reported by Townend *et al.* (2002, p.489)

7. Review therapy tapes ('essential', Liese & Beck, 1997, p.123)	18% of respondents reported reviewing tapes (Townend *et al.*, 2002, p.492). Tapes reviewed on only 6% of observed baseline occasions (Milne & James, 2002, p.64); and on 20% of baseline occasions in a related study (Milne & Westerman, 2001, p.451)
8. Include role-plays (Padesky, 1996, p.281)	19% reported using role-plays in a survey (Townend *et al.*, 2002, p.492–493). Only observed on 7% of baseline interactions in Milne & James (2002, p.63); and 0% in Milne & Westerman (2001, p.451)
E. Use of feedback and evaluation 9. Elicit feedback	Not reported in Townend *et al.* (2002). Feedback observed on only 3% of baseline occasions in both Milne & James (2002, p.64) and Milne & Westerman (2001, p.451)
10. Provide feedback based on instruments assessing therapist competence	Not reported in Townend *et al.* (2002). Note: supervisors can be trained to use CTS-R fairly reliably (Reichelt *et al.*, 2003)

Source: Milne, D.L. (2008b). Reproduced with permission of Cambridge University Press.

4. Clarify your model of practice

It is essential in practice (as it is in research) to be as specific as possible about the ideas that are guiding our work. By making comparisons with closely competing and widely divergent models we can enhance this specification effort. Discussions with peers and supervisor trainers can also sharpen an awareness of our approach, as can the more searching evaluations of the process of supervision (for useful methods see Chapter 8). I strongly recommend that, at the very least, supervisors tape a representative session and consider it against an instrument like SAGE (see Table 8.3), ideally within supervision-of-supervision, so that different perspectives can be considered. Such reality checks tend to furnish surprising data, a great platform for improved awareness and development (e.g. Milne *et al.*, 2002). Clarifying one's supervision model starts with definition, and suitably Chapter 1 in this book detailed an empirically derived definition. Amongst other things, this definition was intended to discourage illogical and misguided models such as 'peer supervision', whilst encouraging a systematic approach to EBCS.

Sometimes, clarifying our model of practice is straightforward, based on the extension of a therapy-based approach (e.g. CBT supervision). At other times it can prove tricky to draw out boundaries and distinctions. A feature of this second edition has been the clarification of evidence-based CBT supervision as a new, fourth wave approach. It unifies the earlier waves of CBT supervision with the EBCS model, which was presented as distinct in the first edition of this book. However, these two models still contain some differences of emphasis, as set out in Table 3.3. A clear model, such as the evidence-based CBT supervision tandem, is an enormous aid to practice ('there's nothing as practical as a good theory'), guiding the supervisor in the first instance, and providing inspiration to figure out solutions when problems arise subsequently. By contrast, appeals to an 'eclectic' approach may be tempting, but surely cannot represent the basis for informed practice. Classic instances are supervising as you were supervised, or transferring a few methods from your therapy model to your supervision work (Falender & Shafranske, 2014).

A clear model also helps research, for instance by pinpointing what is supposed to be happening and the related outcomes. Table 9.1 summarizes data drawn from nine empirical analyses of CBT supervision, indicating that the CBT supervisors in these studies struggled to integrate theory with their practice, as most of the 10 comparisons indicated low fidelity to the model (as defined by the experts listed in column 2 of Table 9.1). For instance, in the key dimension of the supervision techniques (D: The

Methods), comparisons 7 and 8 indicate that, on average, these experiential methods occurred on only 9 per cent of observed occasions. A more detailed discussion of this analysis can be found in Milne (2008a). Thankfully, a recent survey suggested a far greater degree of theory–practice integration, at least amongst CBT supervision leaders (Reiser & Milne, 2016).

5. Cultivate the supervision alliance

This much-endorsed principle lies at the traditional heart of supervision, regardless of the model. It is thought to sit at the interface of supervisor and supervisee input, determining the resultant outcomes (as indicated by the old idea of 'the analytic pact'). It centres on agreeing the goals of supervision, followed by mutual engagement in pursuing them, and an emergent emotional bond. But the evidence for the role of the alliance in supervision is surprisingly minimal, and is marked by complex interactions with other variables (as is true in clinical research). A case in point is whether the bond is a cause or effect, with some reason to believe that it grows as a consequence of the goal-setting and collaboration. Another illustration of the complexity is transactional 'game-playing', which can confuse the supervisor and the researcher alike.

Notwithstanding these continuing uncertainties, for professional practice reasons supervisors should treat the alliance as the foundation for their work, but a foundation that needs consideration and regular maintenance (e.g. ensuring the 'rupture–repair' cycle succeeds). A critical phase in the alliance is the management of endings, discussed at the start of this chapter, but a critical task throughout supervision is responsivity: the capacity to attune to the supervisee and to adapt the unfolding interaction so as to maximize progress. This includes attending to personal and interpersonal dynamics affecting therapy and supervision. Other significant tasks are collaboration, participative decision-making, reflective education and providing a professional role model.

6. Facilitate learning

As in related interventions, such as staff training and therapy, it is sometimes tempting to proceed quickly to what might appear to be the 'heart' of the business at hand, the supervision interventions that are designed to enhance competence (e.g. instructing or demonstrating). But a principled approach requires that supervisors exercise just as much care and attention over their leadership role, and over preliminaries such as educational needs assessment, the collaborative setting of learning objectives and the evaluation of progress. In short, we should engage with the full supervision cycle. These inter-dependent steps are best construed as necessary elements within a system, with attention to one inevitably influencing the others. As an expression of the dynamic nature of this system, even within a supervisory hour the effective supervisor will tend to complete a 'lap' of this cycle (possibly including a couple of steps back or across the cycle, as illustrated in Figure 6.3).

When it comes to intervention, the evidence clearly supports the responsive use of a blend of methods, each emphasizing different learning modalities (iconic, enactive, symbolic). Not for the first time we find the strongest evidence for blended learning within the staff development and instructional design literatures. Examples include deliberate practice (Ericsson, 2009), Vygotsky's (1978) Zone of Proximal Development, crite-rion-referenced instruction (Mager, 1997), performance-related feedback (Locke & Latham, 2006) and mastery learning (McGaghie *et al.*, 2014). Reviews of therapist training continue to recommend these methods of facilitating learning, adding contextual and systemic emphases (e.g. Beidas & Kendall, 2010; Rakovshik & McManus, 2010). The steps in deliberate practice are summarized below, but I still like this 'golden oldie' of a summary from Shanfield *et al.* (1992). They invited experts to observe supervision for elements of excellence, finding that it was the core condi-tions of supervision that carried the greatest weight (e.g. empathy from the supervisor accounted for 72 per cent of the variance in experts' ratings of excellence). When empathy was removed from the analysis, an experiential orientation next accounted for 60 per cent of the remaining variance in the ratings of excellence. In summary, 'supervisors judged to be excellent were empathic and focused on the immediate concerns of the trainee. They had an experiential orientation and tailored their comments to the residents' concerns . . . they were teachers who reflected with residents on their actions as therapists and supervisees' (Shanfield *et al.*, 1992, p.355).

7. Empower the supervisee

There is nothing new in emphasizing the part played in supervision by the supervisee, but surprisingly little empirical work has studied the supervisee's role, nor how the supervisor might best enhance it. In a rare text on the topic, Falender and Shafranske (2012) encouraged supervisees to orientate their supervisors to their developmental needs, to seek and to offer feedback, to engage in reflective practice, to foster their learning alliances, to prepare and plan and to aspire to ethical practice and personal effectiveness (e.g. self-regulation when experiencing challenging emotions). Embedded within this summary is 'learning expertise', something that supervisors should access and foster. Bransford and Schwartz (2009, p.433) defined it this way: 'Learning expertise involves the degree to which would-be experts continually attempt to refine their skills and attitudes to learning: skills and attitudes that include practicing, self-monitoring and finding ways to avoid plateaus and move to the next level.' They cited deliberate practice as a 'powerful example' of such skill refinement (see Chapter 2, and below). A nice illustration of learning expertise within clinical supervision appeared in an IAPT study reported by Green *et al.* (2014), who found that the most effective therapists were more proactive, more experiential and better prepared for supervision. These are vital qualities to foster, as 'it takes expertise to make expertise', including the expertise of the supervisee and the supervisor (Bransford & Schwartz, 2009, p.432).

But just as there can be ruptures to the supervision alliance, so there can be problems in empowering the supervisee, including tensions and complications. This is now illustrated with an example from my own experience, when I was acting as a consultant to an experienced CBT supervisor (Caroline Leck). This consultancy was within our joint programme of action research, and included listening to her supervision tapes on a weekly basis. In listening, I noticed that one of her supervisees described the clinical material at great length, creating a tedious and stupefying atmosphere, one that almost put me to sleep whilst listening to the tapes. This can be considered a transactional 'game', designed to reduce the effective functioning of the supervisor. In going along with this game, the supervisor is colluding with a supervisee-led process in which functions such as threat-reduction (e.g. not allowing one's competence to be judged) are being managed, to the possible detriment of the patient (Kadushin, 1968).

In order to help Caroline to make sense of this experience, the procedure described in 'self-reflection' (Bennett-Levy & Thwaites, 2007) was utilized within one of our consultancy sessions. Their six-stage process model for dealing with relationship difficulties within a CBT framework was applied, in order to make sense of this problematic relationship. The stages are: focused attention, where the problem is framed as a question; the

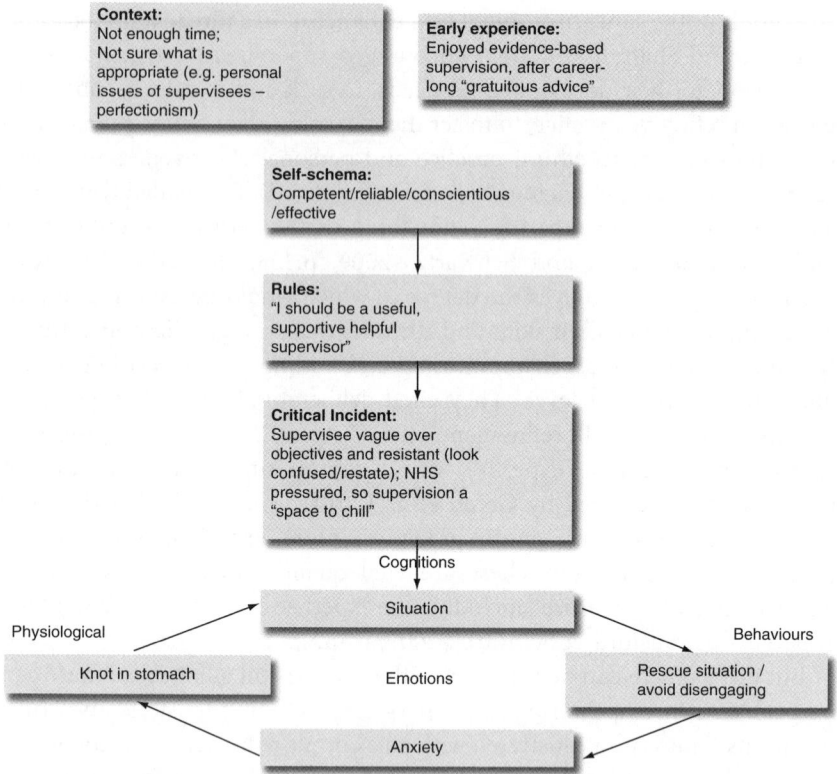

Figure 9.1   A CBT formulation of collusion in supervision, resulting from consultant-facilitated self-reflection, self-practice.
Source: Milne *et al.* (2009). Reproduced with permission of Cambridge University Press.

reconstruction of the experience; clarifying the emotions, thoughts and behaviours that accompanied the experience; trying to make sense of what was occurring (an interpersonal conceptualization); role-play and the rehearsal of ways to deal with the supervisee using the new strategies; and trying out these strategies as homework. This process is summarized in Milne *et al.* (2009). In relation to the fourth of these stages, conceptualizing the experience, we felt it was appropriate to adopt the kind of CBT formulation that Caroline used routinely within her clinical and supervisory work, only this time it was applied reflexively, to her experience of this unresponsive supervisee. Figure 9.1 provides a summary of this formulation, which illustrates how one might address, in a suitably empowering way, problems in engaging the supervisee.

8. Evaluate

As indicated in Table 9.1, evaluation is another necessary element within supervision. It provides an essential corrective link between all the other elements within the supervision process, and at a systemic level of analysis it should provide the kind of information needed to adjust and develop supervision. In Chapter 8, the fidelity framework was introduced as a unifying device, drawing together some complementary aspects of evaluation to address the basic questions in any problem-solving process (e.g. 'What is the right thing to do?'; 'Was it done right?'). The dominant reason for evaluation in supervision is to provide valid feedback to the supervisee, a major spur to the acquisition of adherence and competence. Measurement and feedback feature strongly in deliberate practice (Ericsson, 2009), where systematic, ongoing, formal feedback is deemed essential (i.e. from empirical outcome measures, and from experts such as supervisors). Secondly, it is necessary that feedback is utilized (e.g. learning from any errors made, by developing and executing an improvement plan).

Evaluation of the supervision system (e.g. before and after supervisor training) using the full framework is an exacting business, so I suggested in Chapter 8 that the minimum aim should be a structure–process–outcome evaluation. Whatever the focus, the received wisdom on evaluation is to employ multiple measures, including both qualitative methods (e.g. episode analysis) and quantitative methods (e.g. direct observation methods, such as SAGE: see Table 8.3).

Although the ideas in this book have support from research, theory and expert consensus, it is incumbent upon supervisors as professionals to gather their own data and verify for themselves whether important features hold up in their own context (based on the kind of critical engagement outlined in principle 3). An experimental orientation affords a way of developing supervision, as reflected in this poem:

> The road to wisdom?
> Well, it's plain and simple to express:
> Err and err and err again,
> But less and less, and less. (Aldwin, 2007, p.viii)

9. Seek support and guidance

The range and adequacy of support for supervisors generally appears to be distinctly poor (Milne & Reiser, 2016). In this unsupportive context, supervisors may need to invent their own support mechanisms, preferably in conjunction with course organizers or employers, and also draw on their personal coping repertoires. In the second EBCS manual (Milne & Reiser, 2017), we identified the need to start by clarifying the situation: what is it about the workplace that is challenging? Through a range of methods, such as supervision-of-supervision and metasupervision groups, supervisors and supervisees should be encouraged to process challenging experiences emotionally, and efforts should be made to strengthen their coping strategies. A key way to bolster coping is encourage supervisors and supervisees to make use of social support, especially from peers. The best-established way that supervisors can aid supervisees' coping strategies is through emotional support, modelling professional coping strategies and collaboration (Beinart, 2014). The goals of such methods are to boost effectiveness, morale, motivation and job satisfaction.

It is also appropriate at times to acknowledge the need to recognize, and where possible address, causal factors within the wider social context (e.g. public criticism of care staff), factors that have little or nothing to do with individuals (Azar, 2000). Using examples related to CBT supervision, Azar (2000) proposed normalizing therapists' reactions (e.g. through supervisor self-disclosure); cognitive restructuring within a highly supportive, safe space (or 'affective atmosphere'); and helping supervisees to develop more adaptive assumptions and practices (e.g. negotiating realistic, acceptable objectives).

Successes and Weaknesses

Another element within the above advice on successful endings is for the supervisor and supervisee to pause, so as to credit their successes and to acknowledge any weaknesses. In terms of successes, in this book I believe that I have provided supervisors (and those who work with them, especially supervisees, tutors and researchers) with a fresh, evidence-based account of CBT supervision that could 'compute' (Watkins, 1997), so bridging the gulf between research and practice. I have also tried to infuse this account with a critical, scholarly style, so that the available material was suitably refined and balanced. Another positive is that this second edition has benefited from recent, better-quality research, such as the studies of clinical outcome monitoring (Reese *et al.*, 2009; Swift *et al.*, 2014), studies of specific techniques (e.g. Braun *et al.*, 2015) and studies of feedback (Weck *et al.*, 2016). That this recent research builds on earlier work is a particular strength, as in the psychometric and other analyses that have been used to develop the competence frameworks (Olds & Hawkins, 2014; Gonsalvez *et al.*, 2015a,b), and in the surveys of unethical supervision (Ellis *et al.*, 2014; 2015a). I am particularly pleased to have been able to include long overdue examples of programmatic research. This is exemplified by the work of Gonsalvez and colleagues in Australia (e.g. Gonsalvez *et al.*, 2015a,b) and by the concerted analyses of multisystemic therapy in the USA by Schoenwald and colleagues (e.g. Schoenwald *et al.*, 2009; Schoenwald, 2016).

In this second edition, neighbouring literatures have also continued to repay attention (e.g. regarding training methods: Beidas & Kendall, 2010; Rakovshik & McManus, 2010), and it is exciting to consider a new theoretical perspective from the expertise literature (new for the supervision literature: e.g. Fischer *et al.*, 2003; Ericsson, 2009; McMahon, 2014; Tracey *et al.*, 2014). Another pillar of EBCS is expert consensus statements and guidance, and this aspect has also continued to develop, such as the long-overdue attention to establishing a toolkit of sound measures, linked to practice networks (Wheeler & Barkham, 2014), and the development of the EBCS manual (Milne & Reiser, 2017). In this second edition I have continued to bolster and enliven this summary of other people's work with findings and examples from the programme of applied research that I and my colleagues in the north-east of England have been engaged in for the past 30 years.

Given my own involvement in supervision research and development, this book was not intended to be a completely neutral, disinterested review of the field. Rather, this is a perspective that you might expect from a committed scientist-practitioner, someone who spent 33 years as an employee and vigorous supporter of Britain's National Health Service, written as if engaged in trying to guide supervisors (and those who support them), so that multidisciplinary staff and the mental health services can develop. Like any decisive stance, this platform brings with it potential weaknesses, including some distinct biases and blind spots, and so I wish to recognize the possibility that some of these may have diminished my open-mindedness. I am keenly aware (particularly from presenting the material to colleagues at meetings and conferences) that in my case the delicate balance between evidence and enthusiasm can sometimes become disturbed, resulting at times in what can seem to be an overly prescriptive and opinionated account. My apologies if the book has at times appeared to have taken on that kind of unappealing stance: please attribute it to my enthusiasm getting the better of my judgement. I trust that you will correct this imbalance with your own critical engagement. In time, careful evaluations will, no doubt, also moderate my enthusiasm.

As a case in point, a major part of my approach has been to base these principles, and the associated supervision practices, on a series of systematic reviews of the research literature (e.g. Milne & James, 2000; Milne, 2007b). The reviews were of a particularly optimistic, constructive kind, namely the best evidence synthesis (BES; Petticrew & Roberts, 2006). This is an example where imbalance and attendant collegial resistance may arise, directed at the ironic possibility that the BES yields an unacceptably biased account of 'what is the right thing to do'. In particular, there is a concern that, by carefully excluding unsuccessful manipulations of supervision, some important (possibly even contrary) information is lost, leading to faulty conclusions about what to believe and do.

This raises the question as to whether it is valid to refer to the tandem model as 'evidence-based'. Is this another weakness, in terms of faulty reasoning? Am I being rather too liberal in my use of the term? The popular definition of EBP is that it is 'the conscientious, explicit, and judicious use of current best evidence in making decisions about the care of patients' (Sackett *et al.*, 1996, p.71). On this logic, clinical expertise should be combined with the 'best available external clinical evidence from systematic research' (p.71), evidence that is not restricted to the randomized controlled trial (RCT). In this sense, the tandem model appears to satisfy the definition of EBP, though the research evidence only approximates to 'systematic' if one regards the EBCS framework as an assembly of various foundations of well-established psychological knowledge (e.g. the evidence justifying the learning needs assessment and feedback from the education literature; goal-setting from the training literature; learning from experimental psychology). This definition is less anchored in rigorous research evidence and more concerned with an evidence-based approach to one's work. On this view, EBP is a process of career-long learning, in which such evidence as can be located is critically appraised and applied to answerable questions about our clinical practice, leading to evaluation of our performance (Sackett *et al.*,

1996). On this definition, EBP is an approach to professional practice that is intended to limit the problems associated with relying on our initial training for an evidence-base (or relying on how we do therapy, or were supervised). It is an approach that encourages a healthy engagement with the full EBP spectrum (as per Figure 3.5), as an antidote to complacency and inconsistency. EBCS clearly satisfies this definition, attempting as it does to close the gap between the knowledge-base and supervisory practice, in the tradition of the scientist-practitioner.

There is a second and more exacting definition of EBP, one that requires not just the 'best available' evidence but the successful completion of the most rigorous and large-scale research. As expressed by Parry *et al.* (1996), EBP is initially a broad developmental process that works to combine information from diverse sources, including small-scale, rigorous research (e.g. they endorse the $n = 1$ design as part of this development work), clinical consensus, continuing professional development, audits, and so forth (see Figure 3.5). But, according to them, these various EBP-related activities are merely part of the necessary work that ultimately needs to lead to 'formal evaluation', to research that 'conforms to the most rigorous standards of enquiry' (p.49), which they appear to regard as the RCT. Then, once research with high internal validity has demonstrated efficacy, service-based evaluations can address external validity and implementation issues. On this definition it is harder to assert that EBCS is 'evidence-based', at least in so far as it has not yet been subjected to an explicit RCT.

Therefore, on this exacting logic we need to ask: what is the status of EBCS? Following the National Institute for Health and Care Excellence approach (NICE, 2007), such evidence as exists at any one time is graded against an eight-step hierarchy of research rigour, ranging from expert consensus up to the RCT. In turn, the recommendations that then emerge within NICE guidelines draw on this classification of the evidence to grade all the included evidence on a three-point scale (A = at least one RCT, in good quality literature addressing the specific recommendation, without extrapolation; B = no RCTs, but good clinical studies; C = expert consensus, in the absence of good quality studies). In my opinion, EBCS merits the 'B' grading, as there are several high-quality systematic reviews of controlled research in supervision, a few RCTs that test tandem model type assumptions and some well-conducted case–control type research that is either explicit or highly related (i.e. research where there is a moderate probability that the relationship is causal). I feel reassured that this position is bolstered by extrapolation to those assembled neighbouring literatures, which would surely support one or more 'A' gradings.

But in practice, as Parry *et al.* (1996) note, 'few if any psychotherapies have been programmatically taken through this full cycle', and so they recognize that 'It would be impractical and indeed unnecessary to insist that research findings should be integrated across all these levels before being applied to clinical guidelines and standards of practice' (p.50). Indeed, the shortcomings in research 'are overcome through interpretation', as per expert judgement and systematic consensus-building. Therefore, I conclude that my use of the term 'EBCS' is indeed appropriate. However, as is to be hoped is evident from my emphasis on research and development, it is of course highly desirable for RCTs (and other forms of rigorous research) to be undertaken on the tandem model, to advance it beyond its present intermediate status as EBP. The material within this book should facilitate such progress. In the meantime, supervisors should exercise careful judgement about the application of the material within this book, and should evaluate their work.

Action Plan

A further element within the above advice on successful endings is for the supervisor and supervisee to devote time 'that is focused on deciding what to believe or do' (Ennis, 1985). In relation to the material covered within this book, what we continue to need to do is more and better research, within a pluralistic and programmatic ethos that is summarized in the section above. We need more sophisticated evaluations of supervision, such as dismantling studies that systematically tease apart the relative value of the different components in supervision. We also need comparative evaluations, such as the one reported by Bambling *et al.* (2006), so that we can judge whether one option is preferable to another. Of course, the tandem model itself should be subjected to further experimentation, including dismantling and comparative evaluations. When related to the 'pyramid of research knowledge' (Milne *et al.*, 2007), it can be seen that, at best, EBCS has progressed from the 'knowledge synthesis' stage (i.e. where the available knowledge is synthesized and guidelines are developed), through the 'mapping and modelling' stage, to some 'pilot investigations'. This work should next be replicated, and then, if promising, progressed on to the stages of 'definitive investigation' and 'long-term implementation'. With Ellis (1991), I favour a 'scientific agenda' (p.248), which is based on 'vigorously testing theoretical propositions about what supervision techniques will result in what outcomes' (p.246).

Consistent with the EBCS approach to evidence, such research activity must be integrated with other vehicles of progress, particularly expert consensus building, alongside theory development and its careful application to supervision. These are part of the EBCS framework (see Figure 3.5), and it follows that the other parts of that framework also need attention. To illustrate, workshops and other forms of training for most supervisors still appear to follow traditional topics, methods and formats, and are concluded by simple, non-threatening evaluations (e.g. delegates' satisfaction with the training). The review by Falender and Shafranske (2014) noted data indicating that the majority of internships (i.e. the final year of training in clinical psychology in the USA) offered no training in how to supervise, and that trainees judged the main influence on their approach to be their personal experiences of receiving supervision. Consequently, Falender and Shafranske (2014, p.10) concluded that the 'requisite supervisor competencies . . . are not being transmitted'. At least future action on this part of the framework can draw inspiration from some modern approaches (e.g. Watkins & Wang, 2014; Ferguson *et al.*, 2016).

I have suggested that the whole EBCS framework represents a promising problem-solving cycle, a rationale for research, and generally an effective developmental strategy. Preparing this second edition has added perspective and made me keenly aware of the way that successive cycles of activity around the EBCS framework have indeed resulted in refinements to the tandem model. For example, in the case of the best-evidence literature reviews (e.g. Milne & James, 2000; Reiser & Milne, 2014), this activity effectively started with an empirical definition and evidence-based model, before progressing to issues such as the most appropriate methods to employ, and then on to considering the best ways of training supervisors in those methods. These reviews were accompanied by complementary applied work, serving to integrate theory with routine practice (e.g. Culloty *et al.*, 2010; Milne, 2010; Milne *et al.*, 2013). Another useful action would be to ensure that this EBCS framework is itself suitably shaped and guided by progress now being made in the emergent field of implementation science (e.g. Rotheram-Borus *et al.*, 2012; Beidas *et al.*, 2013).

A significant upshot of all this activity has been the development of the first 'fourth wave' CBT supervision model, significant because it represents real progress towards a supervision-specific model, and with it the implication that CBT supervision has finally arrived as a professional specialization.

Farewell

It is indeed heartening to reflect on these promising developments and all that has been achieved latterly. This progress is particularly heartening for me personally, because my own minor contribution has been achieved by means of multidisciplinary partnerships and collaboration within mental health services, learning from our collective experience. In a book I wrote on training behaviour therapists over 30 years ago (Milne, 1986), I noted the likelihood that much supervision was 'superstitious', in the sense that supervisors probably engaged in many functionally irrelevant activities, owing to inadequate training and feedback. In those days, supervision was a mundane administrative duty that came automatically with seniority, with no recognition that it might become a distinctive and deeply stimulating professional specialization. How things have changed! Now there is international recognition of the need for proper supervisor training, accompanied by a number of effective options for ensuring effective feedback. This improved situation allows us to replace superstition with applied science (Watkins & Milne, 2014; Milne & Reiser, 2017), and to make the whole supervision business 'compute' (Watkins, 1997). Even the reflections in this chapter indicate that what we now know about supervision has advanced since the 1980s, and so knowing what to believe or do in supervision is thankfully more straightforward. It is deeply satisfying for me to witness this progress, and to find that supervision is now being taken seriously throughout professional life. I feel a celebration coming on! I hope that this book has also conveyed to you, the reader, new ways of making the profound business of clinical supervision compute.

References

Agnew-Davies, R., Stiles, W.B., Hardy, G.E., Barkham, M. & Shapiro, D.A. (1998). Alliance structure assessed by the Agnew relationship measure (ARM). *British Journal of Clinical Psychology, 37,* 155–172.

Aldwin, C.M. (2007). *Stress, coping and development.* New York: Guilford Press.

Alliger, G.M., Tannenbaum, S.I., Bennett, J.R., Traver, H. & Shotland, A. (1997). A meta-analysis of the relations among training criteria. *Personnel Psychology, 50,* 341–358.

American Psychological Association (APA). (2002). *Guidelines on multicultural education, training, research, practice, and organizational change for psychologists.* Washington, DC: APA.

American Psychological Association (APA). (2006). Evidence-based practice in psychology. *American Psychologist, 61,* 271–285.

American Psychological Association (APA). (2015). Guidelines for clinical supervision in health service psychology. *American Psychologist, 70,* 33–46.

Andrusyna, T.P., Tang, T.Z., DeRubeis, R.J. & Luborsky, L. (2001). The factor structure of the Working Alliance Inventory in CBT. *Journal of Psychotherapy Practice and Research, 10,* 173–178.

Anthony, S. & Pagano, G. (1998). The therapeutic potential for growth during the termination process. *Clinical Social Work Journal, 26,* 281–296.

Armstrong, P.V. & Freeston, M.H. (2005). Conceptualising and formulating cognitive therapy supervision. In N. Tarrier (Ed.) *Case formulation in cognitive-behaviour therapy.* New York: Brunner-Routledge.

Ayers, T.D. (1987). Stakeholders as partners in evaluation: A stakeholder-collaborative approach. *Evaluation and Programme Planning, 10,* 263–271.

Evidence-Based CBT Supervision: Principles and Practice, Second Edition. Derek L. Milne.
© 2018 John Wiley & Sons Ltd. Published in 2018 by the British Psychological Society and John Wiley & Sons Ltd.

Azar, S.T. (2000). Preventing burnout in professionals and para-professionals who work with child abuse and neglect cases: A cognitive-behavioural approach to supervision. *Journal of Clinical Psychology, 56*, 643–663.

Bagnall, G. & Sloan, G. (2014). A qualitative approach for measuring competence in clinical supervision. In C.E. Watkins & D.L. Milne (Eds) *The Wiley international handbook of clinical supervision* (pp. 431–444). Chichester: Wiley.

Bahrick, A.S. (1990). Role induction for counsellor trainees: Effects on the supervisory working alliance. *Dissertation Abstracts International, 51*, 1484B (University microfilms No. 90-14, 392).

Baltes, P.B., Lindenberger, U. & Staudinger, U.M. (1998). Lifespan theory in developmental psychology. In W. Damon & R.M. Lerner (Eds) *Handbook of child psychology*, 5th edn. (pp. 1029–1144). New York: Wiley.

Baltimore, M.L. & Crutchfield, L.B. (2003). *Clinical supervisor training: An interactive CD ROM training programme for the helping professions.* London: Allyn & Bacon.

Bambling, M. (2014). Creating positive outcomes in clinical supervision. In C.E. Watkins & D.L. Milne (Eds) *Wiley international handbook of clinical supervision* (pp. 445–457). Chichester: Wiley.

Bambling, M., King, R., Raue, P., Schweitzer, R. & Lambert, W. (2006). Clinical supervision: Its influence on client-rated working alliance and client symptom reduction in the brief treatment of major depression. *Psychotherapy Research, 16*, 317–331.

Barker, C., Pistrang, N. & Elliott, R. (2002). *Research methods in clinical psychology: An introduction for students and practitioners*, 2nd edn. Chichester: Wiley.

Barker, K.K. & Hunsley, J. (2013). The use of theoretical models in psychology supervisor development research from 1994 to 2010: A systematic review. *Canadian Psychology, 54*, 176–185.

Barkham, M., Evans, C., Margison, F., McGrath, G., Mellor-Clark, J., Milne, D.L. et al. (1998). The rationale for developing and implementing core outcome batteries for routine use in service settings and psychotherapy outcome research. *Journal of Mental Health, 7*, 35–47.

Barkham, M., Hardy, G.E. & Mellor-Clark, J. (Eds) (2010). *Developing and delivering practice-based evidence: A guide for the psychological therapies.* Chichester: Wiley.

Barlow, D.H., Hayes, S.C. & Nelson, R.O. (1984). *The scientist-practitioner.* London: Pergamon.

Barron, R. & Kenny, D. (1986). The moderator–mediator variable distinction in social psychological research: Conceptual, strategic and statistical considerations. *Journal of Personality and Social Psychology, 51*, 1173–1182.

Barrow, M. & Domingo, R.A. (1997). The effectiveness of training clinical supervisors in conducting the supervisory conference. *The Clinical Supervisor, 16*, 55–78.

Baum, N. (2006). End-of-year treatment termination: Responses of social work student trainees. *British Journal of Social Work, 36,* 639–656.

Baum, N. (2007). Field supervisors' feelings and concerns at the termination of the supervisory relationship. *British Journal of Social Work, 37,* 1095–1112.

Baum, N. (2011). Social work students' feelings and concerns about the ending of their fieldwork supervision. *Social Work Education, 30,* 83–97.

Bearman, S.K., Weisz, J.R., Chorpita, B.F., Hoagwood, K., Ward, A., Ugueto, A.M. *et al.* (2013). More practice, less preach? The role of supervision processes and therapist characteristics in EBP implementation. *Administrative Policy and Mental Health, 40,* 518–529.

Bebbington, P.E., Marsden, L. & Brewin, C.R. (1997). The need for psychiatric treatment in the general population: The Camberwell Needs for Care Survey. *Psychological Medicine, 27,* 821–834.

Beck, A., Steer, R. & Garbin, M. (1987). *Psychometric properties of the Beck Depression Inventory: 25 years of evaluation. A handbook for practitioners.* London: Pearson Education.

Beck, A.T., Rush, J.A., Shaw, B.F. & Emery, G. (1979). *Cognitive therapy of depression.* New York: Guilford Press.

Beidas, R.S., Aarons, G., Barg, F., Evans, A., Hadley, T., Hoagwood, K., *et al.* (2013). Policy to implementation: Evidence-based practice in community mental health – study protocol. *Implementation Science, 20,* 138: 38. DOI: 10.1186/1748-5908-8-38

Beidas, R.S. & Kendall, P.C. (2010). Training therapists in evidence-based practice: A critical review of studies from a systems-contextual perspective. *Clinical Psychology: Science and Practice, 17,* 1–30.

Beinart, H. (2004). Models of supervision and the supervisory relationship and the evidence base. In I. Fleming & L. Steen (Eds) *Supervision and clinical psychology: Theory, practice and perspectives* (pp. 36–50) Hove: Brunner-Routledge.

Beinart, H. (2014). Building and sustaining the supervisory relationship. In C.E. Watkins & D.L. Milne (Eds) *The Wiley international handbook of clinical supervision* (pp. 257–281) Chichester: Wiley.

Belfield, C., Thomas, H., Bullock, A., Eynon, R. & Wall, D. (2001). Measuring the effectiveness for best medical education: A discussion. *Medical Teacher, 23,* 164–170.

Bennardo, G. (2014). The fundamental role of causal models in cultural models of nature. *Frontiers in Psychology, 5.* DOI: 10.3389/fpsyg.2014.01140

Bennett, A. & Elman, C. (2006). Complex causal relations and case study methods: The example of path dependence. *Political Analysis, 14,* 250–267. DOI: 10.1093/pan/mpj020

Bennett-Levy, J. (2006). Therapist skills: Cognitive model of their acquisition and refinement. *Behavioural and Cognitive Psychotherapy, 34,* 57–78.

Bennett-Levy, J. & Beedie, A. (2007). The ups and downs of cognitive therapy training. *Behavioural and Cognitive Psychotherapy*, *35*, 61–75.

Bennett-Levy, J., Lee, N., Travers, K., Pohlman, S. & Hanernik, E. (2003). Cognitive therapy from the inside: Enhancing therapists' skills through practicing what we preach. *Behavioural and Cognitive Psychotherapy*, *31*, 143–158.

Bennett-Levy, J. & Thwaites, R. (2007). Self and self reflection in the therapeutic relationship: A conceptual map and practical strategies for the training, supervision and self supervision of interpersonal skills. In P. Gilbert & R.L. Leahy (Eds) *The therapeutic relationship in the cognitive behavioural therapy* (pp. 255–281). London: Routledge.

Bennett-Levy, J., Thwaites, R., Haarhoff, B. & Perry, H. (2015). *Experiencing CBT from the inside out. A self-practice/self-reflection workbook for therapists.* New York: Guilford Press.

Bennett-Levy, J., Turner, F., Beaty, T., Smith, M., Paterson, B. & Farmer, S. (2001). The value of self-practice of cognitive therapy techniques and self-reflection in the training of cognitive therapists. *Behavioural and Cognitive Psychotherapy*, *29*, 203–220.

Bernard, J.M. (1997). The discrimination model. In C.E. Watkins (Ed.) *Handbook of psychotherapy supervision* (pp. 310–327). New York: Wiley.

Bernard, J.M. & Goodyear, R.K. (2004). *Fundamentals of clinical supervision*. Upper Saddle River, NJ: Merrill.

Bernard, J.M. & Goodyear, R.K. (2009). *Fundamentals of clinical supervision*, 4th edn. Upper Saddle River, NJ: Merrill.

Bernard, J.M. & Goodyear, R.K. (2014). *Fundamentals of clinical supervision*, 5th edn. London: Pearson.

Bertsch, K.N., Bremer-Landau, J.D., Inman, A.G., DeBoer-Kreider, E.R., Price, T.A. & DeCarlo, A.L. (2014). Evaluation of the critical events in supervision model using gender-related events. *Training and Education in Professional Psychology*, *8*, 174–181.

Beutler, L.E. (2001). Comparisons among quality assurance systems: From outcome assessment to clinical utility. *Journal of Consulting and Clinical Psychology*, *69*, 197–204.

Bhanthumnavin, D. (2000). Importance of supervisory social support and its implications for HRD in Thailand. *Psychology and Developing Societies*, *12*, 155–166.

Bibring, E. (1937). The four countries conference: Discussion on control analysis. *Internal Journal of Psychoanalysis*, *18*, 369–371.

Binder, J.L. (1993). Is it time to improve psychotherapy training? *Clinical Psychology Review*, *13*, 301–318.

Binder, J.L. & Strupp, H.H. (1997). Supervision of psychodynamic psychotherapies. In C.E. Watkins (Ed.) *Handbook of psychotherapy supervision* (pp. 44–62). New York: Wiley.

Bjork, R. (2006). *Shedding light on learning.* [This appeared in a conference report, by S. Cleland, published in *The Psychologist,* August, 463.]

Blackburn, I-M., James, I.A., Milne, D.L., Baker, C., Standart, S.H., Garland, A. *et al.* (2001). The revised Cognitive Therapy Scale (CTS-R) psychometric properties. *Behavioural and Cognitive Psychotherapy, 29,* 431–446.

Bloom, B.S., Englehart, M.D., Furst, E.J., Hill, W.H. & Krathwohl D.R. (1956). *Taxonomy of educational objective, handbook I: Cognitive domain.* New York: McKay.

Borders, L.D. (2012). Dyadic, triadic, and group models of peer supervision/consultation: What are their components, and is there evidence of their effectiveness? *Clinical Psychologist, 16,* 59–71.

Bordin, E.S. (1979). The generalisability of the psychoanalytic concept of the working alliance. *Psychotherapy: Theory, Research, Practice, 16,* 252–260.

Bordin, E.S. (1983). Supervision in counselling: Contemporary models of supervision – A working alliance-based model of supervision. *The Counselling Psychologist, 11,* 35–42.

Borelli, B., Sepinwall, D., Ernst, D., Bellg, A.J., Czajkowski, S., Breger, R. *et al.* (2005). A new tool to assess treatment fidelity and evaluation of treatment fidelity across 10 years of health behaviour research. *Journal of Consulting and Clinical Psychology, 73,* 852–860.

Borkovec, R. & Bauer, R.M. (2010). Experimental designs in group outcome research. In A.S. Bellack, M. Hersen & A.E. Kazdin (Eds) *International handbook of behavior modification and therapy* (pp. 139–164). New York: Springer.

Boswell, J.F. (2013). Intervention strategies and clinical process in transdiagnostic CBT. *Psychotherapy, 50,* 381–386.

Bouchard, M.A., Wright, J., Mathieu, M., Lalonde, F., Bergeron, G. & Toupin, J. (1980). Structured learning in teaching therapists social skills training: Acquisition, maintenance, and impact on client outcome. *Journal of Consulting and Clinical Psychology, 48,* 491–502.

Boud, D., Keogh, R. & Walker, D. (1985). *Reflection: Turning experience into learning.* London: Routledge.

Bouwen, R. & Taillieu, T.J. (2004). Multi-party collaboration as social learning for interdependence: Developing relational knowing for sustainable natural resource management. *Community and Applied Social Psychology, 14,* 137–153.

Bower, P., Gilbody, S., Richards, D,. Fletcher, J. & Sutton, A. (2006). Collaborative care for depression in primary care. *British Journal of Psychiatry, 189,* 484–493.

Bransford, J., Brown, A. & Cocking, R. (2000). *How people learn: Brain, mind, and experience and school.* Washington, DC: National Academy Press.

Bransford, J.D. & Schwartz, D.L. (2009). It takes expertise to make expertise: Some thoughts about why and how and reflections on the themes in chapters 15–18. In K.A. Ericsson (Ed.) *Development of professional expertise* (pp. 432–448) Cambridge: Cambridge University Press.

Braun, J.D., Strunk, D.R., Sasso, K.E. & Cooper, A.A. (2015). Therapist use of Socratic questioning predicts session-to-session symptom change in cognitive therapy for depression. *Behavior Research and Therapy, 70,* 32–37.

Breese, L., Boon, A. & Milne, D.L. (2012). Detecting excellent episodes in clinical supervision: A case study, comparing two approaches. *The Clinical Supervisor, 31,* 121–137.

British Psychological Society (BPS). (2002). *Guidelines on clinical supervision.* Leicester: BPS.

British Psychological Society (BPS). (2003). *Policy guidelines on supervision in the practice of clinical psychology.* Leicester: BPS.

British Psychological Society (BPS). (2007). *Criteria for the accreditation of postgraduate training programmes in clinical psychology.* Leicester: BPS.

British Psychological Society (BPS). (2009). *Code of ethics and conduct.* Leicester: BPS.

Brown, J.F. & Ash, B. (2001). Two heads with different tails: A look at the supervision process. *Clinical Psychology, 2,* 11–13.

Bruce, S. & Paxton, R. (2002). Ethical principles for evaluating mental health services: A critical examination. *Journal of Mental Health, 11,* 267–279.

Bruner, J.S. (1966). *Toward a theory of instruction.* Cambridge, MA: Harvard University Press.

Bryson, B. (2004). *A short history of nearly everything.* London: Black Swan.

Buus, N., Lisa Lynch, L. & Gonge, H. (2016). Developing and implementing 'meta-supervision' for mental health nursing staff supervisees: Opportunities and challenges. *The Cognitive Behaviour Therapist, 9,* e22. DOI: 10.1017/S1754470X15000434

Callahan, J.L., Almstrom, J.L., Swift, J.K., Borja, S.E. & Heath, C.J. (2009). Exploring the contribution of supervisors to intervention outcomes. *Training and Education for Professional Practice, 3,* 72–77.

Campbell, J.M. (2006). *Essentials of clinical supervision.* Chichester: Wiley.

Cape, J. & Barkham, M. (2002). Practice improvement methods: Conceptual base, evidence based research, and practice based recommendations. *British Journal of Clinical Psychology, 41,* 285–307.

Capra, F. (1996). *The web of life: A new scientific understanding of living systems.* New York: Doubleday.

Care Quality Commission. (2013). *Supporting information and guidance: Supporting effective clinical supervision.* Newcastle upon Tyne: Care Quality Commission.

Carroll, M. (2007). Clinical psychology supervision. *Clinical Psychology Forum, 174,* 35–37.

Carroll, M. & Gilbert, M.C. (2005). *On being a supervisee: Creating learning partnerships.* London: Vukani.

Case, R. (1992). Neo-Piagetian theories of intellectual development. In H. Beilin & P.B. Pufall (Eds) *Piaget's theory: Prospects and possibilities.* Hillsdale, NJ: Lawrence-Erlbaum.

Castonguay, L.G., Goldfried, M.R., Wiser, S., Raue, P.J. & Hayes, A.M. (1996). Predicting the effect of cognitive therapy for depression: A study of unique and common factors. *Journal of Consulting and Clinical Psychology, 64,* 497–504.

Chambers, M. & Cutcliffe, J.J.R. (2001). The dynamics and processes of 'ending' in clinical supervision. *British Journal of Nursing, 10,* 1403–1411.

Chen, H. (1990). *Theory-driven evaluation.* Newbury Park, CA: Sage.

Clark, D.M., Layard, R., Smithies, R., Richards, D.A., Suckling, R. & Wright, B. (2009). Improving access to psychological therapy: Initial evaluation of two UK demonstration sites. *Behavior Research and Therapy, 47,* 910–920.

Cleary, M. & Freeman, A. (2006). Fostering a culture of support in mental health settings: Alternatives to traditional models of clinical supervision. *Issues in Mental Health Nursing, 27,* 985–1000.

Cliffe, T. & Milne, D.L. (2012). Can a new observational tool distinguish between CBT, systemic and psychodynamic supervision? *Clinical Psychology Forum, 234,* 9–14.

Cogswell, D. & Stubblefield, H. (1988). Assessing the training and staff development needs of mental health professionals. *Administration and Policy in Mental Health and Mental Health Services Research, 16,* 14–24.

Colquitt, J.A., LePine, J.A. & Noe, R.A. (2000). Toward an integrative theory of training motivation: A meta-analytic path analysis of twenty years of research. *Journal of Applied Psychology, 85,* 678–707.

Concise Oxford English Dictionary. (2004). Oxford: Oxford University Press.

Cowen, E.L. (1982). Help is where you find it. *American Psychologist, 37,* 385–395.

Culloty, T., Milne, D.L. & Sheikh, A.I. (2010). Evaluating the training of clinical supervisors: A pilot study using the fidelity framework. *The Cognitive Behaviour Therapist, 3,* 132–144.

Davies, P. (2000). Approaches to evidence based teaching. *Mental Teacher, 22,* 14–21.

Davy, J. (2002). Discursive reflections on a research agenda for clinical supervision. *Psychology and Psychotherapy: Theory, Research and Practice, 75,* 221–238.

DeBell, D.E. (1963). A critical digest of the literature on psychoanalytic supervision. *Journal of the American Psychoanalytic Association, 11,* 546–575.

Deery, R. (2004). An action research study exploring midwives' support needs and the effect of group clinical supervision. *Midwifery, 21,* 161–176.

Demchak, M. & Browder, D.M. (1990). An evaluation of the pyramid model of staff training in group homes for adults with severe handicaps. *Education and Training in Mental Retardation, 25,* 150–163.

Dennin, M.K. & Ellis, M.V. (2003). Effects of a method of self-supervision for counsellor trainees. *Journal of Counselling Psychology, 50,* 69–83.

Department of Health. (1993). *A vision for the future.* London: Department of Health.

Department of Health. (1998). *A first class service: Quality in the new NHS*. London: Department of Health.

Department of Health. (2000). *A health service of all the talents: Developing the NHS workforce*. London: Department of Health.

Department of Health. (2001). *Working together – learning together: A framework for life long learning for the NHS*. London: Department of Health.

Department of Health. (2004a). *Organising and delivering psychological therapies*. London: Department of Health.

Department of Health. (2004b). *The ten essential shared capabilities*. London: Department of Health.

Department of Health. (2004c). *National standards, local action*. London: Department of Health.

Department of Health. (2007). *A learning and development toolkit for the whole of the mental health workforce, across both health and social care*. London: Department of Health.

Department of Health. (2008). *Improving Access to Psychological Therapies (IAPT) commissioning toolkit*. London: Department of Health.

Department of Health. (2012). *The NHS Outcomes Framework*. London: Department of Health (available from www.dh.gov.uk).

Dewald, P.A. (1997). The process of supervision in psychoanalysis. In C.E. Watkins (Ed.) *Handbook of psychotherapy supervision* (pp. 31–43). New York: Wiley.

Dewey, J. (1910). *How we think*. Lexington, NA: D.C. Heath.

Dewey, J. (1933). *How we think: A restatement of the relation of reflective thinking to the educative process*. Boston: D.C. Heath.

Dewey, J. (1938). *Experience and education*. New York: Touchstone.

Dewey, J. (1955). *Democracy and education: An introduction to the philosophy of education*. New York: Macmillan.

Docchar, C. (2007). *Mapping of UK supervision courses for counsellors and psychotherapists*. Paper presented at the 'Supervision Today' conference, British Association for Counselling and Psychotherapy, Birmingham, 4 December.

Donabedian, A. (1988). The quality of care: How can it be assessed? *Journal of the American Medical Association, 260*, 1743–1748.

Donabedian, A. (2005). Evaluating the quality of care. *The Milbank Quarterly, 83*, 691–729. [Reprinted from *The Milbank Memorial Fund Quarterly*, 1966, *44*, 166–203.]

Dorsey, S., Pullmann, M.D., Deblinger, E., Berliner, L., Kerns, S.E., Thompson, K. *et al.* (2013). Improving practice in community-based settings: A randomized trial of supervision–study protocol. *Implementation Science, 8*, 89.

Dreyfus, H.L. & Dreyfus, S.E. (1986). *Mind over machine: The power of human intuition and expertise in the era of the computer*. Oxford: Blackwell.

Driscoll, J. (1999). Getting the most from clinical supervision. Part I: The supervisee. *Mental Health Practice, 2*, 28–35.

Duan, C. & Roehlke, H. (2001). A descriptive 'snapshot' of cross-racial supervision in university counseling center internships. *Journal of Multicultural Counseling and Development, 29*, 131–146.

Dunning, D., Johnson, K., Ehrlinger, J. & Kruger, J. (2003). Why people fail to recognize their own incompetence. *Current Directions in Psychological Science, 12*, 83–87. DOI: 10.1111/1467-8721.01235

Eagle, G. & Long, C. (2014). Supervision of psychoanalytic/psychodynamic psychotherapy. In C.E. Watkins & D.L. Milne (Eds) *Wiley international handbook of clinical supervision* (pp. 471–492). Chichester: Wiley.

Edmunds, J.M., Kendall, P.C., Ringle, V.A., Read, K.L., Brodman, D.M., Pimentel, S.S. *et al.* (2013). An examination of behavioral rehearsal during consultation as a predictor of training outcomes. *Administrative Policy in Mental Health Services Research, 40*, 456–466.

Edwards, E., Bernard, P., Hamigan, B., Cooper, L., Adams, J., Juggessur, T. *et al.* (2006). Clinical supervision and burn out: The influence of clinical supervision for community mental health nurses. *Journal of Clinical Nursing, 15*, 1007–1015.

Efstation, J.F., Patton, M.J. & Kardish, C.M. (1990). Measuring the working alliance in counsellor supervision. *Journal of Counseling Psychology, 37*, 322–329.

Ellis, M.V. (1991). Research in clinical supervision: Revitalizing a scientific agenda. *Counselor Education and Supervision, 30*, 238–251.

Ellis, M.V., Berger, L., Hanus, A.E., Ayala, E.E., Swords, B.A. & Siembor, M. (2014). Inadequate and harmful supervision: Testing a revised framework and assessing occurrence. *The Counseling Psychologist, 42*, 434–472.

Ellis, M.V., Creaner, M., Hutman, H. & Timulak, L. (2015a). A comparative study of clinical supervision in the Republic of Ireland and the United States. *Journal of Counseling Psychology, 62*, 621–631.

Ellis, M.V. & Douce, L.A. (1994). Group supervision of novice clinical supervisors: Eight recurring issues. *Journal of Counselling and Development, 72*, 520–525.

Ellis, M.V., Hutman, H. & Chapin, J. (2015b). Reducing supervisee anxiety: Effects of a role induction intervention for clinical supervision. *Journal of Counseling Psychology, 62*, 608.

Ellis, M.V. & Ladany, N. (1997). Inferences concerning supervisees and clients in clinical supervision: An integrative review. In C.E. Watkins (Ed.) *Handbook of psychotherapy supervision* (pp. 447–507). New York: Wiley.

Ellis, M.V., Ladany, N., Krengel, M. & Schult, D. (1996). Clinical supervision research from 1981–1993: A methodological critic. *Journal of Counselling Psychology, 43*, 35–40.

Ennis, R.H. (1985). A logical basis for measuring critical thinking skills. *Educational Leadership, 43*, 44–48.

Ericsson, K.A. (2006). The influence of experience and deliberate practice on the development of superior expert performance. In K.A. Ericsson, N. Charness,

P.J. Feltovich & R.R. Hoffman (Eds) *The Cambridge handbook of expertise and expert performance* (pp. 683–703). Cambridge: Cambridge University Press.

Ericsson, K.A. (2009). *Development of professional expertise.* Cambridge: Cambridge University Press.

Ericsson, K.A., Krampe, R.T. & Tesch-Romer, C. (1993). The role of deliberate practice in the acquisition of expert performance. *Psychological Review, 100,* 363–406.

Faith, M. & Thayer, J.F. (2001). A dynamical systems interpretation of a dimensional model of emotion. *Scandinavian Journal of Psychology, 42,* 121–133.

Falender, C., Cornish, J.A.E., Goodyear, R., Hatcher, R., Kaslow, N.J., Leventhal, G. *et al.* (2004). Defining competencies in psychology supervision: A consensus statement. *Journal of Clinical Psychology, 60,* 771–785.

Falender, C.A. & Shafranske, E. (2004). *Clinical supervision: A competency based approach.* Washington, DC: American Psychological Association.

Falender, C.A. & Shafranske, E.P. (2012). *Getting the most out of supervision: A guide for practicum students and interns.* Washington, D.C: American Psychological Association.

Falender, C.A. & Shafranske, E. (2014). Clinical supervision: The state of the art. *Journal of Clinical Psychology, 70,* 1030–1041. DOI: 10.1002/jclp.22124

Fall, M. & Sutton, J.M. (2004). *Clinical supervision: A handbook for practitioners.* Boston: Pearson.

Farber, B.A. & Hazanov, V. (2014). Informal sources of supervision in clinical training. *Clinical Psychology: In Session, 70,* 1062–1072.

Ferguson, S., Harper, S., Platz, S., Sloan, G. & Smith, K. (2016). Developing specialist CBT supervision training in Scotland using blended learning: Challenges and opportunities. *The Cognitive Behaviour Therapist, 9,* e26. DOI: 10.1017/S1754470X15000732

Fischer K.W. & Immordino-Yang, H.M. (2002). Cognitive development and education: From dynamic general structure to specific learning and teaching. *Essay for the Spencer Foundation* (The Spencer Foundation, 625 North Michigan Ave, Suite 1600, Chicago, IL 60611).

Fischer, K.W., Shaver, P.R. & Carnochan, P. (1989). How emotions develop and how they organize development. *Cognition and Emotion, 4,* 81–127.

Fischer, K.W., Yan, Z. & Stewart, J. (2003). Adult cognitive development: Dynamics in the developmental web. In J. Valsiner & K. Connolly (Eds) *Handbook of developmental psychology* (pp. 491–516). Thousand Oaks, CA: Sage.

Fleming, I., Gone, R., Diver, A. & Fowler, B. (2007). Risk supervision in Rochdale. *Clinical Psychology Forum, 176,* 22–25.

Fleming, R.K., Oliver, J.R. & Bolton, D.M. (1996). Training supervisors to train staff: A case study in a human service organization. *Journal of Organizational Behaviour Management, 16,* 3–25.

Fleming, R.K. & Sulzer-Azaroff, B. (1989). Enhancing quality of teaching by direct care staff through performance feedback on the job. *Behavioral Residential Treatment, 4*, 377–395.

Follette, V.M. & Batten, S. (2000). The role of emotion in psychotherapy supervision: A contextual behavioural analysis. *Cognitive and Behavioural Practice, 7*, 306–312.

Fonagy, P., Target, M., Cottrell, D., Phillips, J. & Kurtz, Z. (2002). *What works for whom? A critical review of treatments for children and adolescents.* New York: Guilford Press.

Fraser, S.W. & Greenhalgh, T. (2001). Complexity science: Coping with complexity – Educating for capability. *British Medical Journal, 323*, 799–803.

Freud, S. (1912). *The standard edition of the complete psychological works of Sigmund Freud* (Vol. 12, pp. 98–108) London: Hogarth Press.

Friedlander, M.L. & Ward, L.G. (1984). Development and validation of the supervisory styles inventory. *Journal of Counselling Psychology, 31*, 541–557.

Friedman, D. & Kaslow, N.J. (1986). The development of professional identity in psychotherapists: Six stages in supervision process. In F.W. Kaslow (Ed.) *Supervision and training: Models, dilemmas, challenges.* New York: Howarth.

Furr, S.R. & Carroll, J.J. (2003). Critical incidents in student counselor development. *Journal of Counselling and Development, 81*, 483–489.

Gabbay, M.B., Kiemle, G. & Maguire, C. (1999). Clinical supervision for clinical psychologists: Existing provision and unmet needs. *Clinical Psychology and Psychotherapy, 6*, 404–412.

Gilbody, S., Bower, P., Fletcher, J., Richards, D. & Sutton, A.J. (2006). Collaborative care for depression: A meta analysis and review of longer-term outcomes. *Archives of Internal Medicine, 166*, 2314–2320.

Gillmer, B. & Marckus, R. (2003). Personal professional development in clinical psychology training: Surveying reflective practice. *Clinical Psychology Forum, 27*, 20–23.

Godfrey, E., Chalder, T., Ridsdale, L., Seed, P. & Ogden, J. (2007). Investigating the active ingredients of cognitive behaviour therapy and counselling for patients with chronic fatigue in primary care: Developing a new process measure to assess treatment fidelity and predict outcome. *British Journal of Clinical Psychology, 46*, 253–272.

Goldstein, I.L. & Ford, J.K. (2002) *Training in organizations: Needs assessment, development, and evaluation,* 4th edn. Belmont, CA: Brooks/Cole.

Goldstein, I.L. & Gilliam, P. (1990). Training system issues in the year 2000. *American Psychologist, 45*, 134–143.

Gonsalvez, C.J. (2014). Establishing supervision goals and formalizing a supervision agreement: A competency-based approach. In C.E. Watkins & D.L. Milne (Eds) *Wiley international handbook of clinical supervision* (pp. 282–307). Chichester: Wiley.

Gonsalvez, C.J., Brockman, R. & Hill, H.R.M. (2016). Video feedback in CBT supervision: Review and illustration of two specific techniques. *The Cognitive Behaviour Therapist, 9*, e21. DOI: 10.1017/S1754470X1500029X

Gonsalvez, C.J., Deane, F.P. & Caputi, P. (2015a). Consistency of supervisor and peer ratings of assessment interviews conducted by psychology trainees. *British Journal of Guidance and Counselling, 44*, 516–529. DOI: 10.1080/03069885.2015.1068927

Gonsalvez, C.J., Deane, F.P., Knight, R., Nasstasia, Y., Shires, A., Perry, K.N. *et al.* (2015b). The hierarchical clustering of clinical psychology practicum competencies: A multi-site study of supervision ratings. *Clinical Psychology: Science and Practice, 22*, 390–403.

Gonsalvez, C.J., Oades, L.G. & Freestone, J. (2002). The objectives approach to clinical supervision: Towards integration and empirical evaluation. *Australian Psychologist, 37*, 68–77.

Goodyear, R.K. (2014). Supervision as pedagogy: Attending to its essential instructional and learning processes. *The Clinical Supervisor, 33*, 82–99. DOI: 10.1080/07325223.2014.918914

Goodyear, R.K. & Nelson, M.L. (1997). The major formats of psychotherapy supervision. In C.E. Watkins, Jr. (Ed.) *Handbook of psychotherapy supervision* (pp. 328–344). New York: Wiley.

Gordon, P.K. (2012). Ten steps to cognitive-behavioural supervision. *The Cognitive Behaviour Therapist, 5*, 71–82. DOI. org/10.1017/S1754470X12000050

Gosselin, J., Barker, K.K., Kogan, C.S., Myriam Pomerleau, M. & Pitre d'Ioro, M-P. (2015). Setting the stage for an evidence-based model of psychotherapy supervisor development in clinical psychology. *Canadian Psychology, 56*, 379–393.

Granello, D.H., Kindsvatter, A., Granello, P.F., Underfer-Babalis, J. & Moorhead, H.J.H. (2008). Multiple perspectives in supervision: Using a peer consultation model to enhance supervisor development. *Counselor Education and Supervision, 48*, 32–47.

Grant, J., Schofield, M.J. & Crawford, S. (2012). Managing difficulties in supervision: Supervisors' perspectives. *Journal of Counselling Psychology, 59*, 528–541.

Gray, I. (2006). The policy context. In L. Golding & I. Gray (Eds) *Continuing professional development for clinical psychologists* (pp. 23–46). Oxford: BPS Blackwell.

Gray, L.A., Ladany, N., Walker, J.A. & Ancis, J.R. (2001). Psychotherapy trainees' experience of counter-productive events in supervision. *Journal of Counseling Psychology, 48*, 371–383.

Green, D. (2004). Organising and evaluating supervisor training. In I. Fleming & L. Steen (Eds) *Supervision and clinical psychology* (pp. 93–107). Hove: Brunner-Routledge.

Green, H., Barkham, M., Kellett, S. & Saxon, D. (2014). Therapist effects and IAPT Psychological Wellbeing practitioners (PWP's): A multi-level modelling and mixed methods analysis. *Behavior Research and Therapy, 63,* 43–54.

Greenburg, L.S. & Malcolm, W. (2002). Resolving unfinished business: Relating process to outcome. *Journal of Consulting and Clinical Psychology, 70,* 406–416.

Greenspan, R., Hamfling, S., Parker, E., Primm, S. & Waldfogel, D. (1991). Supervision of experienced agency workers; a descriptive study. *The Clinical Supervisor, 9,* 31–42.

Grencavage, L.M. & Norcross, J.C. (1990). What are the commonalities among therapeutic common factors? *Professional Psychology: Research and Practice, 21,* 372–378.

Grossl, A.B., Reese, R.J., Norsworthy, L.A. & Hopkins, N.B. (2014). Client feedback data in supervision: Effects on supervision and outcome. *Training and Education in Professional Psychology, 8,* 182.

Haines, C. (2006). The experiential learning process in clinical supervision: An observational analysis. BSc thesis, School of Psychology, Newcastle University, UK.

Hall-Marley, S. (2000). *Therapist evaluation checklist: Unpublished instrument.* Reported in Falender & Shafranske (2004). pp. 277–280 (Appendix L).

Hambrick, D.Z., Altmann, E.M., Oswald, F.L., Meinz, E.J., Gobet, F. & Campitelli, G. (2014a). Accounting for expert performance: The devil is in the details. *Intelligence, 45,* 112–114.

Hambrick, D.Z., Oswald, F.L., Altmann, E.M., Meinz, E.J., Gobet, F. & Campitelli, G. (2014b). Deliberate practice: Is that all it takes to become an expert? *Intelligence, 45,* 34–45.

Hansebo, G. & Kihlgren, M. (2004). Nursing home care: Changes after supervisions. *Journal of Advanced Nursing, 45,* 269–279.

Harden, R.M., Grant, J., Buckley, G. & Hart, I.R. (1999). Best evidence medical education. *Medical Teacher, 21,* 553–562.

Harkness, D.R. (1987). Social work supervision in community mental health: Effects of normal and client focussed supervision on client satisfaction and generalised contentment. *Dissertation Abstracts International, 49,* 1271–A.

Harkness, D. & Poertner, J. (1989). Research and social work supervision: A conceptual review. *Social Work, 34,* 115–119.

Harmon, S.C., Lambert, M.J., Smart, D.M., Hawkins, E., Nielsen, S.L., Slade, K. *et al.* (2007). Enhancing outcome for potential treatment failures: Therapist–client feedback and clinical support tools. *Psychotherapy Research, 17,* 379–392.

Harmse, A.D. (2001). Support systems for supervisors in the social work profession. *Dissertation Abstracts International, A: The Humanities and Social Sciences, 61,* 3351.

Hatcher, R.L. & Lassiter, K.D. (2007). Initial training in professional psychology: The practicum competencies outline. *Training and Education in Professional Psychology, 1*, 49–63.

Hattie, J. & Timperley, H. (2007). The power of feedback. *Review of Educational Research, 77*, 81–112.

Hawkins, P. & Shohet, R. (2000). *Supervision in the helping professions: An individual, group and organizational approach.* Milton Keynes: Open University Press.

Hayes, S.C., Barlow, D.H. & Nelson-Gray, R.O. (1999). *The scientist-practitioner: Research and accountability in the age of managed care.* Boston: Allyn & Bacon.

Hayes, S.C., Luoma J.B., Bond F.W., Masuda, A. & Lillis, J. (2006). Acceptance and commitment therapy: Model, processes, and outcomes. *Behavior Research and Therapy, 44*, 1–26.

Hays, P.A. (2001). *Addressing cultural complexities in practice: A framework for clinicians and counselors.* Washington, DC: APA.

Health Professions Council. (2007). *Standards of education and training guidance.* London: HPC.

Henggeler, S.W., Schoenwald, S.K., Liao, J.G., Letourneau, E.J. & Edwards, D.L. (2002). Transporting efficacious treatments to field settings: The link between supervisory practices and therapist fidelity in MST programmes. *Journal of Clinical Child Psychology, 31*, 155–167.

Henry, W.P., Schacht, T.E., Strupp, H.H., Butler, S.F. & Binder, J.L. (1993). Effects of training in time-limited psychodynamic psychotherapy: Mediators of therapists' response to training. *Journal of Consulting and Clinical Psychology, 61*, 441–447.

Heppner, P.P., Kivlighan, D.M., Burnett, J.W., Berry, T.R., Goedinghaus, M., Doxsee, D.J. *et al.* (1994). Dimensions of characterise supervisor interventions delivered in context of live supervision of practical counsellors. *Journal of Counselling Psychology, 41*, 227–235.

Heppner, P.P. & Roehlke, H.J. (1984). Differences among supervisees at different levels of training; implications for a developmental model of supervision. *Journal of Counselling Psychology, 31*, 76–90.

Hersen, M. (2010). Single case experimental designs. In A.S. Bellack, M. Hersen & A.E. Kazdin (Eds) *International handbook of behavior modification and therapy* (pp. 167–201). New York: Springer.

Hess, A.K. (1987). Psychotherapy supervision: Stages, Buber and the theory of relationship. *Professional Psychology: Research and Practice, 18*, 251–259.

Hilsenroth, M.J., Defife, J.A., Blagys, D. & Ackerman, S.J. (2006). Effects of training in short-term psychodynamic psychotherapy: Changes in graduate clinician technique. *Psychotherapy Research, 16*, 295–305.

Hofmann, S.G., Sawyer, A.T. & Fang, A. (2010). The empirical status of the 'New Wave' of CBT. *Psychiatric Clinics of North America, 33*, 701–710. DOI: 10.1016/j.psc.2010.04.006

Holloway, E.L. (1997). Structures for the analysis and teaching of supervision. In C.E. Watkins (Ed.) *Handbook of psychotherapy supervision* (pp. 249–276). New York: Wiley.

Holloway, E.L. (2014). Supervisory roles within systems of practice. In C.E. Watkins & D.L. Milne (Eds) *Wiley international handbook of clinical supervision* (pp. 598–621). Chichester: Wiley.

Holloway, E.L. (2016). *Supervision essentials for a systems approach to supervision.* Washington, DC: American Psychological Society.

Holloway, E.L. & Neufeldt, S.A. (1995). Supervision: Its contribution to treatment efficacy. *Journal of Consulting and Clinical Psychology, 63,* 207–213.

Holloway, E.L. & Poulin, K.L. (1995). Discourse in supervision. In J. Siegfried (Ed.) *Therapeutic and everyday discourse in behaviour change: Towards micro-analysis in psychotherapy process research* (pp. 245–273). Norwood: Ablex.

Holloway, E.L. & Wolleat, P.L. (1994). Supervision: The pragmatics of empowerment. *Journal of Educational and Psychological Consultation, 5,* 23–43.

Holman, D., Pavlica, K. & Thorne, R. (1997). *Re-thinking Kolb's theory of experiential learning in management education.* Management Learning Textbook. London: Sage.

Hook. K. & Bunce, D. (2001). Immediate learning in organisational computer training as a function of training intervention, affective reaction and session impact measures. *Applied Psychology: An International Review, 50,* 436–454.

Hundert, J. & Hopkins, B. (1992). Training supervisors in a collaborative team approach to promote peer interaction of children with disabilities in integrated pre-schools. *Journal of Applied Behaviour Analysis, 25,* 385–400.

Huppert, J.D., Bufka, L.F., Barlow, D.H., Gorman, J.M., Shear, M.K. & Woods, S.W. (2001). Therapists, therapists' variables, and cognitive behavioral therapy outcomes in a multicenter trial for panic disorder. *Journal of Consulting and Clinical Psychology, 69,* 747–755. DOI 10.1037/0022-006X.69.5.747

Hyrkas, K. & Lehti, K. (2003). Continuous quality improvement through team supervision supported by continuous self-monitoring of work and systematic patient feedback. *Journal of Nursing Management, 11,* 177–188.

Inman, A.G., Hutman, H., Pendse, A., Devdas, L., Luu, L. & Ellis, M.V. (2014). Current trends concerning supervisors, supervisees, and clients in clinical supervision. In C.E. Watkins & D.L. Milne (Eds) *Wiley international handbook of clinical supervision* (pp. 61–102). Chichester: Wiley.

Inskipp, F. & Proctor, B. (1993). *Making the most of supervision: Professional development for counsellors, psychotherapists, supervisors and trainees.* London: Cascade.

James, I.A. (2015). The rightful demise of the sh*t sandwich: Providing effective feedback. *Behavioural and Cognitive Psychotherapy, 43,* 759–766. DOI: 10.1017/S1352465814000113

James, I.A., Allen, K. & Collerton, D. (2004). A post-hoc analysis of emotions in supervision: A new methodology for examining process features. *Behavioural and Cognitive Psychotherapy, 32*, 507–513.

James, I.A., Blackburn, I-M., Milne, D.L. & Reichelt, F.K. (2001). Moderators of trainee therapists' competence in cognitive therapy. *British Journal of Clinical Psychology, 40*, 131–141.

James, I.A., Milne, D.L., Blackburn, I-M. & Armstrong, P. (2006). Conduction successful supervision: Novel elements towards an integrative approach. *Behavioural and Cognitive Psychotherapy, 35*, 191–200.

James, I.A., Milne, D.L. & Morse, R. (2008). Microskills of clinical supervision: Scaffolding skills. *Journal of Cognitive Psychotherapy, 22*, 29–36.

James, I.A. & Morse, R. (2007). The use of questions in cognitive behaviour therapy: Identification of question type, function and structure. *Behavioural and Cognitive Psychotherapy, 35*, 507–511.

James, W. (1890). *The principles of psychology.* New York: Holt.

Joffe, M. & Mindell, J. (2006). Complex causal process diagrams for analyzing the health impacts of policy interventions. *American Journal of Public Health, 96*, 473–479. DOI: 10.2105/AJPH.2005.063693

Johnson, W.B. (2007). Transformational supervision: When supervisors mentor. *Professional Psychology: Research and Practice, 38*, 259–267.

Johnston, L.H. & Milne, D.L. (2012). How do supervisee's learn during supervision? A grounded theory study of the perceived developmental process. *The Cognitive Behaviour Therapist, 5*, 1–23.

Jones, J. & Hunter, D. (1995). Consensus methods for medical and health services. *British Medical Journal, 311*, 376–380.

Joyce, B. & Showers, B. (2002). *Student achievement through staff development.* Alexandra, VA: Association for Supervision and Curriculum Development.

Juwah, C., Macfarlane-Dick, D., Matthew, B., Nicol, D. & Smith, B. (2004). *Enhancing student learning though effective formative feedback.* York: The Higher Education Academy.

Kadushin, A. (1968). Games people play in supervision. *Social Work, 13*, 23–32.

Kadushin, A. (1976). *Supervision in social work.* New York: Columbia University Press.

Kagan, H. & Kagan, N.I. (1997). Interpersonal process recall: Influencing human interaction. In C.E. Watkins (Ed.) *Handbook of psychotherapy supervision* (pp. 296–309) New York: Wiley.

Kaslow, N.J., Borden, K.A., Collins, F.L., Forrest, L., Illfelder-Kaye, J., Nelson, P.D., *et al.* (2004). Competencies conference: Future directions in education and credentialing in professional psychology. *Journal of Clinical Psychology, 60*, 699–712.

Katon, W., Von Korff, M. & Lin, E. (2001). Rethinking practitioner roles in chronic illness: The specialist primary care physician and the practice nurse. *General Hospital Psychiatry, 23*, 138–144.

Kaufman, J. & Schwartz, T. (2003). Models of supervision: Shaping professional identity. *The Clinical Supervisor, 22,* 143–159.

Kavanagh, D.J., Spence, S.H., Strong, J., Wilson, J., Sturk, H. & Crow, N. (2003). Supervision practices in allied mental health: Relationships of supervision characteristics to perceived impact and job satisfaction. *Mental Health Services Research, 5,* 187–195.

Kayes, D.C. (2002). Experiential learning and its critics: Preserving the role of experience in management learning and education. *Academy of Management Learning and Education, 1,* 137–149.

Kazdin, A.E. (1998). *Research design in clinical psychology.* Boston: Allyn & Bacon.

Keenan-Miller, D. & Corbett, H.I. (2015). Metasupervision: Can students be safe and effective supervisors? *Training and Education in Professional Psychology, 9,* 315–321.

Kiesler, D.J. (1983). The 1982 interpersonal circle: A taxonomy for complementarity in human transactions. *Psychological Review, 90,* 185–214.

Kilburg, R.R. & Diedrich, R.C. (2007). *The wisdom of coaching: Essential papers in consulting psychology for a world of change.* Washington, DC: APA.

Kirkpatrick, D.L. (1967). Evaluation of training. In R.L. Craig & L.R. Bittel (Eds) *Training and development handbook* (pp. 87–112). New York: McGraw-Hill.

Klein, M.H., Mathieu-Coughlan, P.L. & Kiesler, D.J. (1986). The experiencing scale. In L.S. Greenberg & W.M. Pinsof (Eds) *The psychotherapy process: A research handbook* (pp. 21–71). New York: Guilford Press.

Knapp, M.R.J. (1997). Economic evaluations and interventions for children and adolescents with metal health problems. *Journal of Child Psychology and Psychiatry, 38,* 3–25.

Knapp, S. & VandeCreek, L. (1997). Ethical and legal aspects of clinical supervision. In C.E. Watkins (Ed.) *Handbook of psychotherapy supervision* (pp. 589–602) New York: Wiley.

Knapp, S.J. & VandeCreek, L.D. (2006). *Practical ethics for psychologists: A positive approach.* Washington, DC: American Psychological Association.

Knowles, M. (1990). *The adult learner: A neglected species.* Houston, TX: Gulf Publishing Company.

Knudsen, H.K., Ducharme, L.J. & Roman, P.M. (2008). Clinical supervision, emotional exhaustion, and turnover intention: A study of substance abuse treatment counsellors in NIDA's Clinical Trials Network. *Journal of Substance Abuse and Treatment, 35,* 387–395.

Kolb, D.A. (1984). *Experiential learning: Experience as the source of learning and development.* Englewood Cliffs, NJ: Prentice-Hall.

Kolb, D.A. (2014). *Experiential learning: Experience as the source of learning and development,* 2nd edn. Englewood Cliffs, NJ: Prentice-Hall.

Korinek, A.W. & Kimball, T.G. (2003). Managing and resolving conflict in the supervisory system. *Contemporary Family Therapy, 25,* 295–310.

Kovacs, V. (1936). Training and control analysis. *International Journal of Psycho-analysis*, *17*, 346–354.

Kraemer, H.C., Wilson, G.T., Fairburn, C.G. & Agras, W.S. (2002). Mediators and moderators of treatment effects in RCT-S. *Archives of General Psychiatry*, *59*, 877–883.

Kraiger, K., Ford, J.K. & Salas, E. (1993). Application of cognitive skills-based and effective theories of learning outcomes to new methods of training evaluation. *Journal of Applied Psychology*, *78*, 311–328.

Krathwohl, D.R., Bloom, B.S. & Masia, B.B. (1964). *Taxonomy of educational objectives. The classification of educational goals, handbook II: Affective domain*. New York: McKay.

Kruger, J. & Dunning, D. (1999). Unskilled and unaware of it: How difficulties in recognising one's own incompetence lead to inflated self assessments. *Journal of Personality and Social Psychology*, *77*, 1121–1134.

Ladany, N. (2002). Psychotherapy supervision: How dressed is the emperor? *Psychotherapy Bulletin*, *37*, 14–18.

Ladany, N., Ellis, M.V. & Friedlander, M.L. (1999). The supervisory working alliance, trainee self-efficacy and satisfaction. *Journal of Counseling and Development*, *77*, 447–455.

Ladany, N., Friedlander, M.L. & Nelson, M.L. (2005). *Critical events in psycho-therapy supervision: An interpersonal approach*. Washington, DC: American Psychological Association.

Ladany, N., Hill, C.E., Corbett, M.M. & Nutt, E.A. (1996). Nature, extent, and importance of what psychotherapy trainees do not disclose to their supervi-sors. *Journal of Counselling Psychology*, *43*, 10–24.

Laireiter, A-R. & Willutzki, U. (2003). Self reflection and self practice in training of cognitive behavioural therapy: An overview. *Clinical Psychology and Psycho-therapy*, *10*, 19–30.

Lakeman, R. & Glasgow, C. (2009). Introducing peer-group clinical supervision: An action research project. *International Journal of Mental Health Nursing*, *18*, 204–210.

Lambert, N.J. & Bergin, A.E. (1994). The effectiveness of psychotherapy. In A.E. Burgin & S.L. Garfield (Eds) *Handbook on psychotherapy and behaviour change*, 4th edn. (pp. 143–189). New York: Wiley.

Lambert, N.J. & Ogles, B.M. (1997). The effectiveness of psychotherapy supervision. In C.E. Watkins (Ed.) *Handbook of psychotherapy supervision* (pp. 421–446). New York: Wiley.

Latham, M. (2006). *Supervisor and training accreditation* (Training Newsletter, February, p. 3). Accrington: British Association for Behavioural and Cognitive Psychotherapies.

Lavender, A. & Thompson, L. (2000). Attracting newly qualified clinical psycholo-gists to NHS Trusts. *Clinical Psychology Forum*, *139*, 35–40.

Layard, R. (2005). *Therapy for all on the NHS.* Sainsbury Centre Lecture, 6 September. London: Sainsbury Centre.

Lazarus, R.S. & Folkman, S. (1984). *Stress, appraisal, and coping.* New York: Springer.

Leary, T. (1957). *Interpersonal diagnosis of personality.* New York: Ronald Press.

Lehrman-Waterman, D. & Ladany, N. (2001). Development and validation of the evaluation process within supervision inventory. *Journal of Counselling Psychology, 48,* 168–177.

Lerner, R.M. (1998). Theories of human development: Contemporary perspectives. In W. Damon & R.M. Lerner (Eds) *Handbook of child psychology,* 5th edn. (pp. 1029–1144). New York: Wiley.

Lewandowsky, S. & Thomas, J. L. (2009). Expertise: Acquisition, limitations, and control. *Reviews of Human Factors and Ergonomics, 5,* 140–165.

Lewin, K. (1951). *Field theory in social science.* New York: Harper.

Lewis, K. (2005). The supervision of cognitive and behavioural psychotherapists. *BABCP Magazine,* Supervision Supplement, 33. Accrington: BABCP.

Lewis, K.E. & Hendricks, K.E. (2014). A model and guide for evaluating supervision outcomes in cognitive–behavioral therapy-focused training programmes. *Training and Education in Professional Psychology, 8,* 165–173.

Liese, B.S. & Beck, J.S. (1997). Cognitive therapy supervision. In C.E. Watkins (Ed.) *Handbook of psychotherapy supervision* (pp. 114–133). New York: Wiley.

Liness, S., Lea, S., Nestler, S., Parker, H. & Clark, D.M. (2016). What IAPT CBT high-intensity trainees do after training. *Behavioural and Cognitive Psychotherapy, 45,* 16–30. DOI: 10.1017/S135246581600028X

Lister, P.G. & Crisp, B.R. (2005). Clinical supervision in child protection for community nurses. *Child Abuse Review, 14,* 57–72.

Livni, D., Crowe, T.P. & Gonsalvez, C.J. (2012). Effects of supervision modality and intensity on alliance and outcomes for the supervisee. *Rehabilitation Psychology, 57,* 178–186.

Llewellyn, S.P. (1988). Psychological therapy as viewed by clients and therapists. *British Journal of Clinical Psychology, 27,* 105–114.

Locke, E.A. & Latham, G.P. (2006). New directions in goal-setting theory. *Current Directions in Psychological Science, 15,* 265–268.

Lomax, J.W., Andrews, L.B., Burruss, J.W. & Moorey, S. (2005). Psychotherapy supervision. In Gabbard, G.O., Beck, J. & Holmes, J. (Eds) *Oxford Textbook of Psychotherapy* (pp. 495–503). Oxford: Oxford University Press.

Lombardo, C., Milne, D.L. & Proctor, R. (2009). Getting to the heart of clinical supervision: A theoretical review of the role of emotions in professional development. *Behavioural and Cognitive Psychotherapy, 37,* 207–219.

Lovell, C.W. (2002). Development and disequilibration: Predicting councillor trainee gain and loss scores on the Supervisee Levels Questionnaire. *Journal of Adult Development, 9,* 235–240.

Lucock, M., Halstead, J., Leach, C., Barkham, M., Tucker, S., Randal, C., *et al.* (2015). A mixed-method investigation of patient monitoring and enhanced feedback in routine practice: Barriers and facilitators. *Psychotherapy Research, 25,* 633–646.

Lucock, M.P., Hall, P. & Noble, R. (2006). A survey of influences on the practice of psychotherapists and clinical psychologists in training in the UK. *Clinical Psychology and Psychotherapy, 13,* 123–130.

Lynch, L. & Happell, B. (2008). Implementation of clinical supervision in action: Part 3: The development of a model. *International Journal of Mental Health Nursing, 17,* 73–82.

Lyons, J.S., Howard, K.I., O'Mahoney, M.T. & Lish, J.D. (1997). *The measurement and management of clinical outcomes in mental health.* Chichester: Wiley.

Lyth, G.M. (2000). Clinical supervision: A concept analysis. *Journal of Advanced Nursing, 31,* 722–729.

Macdonald, J. & Mellor-Clark, J. (2014). Correcting psychotherapists' blindsidedness: Formal feedback as a means of overcoming the natural limitations of therapists. *Clinical Psychology and Psychotherapy, 22,* 249–257. DOI: 10.1002/cpp.1887

Machado, A. & Silva, F.J. (2007). Toward a richer view of the scientific method. *American Psychologist, 62,* 671–681.

Mager, R.F. (1997). *Preparing instructional objectives: A critical tool in the development of effective instruction,* 3rd edn. Atlanta, GA: Center for Effective Practice.

McFadyen, K.M., Darongkamas, J., Crowther-Green, R. & Williams, O. (2011). Primary care mental health workers' views of clinical supervision. *The Cognitive Behaviour Therapist, 4,* 101–113. DOI: 10.1017/S1754470X11000055

McGaghie, W.C., Issenberg, S.B., Barsuk, J.H. & Wayne, D.B. (2014) A critical review of simulation-based mastery learning with translational outcomes. *Medical Education, 48,* 375–385.

McIntosh, N., Dircks, A., Fitzpatrick, J. & Shuman, C. (2006). Games in clinical genetic counselling supervision. *Journal of Genetic Counselling, 15,* 225–243.

McMahan, E.H. (2014). Supervision: A non-elusive component of deliberate practice toward expertise. *American Psychologist, 69,* 712–713.

McMahon, A. & Errity, D. (2013). From new vistas to lifelines: Psychologists' satisfaction with supervision and confidence in supervising. *Clinical Psychology and Psychotherapy, 21,* 264–275. DOI: 10.1002/cpp1835

Methot, L.L., Williams, W.L., Cummings, A. & Bradshaw, B. (1996). Measuring the effects of a manager's supervisor training programme through the generalised performance of managers, supervisors, front line staff and clients in a human service setting. *Journal of Organizational Behavioural Management, 16,* 3–34.

Miller, W.R., Yahne, C.E., Moyers, T.B., Martinez, J. & Pirritano, M. (2004). A randomized trial of methods to help clinicians learn motivational interviewing. *Journal of Consulting and Clinical Psychology, 72,* 1050–1062.

Milne, D.L. (1986). *Training behaviour therapists: Methods, evaluation, and implementation with parent, nurses and teachers.* London: Croom-Helm.

Milne, D.L. (1991). Why supervise? A survey of costs and benefits. *Clinical Psychology Forum, April, 27*–29.

Milne, D.L. (1998). Clinical supervision: Time to reconstruct or to retrench? *Clinical Psychology and Psychotherapy, 5,* 199–203.

Milne, D.L. (2007a). CPD workshop for new clinical supervisors: A tutor's guide. Unpublished document, available from www.wiley.com/go/milne.

Milne, D.L. (2007b). An empirical definition of clinical supervision. *British Journal of Clinical Psychology, 46,* 437–447.

Milne, D.L. (2007c). Developing clinical supervision through reasoned analogies with therapy. *Clinical Psychology and Psychotherapy, 13,* 215–222.

Milne, D.L. (2008a). Evaluating and enhancing supervision: An experiential model. In C. Falender & E. Shafranske (Eds) *Clinical supervision: A competency-based approach – casebook.* Washington, DC: American Pyschological association.

Milne, D.L. (2008b). CBT supervision: From reflexivity to specialisation. *Behavioural and Cognitive Psychotherapy, 36,* 779–786.

Milne, D.L. (2009). *Evidence-based clinical supervision: Principles and practice.* Chichester: Wiley. [First edition.].

Milne, D.L. (2010). Can we enhance the training of clinical supervisors? A national pilot study of an evidence-based approach. *Clinical Psychology and Psychotherapy, 17,* 321–328.

Milne, D.L. (2014a). Toward an evidence-based approach to clinical supervision. In C.E. Watkins & D.L. Milne (Eds) *Wiley international handbook of clinical supervision* (pp. 38–60). Chichester: Wiley.

Milne, D.L. (2014b). Beyond the 'acid test': A conceptual review and reformulation of outcome evaluation in clinical supervision. *American Journal of Psychotherapy, 68,* 213–230.

Milne, D.L. (2016). Guiding CBT supervision: How well do manuals and guidelines fulfil their promise? *The Cognitive Behaviour Therapist, 9,* doi: 10.1017/S1754470X15000720.

Milne, D.L., Aylott, H., Fitzpatrick, H. & Ellis, M.V. (2008a). How does clinical supervision work? Using a Best Evidence Synthesis approach to construct a basic model of supervision. *The Clinical Supervisor, 27,* 170–190.

Milne, D.L. & Dunkerley, C. (2010). Towards evidence-based clinical supervision: The development and evaluation of four CBT guidelines. *The Cognitive Behaviour Therapist, 3,* 43–57.

Milne, D.L., Freeston, M., Paxton, R., James, I.A., Cooper, M. & Knibbs, J. (2007). A new pyramid of research knowledge for the NHS. *Journal of Mental Health, 16,* 1–11.

Milne, D.L. & Gracie, J. (2001). The role of the supervisee: 20 ways to facilitate clinical supervision. *Clinical Psychology, 5,* 13–15.

Milne, D.L. & James, I. (2000). A systematic review of effective cognitive-behavioural supervision. *British Journal of Clinical Psychology, 39*, 111–127.

Milne, D.L. & James, I.A. (2002). The observed impact of training on competence in clinical supervision. *British Journal of Clinical Psychology, 41*, 55–72.

Milne, D.L. & James, I. (2005). Clinical supervision: 10 tests of the tandem model. *Clinical Psychology Forum, 151*, 6–9.

Milne, D.L., James, I.A., Keegan, D. & Dudley, M. (2002). Teachers' PETS: A new observational measure of experiential training interactions. *Clinical Psychology and Psychotherapy, 9*, 187–199.

Milne, D.L., Kennedy, E., Todd, H., Lombardo, C., Freeston, M. & Day, A. (2008b). Zooming in on CBT supervision: A comparison of two levels of effectiveness research. *Behavioural and Cognitive Psychotherapy, 36*, 619–624.

Milne, D.L., Leck, C. & Choudhri, N. (2009). Collusion in clinical supervision: Review and case study in self-reflection. *The Cognitive Behaviour Therapist, 2*, 106–114.

Milne, D.L., Leck, C., Procter, R., Ramm, L., Weetman, J.R., Wilkinson, J. *et al.* (2012). High fidelity in clinical supervision research. In I. Fleming & L. Steen (Eds) *Supervision and Clinical Psychology*, 2nd edn. (pp. 142–158). London: Routledge.

Milne, D.L. & Noone, S. (1996). *Teaching and training for non-teachers*. Leicester: BPS.

Milne, D.L. & Oliver, V. (2000). Flexible formats of clinical supervision: Description, evaluation and implementation. *Journal of Mental Health, 9*, 291–304.

Milne, D.L., Pilkington, J., Gracie, J. & James, I.A. (2003). Transferring skills from supervision to therapy: A qualitative and quantitative N = 1 analysis. *Behavioural and Cognitive Psychotherapy, 31*, 193–202.

Milne, D.L., Reichelt, K. & Wood, E. (2001). Implementing HoNOS: An eight-stage approach. *Clinical Psychology and Psychotherapy, 8*, 106–116.

Milne, D.L. & Reiser, R.P. (2010). The systematic review as an empirical approach to improving CBT supervision. *International Journal of Cognitive Therapy, 3*, 278–294.

Milne, D.L. & Reiser, R.P. (2011). Observing competence in CBT supervision: A systematic review of the available instruments. *The Cognitive Behaviour Therapist, 4*, 123–138.

Milne, D.L. & Reiser, R.P. (2014). SAGE: A scale for rating competence in CBT supervision. In C.E. Watkins & D.L. Milne (Eds) *Wiley international handbook of clinical supervision* (pp. 402–415). Chichester: Wiley.

Milne, D.L. & Reiser, R.P. (2016a). Evidence-based supervisory practices in CBT. In D.M. Sudak, R. Trent Codd, J.W. Ludgate, L. Sokol, M.G. Fox, R.P. Reiser & D.L. Milne (Eds) *Teaching and supervising cognitive behavioral therapy* (pp. 207–225). Hoboken, NJ: Wiley.

Milne, D.L. & Reiser, R.P. (2016b). Supporting our supervisors: Sending out an SOS. *The Cognitive Behaviour Therapist, 9*, e19. DOI: 10.1017/S1754470X15000616

Milne, D.L. & Reiser, R.P. (2017). *A manual of evidence-based CBT supervision*. Chichester: Wiley-Blackwell.

Milne, D.L., Reiser, R.P. & Cliffe, T. (2013). An $n = 1$ evaluation of enhanced CBT supervision. *Behavioural and Cognitive Psychotherapy, 41*, 210–220.

Milne, D.L., Reiser, R.P., Cliffe, T., Breese, L., Boon, A., Raine, R. *et al.* (2011a). A qualitative comparison of cognitive-behavioural and evidence-based clinical supervision. *The Cognitive Behaviour Therapist, 4*, 152–166.

Milne, D.L., Reiser, R.P., Cliffe, T. & Raine, R. (2011b). SAGE: An instrument for observing competence in CBT supervision. *The Cognitive Behaviour Therapist, 4*, 123–138.

Milne, D.L., Sheikh, A.I., Pattison, S. & Wilkinson, A. (2011c). Evidence-based training for clinical supervisors: A systematic review of 11 controlled studies. *The Clinical Supervisor, 30*, 53–71.

Milne, D.L. & Watkins, C.E. (2014). Defining and understanding clinical supervision. In C.E. Watkins & D.L. Milne (Eds) *Wiley international handbook of clinical supervision* (pp. 3–19). Chichester: Wiley.

Milne, D.L. & Westerman, C. (2001). Evidence-based clinical supervision: Rationale and illustration. *Clinical Psychology and Psychotherapy, 8*, 444–445.

Mithaug, D.E., Mithaug, D.K., Agran, M., Martin, J.E. & Wehmeyer, M.L. (2003). *Self-determined learning theory: Construction, verification and evaluation*. London: Lawrence-Erlbaum.

Moran, A.M., Coyle, J., Boxall, D., Nancrow, S.A. & Young, J. (2014). Supervision, support and mentoring interventions for health practitioners in rural and remote contexts: An integrative review and thematic synthesis of the literature to identify mechanisms for successful outcomes. *Human Resources for Health, 12*, 10. DOI: 10.1186/1478-4491-12-10

Morgan, B. (1997). *The S___ word: What teachers consider important in the supervision of paraeducators*. Paper presented at 16th Annual Conference on the Training and Employment of the Paraprofessional Workforce in Education, Los Angeles.

Moseley, D., Baumfield, V., Elliott, J., Higgins, S., Miller, J. & Newton D.P. (2005). *Frameworks for thinking: A handbook for teachers and learning*. Cambridge: Cambridge University Press.

Mueller, W.J. & Kell, B.L. (1972). *Coping with conflict:Supervising counsellors and psychotherapists*. Englewood Cliffs, NJ: Prentice-Hall.

Muse, K. & McManus, F. (2013). A systematic review of methods for assessing competence in CBT. *Clinical Psychology Review, 33*, 484–489.

Nathan, P.E., Stuart, S.P. & Dolan, S.L. (2000). Research on psychotherapy efficacy and effectiveness: Between Scylla and Charybdis? *Psychological Bulletin, 128*, 964–981.

National Health Service (1998). *Our healthier nation*. London: Department of Health.

National Institute for Health and Care Excellence (NICE). (2007). *Guidelines Manual*. London: NICE.

Nel, P.W. (2006). Trainee perspectives on their family therapy training. *Journal of Family Therapy, 28*, 307–328.

Nelson, M.L. & Friedlander, M.L. (2001). A close look at conflictual supervisory relationships: The trainee's perspective. *Journal of Counseling Psychology, 48*, 384–395.

Nelson, M.L. & Holloway, E.L. (1990). Relation of gender to power and involvement is supervision. *Journal of Counseling Psychology, 37*, 473–481.

Neufeldt, S.A. (1994). Use of a manual to train supervisors. *Councillor Education and Supervision, 33*, 327–336.

Newman, C.F. (1998). Therapeutic and supervisory relationships in CBT: Similarities and differences. *Journal of Cognitive Psychotherapy, 12*, 95–108.

Newman, C.F. (2010). Competency in conducting CBT: Foundational, functional, and supervisory aspects. *Professional Psychology, Research and Practice, 47*, 12–19.

Newman, C.F. (2013). Training cognitive behavioural therapy supervisors: Didactics, simulated practice, and 'meta-Supervision'. *Journal of Cognitive Psychotherapy, 27*, 5–18.

Newman, C.F. & Kaplan, D.A. (2016). *Supervision essentials for CBT*. Washington, DC: American Psychological Society.

Newman, C.F., Reiser, R.P. & Milne, D.L. (2016). Supporting our supervisors: A summary and discussion of the special issue on CBT supervision. *The Cognitive Behaviour Therapist, 9*, e29. DOI: 10.1017/S1754470X16000106

Newman, D., Griffin, P. & Cole, M. (1989). *The construction zone: Working for cognitive change in school*. Cambridge: Cambridge University Press.

Newman-Taylor, K., Gordon, K., Grist, S. & Olding, C. (2013). Developing supervisory competence: Preliminary data on the impact of CBT supervision training. *The Cognitive Behaviour Therapist, 5*, 83–92. DOI: 10.1017/S1754470X13000056

Norcross, J.C. (2001). Empirically supported therapy relationships: Summary report of the division 29 task force. *Psychotherapy, 38*, 4.

Norcross, J.C. (2002). *Psychotherapy relationships that work*. Oxford: Oxford University Press.

Norcross, J.C. & Halgin, R.P. (1997). Integrative approaches to psychotherapy supervision. In C.E. Watkins (Ed.) *Handbook of psychotherapy supervision* (pp. 203–222). New York: Wiley.

Norcross, J.C. & Wampold, B.E. (2011). Evidence-based therapy relationships: Research conclusions and clinical practices. *Psychotherapy, 48*, 98–102.

Oakley, A., Strange, V., Bonell, C., Allen, E. & Stephenson, J. (2007). Process evaluation in randomised controlled trials of complex interventions. *British Medical Journal, 332*, 413–416.

O'Donovan, A. & Kavanagh, D.J. (2014). Measuring competence in supervisees and supervisors: Satisfaction and related reactions to supervision. In C.E. Watkins & D.L. Milne (Eds) *Wiley international handbook of clinical supervision* (pp. 458–467). Chichester: Wiley.

Ogren, M-L. & Boethius, S.B. (2014). Developing understanding in clinical supervision. In C.E. Watkins & D.L. Milne (Eds) *Wiley international handbook of clinical supervision* (pp. 342–363). Chichester: Wiley.

Olds, K. & Hawkins, R. (2014). Precursors to measuring outcomes in clinical supervision: A thematic analysis. *Training and Education in Professional Psychology, 8,* 158–164. DOI: 10.1037/tep0000034

Olsen, S. & Neale, G. (2005). Clinical leadership in the provision of hospital care. *British Medical Journal, 330,* 1219–1220.

Orford, J. (2008). *Community psychology: Challenges, controversies and emerging consensus,* Chichester: Wiley.

Orlinsky, D.E. & Ronnestad, M.H. (2005). *How psychotherapists develop: A study of therapeutic work and professional growth.* Washington, DC: American Psychological Association.

Padesky, C.A. (1996). Developing cognitive therapist competency: Teaching and supervision models. In P.M. Salkovskis (Ed.) *Frontiers of cognitive therapy* (pp. 266–292) London: Guilford Press.

Palomo, M., Beinart, H. & Cooper, M.J. (2010). Development and validation of thesupervisory relationship (SRQ) in UK trainee clinical psychologists. *British Journal of Clinical Psychology, 49,* 131–149.

Paris, M. & Hoge, M.A. (2010). Burnout in the mental health workforce: A review. *Journal of Behavioral Health Services and Research, 37,* 519–528.

Parker, R.M. & Thomas, K.R. (1980). Fads, flaws, fallacies and foolishness in evaluation of rehabilitation programmes. *Journal of Rehabilitation, 46,* 32–34.

Parry, G. (2000). Developing treatment choice guidelines in psychotherapy. *Journal of Mental Health, 9,* 273–281.

Parry, G., Roth, A. & Fonagy, P. (1996). Psychotherapy research, funding & evidence-based practice. In A. Roth & P. Fonagy (Eds) *What works for whom?* (pp. 37–56). New York: Guilford Press.

Patton, M.J. & Kivlighan, D.M. (1997). Relevance of the supervisory alliance to the counselling alliance and to treatment adherence in counsellor training. *Journal of Counseling Psychology, 44,* 108–115.

Pauls, F., Macha, T. & Petermann, F. (2013). U-shaped development: An old but unsolved problem. *Frontiers in Psychology, 4,* 301. DOI: 10.3389/fpsyg.2013.00301

Pearce, N., Beinart, H., Clohessy, S. & Cooper, M. (2013). Development and validation of The Supervisory Relationship Questionnaire: A self-report questionnaire for use with supervisors. *British Journal of Clinical Psychology, 52,* 249–268.

Pearson, Q.M. (2004). Getting the most out of clinical supervision: Strategies for mental health. *Journal of Mental Health Counseling, 26*, 361–373.

Penman, R. (1980). *Communication processes and relationships*. London: Academic Press.

Perris, C. (1994). Supervising cognitive psychotherapy and training supervisors. *Journal of Cognitive Psychotherapy, 8*, 83–103.

Petticrew, M. & Roberts, H. (2006). *Systematic reviews in the social sciences: A practical guide*. Oxford: Blackwell.

Pilling, S. & Roth, A.D. (2014). The competent clinical supervisor. In C.E. Watkins & D.L. Milne (Eds) *Wiley international handbook of clinical supervision* (pp. 20–37). Chichester: Wiley.

Popper, K.R. (1972). *Conjectures and refutations: The growth of scientific knowledge*. London: Routledge & Kegan Paul.

Prince, M.J. & Felder, R.M. (2006). Inductive teaching and learning methods: Definitions, comparisons, and research bases. *Journal of Engineering Education, 95*, 123–138.

Proctor, B. (1988). A cooperative exercise in accountability. In M. Marken & M. Payne (Eds) *Enabling and ensuring* (pp. 21–34). Leicester: Leicester National Youth Bureau and Council for Education and Training in Youth and Community Work.

Proctor, B. (1992). On being a trainer and supervision for counselling. In P. Hawkins & R. Shohet (Eds) *Supervision in the helping professions*. Milton Keynes: Open University Press.

Proctor, B. & Inskipp, F. (2001). Group supervision. In J. Scaife (Ed.) *Supervision in the mental health professions: A practitioner's guide* (pp. 99–121). Hove: Brunner-Routledge.

Quality Assurance Agency. (2005). Major healthcare review: University of Newcastle upon Tyne and Northumberland, Tyne and Wear NHS trust. Retrieved 30 October 2007 from http://www.qaa.ac.uk/reviews/health/Newcastle06.pdf

Radcliffe, K. & Milne, D. (2010). The meaning of satisfaction with clinical supervision: Is it simply getting what you want? *Clinical Psychology Forum, 211*, 15–20.

Rakovshik, S.G. & McManus, F. (2010). Establishing evidence-based training in CBT: A review of current empirical findings and theoretical guidance. *Clinical Psychology Review, 30*, 496–516.

Rakovshik, S.G., McManus, F., Vazquez-Montes, M., Muse, K. & Ougrin, D. (2016). Is supervision necessary? *Journal of Consulting and Clinical Psychology, 84*, 191–199.

Reese, R.J., Usher, E.L., Bowman, D.C., Norsworthy, L.A., Halstead, J.L., Rowlands, S.R. *et al.* (2009). Using client feedback in psychotherapy training: An analysis of its influence on supervision and counsellor self-efficacy. *Training and Education in Professional Psychology, 3*, 157–168.

Reichelt, F.K., James, I.A. & Blackburn, I-M. (2003). Impact of training on rating competence in cognitive therapy. *Journal of Behaviour Therapy and Experimental Psychiatry, 34*, 87–99.

Reilly, C.E. (2000). The role of emotion in cognitive therapy, cognitive therapists, and supervision. *Cognitive and Behavioural Practice, 7*, 343–345.

Reis, H.T., Collins, W.A. & Berscheid, E. (2000). The relationship context of human behavior and development. *Psychological Bulletin, 126*, 844–872.

Reiser, R.P. (2014). Supervising cognitive and behavioral therapies. In C.E. Watkins & D.L. Milne (Eds) *Wiley international handbook of clinical supervision* (pp. 493–517). Chichester: Wiley.

Reiser, R.P. & Milne, D.L. (2014). A systematic review and reformulation of outcome evaluation in clinical supervision: Applying the fidelity framework. *Training and Education in Professional Psychology, 8*, 149–157.

Reiser, R.P. & Milne, D.L. (2016). A survey of CBT supervision in the UK: Methods, satisfaction and training, as viewed by a selected sample of CBT supervision leaders. *The Cognitive Behaviour Therapist, 9*, e20. DOI: 10.1017/S1754470X15000689

Reynolds, M. (1997). Learning styles: A critique. *Management Learning, 28*, 115–133.

Richards, D.A. (2008). Clinical case supervision in high-volume CBT environments. Paper presented at the BABCP Spring Conference, University of Westminster, London, 18 April.

Richards, D.A. (2014). Clinical case management supervision: Using clinical outcome monitoring and therapy progress feedback to drive supervision. In C.E. Watkins & D.L. Milne (Eds) *Wiley international handbook of clinical supervision* (pp. 518–529). Chichester: Wiley.

Richards, D.A., Hill, J.J., Gask, L., Lovell, K., Chew-Graham, C., Bower, P., *et al.* (2013). Clinical effectiveness of collaborative care for depression in UK primary care (CADET): Cluster RCT. *British Medical Journal, 347*, f4913. DOI: 1136/bmj/f4913

Richards, D.A. & Suckling, R. (2013). Improving access to psychological therapies: Phase IV prospective cohort study. *British Journal of Clinical Psychology, 48*, 377–396.

Rieck, T., Callahan, J.L. & Watkins, C.E. (2015). Clinical supervision: An exploration of possible mechanisms of action. *Training and Education in Professional Psychology, 9*, 187–194.

Rigazio-DiGilio, S.A., Daniels, T.G. & Ivey, A.E. (1997). Systemic cognitive-developmental supervision: A developmental-integrative approach to psychotherapy supervision. In C.E. Watkins (Ed.) *Handbook of psychotherapy supervision* (pp. 233–248). New York: Wiley.

Rodolfo, E., Bent, R., Eisman, E., Nelson, P., Rehm, L. & Ritchie, P. (2005). A cube model for competence development: Implications for psychology educators and regulators. *Professional Psychology: Research and Practice, 36*, 347–354.

Rodolfo, E., Greenberg, S., Hunsley, J., Smith-Zoeller, M., Cox. D., Sammons, M. *et al.* (2013). A competency model for the practice of psychology. *Training and Education in Professional Psychology*, *7*, 71–83.

Rosenberg, J.I. (2006). Real-time training: Transfer of knowledge through computer-mediated, real-time feedback. *Professional Psychology: Research and Practice*, *37*, 539–546.

Rossi, P.H., Freeman, H.E. & Lipsey, M.W. (2003). *Evaluation: A systematic approach*, 7th edn. Thousand Oaks, CA: Sage.

Roth, A. & Fonagy, P. (1996). *What works for whom? A critical review of psychotherapy research*. New York: Guilford Press.

Roth, A. & Pilling, S. (2007). Clinical practice and the CBT competence framework: An update for clinical and counselling psychologists. *Clinical Psychology Forum*, *179*, 53–55 [Framework available from: www.ucl.ac.uk/CORE/].

Roth, A.D. & Pilling, S. (2008). Using an evidence-based methodology to identify the competencies required to deliver effective cognitive and behavioural therapy for depression and anxiety disorders. *Behavioural and Cognitive Psychotherapy*, *36*, 129–147.

Roth, A.D., Pilling, S. & Turner, J. (2010). Therapist training and supervision in clinical trials: Implications for clinical practice. *Behavioural and Cognitive Psychotherapy*, *38*, 291–302.

Rotheram-Borus, M.J., Dallas Swendeman, D. & Chorpita, B.F. (2012). Disruptive innovations for designing and diffusing evidence-based interventions. *American Psychologist*, *67*, 463–476.

Rousmaniere, T. (2014). Using technology to enhance clinical supervision and training. In C.E. Watkins & D.L. Milne (Eds) *Wiley international handbook of clinical supervision* (pp. 204–237). Chichester: Wiley.

Rousmaniere, T.G., Swift, J.K., Babins-Wagner, R., Whipple, J.L. & Berzins, S. (2014). Supervisor variance in psychotherapy outcome in routine practice. *Psychotherapy Research*, *26*, 196–205. DOI. 10.1080/10503307.2014.963730

Russell, R.K., Crimmings, A.M. & Lint, R.W. (1984). Counsellor training and supervision: Theory and research. In S.D. Brown & R.W. Lint (Eds) *Handbook of counselling psychology* (pp. 625–681). New York: Wiley.

Russell, R.K. & Petrie, T. (1994). Issues in training effective supervisors. *Applied and Preventive Psychology*, *3*, 27–42.

Sackett, D.L., Rosenberg, W.M.C., Gray, J.A.M. & Richardson, W.S. (1996). Evidence-based medicine: What it is and what it isn't. *British Medical Journal*, *312*, 71–72.

Saccuzzo, D.P. (1997). Liability for failure to supervise adequately mental health assistants, unlicensed practitioners and students. *Californian Western Law Review*, *34*, 115–138.

Sackett, D.L., Straus, S.E., Richardson, W.S., Rosenberg, W. & Haynes, R.B. (2000). *Evidence-based Medicine*, NY: Churchill Livingstone.

Safran, J.D. & Muran, J.C. (2000). *Negotiating the therapeutic alliance: A relational treatment guide.* New York: Guilford Press.

Safran, J.D., Muran, C.J., Stevens, C. & Rothman, M. (2007). A relational approach to supervision: Addressing ruptures in the alliance. In C.A. Falender & E.P. Shafranske (Eds) *Casebook for Clinical Supervision: A competency-based approach* (pp. 137–157). Washington DC: American Psychological Association.

Safran, J.D. & Segal, Z.V. (1990). *Interpersonal process in cognitive therapy.* New York: Basic Books.

Salkovskis, P.M. (1995). Demonstrating specific effects in CBT. In M. Aveline & D.A. Shapiro (Eds) *Research foundations for psychotherapy practice.* NY: Wiley.

Salzberger-Wittenberg, I., Henry, G. & Osborne, E. (1983). *The emotional experience of learning and teaching.* London: Routledge.

Scaife, J. (2001). *Supervision in the mental health professions: A practitioner's guide.* Hove: Brunner-Routledge.

Schindler, N.J. & Talen, M.R. (1994). Focus supervision: Management format for supervision practices. *Professional Psychology: Research and Practice, 25,* 304–306.

Schoen, D. (1987). *Educating the reflective practitioner.* San Francisco: Josey-Bass.

Schoenwald, S.K. (2016). Clinical supervision in a quality assurance/quality improvement system: Multisystemic therapy as an example. *The Cognitive Behaviour Therapist, 9,* e21. DOI: 10.1017/S1754470X15000604

Schoenwald, S.K., Sheidow, A.J. & Chapman, J.E. (2009). Clinical supervision in treatment transport: Effects on adherence and outcomes. *Journal of Consulting and Clinical Psychology, 77,* 410–421. DOI: 10.1037/a0013788

Shadish, W.R., Cook, T.D. & Campbell, D.T. (2000). *Experimental and quasi-experimental designs for generalised causal inference.* New York: Houghton Mifflin.

Shakow, D. (2007). *Clinical psychology as science and profession.* London: Aldine Transaction.

Shanfield, S.B., Matthews, K.L. & Hetherly, V. (1993). What do excellent psychotherapy supervisors do? *American Journal of Psychiatry, 150,* 1081–1084.

Shanfield, S.B., Mohl, P.C., Matthews, K.L. & Hetherly, V. (1989). A reliability assessment of the psychotherapy supervisory inventory. *American Journal of Psychiatry, 146,* 1447–1450.

Shanfield, S.B., Mohl, P.C., Matthews, K.L. & Hetherly, V. (1992). Quantitative assessment of the behaviour of psychotherapy supervisors. *American Journal of Psychiatry, 149,* 352–357.

Shapiro, D.A. (1995). Finding out how psychotherapies help people change. *Psychotherapy Research, 5,* 1–21.

Sharpless, B.A. & Barber, J.P. (2009). A conceptual and empirical review of the meaning, measurement, development, and teaching of intervention competence in clinical psychology. *Clinical Psychology Review, 29,* 47–56.

Siegler, R.S. (1995). How does change occur? A microgenetic study of number conservation. *Cognitive Psychology, 28*, 225–273.

Siegler, R.S. (2002). Microgenetic studies of self-explanation. In N. Granott & J. Parziale (Eds) *Microdevelopment: Transition processes in development and learning* (pp. 31–58). Cambridge, MA: Cambridge University Press.

Skovholt, T.M. & Ronnestad, M.H. (1992). Themes in therapist and counsellor development. *Journal of Counseling and Development, 70*, 505–515.

Smail, D. (1991). Towards a radical environmentalist psychology of help. *The Psychologist, 2*, 61–65.

Smith, R. (1998). All changed, changed utterly. *British Medical Journal, 316*, 1917–1918.

Solomon, P. (1992). Learning contracts in clinical education: Evaluation by clinical supervisors. *Medical Teacher, 14*, 205–210.

Stallard, P., Utwin, O., Goddard, M. & Hibbert, S. (2007). The availability of cognitive behaviour therapy within specialist child and adolescent mental health services (CAMHS): A national survey. *Behavioural and Cognitive Psychotherapy, 35*, 501–505.

Stiles, W.B., Elliott, R., Llewelyn, S.P., Firth-Cozens, J.A., Margison, F.A. & Shapiro, D. (1990). Assimilation of problematic experiences by clients in psychotherapy. *Psychotherapy: Theory, Research, Practice and Training, 27*, 411–420.

Stiles, W.B., Glick, M.J., Osatuke, K., Hardy, G.E., Shapiro, D.A., Agnew-Davies, R., *et al.* (2004). Patterns of alliance development and the rupture–repair hypothesis: Are productive relationships U-shaped or V-shaped? *Journal of Counseling Psychology, 51*, 81–92.

Stiles, W.B. & Shapiro, D.A. (1994). Disabuse of the drug metaphor: Psychotherapy process–outcome correlations. *Journal of Consulting and Clinical Psychology, 62*, 942–948.

Stirman, S.W., Pontoski, K., Creed, T., Xhezo, R., Evans, A.C., Beck, A.T. *et al.* (2015). A non-randomized comparison of strategies for consultation in a community-academic training programme to implement evidence based therapy. *Administration and Policy in Mental Health Mental Health Services, 44*, 55–66. DOI: 10.1007/s10488-015-0700-7

Stoltenberg, C.D., Bailey, K.C., Cruzan, C.B., Hart, J.T. & Ukuku, U. (2014). The integrative developmental model of supervision. In C.E. Watkins & D.L. Milne (Eds) *Wiley international handbook of clinical supervision* (pp. 576–597). Chichester: Wiley.

Stoltenberg, C.D. & Delworth, U. (1987). *Supervising counselors and therapists.* San Francisco, CA: Jossey-Bass.

Stoltenberg, C.D. & McNeill, B.W. (1997). Clinical supervision from a developmental perspective: Research and practice. In C.E. Watkins (Ed.) *Handbook of psychotherapy supervision* (pp. 184–202). New York: Wiley.

Stoltenberg, C.D., McNeill, B.W. & Crethar, H.C. (1994). Changes in supervision as counselors and therapists gain experience: A review. *Professional Psychology: Research and Practice, 25,* 416–449.

Strauss, S. (1993). Theories of learning and development for academics and educators. *Educational Psychologist, 28,* 191–203.

Sudak, D.M., Codd, R.T., Ludgate, J.W., Sokol, L., Fox, M.G., Reiser, R.P. *et al.* (2016). *Teaching and supervising cognitive behavioral therapy.* Hoboken, NJ: Wiley.

Sue, D.W. & Torino, G.C. (2005). Racial/cultural competence: Awareness, knowledge and skill. In R.T. Carter (Ed.) *Handbook of racial/cultural psychology and counselling: Training and Practice* (pp. 3–18). New York: Wiley.

Sugarman, L. (1986). *Lifespan development: Concepts, theories and interventions.* New York: Methuen.

Swift, J.K., Callahan, J.L., Rousmaniere, T.G., Whipple, J.L., Dexter, K. & Wrape, E.R. (2014). Using client outcome monitoring as a tool for supervision. *Psychotherapy, 52,* 180–184. DOI: 10.1037/a/0037659

Talen, M.R. & Schindler, N. (1993). Goal-directed supervision plans. *The Clinical Supervisor, 11,* 77–98.

Tangen, J.L. & Borders, L.D. (2016). The supervisory relationship: A conceptual and psychometric review of measures. *Counselor Education and Supervision, 55,* 159–182.

Temple, S. & Bowers, W.A. (1998). Supervising cognitive therapists from diverse fields. *Journal of Cognitive Psychotherapy, 12,* 139–151.

Tharenou, P. (2001). The relationship of training motivation to participation in training and development. *Journal of Organizational Psychology, 74,* 599–621.

Thelen, E. & Smith, L.B. (1998). Dynamic systems theories. In W. Damon & R. Lerner (Eds) *Handbook of child psychology: Vol. 1. Theoretical models of child development* (pp. 563–634) New York: Wiley.

Thomas, J.T. (2014). International ethics for psychotherapy supervisors: Principles, practices, and future directions. In C.E. Watkins & D.L. Milne (Eds) *Wiley international handbook of clinical supervision* (pp. 131–154). Chichester: Wiley.

Thorn, B.E. (2007). Evidence-based practice in psychology. *Journal of Clinical Psychology, 63,* 607–609.

Tight, M. (1996). *Key concepts in adult education and training.* London: Routledge.

Townend, M. (2004). *Supervision contracts in cognitive behavioural psychotherapy.* BABCP: Accrington.

Townend, M., Iannetta, L. & Freeston, M.H. (2002). Clinical supervision in practice; a survey of UK cognitive behavioural psychotherapists accredited by the BABCP. *Behavioural and Cognitive Psychotherapy, 30,* 485–450.

Tracey, T.J.G. (2002). Stages of counseling and therapy: An examination of complementarity and the working alliance. In G.S. Tryon (Ed.) *Counselling based on process research: Applying what we know* (pp. 265–297). Boston: Allyn & Bacon.

Tracey, T.J.G., Wampold, B.E., Lichtenberg, J.W. & Goodyear, R.K. (2014). Expertise in psychotherapy: An elusive goal? *American Psychologist, 69*, 218–229.

Triantafillou, N. (1997). A solution-focused approach to mental health supervision. *Journal of Systemic Therapies, 16*, 305–328.

Tryon, G.S. & Winograd, G. (2011). Goal consensus and collaboration. *Psychotherapy, 48*, 50–57. DOI: 10.1037/a0022061

Vec, T., Vec, T.R. & Zorga, S. (2014). Understanding how supervision works and what it can achieve. In C.E. Watkins & D.L. Milne (Eds) *Wiley international handbook of clinical supervision* (pp. 103–127). Chichester: Wiley.

Veilleux, J.C., Sandeen, E. & Levensky, E. (2013). Dialectical tensions, supervisor attitudes and contextual influences in psychotherapy supervision. *Journal of Contemporary Psychotherapy, 44*, 31–41. DOI 10.1007/s10879-013-9245-9

Veloski, J., Boex, J.R., Grasberger, M.J., Evans, A. & Wolfson, D.B. (2006). Systematic review of the literature on assessment, feedback and physicians' clinical performance. *Medical Teacher, 28*, 117–128.

Vermunt, J.D. & Verloop, N. (1999). Congruence and friction between learning and teaching. *Learning and Instruction, 9*, 257–280.

Vespia, K.M., Heckman-Stone, C. & Delworth, U. (2002). Describing and facilitating effective supervision behaviour in counselling trainees. *Psychotherapy: Theory/Research/Practice/Training, 39*, 50–65.

Vygotsky, L.S. (1978). *Mind in society: The development of higher psychological processes.* Cambridge, MA: Harvard University Press.

Waller, H., Garety, P., Jolley, S., Fornells-Ambrajo, M. Kuipers, E., Onwumere, J. et al. (2015). Training frontline mental health staff to deliver 'low intensity' psychological therapy for psychosis: A qualitative analysis of therapist and service user views on the therapy and its future implementation. *Behavioural and Cognitive Psychotherapy, 43*, 298–313.

Wampold, B.E., David, B. & Good, R.H. (1990). Hypothesis validity of clinical research. *Journal of Consulting and Clinical Psychology, 58*, 360–367.

Wampold, B.E. & Holloway, E.L. (1997). Methodology, design and evaluation in psychotherapy supervision research. In C.E. Watkins (Ed.) *Handbook of psychotherapy supervision* (pp. 11–30). New York: Wiley.

Warr, P.B. (1980). An introduction to models in psychological research. In A.J. Chapman & D.M. Jones (Eds) *Models of man* (pp. 291–310). Leicester: BPS.

Warr, P. & Downing, J. (2000). Learning strategies, learning anxiety and knowledge acquisition. *British Journal of Psychology, 91*, 311–333.

Watkins, C.E. (1995). Psychotherapy supervisor development: On musings, models, and metaphor. *Journal of Psychotherapy Practice and Research, 4*, 150–158.

Watkins, C.E. (Ed.) (1997). *Handbook of psychotherapy supervision.* New York: Wiley.

Watkins, C.E. (2011). Does psychotherapy supervision contribute to patient outcomes? *Considering thirty years of research. The Clinical Supervisor, 30*, 235–256.

Watkins, C.E. (2014a). The supervision alliance as quintessential integrative variable. *Journal of Contemporary Psychotherapy, 44*, 151–161.

Watkins, C.E. (2014b). The supervisory alliance: A half century of theory, practice, and research in critical perspective. *American Journal of Psychotherapy, 68*, 1–37.

Watkins, C.E. (2014c). Supervisory alliance research: The first twenty-five years. Paper presented at the annual meeting of the American Psychological Association, Washington, DC, 8 August 2014.

Watkins, C.E. (2014d). Leading and learning in the psychotherapy supervision seminar: Some thoughts on the beginnings of supervisor development. *Journal of Contemporary Psychotherapy, 44*, 233–243.

Watkins, C.E. & Milne, D.L. (2014). *Wiley international handbook of clinical supervision* (pp. 61–102). Chichester: Wiley.

Watkins, C.E. & Wang, D.C. (2014). On the education of clinical supervisors. In C.E. Watkins & D.L. Milne (Eds) *Wiley international handbook of clinical supervision* (pp. 177–203). Chichester: Wiley.

Watson, J.D. (1999). *The double helix: A personal account of the discovery of the structure of DNA*. London: Penguin.

Webb, N. (2006). *A definitive critique of experiential learning theory*. Retrieved 5 December 2006 from http://cc.wiresu.edu/nmnweb.

Weck, F., Kaufmann, Y.M. & Hofling, V. (2016). Competence feedback improves CBT competence in trainee therapists: A randomized controlled pilot study. *Psychotherapy Research*, 2016. DOI: org/10.1080/10503307.2015.1132857

Wells, A. (1997). *Cognitive therapy of anxiety disorders*. Chichester: Wiley.

Whaley, A.L. & Davis, K.E. (2007). Cultural competence and evidence based practice in mental health services: A complimentary perspective. *American Psychologist, 62*, 563–574.

Wheeler, S. (2004). A review of supervisor training in the UK. In I. Fleming & L. Steen (Eds) *Supervision and clinical psychology: Theory, practice and perspectives* (pp. 15–35). New York: Brunner-Routledge.

Wheeler, S. & Barkham, M. (2014). A core evaluation battery for supervision. In C.E. Watkins & D.L. Milne (Eds) *Wiley international handbook of clinical supervision* (pp. 367–385). Chichester: Wiley.

Wheeler, S. & King, D. (2000). Do counselling supervisors want or need to have their supervision supervised? An exploratory study. *British Journal of Guidance and Counselling, 28*, 279–290.

Wheeler, S. & Richards, K. (2007). The impact of clinical supervision on counsellors and therapists, their practice and their clients. A systematic review of the literature. *Counselling and Psychotherapy Research, 7*, 54–65.

White, E. & Winstanley, J. (2014) Clinical Supervision and the helping professions: An interpretation of history. *The Clinical Supervisor, 33*, 3–25.

Wilkes, M. & Bligh, J. (1999). Evaluating educational interventions. *British Medical Journal, 318,* 1269–1272.

Wilson, M. (2007). Can experiences of supervision be quantified? My PETS: A new tool for measuring supervisee's perceived satisfaction with clinical supervision. Undergraduate thesis, Psychology Department, Newcastle University, UK. [Summary presented in Milne *et al.* (2012).].

Winstanley, J. (2000). Manchester Clinical Supervision Scale. *Nursing Standard, 14,* 31–32.

Witmer, L. (1907). Clinical psychology. *The Psychological Clinic, 1,* 1–9.

Wood, D., Bruner, J.S. & Ross, G. (1976). The role of tutoring in problem-solving. *Child Psychology and Psychiatry, 17,* 89–100.

Wood, J.A.V., Miller, T.W. & Hargrove, D.S. (2005). Clinical supervision in rural settings: A telehealth model. *Professional Psychology: Research and Practice, 36,* 173–179.

Worthen, V.E. & Isakson, R.L. (2000). *Supervision outcomes survey: Unpublished scale.* Reported in Falender & Shafranske (2004), pp. 271–272, Appendix J.

Worthen, V.E. & Lambert, M.J. (2007). Outcome-oriented supervision: Advantages of adding systematic client tracking to supportive consultations. *Counselling and Psychotherapy Research, 7,* 48–53.

Worthington, E.L. (1987). Changes in supervision as counsellors and supervisors gain experience. *Professional Psychology: Research and Practice, 18,* 189–208.

Ybrandt, H., Sundin, E.C. & Capone, G. (2016). Trainee therapists' views on the alliance in psychotherapy and supervision: A longitudinal study. *British Journal of Guidance and Counselling, 44,* 530–539. DOI: org/10.1080/03069885.2016.1153037

York University. (2007). *Patient case management information system.* Department of Health Sciences, York University.

Zorga, S. (2002). Supervision: The process of life long learning in social and educational professions. *Journal of Inter Professional Care, 16,* 265–276.

Index

Evidence-Based CBT Supervision: Principles and Practice, Second Edition. Derek L. Milne.
© 2018 John Wiley & Sons Ltd. Published in 2018 by the British Psychological Society and
John Wiley & Sons Ltd.